The Chinese in Indonesia : Five Essays

The Chinese in Indonesia

Five Essays
Edited by J. A. C. Mackie

The University Press of Hawaii, Honolulu
in association with
The Australian Institute of International Affairs

Library of Congress Cataloging in Publication Data
Main entry under title:

The Chinese in Indonesia.

   Bibliography: p.
   Includes index.
   1. Chinese in Indonesia—Addresses, essays, lectures.
   2. Indonesia—Politics and government—20th century—
Addresses, essays, lectures.   I. Mackie, J. A. C.
DS632.3.C5C45   301.45'19'510598   76-000139
ISBN 0-8248-0449-X

© The Australian Institute of International Affairs 1976

*Having as its object the scientific study of international
questions, The Australian Institute of International
Affairs, as such, does not express opinions or advocate
policies. The views expressed in this book are therefore
the authors' own.*

This book is copyright. Apart from any fair
dealing for the purpose of private study, research,
criticism or review, as permitted under the
Copyright Act, no part may be reproduced by
any process without written permission. Inquiries
should be addressed to the publishers.

This edition published by arrangement with
Thomas Nelson (Australia) Limited

Filmset in Hong Kong by Asco Trade Typesetting Ltd.
Manufactured in the United States of America

Contents

Preface

These essays had their origin in a series of discussions between the authors and several others from Monash University during the years 1966–68, at a time when the predicament of the Chinese inhabitants of Indonesia seemed desperately bleak and reliable information about it was extremely difficult to obtain. An opportunity to pursue some of our lines of enquiry further through field research by Messrs Coppel and Thomas was opened up by the award of a research grant from the Ford Foundation, through the Australian Institute of International Affairs, whose assistance we gratefully acknowledge. Since then the general situation confronting the Indonesian Chinese has improved a good deal, fortunately, although it is still not easy to get precise data about many matters on which one would like to know much more than we do.

The conclusions we drew and the information we obtained from these enquiries, although limited in scope, have raised many of the broader questions that arise in an attempt to understand how the Chinese have fitted into Indonesian society in the rapidly changing circumstances of the twentieth century. We have therefore tried to set the more specialised essays which form the core of this book into a broader context by providing a general introductory sketch of the demographic, legal and socio-political background of the Indonesian Chinese and by concluding with some observations by a non-Indonesian Overseas Chinese, Professor Wang Gungwu, who has been well placed to see the Indonesian situation in the light of the experience of the Overseas Chinese in Malaysia and elsewhere in Southeast Asia.

We are acutely aware that it is perilous and presumptuous for a group of outsiders, most of whom do not speak Chinese, to venture into a field such as this where the questions at issue are complex and controversial, touching many sensitive nerves on both the Chinese side and the Indonesian. (Even on quite rudimentary points of the appropriate terminology to be used, strong feelings are aroused; see the note at the end of this Preface.) It seemed preferable, however, that some preliminary mapping of the problems should be attempted, than that this important topic should be left utterly unexplored, if only for the sake of encouraging others who are more suitably qualified to carry the investigations further and to bring the problems out into the light of day for calm and rational discussion. There may be times when it is wisest to let sleeping dogs lie, lest one arouse passionate arguments, or animosities that might otherwise remain dormant; but to treat problems of this kind as if they were best ignored is a very dubious strategy in the long run, for they are not likely to disappear unless deliberate efforts are made to resolve them—and all friends of Indonesia and of the Overseas Chinese must hope they will be resolved.

Since any analysis of these questions is almost inevitably coloured by one's subjective opinions and value judgments, as well as by the 'objective facts of the matter', it is appropriate to say something at the outset about our aims, sympathies and basic presuppositions. We are not attempting to put forward any simple answers to the problems associated with the Indonesian Chinese. It is extremely doubtful if there are any simple answers. Nor do our sympathies incline us strongly toward one side or the other on all the issues at stake; indeed, the issues are rarely clear-cut and there are frequently more than two sides to choose from. In general, however, we do believe that these problems should be resolved in such a way that all Chinese who are born in Indonesia should have a right to Indonesian citizenship if they continue to live there. (It is at present, as of 1975, very difficult for alien Chinese to become naturalised.) We also believe that the government should try to ensure that this status should not be a hollow one but should entail equal rights for all who hold it, regardless of their ethnic origin. On the other hand, we believe that some Chinese may have to sacrifice certain things they cherish (e.g. a Chinese education) if this is to be achieved. Furthermore, we believe that inter-ethnic friction will only disappear if greater equality of the social and economic status of the Indonesians and Chinese can be achieved; progress toward these desired aims can be achieved by the government's actions—and almost certainly will depend in large part on such actions—but we do not presume to tell the Indonesian government how they should be achieved. (The problem, in any case, is one of allocating priorities between these different and sometimes divergent objectives.) Although we are critical of some courses of action which seem unwise or indefensible on humanitarian grounds, in almost every case the same judgment has been made by many Indonesians in positions of responsibility on the basis of commonly accepted principles which their own government has endeavoured to uphold. Despite our general concordance of views on these questions, however, we differ in minor respects on some points, and the authors of the various chapters are solely responsible for the views expressed therein.

Finally, we wish to record our indebtedness to Professor Herbert Feith, who was the moving spirit in the original discussions which gave rise to this book and who has contributed generously towards it through the provision of his comments, criticism and information which he has collected. We also wish to acknowledge the assistance of the Myer Foundation for a grant in aid of Mr Coppel's field research in 1968–69, the Indonesian Department of Home Affairs for permission to consult the LPKB archives, and the following persons for their kindness in commenting on a draft of one of the chapters or the bibliography: Go Gien Tjwan, Andrew Gunawan, Lau Teik Soon (and the Institute of Southeast Asian Studies, Singapore), Lie Tek Tjeng, Rex Mortimer, Bob Muskens, Robert Reid-Smith, W. D. Sukisman, Leo Suryadinata, Mely Tan, Peter Weldon, and W. F. Wertheim (in consultation with The Siauw Giap). Sue McKemmish has given us valuable help with the index and Pam Sayers with the typing of numerous drafts; to both we wish to record our thanks. Needless to say, responsibility for what is published here remains with the author concerned.

PROBLEMS OF TERMINOLOGY AND SPELLING

The problems of terminology that arise in any discussion of 'the Chinese' in Indonesia involve difficulties of substance as well as style, since the racial and the legal denotations of the term are not identical. We have used the term 'Chinese' to refer to all ethnic Chinese residing in Indonesia, regardless of whether they are Indonesian citizens or aliens, of purely Chinese ancestry or of mixed blood, insofar as they identify or are generally identified as Chinese. There are difficulties even about a broad racial definition, for in Skinner's words 'one cannot determine who is and who is not a Chinese according to any simple racial criterion'. Hence the only satisfactory definition is one given in terms of a person's social identification with other Chinese. In order to distinguish between those Chinese who are Indonesian citizens and those who are not, we will refer to the latter as alien Chinese and to the former apply the commonly accepted expression 'WNI Chinese' (i.e. *Warganegara Indonesia*— Indonesian nationals). We sympathise with the argument frequently advanced by members of this group that use of such a categorisation seems to imply that they are to be distinguished from other 'indigenous' Indonesians (*asli* or *pribumi*)[1] and merely reinforces the tendency to maintain a racial rather than a legal differentiation which is not recognised by Indonesian law; but there is no alternative to the use of these terms if one wishes to talk about ethnic relationships at all fruitfully. Unless one takes the view that it is better not to discuss these sensitive problems at all, one has to make do with a terminology that reflects the socio-cultural distinctions, even though it must be emphasised strongly that this distinction is not a legal one and sometimes not a defensible one. Moreover, in using this terminology, we do not mean to imply (as some Indonesian usage of terms like *asli* and *WNI* does imply) that Indonesian citizens of Chinese extraction are 'any less Indonesian than others'—to use the words of Donald Willmott, with whose conclusions on this thorny problem we fully concur.[2]

We have adopted the official form of spelling the Indonesian and Malay languages established in 1972, except in the cases of quotations from or titles of books or articles written before the introduction of the new spelling. Place names have been changed where appropriate (except in one or two cases where the anglicised form has become generally accepted, like Java), but not names of persons or pre-1972 organisations; it is left to each individual to determine whether to change the spelling of his name: the same rule applied years earlier to the switch from the Dutch 'oe' to the Indonesian 'u' (as in Soekarno = Sukarno). Briefly, the main changes are:

Consonant Change			*New Form*	*Old Form*
y	instead of	j	Surabaya	Surabaja
j	,,	,, dj	Jakarta	Djakarta
sy	,,	,, sj	Masyumi	Masjumi
c	,,	,, tj	Aceh	Atjeh

May 1975   *J. A. C. Mackie*

The Chinese in Indonesia : Five Essays

I

A PRELIMINARY SURVEY
J. A. C. Mackie and Charles A. Coppel

In 1970 there were probably about three million ethnic Chinese scattered throughout Indonesia amidst a total population of about 120 million. In any consideration of Indonesia's political or economic prospects one has to take into account the manifold problems created by and confronting this very important minority.[1] Indonesians often speak about 'the Overseas Chinese problem', which is a convenient shorthand term, although it refers of course not to one single problem but to a complex tangle of issues that differ from place to place and from group to group. In fact almost every individual of Chinese descent in the country has to cope with the general predicament to some degree in his daily life, either as petty discrimination or as personal tragedy. But in this book we will have to approach the several topics we examine from the general rather than the individual level, from the bird's-eye view, as it were, while keeping in mind the very diverse circumstances confronting the Overseas Chinese and the significant differences that mark some of them from others, to which earlier writers have alerted us.[2]

There is no need to elaborate here upon the heterogeneity of the Overseas Chinese, for it seems to have little relevance to the problems with which this book is mainly concerned. Our primary aim is to open up for fuller investigation three quite separate aspects of this very broad subject, so that some of the complexities and ambiguities involved in the attempt to analyse them will be better understood. This introductory chapter is merely to set the scene for them. Much more work will have to be done before any comprehensive analysis or general synoptic survey of the main trends affecting the political, social or economic status of the Indonesian Chinese can be put forward with reasonable confidence.

Assimilation of the Overseas Chinese is often recommended as if it were the ultimate solution to most of the problems and frictions they currently encounter or create. The case for assimilation has been strongly argued by Lea Williams in *The Future of the Overseas Chinese in Southeast Asia*. He shows that there has been an encouraging trend in this direction since the bad old days of colonialism, which had generally exploited and intensified the separateness of the various ethnic minorities.[3] Williams recommends further participation in local government and politics as the most desirable course open to the Overseas Chinese, in preference to standing aloof or engaging in communal politics. One can only hope he is right in his view, but as Charles Coppel shows in Chapter 2, the notion of 'assimilation' itself poses nearly as many questions as it answers. A contrary argument has been put forward by R. J. Coughlin, who queries whether political assimilation is either possible or desirable.[4] The Chinese should cling to their community organisations, which have proved 'resilient buffers against predatory officials and hostile governments', he argues, since their physical survival 'may well depend on the continued vitality of these communities'. He regards as questionable several basic assumptions he attributes to Williams—that the crux of Chinese separatism is political isolation and that if the Chinese community were to participate in politics, the other troublesome problems of social and cultural assimilation would be solved also. According to Coughlin,

> Southeast Asia today is pockmarked by military dictators and assorted political foxes who have reached the top and managed to stay there because of the inability or unwillingness of the people they rule to do anything about it ... If political disinterest and inactivity characterise Southeast Asians, to recommend that Chinese participate actively in politics is asking that they do something that Southeast Asians do not do. Is this assimilation?

Perhaps he has overstated his point—for there are many modes of political activity in this part of the world, amongst the Chinese and others, as Coppel also shows—but we cannot ignore the awkward grain of truth in Coughlin's argument. The separateness of the Overseas Chinese stems as much from their treatment by the host societies and governments as from their own attitudes and behaviour.

The Indonesian side of the relationship is dealt with (in one of its many aspects) in Chapter 3; it also forms an important part of Thomas and Panglaykim's story in Chapter 4. We would hope that the conclusions to be drawn from these would point in the direction of Williams's view of the future rather than Coughlin's, although we realise the need to be cautious in any broad generalisations about these matters. Thomas has found that many of the arguments advanced by economic nationalists for excluding the Chinese from their dominant position in the rubber industry of South Sumatra were based on a very shallow understanding of their economic role and that the attempts made to achieve this aim were simply counterproductive. Fortunately there have been signs that more realistic views about what can be achieved in this field are now prevailing in Indonesia—which is not to say that the goals of the economic nationalists are to be deplored (i.e. reducing Chinese control or ownership over the trading and manufacturing sectors of the Indonesian economy and promoting more effective Indonesian participation in these spheres), but simply that the costs of pursuing these goals should be measured in the light of experiences such as he has described, in terms of both economic and social or human costs. Likewise, the conclusion to be drawn from an examination of the anti-Chinese outbreaks is not that these are part of some mechanistic or inevitable social process which is bound to recur (which would indeed justify Coughlin's pessimism), but that such episodes can be prevented, given the will to do so, if the situations that give rise to them are understood and anticipated, so that the risks of precipitating clashes by unforeseeable incidents may be minimised. There are reasonable grounds for believing that the circumstances that gave rise to those tragic events between 1959 and 1967 may have changed sufficiently since 1968 to justify a cautious optimism on that score, provided that a reasonable degree of economic and social stability can be maintained in Indonesia and that the Indonesians succeed in narrowing the dangerous gap between their own economic weakness and the economic strength of the Chinese.

There is much more to be said, of course, about the pressures working toward and against the assimilation of the Indonesian Chinese within both their own and the host communities. In this book we are concentrating only on three more limited topics. For instance, the social psychology of race relations in Indonesia is an important but still almost unexplored field, which has a direct bearing on all three—although we can make some inferences about the political implications of racial attitudes on the basis of the valuable works by Willmott, Tan Giok-lan, Skinner, Somers, Lea Williams and Suryadinata. At least the general outlines are now sufficiently clear to warrant a modest degree of hope that the record of race relations in Indonesia may be rather more tranquil in the years ahead than it was in the 1960s. A more pessimistic view is often expressed on the basis of much cruder arguments than Coughlin has used in the passage quoted, particularly among those severely 'practical' men who merely extrapolate their notion of the future from selected incidents in the past on the principle of 'more of the same', or who fear that the Overseas Chinese will not be willing to identify with their countries of residence, but will prefer to rely either on Peking or on the collective strength (economic as much as political) of the 'Third

China' in Southeast Asia or on the protection they can find within their particular communal enclaves.[5] These possibilities cannot be ruled out of consideration entirely so long as Southeast Asia remains as unsettled a region as it has been since 1941; but at least we should recognise that this is not the only way to look at this situation—and, hopefully, not the most appropriate one for the 1970s.

THE DEMOGRAPHIC BACKGROUND

Chinese traders and seamen have been plying to and from the Indonesian archipelago for well over a thousand years, even before the time of the great Palembang-based kingdom of Srivijaya in the sixth to twelfth centuries. But China's rulers rarely showed more than a perfunctory interest in exercising military or maritime power in the *Nan Yang* (South Seas) or in encouraging 'colonies' of Chinese settlers there, apart from one brief period of assertiveness under the early Ming dynasty. In fact, overseas trade and settlement was in principle forbidden by the Ch'ing dynasty between 1644 and 1894, though not at all effectively; several concentrations of Chinese immigrants developed, notably in West Kalimantan and Bangka Island. But it was only during the last hundred years that the numbers of the Chinese in Indonesia increased really substantially, from about a quarter of a million in the mid-nineteenth century to an estimated $1\frac{1}{4}$ million by 1930. This sudden growth occurred largely as the consequence of two great surges of immigration. The first of these was an inflow of Chinese labourers to the estate area of North Sumatra and the tin islands between about 1860 and 1890; the second occurred after the Dutch government's relaxation of the earlier restrictions on Chinese entry into and settlement in the colony after 1900 and was more widely dispersed and more heterogeneous, as Chinese traders fanned out throughout the archipelago. The rate of immigration reached its peak in the 1920s when the net inflow was as high as 40000 in some years.[6] But it fell off sharply during the depression and has been restricted since 1950 to a mere trickle of (mostly illegal) immigrants after Indonesia became independent.

Dutch policy towards the Chinese developed in such a way that they came to occupy an important intermediate position in what Wertheim has aptly called the 'colonial caste structure', based on an essentially racial stratification system, between the great mass of the subject Indonesians and the few Europeans who occupied the top levels. They were engaged particularly as tax farmers and operators of pawnshops, the salt monopoly, and the opium trade on behalf of the Dutch government. From these key positions they were able to widen their network of commercial contacts into money-lending, wholesale trade and the purchasing of primary products for the export market, though they were able to make little headway in the sectors of economic life which were dominated by the Dutch, such as plantation agriculture, the export and import trade, wholesaling and banking, until very late in the colonial era.[7] Land ownership outside the towns was debarred to them by the Agrarian Law of 1870 which confined land ownership to the 'natives', although in the few places where Chinese had owned and farmed land prior to that date their rights were maintained. Thus partly because of direct Chinese competition and partly because of indirect Dutch discouragement, the weakly established indigenous trading classes which had begun to emerge in the coastal towns of the archipelago during the great expansion of trade in the sixteenth and seventeenth centuries had almost faded away by the beginning of the twentieth century. Yet the Chinese too were curbed in their activities by the Dutch system of pass and residential restrictions, which were not abolished until the first decade of this century, so that it is really only in the last fifty or sixty years that they have come to play the predominant role in the distributive trade of Indonesia with which they are now so commonly identified.

Since about the beginning of this century, it has been possible to distinguish two groups of Chinese in Indonesia, on the one hand the *totoks* (literally, 'of pure blood') being those who had recently immigrated, spoke Chinese and were culturally oriented towards China, and on the other the much older *peranakan* communities being characterised by the use of the vernacular language for everyday purposes and by a distinctive set of cultural traits which were neither wholly Chinese nor wholly Indonesian.[8] As G. W. Skinner has forcefully pointed out, these terms refer not merely to differences of ethnic purity or birthplace or daily language of individual Chinese, but to a socio-cultural cleavage between quite distinct communities, whose political and social interests have quite frequently diverged and between which there has often been relatively little communication or even possibility of social intercourse.[9] The significance of this cleavage and the historical background to it will be spelled out more fully in the following pages. So too will some of the pressures which have at times tended to pull some of the peranakan intellectuals in the direction of greater Chineseness and at other times to push them in opposite directions.

The many Chinese communities scattered throughout the archipelago have differed from one another in many ways—by reason of their length of settlement, the languages and occupations of the settlers and the degree of isolation of one community from another, as well as differences related to the culture and relative size of the indigenous societies among which they settled. Before 1900 various governmental measures combined with natural or geographic factors to inhibit contact between the different Chinese communities and yet to concentrate them in certain areas. At that time, Chinese were required to obtain a government pass if they wished to travel outside their own town, and government regulations compelled them to live in specified quarters of the towns.[10] The rich Priangan region of West Java had only recently been opened for Chinese settlement and, despite the rapid influx to fill this vacuum after 1872, the bulk of the Chinese population of Java remained concentrated along the north coast, as it had been for centuries, especially in the major cities of Batavia, Semarang and Surabaya, but also in the smaller towns and, in a few areas, outside them. Except for a few long-settled areas, particularly near Batavia and Cirebon, the Chinese in Java were overwhelmingly urban; this pattern of distribution had been reinforced by the Agrarian Law of 1870 which prohibited the purchase of land by non-natives. The concentration along the north coast reflected the main arteries of trade; in Java, most of the harbours were to be found there.[11]

At the turn of the century the Chinese population in Java had not reached 300000 and its growth rate was slight compared with that of the Chinese in the Outer Provinces. Numbers rose in the next thirty years. In Java the number of Chinese almost doubled between 1905 and 1930, largely as a result of a dramatic increase in the numbers of immigrants. Despite this increase, however, the 1930 census showed that the percentage born in the Indies was still as high as 79.4 per cent and that, of this group, no less than 80 per cent had fathers who were also born in the Indies.[12]

The Chinese of Java were by no means uniform in language. The new arrivals spoke the speech of their place of origin in China. In Java most immigrants had been Hokkien speakers, but the composition of the immigrants was changing and the numbers of Hakka and Cantonese speaking immigrants would come to surpass those of the Hokkiens. These three speech groups are mutually unintelligible, and since few of the immigrants could speak Mandarin (*kuo-yü*, the national language) or were literate (and thus able to read Chinese characters which bridge speech-group differences), there were barriers to a united Chinese community even among the new arrivals.

There was, moreover, a linguistic chasm between the totok immigrants and the Indies-born peranakan Chinese. The peranakan community had developed over the centuries as a result of the alliances concluded between immigrant (mostly Hokkien) men and native women. A stable community evolved in which the numbers of women came to match those of the men, although immigration had always been primarily a male affair. This community developed a culture of its own which was something more than a mere mixture of Chinese and indigenous elements. One mark of the peranakan was the use of Indonesian (Malay) or a regional Indonesian language as his daily tongue. Less than one-third of the total Chinese population of Java in 1920 used

Chinese as their main language of daily intercourse.[13] Of these, most must have been first generation immigrants. Before this century, few of the peranakan Chinese were able to speak the language of their ancestors, since Chinese language education was poor and scarce. But they still considered themselves Chinese, an identification which Dutch colonial policy helped to confirm by preventing them from assimilating to either the indigenous population or the Dutch.

In Java the Chinese most closely approached the stereotype of the trading community. Few of them engaged in agriculture (a pattern intensified by the 1870 Dutch land law) and few were workers in mines and plantations which attracted so many Chinese to the Outer Provinces.[14] Although more than half of the Chinese of Java who were in gainful employment were found in 1930 to be engaged in trade of some kind, it should not be forgotten that a trader might be anything from a pedlar to a magnate, and that pedlars are notoriously more plentiful than magnates. After trade came industry, at least at the time of the 1930 census. Again this classification incorporated unskilled labourers and skilled artisans as well as factory owners.

There is no doubt that the average Chinese was wealthier than the average indigenous Indonesian. Figures of the 1920s and 1930s show that he paid more income tax, his house was more likely to be made from brick, and he was more likely to own a motor car.[15] By the same criteria, the average European was vastly better off than the average Chinese.

Outside Java, Chinese society was even more diversified.[16] In some scattered areas, notably Padang and a few towns in Eastern Indonesia, the picture was somewhat similar to that in the small towns of Java, with an established, mainly urban trading community of Hokkien origin but speaking Indonesian or a regional Indonesian language and heavily acculturated to local patterns of life. More isolated than similar communities in Java, these peranakan communities were, like them, small in comparison with the total population of their areas.

In other areas, such as Bangka and West Kalimantan, although there had been Chinese settlements for centuries and the greater part of the Chinese population was locally born, the Chinese remained overwhelmingly Chinese in speech. Most members of these communities were employed in mining and small-scale agriculture.[17]

Along the east coast of Sumatra and on the islands of Belitung and the Riau archipelago there were large concentrations of Chinese, almost all Chinese-speaking, and mostly new arrivals.[18] It was only in Sumatra that the new arrivals outnumbered the locally born in 1930. Here the great wave of coolie immigration which had begun in the middle of last century had its greatest impact, and thousands of Chinese entered Sumatra to work in the tin mines and plantations. Others worked in the *panglongs* (or timber and fuel businesses) of the Riau archipelago, supplying wood and charcoal for the growing market of near-by Singapore, while further north a great concentration of Chinese built up one of the world's largest fishing ports at Bagan Siapiapi.

In the Chinese-speaking communities of East Sumatra, Riau, Bangka, Belitung, and West Kalimantan (Borneo), the proportion of Chinese to the total population was far higher than elsewhere, as was the extent of Chinese settlement in rural areas. Situated in a tight arc around Singapore and Malaya, these areas developed strong trading links with them. Here, as in Malaya and Singapore, the diversity of speech groups was greater than in Java.[19]

After 1860 the Chinese population grew more quickly outside Java than within it. Whereas in 1860 two out of every three Chinese in Indonesia lived in Java, by 1905 the proportion had dropped to about one in two. Most of the increase outside Java occurred in Sumatra. In the following twenty-five years, the total Chinese population of Indonesia more than doubled, the increase again being disproportionately great outside Java. Then the great wave of immigration faded away under the influence of the depression, and thereafter the Chinese population grew almost entirely through natural increase alone.[20]

The immigrants of the first three decades of this century included, for the first time, significant numbers of women. As a result, it now became possible for an immigrant to take a China-born wife, rather than an indigenous Indonesian or a local born Chinese of mixed ancestry. This development, which coincided with a growth of Chinese national pride among the immigrants, tended to harden the lines of division between the immigrants and the locally rooted Chinese population in those areas where, as in Java, the locally rooted population no longer used the Chinese language in daily speech. Many immigrants no longer needed (or wished) to assimilate to peranakan society and their numbers grew to a size which could support a separate totok community, of which their Indies-born children were also members.[21] Something of the same kind of split developed even in the areas of Chinese-speaking Chinese communities outside Java, especially the longer established ones.

The occupations of the Sumatran Chinese were quite differently distributed from those of the Chinese in Java. Where in Java only 9 per cent of those gainfully employed were engaged in the production of raw materials in 1930 and 58 per cent in trade, in Sumatra the corresponding figures were 50 per cent and 18 per cent.[22] Although separate figures for West Borneo are lacking, it is likely that they would be close to those of Sumatra. Because the Chinese outside Java was more likely to be a peasant farmer, plantation coolie, mine-worker, market gardener or fisherman than his fellow in Java, the gap between average income of Chinese and Indonesians was smaller there than in Java. But the gap still existed.

CIVIL STATUS

Legal problems about the civil status of the Chinese in Indonesia were one of the many tangled legacies of the colonial era.[23] Dutch legislation of 1854 put the Chinese, along with the 'natives', on an inferior level to Europeans in matters of law and administration within the colony, although all persons born in the Netherlands or its colonies were considered to be Dutch citizens, including persons of Chinese descent. Later, however, the Indies Chinese were designated as 'foreigners' and, later still, categorised for statistical and administrative purposes as 'Foreign Orientals', distinct from the other two categories of 'Europeans' and 'Natives'. This categorisation rankled and as Chinese nationalism grew at the turn of the twentieth century, both in China and among the South Seas Chinese, demands for its abolition arose. At about the same time the Manchu government began to press the Dutch to permit the stationing of its consuls in the colony and to eliminate the various forms of legal discrimination applied against the Chinese in the Indies. In 1909 China promulgated a citizenship law which has been the crux of the problem of the dual nationality of the Overseas Chinese ever since, for it embodied the principle of *jus sanguinis*—i.e. that every child of a Chinese father or mother was a citizen of China, regardless of birthplace. The Dutch countered this in 1910 with a nationality law embodying the principle of *jus soli* (i.e. birthplace as the key consideration) which also distinguished between Dutch 'citizens' and Dutch 'subjects', defining the latter as all persons born in the colony of parents who were domiciled there.[24] These conflicting principles were not reconciled until the Sino-Indonesian Treaty abolishing dual nationality in 1960. When the Dutch and the Chinese governments reached agreement on a consular convention in 1911, the latter conceded that her consuls would not have jurisdiction over Dutch subjects while they were resident in the Indies, although in practice her consuls did not always confine their actions to the totok Chinese as the convention bound them to. However, later Chinese governments specifically refused to abandon the principle of *jus sanguinis*, but no major disputes arose on either score before the end of the colonial era.

When the Republic of Indonesia came to tackle the problems of clarifying the legal status of its Chinese inhabitants after the declaration of independence in 1945, the difficulties it faced were quite different from those confronting the Dutch.[25] It had little difficulty in persuading the Communist government in Peking to drop its insistence on the principle of *jus sanguinis*, to allow the Overseas Chinese to make their own choice between Indonesian or Chinese nationality (principles which in 1955 Peking proclaimed in respect of all Overseas Chinese residing in countries whose governments were willing to negotiate with it on the dual nationality issues) and even to negotiate with the principles and procedures which should be applied henceforth. But it was no easy matter to induce the Indonesia-born Chinese to opt for Indonesian nationality rather than Chinese, nor to obtain agreement among them and the Indonesian politicians about the methods to be adopted for executing their choice. In the first flush of enthusiasm to win the allegiance of its Chinese inhabitants in 1946 during the struggle against the Dutch, the Republican government had promulgated a Citizenship Law which provided that all Chinese who were born in the Indies and had resided there continuously for five years would automatically assume Indonesian nationality unless they took certain steps to reject it in favour of Chinese nationality. This became known as the 'passive system' of choice. Relatively few Chinese took any action to register their choice, however, for there was neither need nor incentive for them to do so; they would retain their Chinese nationality under the principle of *jus sanguinis* in any case, a matter on which the (then Nationalist) Chinese consulate publicly reassured them. But the consequence was to raise doubts in Indonesian minds about the real allegiance of Chinese who later claimed to be Indonesian citizens. Under further transitional regulations of 1949–50, quite a large number of Indonesia-born Chinese did reject Indonesian citizenship, this being a time when Chinese nationalism was invigorated by the victory of Mao Tse-tung in China.

In 1953, because of problems faced by Indonesian Chinese in establishing documentary proof of Indonesian nationality under the existing legislation, coupled with doubts about the validity of the 1946 Law, the Ali Sastroamidjojo government proposed new legislation to clarify the matter, this time proposing a system of 'active choice', whereby certain categories of foreigners born in Indonesia, including most of the peranakan Chinese, would be entitled to apply for Indonesian citizenship, according to procedures which included the specific repudiation of any other nationality. At about the same time, negotiations on the dual nationality problem were begun with Peking. The new bill had the advantages of leaving no doubt about who held Indonesian citizenship and who did not, as well as of requiring an unequivocal act of choice. It was extremely unpopular, however, among those Indonesian Chinese who claimed that they had already demonstrated their choice by identifying themselves with the Republic in various ways and who resented having to repeat the process. It was also criticised, but for quite opposite reasons, by some Indonesian politicians who wanted to make it even harder for the Chinese to obtain citizenship and to minimise the number of those who could (since it would henceforth be harder to deny them equality of rights). Consequently the question remained unsettled until 1958, when a Citizenship Law was finally approved by the parliament.[26] In the meantime, the Chou En-lai—Sunario Treaty on the abolition of dual nationality was signed during the Afro-Asian Conference at Bandung in April 1955, marking an important step towards the ultimate settlement of the problem, although it was still necessary to conduct further negotiations on certain details of just who did or did not hold dual nationality (i.e. which of the Indonesian Chinese were assumed to have already acquired Indonesian citizenship under the earlier regulations).[27] But before the ratification of the Treaty was completed, a serious rift developed in Sino-Indonesian relations at the end of 1959 over Indonesia's move to ban all alien shopkeepers, nearly all of them Chinese, from her rural areas. The story of that episode is told more fully in Chapter 3. Here it is sufficient to note that it slightly delayed and cast a cloud of mutual distrust and antagonism over the last stages of the negotiations about the detailed implementation of the choices of nationality by Chinese with dual nationality. However, the rift was soon patched up and during the two year period following the exchange of instruments of ratification in January 1960 most of the million or so Indonesian Chinese with dual nationality registered their choice, with those who opted in favour of Indonesian citizenship being estimated at between 65 per cent (according to the official sources) and 70–90 per cent (according to Chinese leaders).[28]

While the legal status of the Overseas Chinese in Indonesia was finally settled by 1962, other obstacles still remained in the way of their full assimilation and acceptance into Indonesian society. (Moreover, the Treaty was later abrogated by the Indonesian government in 1969.)[29] The scepticism of many Indonesians about the loyalty even of those Chinese who had chosen Indonesian citizenship was still not assuaged entirely. Nor did discrimination against them end completely by any means, although it was no longer as easy for officials to discriminate against WNI Chinese as it had been in the previous decade, when their legal status was still obscure: in fact they had a better chance of obtaining some degree of political protection or redress against flagrantly illegal discrimination under Guided Democracy than earlier. But unofficial forms of discrimination could not easily be prevented in the circumstances of administrative decay and economic chaos that Indonesia experienced between 1961–66. In such conditions, legal distinctions were not always of much significance. The most effective form of self-protection open to the Chinese was bribery of the underpaid officials. But all this merely reinforced stereotyped Indonesian views of the Chinese as wealthy corruptors of lowly-paid Indonesians. As Skinner has put it: 'In the view of many Indonesians, the WNI Chinese differs from the foreign Chinese only in that he found his self-interest best served by the opportunistic assumption of Indonesian citizenship. Indonesian business groups, in fierce competition with WNI Chinese as well as with aliens, are eager to perpetuate the view that all Chinese are the same and, in congruence with their typically Islamic orientation, to define that sameness in religious and moral terms'.[30] This mode of thinking is similar to that which proclaims 'Once a Jew, always a Jew' without noticing the differences within that category.

Such suspicions may even have been intensified by a controversy which raged with some heat among the WNI Chinese in the early 1960s between those who advocated total assimilation into Indonesian society, to the point of abandoning Chinese customs, cultural traits and social exclusiveness, and those who have been described as 'integrationists', advocating political loyalty and identification with Indonesia but not an immediate abandonment of group identity which was claimed to be unnecessary in a multi-ethnic society. This controversy with its important political overtones is elaborated more fully in Chapter 2 below. How far the strong support for the latter approach confirmed the stereotyped view among Indonesians that the WNI Chinese still had more in common with their alien brethren than with their fellow-citizens of Indonesia we can only guess; but it would be very surprising if in the tense political atmosphere of 1961–65 it did not strengthen suspicions of that kind in the minds of the anti-communist, anti-Chinese and anti-Sukarno elements, particularly as they were then feeling threatened by the steady erosion of their power and by Sukarno's increasingly close association with the PKI in domestic politics and the Chinese People's Republic in his foreign policy. Thus political antagonisms tended to reinforce generalised anti-Chinese sentiments just at the time when one might have hoped that the settlement of the dual nationality problem would pave the way for more cordial acceptance.[31] Many WNI Chinese must have had doubts during this period about the value of relying on the assumption of Indonesian citizenship and the protection of the law rather than on whatever political and diplomatic support they might have hoped to obtain from Peking as Chinese nationals. Yet whenever it came to a showdown Peking could do relatively little to save even its own nationals in Indonesia from victimisation, as Chapter 3 reveals. The course of Sino-Indonesian relations has also been a significant factor mitigating the pressures upon the Overseas Chinese in that country in the early sixties, aggravating them after 1965, but the dynamics of the process have been complex and indirect.

CHANGING ECONOMIC ROLES

Before we touch on the international aspects of the question, it is necessary to give a brief sketch of the economic position of the Indonesian Chinese since independence and the attempts made to circumscribe their economic power. It is probably true to say that most Chinese business-men have been steadily extending the scope of their activities since the end of the colonial era—and are, in general, considerably better off than they were before that, both in terms of their net income and of their relative positions vis-à-vis their Indonesian competitors in the socio-economic scale—having gained at the expense of both the Dutch who had formerly been able to exclude them from some of the most lucrative and powerful spheres of activity, and of the Indonesians, of whom only a few have made substantial advances up the ladders of commercial advancement of which the Chinese now occupy the higher rungs.

In 1950 the Chinese played a dominant part in most of the retail trade and purchasing of smallholder agricultural commodities through-out Indonesia and in many spheres of wholesale trade, industry, trans-port services and finance, although the Dutch too were still active in the latter fields (but Indonesians hardly at all), while the commanding heights of the economic system, the major banks, export-import houses (the Dutch 'Big Five') and plantations remained predominantly in Dutch hands.[32] Various piecemeal measures were taken to 'Indones-ianise' the economy in the following years by bringing under public ownership various public utilities, plantations and factories sold by their Dutch owners; but little progress was made in this direction before the large-scale nationalisation of Dutch enterprises in 1957–58 as part of the campaign to recover West Irian. Other steps were taken to promote the development of an Indonesian business class through the granting of preference in the allocation of scarce bank credits or import and for-eign exchange licences, measures which tended to discriminate against their Chinese competitors as well as the Dutch. The most notorious of these schemes was the so-called 'Benteng system' of 1950, under which certain categories of imports were reserved for 'national importers' in the hope of building up their capital backing by giving them a mono-poly over commodities for which there were relatively secure profit margins. The term 'national importers' was at first defined as *bangsa Indonesia asli* with the specific purpose of excluding the WNI Chinese from the privileges of the scheme, although in 1953 the government yielded to Chinese representations on this point and dropped the word 'asli' from the definition.[33] But the scheme was beset by troubles from the start and resulted in the creation of only a handful of Indonesian bona fide importers. Lack of working capital handicapped them throughout and many of the 'national importers' merely sold their licences to Chinese businessmen who actually conducted the transactions. Because of these 'brief-case importers' or 'Ali Baba firms' (Ali the Indonesian front man who obtained the licences, Baba the Chinese with the trading connections and capital) the system soon fell into disrepute, generating a good deal of hostility to both parties for their duplicity. Those of the national businessmen who avoided such arrangements found themselves in severe financial difficulties from time to time because of their inadequate reserves, as the economy lurched between rapid inflation and drastic deflation during the 1950s. Despite the commitment of all Indonesian governments during that period to what Anspach has called the 'indigenisation' of the economy and the fostering of the national businessmen, these objectives often had to be sacrificed to the more pressing exigencies of safeguarding the balance of payments or curbing inflation by liberalising imports, a process which generally brought greater profits to the Dutch and Chinese businessmen who had easier access to capital.[34]

By the mid-1950s, many Indonesians were becoming critical of the very notion of building up an indigenous capitalist class to compete with the foreigners, especially if the process was going to prove so wasteful, corrupting and ineffective; on the other hand the beneficiaries of that process were putting the blame on the Chinese for their inability to compete with them successfully. Their frustrations were expressed in the 'Assaat movement' of 1956, a broadly based grouping of several organisations of the national businessmen demanding greater governmental assistance to 'national enterprise', which it defined in such a way as to discriminate in favour of asli Indonesians and against WNI Chinese. As Feith put it: 'The Assaat movement expressed with shattering directness feelings which Indonesians had long had, but hesitated to express in public'.[35] But the main political parties were reluctant to endorse a doctrine with such blatantly discriminatory implications and the movement soon lost political momentum. In any case, a general reaction against both private enterprise and 'liberal' capitalism developed during the political crisis which swept over Indonesia in the years 1956–58 because of the corruption and misuse of public funds that had been associated with the policies directed towards the creation of an Indonesian middle class. Political and ideological forces also encouraged a more socialistic approach to the problems of economic and social development in Indonesia, a trend reinforced by the fact that nationalisation of the Dutch enterprises in 1957–58 left the government saddled with a vast State-owned sector of the economy to manage. Consequently private businesses, whether Indonesian, Chinese or other, now found themselves operating in an extremely unfavourable political climate. For the Chinese in particular the question of whether they would suffer the same fate as Dutch capital now loomed uncomfortably large because of the intensely nationalist as well as Socialist overtones of the new enthusiasm for Sukarno's emphasis on Socialism and a 'return to the national identity'.[36]

The pressures upon the Chinese increased in the late 1950s from several quarters. According to Skinner, 'by 1957 the avowed policy of the Ministries of Industry and Trade was to move gradually toward the exclusion of aliens from all lines of business'.[37] A substantial head tax on aliens was introduced in 1957. The private Chinese-language school system was largely dismantled and Chinese newspapers were banned at the behest of the military authorities using their martial law powers. And in 1958 all Kuomintang organisations were banned and schools and businesses with KMT connections closed in reprisal for Taiwan's assistance to the PRRI-Permesta regional rebellion of that year. Skinner mentions that the army also took advantage of the broader campaign against foreign Chinese to weaken the Communist partisans within the totok community. The culmination of this series of events was the 1959 ban on alien traders in the rural areas, discussed in Chapter 3. This episode seemed to show that, as Skinner put it shortly afterwards, 'the Chinese had few friends indeed in the recently altered Indonesian power structure. With the decline of the parties and the rise of army power, few checks on anti-Sinitic politics remained', except insofar as Sukarno himself could impose them.[38] In fact, Sukarno's capacity to curb anti-Chinese policies, while by no means unlimited, turned out to be rather greater during the 1960–65 period than the gloomy trend of events leading up to the 1959 crisis suggested. He was at least able to put a stop to overt advocacy of anti-Chinese measures, although covert and unofficial forms of harassment and discrimination undoubtedly continued and one attempt was made in May 1963 to stir up anti-Chinese riots for political purposes. While it is true that 'foreign enterprise continued to be attacked on a wide front'[39] during the era of Guided Democracy, the Chinese suffered less, in general, than American, British and other 'imperialist' enterprises, because the political situation created an ideological and diplomatic motive for attacks in that direction while political considerations, notably Sukarno's distrust of the right wing and increasing reliance on the left, helped to shield the Chinese from directly racial or discriminatory attacks.

After the attempted coup of October 1965, resulting in the destruction of the PKI and the overthrow of Sukarno, the situation confronting the Indonesian Chinese changed radically. For several years they were subject to a variety of pressures and attacks, described more fully in Chapter 3, resulting from the tendency to identify them with the PKI or the Peking government. Since 1968, however, anti-Chinese actions have ceased and the tension has diminished considerably as a result of several developments. The Suharto regime was by then fairly securely established in power and better able to take firmer action against anti-Chinese outbreaks. For the sake of its economic stabilisation programme it had no choice but to try to avoid the economic disruption resulting from attacks on Chinese businessmen; in fact, efforts were being made to attract new investment by them in order to get the economy back on its feet. Many of the generals, moreover, were now engaged in financial arrangements with Chinese businessmen and had a positive interest in discouraging mob outbursts of any kind in that direction. After the suspension of diplomatic relations with Peking in October 1967 there was no longer the immediate irritant and provocation to mass actions that had been an important element in the earlier tensions. But perhaps most significant of all was the fact that the groups which had previously been most inclined to stir up anti-Chinese hostility in order to embarrass the Sukarno government no longer had the same political motivation for doing so, while the opponents of the Suharto regime were either disinclined or tactically unable to exploit anti-Sinicism in the same way.

SINO-INDONESIAN RELATIONS

The state of Indonesia's relations with China has been an important background factor influencing the political dispositions of the Indonesian Chinese and the intensity of the pressures to which they have been subjected, although there is no simple correlation between these variables. During the first ten years after the accession of the Communist regime in Peking in 1949 relations between the two countries were generally cordial, despite the relatively anti-Communist complexion of most Jakarta governments at that time; for it was Russia rather than Peking which was then regarded with most suspicion as the mentor of the world Communist movement and as a potential supporter of the PKI. The Chinese People's Republic was widely admired as another manifestation of the spirit of 'new Asia on the march' which had inspired the Indonesian nationalists themselves during their struggle for independence, a spirit which found its apotheosis at the Afro-Asian Conference in Bandung in 1955. China was not at that time regarded as an imminent threat to Indonesia's independence in the way that the two leaders of the Cold War ideological blocs were felt to be because of their crusading mentalities and suspected interference in domestic politics. China conducted her foreign policies skilfully with the aim of maximising the amount of common ground she shared with non-aligned nations like Indonesia in the struggle against colonialism and imperialism and of working towards the elimination of points of friction like the dual nationality problem. Her strategy was generally successful in creating a favourable climate of opinion towards her within Indonesia and particularly in its impact on Sukarno and those who shared his political attitudes.[40]

The atmosphere changed considerably after the 1959–60 rift over the ban on rural traders, however. The right wing elements in Indonesian political life were henceforth much more suspicious of China's aims, partly because of their fears of increasing PKI influence, which Russian and Chinese policy seemed to be designed to promote, partly because China's dispute with India and handling of the Tibetan revolt could easily be depicted as part and parcel of a more assertive foreign policy such as she had demonstrated towards Indonesia in 1959–60. The spectre of a 'threat from the north' was now more easily evoked and although few Indonesians worried about this as an imminent possibility, those who were apprehensive about PKI influence and antagonistic towards the Overseas Chinese became more inclined to look upon the latter as Trojan horses serving Peking's supposedly devious purposes. But Sukarno was moving towards closer alignment with Peking in his foreign policies, as they became steadily more 'revolutionary' after about 1962. This trend coincided with the Sino-Soviet rift and with the PKI's gradual shift from a position of neutrality in that dispute towards an openly pro-Peking alignment by 1963. Sukarno's relations with the USSR also chilled at that time. The development of the Indonesia-Malaysia conflict in 1963–65 further emphasised the convergence of Chinese and Indonesian foreign policy objectives in seeking to hasten the end of 'imperialist and neo-colonialist' hegemony in Southeast Asia. Thus, as Indonesia's relations with Britain and the USA deteriorated, Sukarno began to put more and more stress on the 'Jakarta-Hanoi-Peking-Pyongyang axis' (as he called it, in order to emphasise its broader character as an association of 'The New Emerging Forces' rather than a mere Indonesian-Chinese entente), partly to disguise the diplomatic isolation of Indonesia. In the negotiations preceding the abortive Second Afro-Asian Conference in Algiers in 1965, Indonesia and China were pursuing very similar policies of extreme anti-imperialist radicalism which alienated them from most other members of that bloc. This is not the place to go into the reasons for Sukarno's foreign policy adventures which drew him into such a close association with Peking, but the effects of this trend on the position of the Indonesian Chinese at that time need to be noticed. Outwardly, their position seemed more secure than before, since the left wing was in the ascendant and behaviour or utterances from the right which could be characterised as 'racialist' or 'counter-revolutionary' were likely to get the exponent into serious political difficulties. The May 1963 riots are a revealing case study of the political dynamics of this sort of thing.[41] But beneath the surface both social and ideological tensions were building up which could all too easily be directed against convenient scapegoats if the political structure was shaken, as it was by the abortive coup of October 1965. It was largely because of the fears aroused among anti-communists by Sukarno's flirtation with Peking that the reaction against the Chinese and the PKI was so vehement.[42]

Immediately after the 1965 coup attempt, Sino-Indonesian relations deteriorated sharply as a result of the violent domestic reaction against the Communists (and suspected Communist sympathisers) and the reversal of Sukarno's pro-China foreign policy. For the Indonesian Chinese this meant a major change in the political environment to which they had to adjust and it ushered in a period of frightening insecurity. A return to Indonesia's traditional foreign policy of non-alignment was proclaimed by the Suharto regime, although it has in fact been so heavily dependent on Western foreign aid that its critics have challenged that categorisation. But Foreign Minister Adam Malik sought to avoid a breach with the Soviet Union and even to maintain diplomatic relations with China as long as possible, until his hand was forced by domestic political pressures during mid-1967.[43] China was at that stage in the throes of the Cultural Revolution and her diplomats were not inclined to subordinate ideological considerations to the advantages of preserving diplomatic relations, even for the sake of upholding the interests of the million or so Chinese nationals who still remained in Indonesia, facing a very bleak future. Fortunately the heat has gone out of the issue since then and the Indonesian Chinese have undoubtedly suffered less harassment and pressure than in the years preceding, for reasons which go well beyond the diplomatic factor.

2

PATTERNS OF CHINESE POLITICAL ACTIVITY IN INDONESIA

Charles A. Coppel

The nature of writing about the Overseas Chinese has changed with time. Early writings tended to concentrate either upon quaint *Chinoiseries*, the place of the Chinese under colonial administration, the chronicling of early Chinese officers, or the history of contacts between China and Southeast Asia. A later generation made macro-sociological and economic studies of the Chinese based largely, in the case of Indonesia, on the 1930 census findings. Since the war there has been added a series of sociological studies based upon extensive periods of field work in particular Chinese communities, with attention being paid mainly to the impact upon the Chinese of local patterns of social organisation and culture.[1]

Another, more recently popular phase in the studies of the Indonesian Chinese has been the study of the Chinese in politics. Before the war this subject had only been touched upon, or, in another kind of work, was part of the political debate itself. Since then, the major contributions to this field have been made by Willmott, Williams, Somers and Suryadinata.[2]

This chapter is a venture into the same territory. It seeks to build upon these earlier works and to refine our analysis of the Indonesian Chinese as political men. It is interesting to observe that Professor Wang Gungwu has recently undertaken the same kind of exercise for the Malayan Chinese. One should not expect the patterns of political activity in different Southeast Asian countries to be identical; plainly they will not be. In fact, the three groups of Chinese in politics distinguished by Wang Gungwu 'rest on the premise that the Chinese do want to remain culturally distinguishable'.[3] The same premise cannot hold for the Indonesian Chinese. By comparing the Chinese in politics in different Southeast Asian countries, however, and by seeing where the differences and similarities lie, we may come to a more advanced understanding of the political behaviour of this important ethnic minority. The stereotypes are still widely held either of the Chinese as mere pawns of one or other of the Chinas (or, in another version, of a Singapore-centred 'Third China') or as politically passive commercial beings. Here the political scientists and historians may conceivably be able to play a role in breaking down prejudice similar to that played by the sociologists in cracking the myths of the supposed uniformity and changelessness of the Overseas Chinese.

Myths often have their foundation in some fact. The suggestion that the Southeast Asian Chinese are quite uninterested in politics and are only concerned with making a profitable living is no exception to this. Uncharitably it is said 'They don't care who hold the Southeast Asian cows, so long as they can milk them.' Even as charitable a friend as Victor Purcell has slipped into this turn of phrase.[4] A Chinese business-man might put it another way: 'Politics is a risky business here, above all for a Chinese; I prefer to play safe looking after my business and my family'. A businessman of this kind may be well informed about politics. He has reason to be, since it can affect his livelihood and the welfare of his family. But he will be very careful to avoid open political activity or commitments. Such a man might hold strong political views or may be apathetic politically. Political developments may also drive a man who has been politically active into inactivity, whether by concentrating his social activity in non-political areas, or, in an extreme case, because he has been forced to leave the country, been jailed or even killed for his political beliefs and actions. Political inactivity and apathy are wide-spread in most societies; the Overseas Chinese societies are not excep-tions. Whether the proportion of activists is lower or higher than among the indigenous people of Southeast Asia is difficult to assess; in terms of income and occupation, the Chinese are far from typical of the population at large and, generally speaking, they live in towns whereas the indigenous people are for the most part peasants.

On the other hand, it is also true that many Overseas Chinese have been politically active. The extent and nature of that activity has not been constant over time. It has expanded, contracted and changed in response to events and developments of many kinds, some occurring or originating from inside the Chinese communities, others from outside them. Some observers have perceived Overseas Chinese political activists either as a 'fifth column' for either the Chinese Communist Party or the Kuomintang, or as collaborators of the rejected colonial powers. Al-though some political activity has also approximated these stereotypes, the totality, at least in Indonesia, has been far more diverse and less static than the stereotypes suggest.

The object of this chapter is therefore to spell out the different patterns of Chinese political activity in Indonesia since the turn of the century and to analyse the factors which have contributed to its variety, extent and change.

SIX PATTERNS OF POLITICAL ACTIVITY

The six patterns (or styles) of politics which have emerged at different times and in response to different historical conditions are,

1   the traditional officer system which, it will be argued, has had two modern variants, one during the Japanese occupation and the other since 1965;
2   the 'nationalist' pattern, in which political activity is primarily an extension of the politics of China;
3   the 'integrationist' pattern, of political parties representing the interests of the Chinese community (or sections of it) in local politics;
4   the 'assimilationist' pattern, which is essentially anti-communal;
5   the 'assimilated' pattern, in which Chinese political activists operate within Indonesian formal politics and political parties as individuals rather than as representatives of the Chinese as a group (but who themselves may or may not be 'assimilated' in a sociological sense); and
6   the 'cukong influence' pattern in which certain Chinese businessmen exercise informal political influence over Indonesian powerholders (army men, bureaucrats, party leaders) with whom they have close business connections.

This dimension of diversity does not tell the whole story, however, since rival political streams have on occasion flowed within the same pattern. The diversity of political behaviour has derived in part from cleavages within the Chinese community along the lines of cultural differences and socio-economic status. In part also it has reflected changes over time—in government and government policy, in education, and in political ideas. Further, political behaviour has been influenced by great events; to name a few, the 1911 revolution in China, the rise of Indonesian nationalism, the Japanese occupation of Indonesia, Indonesian independence, the establishment of the Chinese People's Republic, and the failure of the attempted coup in 1965 in Indonesia. These factors have not worked in isolation one from another, but have interacted; and it is their peculiar constellation at particular times which has formed the environment in which Chinese political activists have made their political choices.

CHINESE POLITICAL ACTIVITY DURING THE COLONIAL PERIOD

As far as can be gleaned from the few available sources, there was little scope or desire in the areas under effective Dutch control for political activity outside the field of colonial administration before the present century. The general pattern of administration over the Chinese (especially in Java) was one which had existed for centuries—the traditional officer system. Furnivall said of this system that 'the Dutch, like the Portuguese, were merely following the general Eastern practice in the great markets where *each people had its own rulers*' and that 'the Chinese and other foreign orientals *were left under headmen of their own race*'.[5]

These passages are misleading if they are taken to mean that the Chinese communities were autonomous under their headmen or that they were free to choose their headmen for themselves. A crucial feature of the system was that the leaders were selected and appointed by the colonial government, and were answerable to it. As Lea Williams stresses, the Chinese were 'in theory and within restricted limits in practice...accountable to their headmen or officers', but 'final and absolute authority was...always in the hands of a Dutch governor general who acted in accordance with directives from the Hague'.[6]

Truly autonomous Chinese communities had existed in West Kalimantan in the late eighteenth and early nineteenth centuries. These *kongsis*, originally formed by the Chinese goldminers of that area, had by 1850 achieved complete de facto independence, from the Dutch, the Malay sultans on the coast, and the indigenous Dayaks. They were 'living under their own laws, levying their own taxes, and punishing criminals according to their own ideas of justice' (Irwin).[7] Only those members of a kongsi who held a share in the exploitation of its mines were entitled to vote at its assemblies and only those born in China were eligible for office. The kongsis, although 'bitterly hostile to one another', were united in regarding the Malay Sultan of Sambas as merely the ruler of a neighbouring State; the Dutch government, too, was seen as simply another outside power. This independent attitude was resented by Dutch and Malay authorities alike. The Dutch government's response was not merely to demand homage from the kongsis, but to set about 'the total dismemberment of the kongsi system of government' and in particular 'to end once and for all the power of the Chinese of Western Borneo to make war'. In its place, they instituted a system of direct Dutch rule, albeit with the help and advice of Chinese headmen. Some contemporaries criticised the removal of these Chinese communal institutions as being inconsistent with the Dutch government's policy of allowing the Javanese to retain theirs.[8] In 1909 the colonial official, van Sandick, cited the forcible abolition of the kongsis in support of his contention that the government had never wanted even partial autonomy for the Chinese or for them to choose their own leaders.

In the case of the officer system as it developed in Java, although the officers were appointed by the colonial government, one of the criteria used in their selection—wealth—was itself highly valued by the Chinese communities themselves. Tenure of office tended to increase the wealth and power of the officers, so that (in pre-nationalist times) their prestige rose too. Willmott writes of three essential prerequisites for appointment as a Chinese officer—wealth, business connections and acquaintance with Dutch officials.[9] These qualifications tended to coalesce, and it was not unusual to find many officers in one family, and for this to be promoted by intermarriage between leading families, giving the office in some places a quasi-feudal, hereditary character, as Lea Williams observes. A further qualification required was loyalty to the Dutch.

> The recruitment of the officers was not based upon a desire to install true representatives of the Chinese community. Wealthy men ordinarily were selected because they appeared to command the respect of their compatriots and because they were thought likely, having a personal stake in the colony, to be loyal to the Dutch. The Netherlands authorities believed, with justification in the pre-nationalist era, that the richest Chinese of a city was likely to be the most highly respected man in his community. He was certain to be a staunch advocate of law and order.[10]

The Chinese officers were instruments of Dutch administration but were not properly part of it—they were 'merely servants of it—and servants without pay at that'.[11] Despite this and despite the fact that they were appointed by the Dutch rather than by the Chinese community, there is reason to see their role as being in part political rather than purely administrative. As the channel of communications between the Dutch and the Chinese, they sometimes advised the Dutch government in matters of direct concern to the Chinese, and transmitted and interpreted Dutch law to the Chinese.[12] When the nationalist movement began to get under way, some officers submitted confidential reports on it to the Dutch authorities, thus constituting a rudimentary intelligence system.[13]

The traditional officer system was an institution which lasted in Java for three centuries. Yet by the 1930s the institution had been abolished in most places and replaced by other forms of political organisation. Why was it superseded?

One reason for the continuing prestige of the officers until the late nineteenth century had been the absence of other forms of leadership and social organisation to rival them. From the evidence available, it seems that the flowering of community organisations which has been so striking a feature in this century is also peculiar to it, and is closely related to the development of Chinese nationalism and the spread of education. In previous centuries 'The Chinese populations were not organised for the determination and expression of their group will'.[14] When this situation changed, the officers no longer held a monopoly of leadership.

In part the institution of Chinese officers failed because its economic basis had been undermined and with it some of the prestige of the office. Most of the officers had held government licences as retailers of opium, and were revenue farmers in other fields, such as running gambling houses or ferries. Many also derived income from rural money-lending. An important aspect of the growing humanitarianism which led to the adoption of the Dutch 'ethical policy' at the turn of the century was the abolition of Chinese revenue farming and a tightening up of the pass and quarter systems applicable to the Chinese. The government also came to intervene directly in the supply of rural credit.[15]

The Dutch introduced a number of measures which were apparently intended to counteract the declining prestige of the officers by granting them special privileges not generally available to the rest of the Chinese population. These included exemption from the pass and quarter systems, immunity to trial by native courts and permission for their children to attend European primary schools. In addition, they introduced an official uniform for the officers. These measures succeeded only in further alienating the officers from the rest of the Chinese population. 'It was as if the regime had taken the list of the major grievances of the Chinese. . . and employed it as a guide for the extension of special rights to the officers.'[16]

The officers were usually local born; in Java, this almost invariably meant that they were not literate in Chinese, and even if they spoke Chinese, it was usually Hokkien, and not Hakka or Cantonese, the speech of an increasing proportion of the newcomers. According to van Sandick this, and the officers' lack of interest in the poor immigrants, made the office redundant in Java. His argument must have become more persuasive in the following two decades as the volume of immigration rose. The officers' lack of literacy in Chinese also was open to condemnation, not merely on grounds of utility (as van Sandick argued), but also as something absurd in a leader of a Chinese community at a time of growing Chinese nationalism.[17]

One of the most important reasons for the collapse of the officer system was that most of the officers failed to identify themselves with the new nationalist currents. Many of them were seen as identified with the Dutch in opposition to Chinese nationalism.

Although the officers, in Java at least, passed away in the 1930s, it will be argued that there have since been two brief but distinct attempts to reintroduce a similar institution in a modified form; first, during the Japanese occupation, and secondly following the abortive coup in 1965. For this reason, analytical discussion of this pattern of political activity is postponed until after the modified versions are introduced.

The second and third patterns, which are here called the 'nationalist' and 'integrationist' patterns, are both styles of communal politics characteristic of a society which is more politically aroused and more open for Chinese political activity than the first. Both emerged in response to the great Chinese nationalist awakening which began to have an impact in Indonesia (and especially in Java) about the turn of this century.[18] The offshoots sprouted in different directions partly because the roots of the nationalist awakening were diverse, partly because of the Dutch government's response to the awakening, partly because of the differences in interest and outlook between totok and peranakan, and partly because of the interplay of these factors.

Some of the roots of the awakening were buried deep in Indonesian soil; others were shared with the growth of Chinese nationalism elsewhere. The former lay in the grievances of the Indies Chinese as a group; in the fact that they had not been assimilated to European status but were treated as 'Foreign Orientals', subject to the native courts.[19] This rankled all the more after Japanese residents of the Indies were accorded European status in 1899. In addition the Chinese were confined to certain quarters of the cities and towns, were allowed to travel only with a special pass, and were denied access to Dutch education. Moreover, as a consequence of the pro-native ethos that led to the introduction of the ethical policy, their position had been worsening. The Agrarian Law of 1870 prevented them (along with other non-natives) from obtaining full title to agricultural land, their revenue-farming privileges were in process of abolition, and there were plans afoot to introduce rural banks which would undermine the dominant Chinese place in the provision of village credit. It seemed to many Chinese (whatever the Indonesians may have thought) that they had the worst of all worlds, since they had the disadvantages of indigenous status in this European colony with none of the privileges of that status which European morality saw fit to dispense; and the tide seemed to be running against them.

Apart from the grievances arising from their peculiar situation, the Indies Chinese, in common with the Chinese everywhere in Southeast Asia, became increasingly conscious of their Chineseness.[20] There was a quickening of interest in Confucianism, in Chinese history, in Chinese customs and current events in China. The desire to unite the Chinese as one community and nation and to promote the learning of the Chinese language, even among those who knew no Chinese, spread rapidly. The schools founded by the *Tiong Hoa Hwe Koan* (itself an organisation formed in 1900 to promote these Pan-Chinese ideals) provided instruction in Mandarin.[21] This helped to link the different speech groups among the newcomers and even the peranakans, who sent their children to school to learn the forgotten language of their ancestors.[22] A Chinese language and Malay language press, catering for the increasingly literate and self-conscious Chinese community, sprang up and flourished. Chambers of commerce were founded which not only defended Chinese economic interests but also performed political and quasi-consular functions to link the Overseas Chinese to their homeland.[23] The Chinese government, too, began to take an increasing interest in the Overseas Chinese; imperial government officials visited Java to supervise education, Chinese warships showed the flag in Javanese ports, and peranakan students were encouraged to study in China. On the other hand, revolutionary ideas aimed at the overthrow of the Manchu emperors also spread and political organisations supporting Sun Yat Sen and his fellow revolutionaries were established under cover of the *Soe Po Sia* reading clubs.[24] The consciousness of Chineseness as nationality was given further shape when the Chinese imperial government promulgated its Nationality Law of 1909, by which statutory effect was given to the principle that a child of a Chinese father, wherever born, was a Chinese national.[25]

One might have expected that the combined effect of all these developments would have led rapidly to the consolidation of a real Chinese community, a *sia hwee Tionghoa* which would embrace all speech groups and totok and peranakan alike.[26] Indeed, many leaders of what is here called the 'nationalist' pattern of political activity hoped that it would and worked to achieve it. They did not succeed because of a continuing sense of difference between many of the peranakans and the rapidly increasing numbers of totoks and because of the success of the measures which were taken by the Dutch government in response to the awakening in maintaining this sense of difference.

The Dutch government responded in stages and selectively to the Chinese awakening. Some Chinese individuals were allowed to qualify for European legal status.[27] A new type of primary school in which Dutch was the medium of instruction was established in 1908 exclusively for Chinese children (HCS—*Hollands Chineesche Scholen*). In 1910 a nationality law was passed by which all Indies-born Chinese whose parents resided in the Indies were declared to be Dutch subjects (*onderdanen*) and in 1911 a consular agreement was entered into with the Chinese (imperial) government under which it was agreed that the nationality of the Chinese should be interpreted in each case in accordance with the law of the country of domicile.[28] There was no provision for rejection or loss of the status of Dutch subject under the Dutch nationality law, except in the case of a Chinese who married an alien, was naturalised elsewhere, or who resided in a foreign country for a stipulated period without registering himself at the Dutch consulate. The combined effect of this law and the consular agreement was, in substance, to exclude the peranakans and Indies-born totoks from the jurisdiction of the Chinese consuls, who began to arrive in the Indies in 1912.[29] When the Dutch established the *Volksraad* (People's Council) in 1918 provision was made for the representation of the Chinese. Finally, many of the legal grievances of the Chinese were removed; they were no longer required to appear before native courts in criminal matters and Dutch civil law was extended to them generally, while the hated pass and quarter systems were abandoned.[30]

It was not immediately apparent that these measures would be successful in checking the movement of the Indies Chinese towards political unity. By 1917 the Chinese press, schools and associations were in full cry, and it seemed that the most vocal and influential sections of Chinese society viewed the Dutch policies at best as inadequate palliatives and at worst as sinister attempts to practise divide and rule upon the Indies Chinese. A conference was called at Semarang in 1917 to discuss the question of Chinese representation in the *Volksraad*. This conference, the largest gathering yet held of the Javanese Chinese, decisively rejected the proposal.[31]

The nationalists started from the premise that the Chinese in the Indies were aliens, whatever Dutch law might proclaim. Even the Dutch conceded, they argued, that the Chinese who were born in China were Chinese nationals. Sooner or later (and probably sooner) the Dutch would allow them European status, as they already had the Japanese. As aliens, the Chinese were entitled to the protection of the Chinese government, which had an embassy in the Hague and consular representation in the Indies. What value was there then in Chinese representation in the *Volksraad*? Since the Chinese were only a small minority in the Indies, they were bound to be outvoted in the *Volksraad*. Moreover, participation in the *Volksraad* would be construed as an admission that the Indies-born Chinese were Dutch subjects as the colonial government claimed. This status was not equivalent to that of the Europeans and was inferior to that which the foreign-born Chinese were bound to enjoy soon. In addition, the status of Dutch subject would bring liability to militia service. For men of this cast of mind, national sentiment and practical considerations were at one in demanding that the Chinese should oppose participation in the *Volksraad* and that they should be entitled to repudiate the status of Dutch subject under the Dutch nationality law. They confidently expected that most Indies-born

Chinese would exercise the right of repudiation if it was conceded to them.

The nationalist viewpoint was forcibly expressed in the columns of the Malay language daily *Sin Po* (and later in its sister Chinese language edition) and the nationalists among the peranakans became known as the *Sin Po* Group.[32] The nationalist pattern of activity was probably always much more widespread among the totoks and in areas where the Chinese were Chinese-speaking than among the peranakans. The chief characteristics of the nationalist pattern suggested here are a rejection of involvement in local Indies politics and a high degree of political orientation towards China. Because so little has been written about the politics of the totoks or of the Chinese communities outside Java, the following discussion of the nationalists should be treated with great caution.

It may be surmised that among those whose politics were China-oriented, there were divisions which followed the lines of cleavage of the politics of China itself. Although this contention is much easier to document for the period after the Second World War than for the period preceding it, it is probable that among the nationalists there were followers both of the Kuomintang and the Communist Party.[33] Although internecine strife between these two factions no doubt existed at certain times, a more typical activity of pre-war nationalist politics was the anti-Japanese campaign for the defence of China. The nationalists called for volunteers to serve in China, funds to be raised and trade boycotts to be instituted against Japanese goods.[34] The response of the peranakans to these appeals was usually disappointing, despite the efforts of *Sin Po*. At times of real crisis in China, there was a stirring of support from other sections of the peranakan community than the nationalists, but their support and political involvement were not sustained. (For a parallel case, one might look to the reactions of non-Zionist Jews in the diaspora to the Six Day War in 1967.) There were many among the peranakans who felt pride in China's ancient civilisation and culture and who felt personally touched when China was under attack; and yet they considered that their interests and destiny lay in the Indies. When people of this kind engaged in political activity, it was not of the nationalist pattern discussed here.

The rejection of participation in Indies politics which was characteristic of the nationalist pattern should not be confused with indifference to or ignorance of the Indies political world. For example, in the 1920s there was some co-operation between Chinese nationalists and Indonesian nationalists (expecially non-cooperators like Sukarno) under the banner of Pan-Asianism.[35] Radical nationalists of both nations thought in terms of a partnership to rid Asia of imperialism and colonialism. In fact radical Indonesian nationalists found their China-oriented 'comrades-in-arms' more congenial than the Indies-oriented and culturally more Indonesianised peranakans who seemed to be allying with the Dutch against the Indonesian nationalist movement and were prepared to work through the *Volksraad*.

Those whose politics were of the nationalist pattern tended to regard the Chinese in Indonesia as one community, and to play down the differences of interest and outlook between totok and peranakan. They wanted to unite the Indonesian Chinese 'on totok terms; through the resinification of the peranakan Community'.[36]

Indeed, it is questionable to what extent and for how long peranakans were attracted to the nationalist fold. Even in 1917, at the peak of the nationalist movement's success, there were not only individuals but even some 'pan-Chinese' organisations which stood aloof from the nationalist political pattern. The earliest pan-Chinese organisation of all, the *Tiong Hoa Hwe Koan*, Batavia, apparently abstained from voting at the Semarang conference of 1917 on the issue of Chinese representation in the *Volksraad*, declined to support the *Sin Po* campaign against the status of Dutch subject and even supported a counter-campaign for the retention of the Chinese officers against attacks from the *Sin Po* group on one side and the colonial government on the other.[37] On the other hand, the *Soe Po Sia* reading clubs, which were more clearly China-oriented politically, were established in disproportionately large numbers outside Java and few peranakans joined.[38]

If, for the nationalists to succeed, it was necessary that the peranakans should be resinified, much turned upon the capacity of Chinese language schools to attract the children of peranakans. Suryadinata points out that even top leaders of the THHK sent their children to Dutch schools rather than the THHK's own Chinese-language schools and cites the observation of a leader of the *Hak Boe Tjong Hwee* (the General Educational Association of Java) that most of the peranakan students who went to THHK schools were those who had failed to enter the Dutch-language schools (HCS). The THHK did not establish secondary schools until the mid-1920s and for tertiary education it remained necessary to go to China. In addition to these handicaps, a Chinese education was of little or no use to those who might wish to enter government service in the Indies. It is small wonder that the greater part of the students attending Chinese language schools were totoks. A *Sin Po* survey in 1934 revealed that the number of Chinese attending Dutch schools was almost as great as of those attending Chinese schools and, in the case of secondary schools, was a little greater. The separation of education for the Chinese into Dutch and Chinese streams was matched by a corresponding duality in Chinese teachers' unions and student associations.[39]

Another factor undermining the appeal of the nationalists to the peranakans was the growing realisation that they were different from the Chinese in China. Some highly nationalist peranakans, including a former editor of *Sin Po*, returned to Java in the 1920s and early 1930s after years in China with second thoughts about the appropriateness of Chinese nationalism for the peranakans and prepared to accept the status of Dutch subjects. The peranakans who continued their studies in China held Dutch passports and were usually careful to register at the Dutch consulate lest they forfeit the opportunity to return to the Indies, and possibly thereby received better treatment from Chinese government officials and police. The Dutch authorities showed that they were quite prepared to refuse re-entry to nationalists who went abroad. The members of a nationalist delegation which attempted vainly in 1920 to enlist the support of the Chinese government for the campaign against Dutch subject status were refused permission to return to Java. Some of the delegates were later allowed to return after recanting on the issue. As time passed, the numbers of peranakan Chinese going to China for further study declined. They far preferred higher education in the Netherlands or elsewhere in Europe.[40]

Dutch laws regulating political activity also helped to divide the totoks from the peranakans and to discourage many Chinese from attempting to engage in political activity of the nationalist pattern. On the one hand, only Netherlands subjects were permitted to participate in local political organisation. Although the separation effected by this law could be circumvented by allowing the China-born Chinese to become associate members without voting rights or by splitting an organisation into political and social sections and restricting membership of the former to the Indies-born, it tended to confirm the belief of many peranakans that their interests were not identical with those of the totoks. On the other hand, another Dutch law prohibited elections being conducted in the Indies for a representative council of a foreign country. In 1936 a number of Indies Chinese who were preparing for the election of representatives to the National Congress of China were arrested for breach of this law.[41]

The appeal of the nationalist argument on grounds of material interest waned as the Dutch made progressive concessions to allay many of the Chinese grievances. On the other hand, the very obstinacy of the Dutch in refusing to concede European status even to the alien Chinese weakened the credibility of the nationalists' strategy. At the time of the Japanese invasion of Java, the Chinese were still classified as Foreign Orientals whilst the Siamese had joined the Japanese among the 'Europeans'.[42]

If support for the nationalists was undermined by skilful Dutch policy, it was also little encouraged by the Chinese government. The Chinese consuls in the Indies did not always observe the Consular agreement of 1911. In fact they repeatedly attempted to register all Chinese living there, both totok and peranakan.[43] But the Chinese government's explanations for this were apologetic. It answered the protests of the Indies government by saying that a mistake had been made and claiming that the registration had been intended only for totoks. Despite a campaign by the Chinese nationalists in the Indies, who sent a delegate to Peking and Nanking to urge the Chinese governments not to renew the Consular agreement, the agreement was renewed by the Peking government (then the one recognised by the Western powers) in May 1927. The nationalists' emissary is said to have had more success in his mission to Nanking, but the damage had been done and when the Nationalist government there came to control China in 1928 it did not attempt to abrogate the treaty renewed by the Peking government in the previous year.[44]

Although Chinese government interest in and contact with the Indies and other Southeast Asian countries increased in the 1930s, this did not work to the advantage of the nationalists. To their embarrassment, the Chinese government gave recognition to their enemy H. H. Kan, the president of the *Chung Hwa Hui*, an arch-collaborator with the Dutch who had accepted nomination to the *Volksraad* in the teeth of the Semarang conference decision of 1917.[45] When the (largely totok) Federation of the *Siang Hwees* (Chambers of Commerce) of the Netherlands Indies was founded in 1934 under the auspices of the Consul-General of China, H. H. Kan was elected President. His daughter married a son of the Consul-General.

But the decisive element in the failure of the nationalists to resinify the peranakans remained the effect of Dutch policy. Apart from its intrinsic socio-cultural significance, the importance of this development for present purposes is that it paved the way for a new pattern of political activity—the integrationist pattern.

The integrationist pattern emerged from the nationalist pattern in the 1920s. To the pride in being Chinese, the sense of their having distinct communal interests and the new organisational forms, which were all products of the new Chinese nationalist awakening, there was now grafted the conception that these things could and should be worked for through participation in Indies politics. Although they also sought totok support in a way rather analogous to the nationalist wooing of the peranakans, the integrationists were quicker than the nationalists to recognise and acknowledge differences of interest between peranakan and totok, and between those who were Dutch subjects and those who were not. The integrationist pattern, like the nationalist, is a form of communal politics; unlike the nationalists, the integrationists were Indies-oriented and a part of Indies politics.

Both (like the three groups of political Chinese in Malaya distinguished by Wang Gungwu) accepted 'the premise that the Chinese want to remain culturally distinguishable'.[46] To the extent that they considered the matter, they were either opposed to the notion of socio-cultural assimilation (absorption) of the Chinese by the indigenous majority or sceptical of its feasibility. Reasons for this varied; apart from the extreme case of active Chinese political nationalism, many were proud of Chinese culture, considered that the Chinese as a group had a distinct economic or other interest, or believed that the indigenous people were unwilling to accept them. Differences of opinion over issues of this kind and differences of attitude towards Indonesian nationalism distinguished one stream of integrationists from another.

As we have seen, even at the peak of the nationalists' power, there were some individuals and organisations which stood aloof. Some of them, like H. H. Kan, accepted government nomination to the *Volksraad* or became members of municipal councils. Three of the five appointed Chinese members of the *Volksraad* before 1931 were also Chinese officers.[47] Until 1927, when for the first time a majority of the Chinese representatives in the *Volksraad* were elected rather than nominated, these politicians seem nearer to our model of traditional officers than to the integrationist pattern. But the reform of the *Volksraad* and the institution of provincial councils in Java acted as a catalyst for political development among the peranakan community and led to the formation of the first integrationist party, the *Chung Hwa Hui* (Chinese Association).[48]

The CHH was formed in 1928 as the result of two Congresses held in Semarang in that and the preceding year by peranakan leaders. It was a time in which political alignments in the Indies were becoming increasingly polarised along racial lines. The association parties were losing ground to parties representing particular racial groups. The colonial authorities, having crushed the Communist rebellions of 1926–27, had moved to a more conservative and repressive policy and the Indonesian nationalist movement had become increasingly radical and non-cooperative. The model which the founders of the CHH had before their eyes was the *Indo-Europeesch Verbond* (IEV), or Indo-European Union, which represented Dutch Eurasians and loyally supported the administration whilst working to advance the claims of the Eurasians to parity with the Dutch.

The founders of the CHH came from three principal sources. One was the group of politicians who had been participating in the *Volksraad* and other councils for a decade or more. A second group was connected with organised Chinese big business and, in particular, the biggest business of all, the Oei Tiong Ham Concern, which had its headquarters in Semarang. The third source was from the ranks of the Dutch-educated peranakans, especially the growing numbers of those who had received secondary and tertiary education in the Netherlands. The participants at the Congresses which led to the foundation of the CHH almost all spoke in Dutch.[49]

The CHH was formed as a political party to represent Chinese interests. Its big business backing soon earned it the derogatory nickname of *'Kaoem Packard'* (the Packard group). In contrast to the nationalists, the CHH did not object to the status of Dutch subject but was content to work for the betterment of the Chinese within the existing constitutional framework of the Netherlands Indies. Its efforts to gain further concessions for the Chinese from the Dutch were not conspicuously successful. A submission that the peranakan Chinese should be allowed the same right of acquiring agricultural land for cultivation as the indigenous people was rejected outright by the government Spit Commission report in 1936. Its claim for the Chinese to be given the same status as Europeans (while remaining Dutch subjects) was no more successful than that of the nationalists who sought to make it possible for Chinese to reject Dutch subject status.[50]

The formation of the CHH met with an unfavourable reception not only from the Chinese nationalists but also from the Indonesians. It was apparent to the latter that the CHH was likely to be unenthusiastic at the prospect of Indonesian independence or even autonomy since H. H. Kan, its president, had voted with the Dutch and Dutch Eurasians to defeat a proposal that there should be a majority of indigenous members in the *Volksraad*. That suspicion was confirmed in practice; H.H. Kan proudly told the *Volksraad* in 1935 that the Chung Hwa Hui was composed of 'loyal Dutch subjects' and the CHH representatives there could not bring themselves to support even the innocuous Soetardjo Petition of 1936 which called for a conference in which eventual self-government might be discussed. The loyalty of the CHH did not go unrewarded by the colonial authorities; nominated places on the *Volksraad* and other bodies usually found a CHH man appointed.[51]

Full membership of the CHH was confined to the Indies-born Chinese; the non-Indies born were only allowed associate membership without voting rights. The party was a patrician one, and its leaders were for the most part highly educated and from wealthy families. The party was an enthusiastic supporter of the government Dutch-language schools for the Chinese and set up schools of its own which were modelled upon them.[52]

It might be thought from this that the CHH was opposed to Chinese language and culture and that its members aspired to a fully Dutch way of life as well as Dutch status. Such a picture would be a false one; although considerably Westernised, Dutch-educated and Dutch-speaking, many of them held strongly to traditional peranakan religious practices and advocated the teaching of Chinese language, history and geography in the government schools for the Chinese. This emphasis on Chinese content in education became more pronounced in the late 1930s and culminated in a plan of the CHH in 1940 to establish six-year primary schools (*Volkschool*) in which the medium of instruction would be Dutch but the Chinese language would be taught. These schools, although to be run by the CHH, were to be geared to the government HCS so that students at the *Volscholen* could move on to the HCS.[53]

The increase in emphasis upon the Chinese content in education coincided with a proposal at the 1935 CHH party congress to divide the party into political and social sections, with the latter open to Chinese who were not Dutch subjects. The proposal was in fact rejected, ostensibly because of the difficulty of distinguishing the social from the political.[54] The attempts to broaden the membership of the party (within the limits allowed by the law) and to increase the Chinese content of Dutch-Chinese education were perhaps related to the increasing number of Indies-born totoks and an increasing Chinese consciousness connected with the Sino-Japanese war. Taken together, they suggest a strategy which, but for the Japanese occupation, might have succeeded: to bring about the *sia hwee Tionghoa* ideal not, as the nationalists planned, by a resinification of the peranakans and a disengagement from Indies politics, but by drawing the totoks into the Dutch-educated and integrationist fold while simultaneously making the peranakans more Chinese. With the decline of Chinese immigration in the depression years of the early thirties, the totok community was becoming increasingly Indies-born and hence eligible for participation in Indies politics. The CHH did not fare too well in the 1935 *Volksraad* elections, and these efforts to tempt the totoks have something to do with the necessity to muster more electoral support. But it is probable that the CHH leaders saw a virtue in the necessity, that of the opportunity for wider community leadership that it opened up. Seen in the context of the time, the policy of the CHH probably struck many Chinese as moving in the right direction. The leaders of the radical Indonesian nationalist movement were in internment and Indonesian independence seemed to most observers of Indies politics to be a long way off. To increase the cohesion of the Chinese community and to demonstrate its reliability and indispensability to the colonial government seemed to be eminently in the community's interest. And maybe the government would eventually see the light and grant European status to the Chinese. But time, as it happened, was not on the side of the leaders of the CHH.

The CHH was not the only integrationist party in the period before the Japanese occupation. In 1932 a rival party, the *Partai Tionghoa Indonesia* (Indonesian Chinese Party), was formed in Surabaya. Its founders included some of the people who had decided at the 1928 *Chung Hwa* Congress to form the CHH but had not gained prominence in it. It also attracted a group of young radical students from the Netherlands who had broken away from the main Chinese student organisation there (the *Chung Hua Hui-Netherlands*) to form a separate organisation closer to the Indonesian nationalist students association.

The PTI was born of a double dissatisfaction with the CHH. Its founders were critical of the negative attitude of the CHH toward the Indonesian nationalist movement, and they felt that the CHH represented only the wealthy Chinese.[55]

The PTI actively supported the demand of the Indonesian co-operating nationalists for independence. It opposed the status of Dutch subject, proposing instead an Indonesian status (*Indonesierschap*) which would be open to all races. The PTI representative in the *Volksraad*, Ko Kwat Tiong, was one of the sponsors of the ill-fated Soetardjo Petition. When the government Visman Commission made its belated inquiry into constitutional reforms in 1940, the PTI argued for full dominion status for Indonesia.[56]

The leaders of the PTI, who included a number of Marxists, sought to appeal to the 'have-nots' in the Chinese community, though their radical image was rather tarnished by the need to forge an electoral alliance against the CHH with a group of Chinese business interests opposed to the CHH.[57] Their radicalism and support for Indonesian independence merged in an anti-colonial sentiment which brought them for a time into harmony with the Chinese nationalists, but the concern by the PTI for the special interests of the peranakans alienated the two groups from each other.

The PTI was smaller, rather more local in its support, and less successful in elections than the CHH.[58] Because of its more radical position, its members did not, like those of the CHH, receive government nomination to the *Volksraad* or municipal councils. Although the PTI regarded itself as an Indonesian nationalist party, the Indonesian nationalists, with a few exceptions, did not fully accept it in that character. When they formed a federation of Indonesian political parties (GAPI) in May 1939, the PTI and the PAI (the sister Arab party) were only offered associate, not full, membership. The PTI, offended, declined to join GAPI on these inferior terms.[59]

The PTI was committed to Indonesian independence and to a common citizenship for all races, but it did not advocate the abandonment of Chinese culture; and it accepted foreign-born Chinese as members by converting itself into a social organisation and then forming an Election Section whose membership was limited to the Indies-born. The PTI had some assimilationist tendencies: it ran a HCS-type school in Surabaya which accepted some non-Chinese students and in 1939 its president, Tjoa Sik Ien, criticised the segregation of government primary schools by race as a policy designed to 'divide and rule'. But these tendencies were limited, as may be seen from the PTI reaction to the assimilationist proposals of Kwee Hing Tjiat in August 1934.[60]

Kwee was a political maverick who had started out as an ardent Chinese nationalist. After editing the Malay edition of *Sin Po* in 1916–18 he had spent about four years in Europe. When he returned to Java in 1923, the colonial authorities refused him permission to land, doubtless because of his criticisms of them which had continued unabated while he was in Europe. He spent the next ten years or so in Shanghai, before returning to Java on the guarantee of Oei Tjong Hauw, the director of the Oei Tiong Ham Concern, to become the editor of a new Semarang newspaper called *Mata Hari*. *Mata Hari* was reputedly financed by the Oei Tiong Ham Concern, and it was presumed that Kwee must have sold out to the CHH.[61] In a rather confused argument, Kwee startled the readers of his opening numbers by announcing that the time had come for all peranakan Chinese to take their place as 'Sons of Indonesia' (*Poetra Indonesia*) and be prepared to shoulder all their responsibilities. These, he explained, required them not merely to work with indigenous Indonesians for Indonesian independence but also to become absorbed or assimilated by the Indonesian people.

Reactions to this statement were very strong. The *Djawa Tengah Review*, which supported the PTI, suggested that Kwee's unhappy experiences in China might have set his wits astray! His views, it said, were in conflict with those of the PTI because the PTI did not urge the Chinese to assimilate themselves to become Indonesians; rather, it urged Chinese totoks and peranakans to work together with Indonesians in various fields so that they understood and respected one another, for the public welfare and for the progress of Indonesia and all its inhabitants.[62]

In retrospect one can see Kwee Hing Tjiat's *Mata Hari* campaign as an isolated case in the pre-war period of our fourth, assimilationist, pattern of political activity: anti-communal, rejecting integrationist politics and urging socio-cultural assimilation.[63] He was roundly attacked from all sides—his sanity, integrity, sincerity, and even his courage were all impugned; his proposal was said to be unnecessary, undesirable and impossible to carry out. *Sin Po* carried an article attacking Kwee's proposals under the heading '*Ajam Tida Bisa Djadi Bebek*' (A Chicken can't become a Duck). Antagonism from the Chinese community, even the peranakans, was only to be expected so soon after the heyday of Chinese nationalism. What is, perhaps, surprising today is to discover how little support for Kwee emerged from the indigenous Indonesians. The reason seems to lie in the fact that most pre-war Indonesian nationalist leaders embraced a nationalism which was not merely political but also cultural and often racial.[64] This may be illustrated by the fact that few Indonesian political parties at that time were prepared to accept even peranakan Chinese as full members.

The PNI constitution, for example, provided that only indigenous Indonesians (*Orang-orang bangsa Indonesia*) could be full members and that other Asians (*Orang-orang bangsa Asia jang lain*) could be associate members. Dutch Eurasians and peranakan Chinese found themselves excluded from full membership under this provision. The *Parindra*, the most powerful nationalist party in the *Volksraad* in the 1930s, decided at its 1938 congress not to allow peranakans of any kind (whether Eurasian, Chinese, Arab or Indian) to become members of the party. Thamrin, whose working paper was accepted by the congress, justified the exclusion of the peranakan Chinese by arguing that although there were those in the PTI who were oriented toward Indonesia and considered it to be their motherland, the Chinese still wanted to maintain their customs and Chinese education. Thamrin's argument foreshadows that of more recent advocates of the assimilation of the Chinese into the indigenous community who equate political loyalty and citizenship with socio-cultural assimilation. It is particularly interesting in view of the hostile reception given only a few years before to Kwee Hing Tjiat's proposals.[65]

In general Indonesian nationalist parties had no Chinese members, but the left wing parties were something of an exception. In the 1920s the Communist Party sought to obtain Chinese support 'apparently inspired by internationalist and anti-racist considerations' though evidently with little success.[66] In 1939 the internationalist and United Front-minded *Gerindo* decided to allow peranakans to become members; among the few who accepted the invitation was Liem Koen Hian, the founder of the PTI, who left the PTI to join *Gerindo*.[67]

The occasional Chinese who thus joined Indonesian political parties were the pioneers of the fifth pattern of political activity suggested here—the 'assimilated'. This category refers solely to the political actions of those concerned, many of whom were far from assimilated in the broader socio-cultural sense. In the pre-war period, the numbers of those practising 'assimilated' politics were few, both because of the reluctance of many parties to accept them and because of the reluctance of most Chinese to join.

Their reluctance is not difficult to understand. Even after the successes of the Chinese nationalists in gaining concessions from the colonial authorities (by the removal of many legal grievances of the Chinese), the conduct of colonial administration suggested communal rather than assimilated politics. The Chinese were provided with Dutch primary schools separate from those of the Indonesians, and the distinction between foreign orientals and natives remained important in various fields. The provision of separate representation by race in the *Volksraad* and other councils itself steered the politics of the Chinese in a communal direction.

Quite apart from these considerations and those of group sentiment, many political Chinese felt that communal political action was the only logical course. They felt that the Chinese were distinctive as a group and that they had group interests to defend. The success of the nationalists in promoting Chinese interests (although limited) showed that communal politics could be effective; the integrationist parties, each in its own way, merely applied that lesson to local politics.

The general climate for Chinese political activity was fairly favourable in the Indies in the 1920s and 1930s. It is true that Dutch policy to some extent moulded the nature of that activity and set limits to it. But it was a period in which a wide range of Chinese community organisations flourished; Dutch and Chinese language schools catered for Chinese children; and rival Chinese political views were expressed through a lively and vigorous Malay and Chinese language press. The different contenders for Chinese political allegiance each had its outlet in a Malay language newspaper: the officers in *Perniagaan*, the nationalists in *Sin Po* and *Keng Po*, the CHH in *Siang Po* and later in *Pelita Tionghoa*, and the PTI in *Sin Tit Po*.

Some patterns of activity were far less important than others in this period. The officer pattern became superseded in the twenties. Officers with a substantial following became active in other ways, particularly as members of the CHH. The 'assimilated' pattern was inhibited less by Dutch policy than by the policies of the Indonesian political parties. The assimilationist pattern was as yet scarcely more than the voice of Kwee Hing Tjiat.

The mainstream of Chinese politics flowed fairly freely within the nationalist and integrationist patterns. In Java, at least, the arguments of the three main groups joined issue in the press. Chinese who wanted to think about politics had a very substantial freedom of choice. Many exercised it, following the promptings of sentiment or carefully weighing costs and benefits or, more commonly, doing both. Then came the Japanese invasion and occupation. With it much of the political initiative passed from the Chinese community.

THE JAPANESE OCCUPATION AND THE INDONESIAN REVOLUTION

One immediate and obvious effect of the Japanese occupation was a sharp decline in the level of political activity among the Indonesian Chinese.[68] In the confusion of the invasion, there was some violence against the Chinese, especially in the Tanggerang district of West Java. This was soon checked by the Japanese authorities, who did not want any disruption to the economy. After a brief easy period, that of the 'Triple A' Movement, when it seemed that even the perennial H. H. Kan might be able to co-operate with the Japanese, hundreds of Chinese political leaders were interned and others went into hiding.[69] The independent (non-collaborating) Chinese press was silenced and all Chinese political organisations banned. Dutch influences, which had become so strong among the peranakan Chinese, were now suddenly stifled. Most Dutch nationals were interned, Dutch-language schools and Dutch businesses closed, and use of the Dutch language barred. Unemployed former students and employees among the peranakans began to learn Mandarin privately or in the Chinese-language schools which, after a brief closure, reopened and apparently expanded in numbers. As a result, the resinification of the peranakans, which had been a fading dream of the nationalists for many years, now began to seem a possibility. Chinese with Western given names began to use Chinese ones instead, and many peranakans found that they had to learn to write their names in Chinese characters to comply with Japanese regulations. The achievement of a united community on totok terms, by some extraordinary paradox, was being assisted by the Japanese! An important factor in this development was the form of social and political organisation which the Japanese sponsored.[70]

In Java, at least, the various Chinese associations (apart from the banned political organisations) were grouped together in a single federation, the *Hua Ch'iao Tsung Hui*, which was established after July 1942 in each locality and with a central headquarters in Jakarta.[71] Represented on the board were peranakans, totok speech groups, and social organisations such as burial insurance societies. Until the end of 1943, the HCTH exercised many of the same political functions as the former Chinese officers. Its leaders, too, were appointed by an authority outside the Chinese community, in this case the Japanese military commanders, and were responsible to them and to the office of Chinese affairs, the *Kakyo Han* in Jakarta, which issued regulations governing the Chinese community. In addition the HCTH collected funds for the war effort, provided relief for poorer Chinese or refugees from insecure areas, and managed Chinese schools.

The HCTH leaders, like the officers, were hand-picked agents of the established government but they also performed services for the Chinese community. Apart from organising relief and education facilities, they succeeded in persuading the Japanese to revoke the alien head tax which had been imposed on all male Chinese early in the occupation and the provision requiring Chinese to obtain travel passes. Since most of the pre-war leaders were interned, the HCTH did not attract the 'natural' leaders of the Chinese community. The chairman of the Jakarta HCTH was a man who had been jailed by the Dutch for pro-Japanese activities not long before the invasion and was the editor of a Malay language newspaper called *Hong Po* during the occupation period.[72]

Although the HCTH lost its formal right to discharge political functions at the end of 1943, it continued to exist as a federation of Chinese associations. Through it and the office of Chinese affairs (to which Liem Koen Hian, the former PTI leader, was recruited), the Japanese treated the Chinese, whether totok or peranakan, as a unified group, separate from the indigenous Indonesians. In the latter part of the occupation, this rigid separation was relaxed slightly. A few peranakan leaders, including Liem Koen Hian, were appointed as members of representative councils to discuss Indonesian independence.[73]

During the three and one half years of the occupation, the two patterns of Chinese political activity which had been dominant in the pre-war period—the nationalist and integrationist patterns—were suppressed by the military authorities. In their place, the Japanese introduced a variant of the officer system which had potentialities for the future. For the first time, many of the old communal associations were bound together in a federation which was later able to be transformed into a potent instrument for the solidarity of the Chinese community.

After the Japanese surrender, the Chinese communities (in Java) themselves built a new federation of Chinese organisations to replace the HCTH which was called the *Chung Hua Tsung Hui*. Like the HCTH, the new CHTH for a time federated totoks and peranakans; unlike it, its leaders were chosen by the Chinese community. There were good reasons for the Chinese to close ranks. Chinese education continued to expand, China had been declared one of the five great powers, and the Indonesian Chinese were occasionally targets of the revolutionary violence which accompanied the attempt of the Indonesian Republic to assert its independence against the returning Dutch administration. Despite all these factors, even the CHTH, which was probably for a while the most all-embracing of all Pan-Chinese organisations ever in Java, did not attract all politically minded Chinese and within a few years lost much of its unity and membership.[74]

An important consideration for the Chinese during the period of revolution against the Dutch was that before very long almost all the major cities were in Dutch hands. Not only was a large proportion of the Chinese population in Java already concentrated in these cities, but many more fled to them from less secure small towns and rural areas. Nevertheless some peranakans were staunch supporters of the Republic and in the Republican strong-hold of Yogyakarta, the local CHTH itself was pro-Republican. Several were prominent members of political parties and held Cabinet posts in the Republican government.[75] Even in the Dutch held city of Surabaya, there was a small organised peranakan political group ('Servants of Society'—SOS) which was led for a time by the former president of the PTI, Dr. Tjoa Sik Ien (who also became a member of the Indonesian delegation to the United Nations). The SOS principally attracted former PTI members.[76] Apart from this, there were a number of individual sympathisers for the Republican cause living in Dutch occupied areas, who helped in various ways, including smuggling supplies. The Republic, for its part, attempted to attract as many Chinese as it could to its support. The Republican citizenship law of 1946 automatically conferred Indonesian citizenship upon all Chinese born in Indonesia who had resided there for five years, unless they repudiated it within a given period. This law demonstrated the desire of the Indonesian government to show its acceptance of peranakans, while permitting the Chinese nationalists among them to reject local citizenship (which was something the Netherlands Indies government had refused to do, despite the protests of the Chinese nationalists). Its attempts to attract Chinese support were handicapped by its inability to control all the irregular units on the Republican side (some of which were prone to harass Chinese communities), by the use of a 'scorched earth' policy so as to deny economic assets to the Dutch (which necessarily hurt the Chinese more than the Indonesians), and the confusion which inevitably arose in areas where one side was advancing and the other retreating. The nationalism of the Indonesian revolutionaries also on occasions had racial and anti-capitalist overtones which led to violence against Chinese as well as Dutch. After the worst of the attacks on the Chinese, in Tanggerang in May and June 1946, even some of the more vocal sympathisers of the Republic among the Chinese became disillusioned at the failure of the Republic to protect the Chinese. These incidents gave rise to the suggestion (originating from the Chinese Consul-General in Jakarta) that the Chinese should form their own self-defence organisation to protect Chinese lives and property. When it was formed, this body, the *Pao An Tui*, appeared to the Indonesians to be fighting with the Dutch against the Republic, a factor which led many Indonesians, particularly in the army, to be sharply resentful of the Chinese.[77]

The Dutch administration, on the other hand, made the most of anti-Chinese incidents in its propaganda against the Republic and adopted a political strategy of appealing to minority groups (including smaller ethnic communities as well as the Chinese) in an endeavour to isolate the Republic. Chinese delegations were invited to conferences sponsored by the administration in 1946 and 1947 to establish states which might eventually be member states of an Indonesian federation, and when at length parliaments were set up for the Dutch-sponsored federal states, the Chinese were allotted a disproportionately large share of the seats. Some Chinese co-operated closely with the Dutch, notably Thio Thiam Tjong, a former CHH leader, who became an official adviser to the Lieutenant Governor General, van Mook.[78]

In the turmoil and uncertainty of the revolutionary period, a common reaction of the Chinese was a studied neutrality. Loa Sek Hie, another former CHH leader, who participated in the Pangkalpinang conference in October 1946, said that the position of the Chinese in Indonesia was 'between the hammer and the anvil'. The colonial government itself was, he said, chiefly to blame for the failure of the Chinese to enter fully into political life, since it had not even given the Chinese the status of the now hated Japanese. The upshot was that the Chinese, for reasons outside their control, and not because of opportunism or fence-sitting, were unable to choose between the parties (Indonesia and the Netherlands). At the Pangkalpinang conference, the Chinese delegates unanimously declined to express their views on problems of state and politics 'until the political horizon becomes clearer'.[79]

The newly found unity in the Chinese community could not survive the conflicting pressure from the Dutch and Indonesian sides on the one hand, and the growing influence of the Chinese civil war on the other. The conflict of interest between peranakans and totoks proved too great and new peranakan associations were formed in many places which in some cases broke away from the CHTH. A notable example was the formation of the *Sin Ming Hui* (New Light Association) in Jakarta in 1946, which sponsored the formation of a new peranakan political party in May 1948, and broke away from the CHTH.[80]

The new party, at first named the *Persatuan Tionghoa*, was an integrationist party in the pre-war tradition. It attracted as leaders some men who had been interned by the Japanese and some who had collaborated with them, some who had been CHH leaders before the war and some, surprisingly, who had then been prominent among the China-oriented *Sin Po* group.[81] The PT claimed to be a political party which did not espouse any 'ism' but was based upon a 'practical-realistic' policy. An article in its 1950 Congress publication demonstrated the integrationist quality of the party in a statement that 'as long as we' (i.e. the Chinese) 'still have specific interests, we must put them forward and defend them'.

Among peranakans who had been impressed by the elevation of China to great power status after the war, there were soon feelings of disappointment at the apparent ineffectiveness of China to protect them in the turbulence of the Indonesian revolution. Although the Chinese government early in the piece supported Indonesian independence, it found itself increasingly compelled to protest against the violence suffered by the Indonesian Chinese. The protests were not able to produce the protection desired by the Indonesian Chinese, and the Chinese government was powerless to intervene.

The Chinese government was of course in dire straits at home. Runaway inflation and the defeats of Nationalist troops by the Communists in late 1948 and early 1949 heralded the flight of the Nationalist government to Taiwan late in 1949, and the establishment of the Communist Chinese People's Republic on the mainland.

These momentous changes had their impact in Indonesia, where the fragile fabric of Chinese solidarity was soon split again, this time amongst the China-oriented totoks. Kuomintang membership in Indonesia declined as the Communists gained ground in China, and new leftist organisations were set up to rival those dominated by pro-Kuomintang leaders. The battle among the totoks between the pro-Communist and pro-Kuomintang Chinese was joined in many spheres.[82] The prize was control—of the schools, the press and the various community organisations. The contest was an unequal one since the Indonesian government soon recognised the Chinese People's Republic as the sole government of China and its first ambassador arrived in Jakarta in August 1950. Thereafter the Kuomintang Chinese were on the defensive, although their ranks were augmented by the arrival of some Nationalist refugees from the mainland. The detailed story of the struggle between these two groups, which continued until the dissolution of the Kuomintang and all its affiliated schools and newspapers in 1958 (and has persisted in more covert forms since then) has never been explored in published research. It is known, however, that in some areas (notably in some parts of Sumatra, around Pontianak in West Borneo, and in Jakarta itself) a substantial number of Kuomintang-oriented schools, newspapers and associations continued to exist right up until their dissolution in 1958. But even in these areas of KMT strength there was something closer to a balance between the two sides rather than a KMT preponderance. Elsewhere, the pro-Communists greatly outnumbered those favouring the KMT.

The Indonesian independence struggle also reached its climax in 1949. At the end of that year the Netherlands at length agreed, at the Hague Round Table Conference agreement, to the transfer of sovereignty to a federal but Sukarno-Hatta-dominated Indonesia. Many Chinese who had been living in the areas under Dutch control now had to make a difficult re-adjustment to a situation in which Indonesian nationalism was triumphant. One aspect of the problem of adjustment was the provision in the Hague agreement that the Chinese born in Indonesia would have Indonesian citizenship but be free to choose within two years to reject it. In some areas at least, leftists urged the Chinese concerned to reject their Indonesian citizenship, while KMT supporters urged them to keep it. Eventually almost 400 000 local-born Chinese repudiated Indonesian citizenship. This surprisingly large group is said to have included Liem Koen Hian, the founder of the PTI, who had also been a member of the Committee for the investigation of Indonesian independence during the last months of the Japanese occupation. Liem's decision was said to be due to his resentment at being jailed by the Sukiman government in August 1951 together with many prominent leftists and other Chinese.[83]

BAPERKI VS THE 'ASSIMILATIONISTS'

The period of constitutional democracy which followed the transfer of sovereignty in December 1949 posed new problems for Chinese political activists. The Indonesians were now masters of their own country and government. The old-style integrationist PT (under its new name of Partai Demokrat Tionghoa Indonesia) was suspect in the eyes of the Indonesians since none of its leaders had sided clearly with the Republic in its struggle for independence and its chairman Thio Thiam Tjong had even been adviser to the Dutch Lieutenant Governor General. But the PDTI found it hard to attract a great deal of Chinese support. By 1953 its parliamentary representatives had all defected to other parties. The PDTI itself attributed this sorry state of affairs to the existence of two distinct schools of political thought in the Chinese peranakan community, one advocating what we are here calling 'assimilated' politics and the other integrationist politics.[84] Both groups acknowledged the existence of a minority problem, it said, both opposed racial discrimination among fellow citizens, and both wanted to work for its elimination. But those favouring 'assimilated' politics were opposed to communal or integrationist parties, since their existence could only sharpen existing differences and isolate the minority concerned. They thought it far better to join general political parties based upon some ideology and work to oppose discrimination from within them. Within this camp there was a small minority which argued for socio-cultural assimilation so that differences between indigenous Indonesians and Indonesian citizens of Chinese descent (hereafter called WNI Chinese) would ultimately disappear, while the remainder were in favour of retaining their Chinese culture and way of life. The second school of thought, however, argued that since it was a fact that there were minorities in Indonesia which were discriminated against in various fields, such a minority was entitled to combine to oppose that discrimination. In their view, membership of general political parties by WNI Chinese was meaningless since in those parties they were also in a minority. Thus where majority and minority interests were in conflict, the latter must lose out. They therefore advocated a party consisting of peranakan Chinese to defend their interests.

The WNI Chinese in parliament in the period before the 1955 elections were scattered among various parties. There were two representing the PSI, two representing the PNI, and one each for the Catholic Party, the Democratic Fraction and the SKI Fraction. Moreover, there were two WNI Chinese members of the first cabinet of Ali Sastroamidjojo (July 1953–July 1955)—one from the PNI and one from the PSII.[85] Despite the presence of WNI-Chinese in the cabinet and the parliament, there was a widespread feeling among politically conscious Chinese that discrimination against them was on the increase. By 1953, economic policies were giving strong preference, not merely to Indonesian citizens over alien Chinese, but to indigenous citizens over those of Chinese descent, particularly in the field of importing. Even where the law and regulations did not discriminate between citizens, officials often required Chinese to prove their Indonesian citizenship.[86] This requirement was at worst impossible or difficult and expensive, and at best humiliating, particularly as it was not made of indigenous Indonesians. With the consequences of alien status worsening, a new citizenship law was in preparation which promised to exclude many Chinese from Indonesian citizenship who were currently entitled to it. From the period of the first Ali cabinet, due to the fact that the scope of legality was shrinking and bureaucratic power and arbitrariness rising, racial discrimination became more common. Despite this, however, many Chinese benefited from the new situation, especially by moving into economic roles which the Dutch were abandoning.

In 1953 an elections law was enacted by the parliament, where-upon electioneering quickly got under way. The government had decided to establish a common roll for all citizens rather than separate communal rolls for the ethnic minorities. Thus, to comply with the constitutional requirement of a stipulated number of representatives of these minority groups, the government proposed, should the voters as a whole fail to elect the number of minority representatives constitutionally guaranteed, to fill the deficiency by appointment. WNI Chinese politicians feared (justifiably, as it later turned out) that the Chinese who would be appointed by the government would not be representative of the minority so much as of the parties comprising the government which appointed them.[87]

Thus many factors—the weakness of the PDTI (and of similar smaller bodies based in Surabaya [Perwitt] and Makasar [Pertip]), the increasing discrimination against both alien and citizen Chinese, the proposed citizenship law and the impending elections—all seemed to point to the need for some new communal organisation which could nominate candidates or back those selected by the political parties and make its platform opposition to racial discrimination among fellow citizens.[88] The proposal, first propagated in the PDTI organ, reached fruition with the formation in March 1954 of *Baperki* (*Badan Permusjawaratan Kewargane-garaan Indonesia*—Consultative Body for Indonesian Citizenship).[89] The PDTI, *Perwitt* and *Pertip* were all absorbed by the new organisation. Membership was open to all Indonesian citizens and the name *Baperki* was preferred to that earlier proposed (*Baperwat*—*Badan Permusjawaratan Warganegara keturunan Tionghoa*—Consultative Body for Citizens of Chinese descent). To try to ensure that it should obtain maximum support, the new body was to be a 'mass organisation' rather than a political party like the PDTI. It was therefore to be limited in its aims and ideologically unaligned. By limiting its aims substantially to the promotion of citizenship and the elimination of discrimination among citizens, Baperki succeeded at its foundation in attracting a remarkably wide political range of leaders and election candidates. Baperki in 1954–55 was the most representative of all the Indonesian integrationist groups before or since. Its leaders and election candidates included members of all the main streams of peranakan politics before and after the war, rightists and leftists, members of different religious groups, employers and union men.[90]

Baperki took root in the peranakan community with great rapidity. By October 1955 it claimed 40 000 members and 142 branches. But although the name and constitution of the organisation were designed to suggest that it was open to Indonesian citizens who were not Chinese, 98 per cent of the members, on its own admission, were of Chinese descent and another 1 per cent were citizens of other foreign descent. Moreover it acted as a communal organisation for the WNI Chinese by proposing its own list of candidates for appointment by the government after the elections to the vacancies for minority representatives in the parliament and constituent assembly.[91]

Although claiming to be a mass organisation rather than a political party, Baperki fielded its own candidates in the 1955 general elections. Its chairman, Siauw Giok Tjhan, was elected on a Baperki ticket to the parliament and, with another Baperki candidate, to the constituent assembly.[92]

As Mary F. Somers has observed, 'such a broad-based coalition could not be expected to endure; it did not even survive until the elections'. Shortly before the elections, several prominent Baperki leaders, including two listed as Baperki candidates, left the organisation.[93] Those who left were associated either with the PSI or with the newspaper *Keng Po* (which supported the PSI). In the next few years, their example was followed by other 'rightists', especially Catholics and Protestants. Although this was not always the reason publicly given, the conviction was spreading among these groups that the chairman of Baperki was steering the organisation into the Communist camp. In the 1957 regional elections, Baperki local branches entered into vote-pooling agreements with the PKI in areas (particularly East and Central Java) where the PKI was strong; they were also areas where Baperki was strong. It was little consolation to the Catholic Chinese of those areas to be told that there were as many vote-pooling agreements with the Catholic Party (elsewhere) as there were with the PKI.[94] The left-wing influence in Baperki was noticeably less strong outside Java.

Although Siauw Giok Tjhan has never described himself as a Communist, his record suggests that he has been in agreement with the PKI's stand on most important issues. His speeches have a Marxist ring to them, even when dealing with race discrimination; his conviction has been that only with the achievement of a socialist Indonesia can discrimination be eliminated, and he has constantly cited the Soviet Union and the Chinese People's Republic as models for the solution of problems of national minorities. He was a personal friend of the PKI leader Tan Ling Djie and was for a short time editor of the PKI newspaper *Harian Rakjat*. Whether or not Siauw was a member of the PKI, its ideas were quite congenial to his own. Moreover, Siauw, who was a powerful figure in Indonesian politics in his own right (he had been a cabinet minister in the Amir Sjarifuddin government in 1947), very soon became the dominant influence in Baperki.[95]

Over a period of time Baperki moved away from the ideological non-alignment expressed in its constitution and in its election platform in 1955, and moved to a position which was increasingly closer to that of the PKI. This shift was made easier by the fact that the whole national political spectrum also shifted to the left in the late fifties, when Indonesia, by decree of President Sukarno, returned to the 1945 Constitution and entered upon the era of 'Guided Democracy'.[96] In 1960 there was a final, belated challenge to Siauw's policies when Yap Thiam Hien, an eminent Protestant lawyer who had been a senior vice-chairman of the organisation from its foundation, accused Siauw of deviating from the original non-aligned policy and betraying Baperki's fundamental policies by supporting the proposal for return to the 1945 constitution in the constituent assembly.[97] This latter was particularly blameworthy in a Baperki representative because the 1945 Constitution provided that the President must be an asli (indigenous) Indonesian, and therefore discriminated against Indonesian citizens who were of foreign descent (unlike the 1950 Constitution which it superseded). Yap's motion of no confidence in Siauw's leadership was overwhelmingly defeated in the Baperki Congress in December 1960 and he ceased to be vice-chairman. The central leadership (now purged of the last of its 'rightists') was able to claim that where its policies converged with those of the PKI, it was doing no more than the President himself.[98] It was now a period in which Indonesia had a state ideology (the *Manipol-USDEK*, or Political Manifesto) and the return to the 1945 constitution was an accomplished fact; circumstances, they said, had changed since the foundation of Baperki. Timorous members could be brought into line by pointing out that dissenting political organisations would now be banned. Any criticism of communist leanings could now be met by accusing the critic of 'Communist-phobia', which the President had condemned. Baperki should now become a member organisation of the *National Front* and its constitution should be revised to conform with the new situation.

Although Baperki now espoused a leftist ideology, it succeeded in

retaining its position as the outstanding representative of the WNI
Chinese. In particular, it continued to receive the support of the greater
part of the Chinese business community. To understand this, one needs
to look at its achievements on behalf of Chinese communal interests (and
not only in the political field) and developments in the alien Chinese
community, as well as the shift in the general Indonesian political
spectrum already mentioned.

Under Siauw's leadership, Baperki conducted a vigorous campaign
against racial discrimination. WNI Chinese rice-millers had reason to
be grateful to Siauw for defending their interests in the face of a bill which
threatened them in 1954, and when in 1956–57 the WNI Chinese were
faced by a full-scale challenge from the 'Assaat Movement', which
sought to gain preferential treatment for indigenous Indonesian businessmen vis-à-vis Indonesian-citizen Chinese, Baperki responded
quickly and firmly.[99] It is debatable to what extent Baperki's activities
actually reduced the amount of discrimination; other factors were
probably more important in bringing about the decline of Assaatism.
But what was clear to many WNI Chinese was that in Baperki they had
found an organisation whose leaders were willing and able to take a
strong and unambiguous stand on the issue of discrimination—a
champion of their rights as citizens—and that in it, the body of the
peranakan community had found a voice.

Its representatives strongly opposed the draft citizenship law of 1954,
and were prominent in the parliamentary debates on citizenship and the
dual nationality treaty entered into between China and Indonesia in
1955. The viewpoint of Baperki (a view held by most members of the
Chinese community) was that dual nationals should not be required to
make an active rejection of Chinese citizenship in order to retain their
Indonesian citizenship. This proving unacceptable to the Indonesian
government, Baperki did its best to ensure that the widest class of dual
nationals possible should be exempted from this requirement under the
treaty. It also pressed for the inclusion amongst those considered to be
dual nationals of the Indonesia-born Chinese who had been minors in
the 1949–51 period and whose parents had at that time rejected Indonesian nationality, a proposal which was ultimately adopted by the
Indonesian government after the personal intervention of President
Sukarno. When the treaty came to be implemented, Baperki was again
active in providing information to those affected and in giving assistance
or criticism as required to Indonesian officials responsible for its implementation.[100]

As well as having one candidate elected to the parliament and two to
the constituent assembly, Baperki succeeded in interposing its demands
in relation to the filling by government nomination of vacancies for

Chinese minority representatives. The government initially planned to nominate Chinese members of the six government parties, but the Baperki campaign against this eventually resulted in several Baperki men being among the appointees.[101]

Baperki's activities were not confined to the political field. Its most notable achievements after 1957 were probably in the field of education. In 1957 it began to set up schools, which spread so rapidly that there were said to be about 100 by 1963. They were national schools, in that their curriculum was Indonesian and the language of instruction was also Indonesian. Admission to them was in principle open to indigenous Indonesians and Chinese, both citizens and aliens. The vast majority of the students in most Baperki schools was Chinese, many of them Indonesian citizens who had, since 1957, been forbidden to attend Chinese-language alien schools. In addition, Baperki established a university in Jakarta with a branch in Surabaya which was well-equipped and staffed, and was prepared to accept graduates of the alien Chinese schools. By its educational endeavours, Baperki won many friends among the Indonesian Chinese who would otherwise have found it difficult or impossible to educate their children in ways they thought appropriate, and played a role in bringing peranakans and totoks together.[102]

As we have already seen, Baperki's appeal was not confined to the WNI Chinese. Although it was set up as a body concerned with Indonesian citizenship, Baperki's economic policies, as articulated by chairman Siauw, were framed in such a way as to serve the interests of Chinese in Indonesia, whether they were alien or citizen.[103] He argued that in Indonesia's current stage of development, the country needed to make full use of all 'domestic capital' without discriminating between indigenous or non-indigenous citizens, or requiring that the capital should be owned by citizens, provided that profits from it were not transferred overseas. Thus the foreign capital which was detrimental to the development of the Indonesian economy was not Chinese capital (which was reinvested in Indonesia and therefore 'domestic') but 'foreign monopoly capital' which repatriated resources to Western countries.[104] Siauw's strategy for the utilisation of Chinese capital found its way into President Sukarno's Political Manifesto doctrine that all 'funds and forces' of a progressive character should be used for Indonesia's national development. This included the funds of alien Chinese who had settled in Indonesia and were prepared to co-operate in the government's programme. On several occasions Baperki's parliamentary representatives defended alien Chinese interests. In 1957, for example, Ang Tjiang Liat, in opposing the alien head tax which had just been introduced, suggested that 'the spirit of Bandung' required that Chinese People's Republic nationals should be exempt from the tax. And Siauw led his National

Progressive Fraction in the parliament into an alliance with the PKI representatives to oppose the 1959 regulation banning retail trade by aliens in rural areas.

The shift to the left in Baperki and in Indonesian politics generally in the late 1950s was to be found also among the alien Chinese. The struggle between the pro-Communist and pro-Kuomintang Chinese ended in a decisive victory for the former in 1958.

In March of that year, the headquarters of the Indonesian army announced that arms originating in Nationalist China had been dropped to the PRRI rebels in Central Sumatra. Leftist and nationalist groups called for radical action against the Kuomintang in Indonesia. The Army Chief of Staff acting as Central War Administrator issued a series of decrees under the martial law then prevailing. The first of these (in April) banned the Chinese language press from publication, then permitted it to publish only by government licence. This initially hit the Communist as well as the Kuomintang press, but in December the leftist newspapers were again allowed to publish. In September and October decrees followed which were aimed specifically at the Kuomintang Chinese. All organisations set up by 'stateless' Chinese were banned and their schools and businesses (or those in which they had a part interest) were placed under government control. The result of these measures was to leave the remaining alien Chinese press, schools and community organisations in the undisputed possession of the leftists. Overt political activity by the Kuomintang-oriented Chinese was suppressed and did not emerge again until the late 1960s.[105]

Siauw Giok Tjhan's policies succeeded in making him an unprecedentedly successful leader of the Chinese in Indonesia. But they were too pro-Communist and too China-minded for some sections of the community. His concern for alien Chinese interests (other than those of the Chinese who favoured the Kuomintang), his campaign to have Indonesian citizenship available to the largest possible number of Indonesian Chinese in the easiest way possible, and the fact that one of his own children was sent to China for schooling aroused suspicions not only among many indigenous Indonesians but also among WNI Chinese who were either anti-Communist, or advocates of assimilation or unsympathetic to the interests and orientations of totoks.

In 1960 some WNI Chinese of this outlook organised a consciously anti-communal movement which came to the surface in the peranakan Chinese community in Java under the banner of assimilation. The WNI Chinese, they urged, should work to put an end to the Dutch-built barriers to their full participation in the Indonesian community. Its leaders were not so much putting forward novel ideas as expressing them for the first time as a coherent programme of political action for the WNI Chinese.

The roots of the movement were various and were not confined either to the Chinese community or to those who were principled advocates of assimilation. Although Kwee Hing Tjiat was perhaps closest to being a spiritual father of the movement, his paternity has not been recognised by the assimilationists. Instead, they have claimed Liem Koen Hian and his PTI as the pioneers of assimilation.[106]

The idea that the WNI Chinese should assimilate to the Indonesian community was not new. From the early days of the revolution, the Indonesian government's Bureau of Peranakan and Alien Affairs (UPBA—*Urusan Peranakan dan Bangsa Asing*) in the Ministry of Home Affairs advocated the assimilation of all minorities, though without spelling out the content of the concept in any detail.[107] Prominent indigenous Indonesians have frequently given voice to the same concept. For example, in April 1958, General Nasution, then Army Chief of Staff, urged all WNI of foreign descent not to mix with aliens but to ally themselves with indigenous Indonesian groups and organisations. It has been a common tenet of nationalism that Indonesia should be 'united and homogeneous' and that 'exclusive' organisations were undesirable. Debate has not been about these ideals but rather about their meaning and what their application entailed.

In 1952 there was a move by the leaders of the Chinese student federation in the Netherlands (the *Chung Hua Hui*) for the dissolution of the federation and its constituent bodies.[108] It was argued that with Indonesia now independent it was no longer appropriate to maintain an organisation consisting exclusively of persons of Chinese origin and in particular one in which some of the members were Dutch nationals and the majority Indonesian. The proposal gained over 60 per cent of the votes cast but failed to gain the two-thirds majority required by the CHH constitution. The leadership thereupon resigned en masse from the CHH and were followed by many of the members. A number of those who left became active in general Indonesian student organisations in the Netherlands. In a pamphlet which they published at the end of 1952 these activists expressed their aim as being 'to move as Indonesian individuals in general Indonesian circles and no longer to constitute a collective grouping from one ethnic group'.

We have noted[109] that before the formation of Baperki there was already a school of thought in the peranakan Chinese community in Indonesia which favoured 'assimilated' politics, and that a radical minority of this group wanted assimilation in a broader socio-cultural sense. They were, however, a collection of individuals rather than an organised movement.

The general feeling against 'exclusivism' had its influence upon communal institutions in the peranakan community. The outward signs of this included the abandonment of Chinese names for newspapers and associations, the exclusion of aliens from membership of associations and the opening of membership to indigenous Indonesians. Beyond this point integrationists and assimilationists began to part company. The former argued that after these changes the communal associations were no longer 'exclusive' (because they allowed indigenous membership) and that they were necessary in order to bring WNI Chinese into Indonesian social and political life. 'Integration' of the WNI Chinese, according to this view, was a group affair. Thus integration could be achieved and exclusivism broken down by WNI Chinese communal organisations joining general Indonesian federations. (For example, the Chinese association of university students, the *Ta Hsueh Hsueh Sheng Hui*, in 1957 renamed *Perhimi*, or *Perhimpunan Mahasiswa Indonesia*, joined the Indonesian student federation PPMI and became very active in it.) For the assimilationists, these measures were insufficient; the associations remained exclusive in spirit and would remain so as long as most of their members were of Chinese origin.

Another source of the assimilationist movement was from the Baperki members who had left Baperki because of its shift to the left. Of these, the most important were the Catholics who were influenced by the anti-Communist and the universalist tenets of their church. Protestants were less active than Catholics in the assimilationist movement, possibly because of the existence of Chinese Protestant churches which were separate from the indigenous churches.[110].

A further factor of importance in the birth of the movement was the emergence of a group of young idealist students whose educational experience had been entirely gained in independent Indonesia, who had attended schools and university with indigenous Indonesians, and who were impatient with 'exclusive' communal associations which they saw as 'old-fashioned' and relics of the racially stratified society of colonial days.

The time at which the movement emerged was one in which stirring nationalist appeals were being made daily. For WNI Chinese, there was additional cause to consider what their duty was in answer to them. A major reason why the movement arose when it did has to do with the pressures exerted on the WNI Chinese by the 1959 regulation banning retail trade by aliens in rural areas (PP 10) which had just been introduced. This regulation was accompanied by a major anti-Chinese campaign launched in anti-Communist sections of the press and led to sharp diplomatic exchanges with Peking. As a result many Chinese were leaving Indonesia to go to China permanently.[111] The WNI Chinese were at a crossroads. They could identify with the harassed aliens, or alternatively dissociate themselves from them entirely and accept the demands of Indonesian nationalism that they be decisive in putting their loyalty to Indonesia first. The dual nationality treaty was at last to be implemented; many were asking themselves 'What does my choice of Indonesian citizenship entail?'

In answering this question, the assimilationists were divided into radical and conservative wings. The more conservative supporters were primarily opposed to communal organisations and particularly to Baperki which was tending in their view to identify the WNI Chinese with the PKI and to isolate them from indigenous Indonesians. Although they were prepared to sign their names to indicate their approval of the process of assimilation and to express their opposition to those who wanted to put obstacles in its way, they tended to drop out of the move-ment at that point, to let nature take its course. The more radical supporters considered that the process of assimilation was not only necessary and inevitable, but that it needed to be prodded and, if possible, speeded up. They actively urged the WNI Chinese to change their Chinese names to Indonesian ones, to marry indigenous In-donesians and to abandon exclusive social groups and Chinese cultural traits. The extremists among these radicals condemned Confucianism and peranakan customs and argued privately that name-changing should be made compulsory for all WNI Chinese. Most, however, were more moderate and more tolerant of differences of belief and custom and consistently denied that they were in favour of assimilation by force. The appeals of the assimilationists were usually couched in nationalist terms; if the WNI Chinese were to be good citizens and true patriots they must cast aside their pride and feelings of superiority (which they could do symbolically by changing their names) and demonstrate their love of their Indonesian motherland by service to it. Only in this way would the indigenous majority fully accept them. The minority problem would be solved with the disappearance of the Chinese as a socially and culturally discrete group.

Like Baperki, the assimilationists were opposed on principle to policies discriminating among fellow citizens on a racial basis. But they stressed the obligations rather than the rights of citizenship, speaking of these in social and cultural rather than political terms, and they were inclined to blame the Chinese themselves at least as much as the indigenous Indonesians for the discrimination which occurred. Baperki's insistence upon equal rights for all citizens was occasionally described by them as a sign of a conditional loyalty motivated by a trader mentality.

If they spoke of 'total assimilation' of the Chinese 'in all fields', their demands nevertheless had limits. They did not advocate conversion to Islam, although the vast majority of indigenous Indonesians is Muslim by religion. Nor did they argue that 'exclusive' Christian schools should be abolished together with Baperki's exclusively Chinese ones. Their reluctance to espouse religious assimilation could be justified by reference to the fifth of the *Pantja Sila* ('Belief in one God') which was interpreted as denying any one State religion. It also had something to do with the prominence of Christian Chinese among the assimilationists. Chinese Muslims are few in Indonesia but it is striking that none of them played a leading role in the movement.[112]

If it was clear that the assimilationists were opposed to Baperki and its schools, it was not so clear how assimilation was to be achieved. While suggesting that there was something alien or to be ashamed of in Chinese (and even Chinese peranakan) culture, they did not explain what was to take its place except by stressing that it must be truly Indonesian. The community of ethnic Indonesians is of course far from culturally homogeneous. Diversity is admitted in the national motto 'Bhinneka Tunggal Ika' (unity in diversity). The assimilationists interpreted the motto as a platform for change, quoting a statement by President Sukarno that Bhinneka (diversity) was 'das Sein' (what is) and Tunggal (unity) was 'das Sollen' (what shall be). For Baperki leaders, the same motto was said to justify cultural pluralism, interpreted conservatively to support the co-existence within one Indonesian nation of many ethnic groups (sukus) of which the peranakan Chinese formed one suku. Sukarno also gave support to this view by expressly referring to the peranakan Chinese as a suku and thus one of the legs of the Indonesian body.[113] Baperki leaders looked to a future in which, with the achievement of Indonesian socialism, all sukus (including the peranakan Chinese) would disappear as distinctive groups. The assimilationists thought that the disappearance of the WNI Chinese as a distinctive group must be given priority because it posed a greater problem.

How was it to be done? Must the Chinese assimilate to the indigenous sukus first, before they were themselves welded into a national whole? Or should they, being so heavily concentrated in the large urban centres, which were often ethnically heterogeneous, assimilate in one jump to the all-Indonesian culture (the 'Indonesian metropolitan superculture' as Hildred Geertz has called it[114]) which was developing there? These questions, and the practical problems which they raised, were never publicly discussed by the assimilationists. Perhaps the difficulties were never clearly perceived by them, since they were themselves for the most part members of the elite group adhering to the metropolitan superculture. Certainly they did not urge their fellow peranakan Chinese to settle in rural areas where most indigenous Indonesians still live. Scarcely any of them had even a smattering of the Chinese language and they were quite unsympathetic to the problems posed by their campaign for the WNI Chinese who came from totok families, those who lived and worked in 'Chinatowns', and those who lived in the areas of Sumatra and Borneo which were overwhelmingly Chinese-speaking. And what was the WNI Chinese to do who lived in an area where his indigenous Indonesian neighbours all took their Islam very seriously?

Ten peranakan Chinese in Jakarta launched the assimilationist movement by publishing a manifesto in the magazine *Star Weekly* in March 1960. It asserted that the only way to solve the minority problems was by voluntary assimilation in every field, supported a statement by President Sukarno which approved marriages between members of different ethnic groups, and disapproved actions or utterances which might impede the process of assimilation. As an example of the latter, it referred to a recent statement by Siauw Giok Tjhan in the Baperki newspaper *Republik* in which he maintained that the solution of the minority problem by means of name-changing and biological assimil- ation was unwise, undemocratic, an invasion of basic human rights, and impracticable. The manifesto was thus a clear challenge to Baperki. The ten signatories included several prominent Catholic Party pol- iticians as well as Injo Beng Goat (the director of *Keng Po*) and Auwjong Peng Koen (who, in addition to being editor of *Star Weekly*, which was printed by Keng Po, was one of the Baperki candidates who had left this organisation before the 1955 general elections).[115]

In the following months, *Star Weekly's* correspondence columns were expanded to give space to letters supporting and opposing the manifesto. They exposed to the public view the split in Baperki between Siauw and vice-chairman Yap Thiam Hien. Although both preferred cultural pluralism to assimilation, Yap supported his argument by referring to Christian ideals and the rule of law, characterising Siauw's approach as the Communist one. Siauw, angered, stamped Yap as a McCarthyist and said that his own view was based upon the Political Manifesto of President Sukarno which, having become State policy, was binding upon all loyal citizens, Communist or not. Most of *Star Weekly's* corres- pondents, who included indigenous Indonesians, supported the magazine's backing of the assimilationists.

The movement was put on an all-Java footing after a conference at Bandungan in Central Java in January 1961 which issued a Charter of Assimilation. In Jakarta, the assimilationists formed a standing com- mittee which proposed to General Nasution (then Minister of Defence and Army Chief of Staff) that a special bureau for the promotion of national unity should be formed under army auspices.[116] This proposal was realised in June 1962 and was the beginning of an association between the assimilationists and a section of the army high command which was to prove of great importance to the politics of the Indonesian Chinese.

The central axis of domestic politics in Indonesia at the time was between the army and the PKI. By accepting army protection the assimilationists made clear their alignment in the general political arena, just as Baperki had declared itself for the left. During the guided democracy period, there was no longer any prospect of elections and the system of political parties was 'simplified' with one major party suppressed. Sukarno's speeches, and particularly the *Manipol—USDEK*, became 'the language of all public political discourse'[117] so that the words of the President were now the authoritative source of ideological legitimacy. Great importance was therefore attached to obtaining his blessing for a particular verbal formula or his presence at a meeting.

The chance of obtaining such a favour depended upon having access to the President either through members of the court circle or by pressure exercised by one of the two main pressure groups and contenders for the succession—the army and the PKI. Presidential decrees were often issued in highly personal ways rather than through the appropriate State organ. After a speech had been made or a decree issued by the President, political argument largely centred on establishing the authenticity of the text, elucidating its meaning and relevance in a way favourable to one's own side, discounting or suppressing texts which might help one's opponents, and accusing them of failing to carry out the President's commands. The President himself was not passive but was a participant in this process, throwing his weight to one side or the other to maintain minimal unity and his own power and prestige. The tactics open to political rivals (like Baperki and the assimilationists) in this period were limited. The chief aim was to have one's opponents' organisation dissolved and its ideas condemned by the President while leaving one's own intact. Failing that, the opponent should be neutralised with his organisation being 'retooled' or its ideas reinterpreted so as to correspond more closely with one's own.

In early 1963 the assimilationists were aware that in the coming May the existing institutional basis for their co-operation with the army would be undermined by the removal of martial law.[118] They approached the President and obtained from him a statement supporting assimilation and asserting that 'a nation with minorities is no nation'. Then they held a conference in Jakarta which was timed to try to steal the thunder from the forthcoming Baperki congress. As well as condemning 'exclusivism', the conference agreed to set up an Institute of Promoters of National Unity (LPKB—*Lembaga Pembina Kesatuan Bangsa*).[119] The unity they sought was to be achieved, in co-operation with the government, by means of assimilation in every field. The institute was to be a mass organisation in form, having members and branches. As in the case of its army-sponsored predecessor, the LPKB included a number of indigenous Indonesians who were civilians and rightist politically. It worked from the same Jakarta headquarters on army property.[120]

The Baperki congress which followed must have been a blow to the assimilationists. The President attended in person and delivered a speech in which he praised Baperki, explained that Indonesia had no minorities but only sukus, and explicitly referred to the peranakan Chinese as one of the sukus. He also disclosed that he personally thought a person's name, like his religion, was his own private affair; he did not need to change his name to be a good citizen.[121]

In the next few months there were successive anti-Chinese riots in various West Java towns and cities of which the most notorious was the '10th May incident' in Bandung. In a number of cases, the riots followed shortly after visits to the towns concerned by LPKB indoctrination teams preaching assimilation. Baperki, in collaboration with the PKI and Partindo, set up a Committee of Helpers of Victims of the Counter-Revolution (PPKK—*Panitia Penolong Korban Kontra-Revolusi*) which ⌐aised funds for those injured or suffering loss as a result of the riots and called for punishment of the racists responsible. Partindo was at that time very close to Baperki; three of its governing board were also Baperki leaders. One consequence of the riots in 1963 was to drive many young WNI Chinese into joining Partindo.[122] The leftist press started to accuse the LPKB activists of being responsible for the riots. By spreading assimilationist propaganda, it was said, they had prepared the ground for the racists, who used 'economic assimilation' as an excuse for their actions.

The assimilationists felt very vulnerable. Already in April they were anxious to obtain a formal link with some sector of the government rather than remain exposed as a private body. They achieved this goal in July when the President was persuaded to sign an Assimilation Message and to form a government body called the Institute for the Promotion of National Unity (also LPKB—but now *Lembaga Pembinaan Kesatuan Bangsa*). The government LPKB was established by Presidential decree and a further special Presidential decree of the same date appointed as its acting head a naval lieutenant who had changed his name to Sindhunatha.[123] Sindhunatha was a WNI Chinese Catholic who was Chairman of the existing LPKB. These two decrees are good examples of unorthodox guided democracy legislation. They were drafted hurriedly, secretly and by a draftsman (a young non-Chinese LPKB member) who was totally inexperienced in drafting legal documents. In his hurry, he accidentally changed the name of the organisation (which led to later suggestions from opponents of the assimilationists that there were really two separate LPKBs—one official and the other not). The operation was carried out so quickly that Sindhunatha himself, who was at the time in Surabaya, first learnt of it after the event from reading the newspapers. The initiative came, in fact, from Col Soetjipto, S.H., who was at that time general secretary of the MPPR (Consultative Council of the Leadership of the Revolution—an advisory council to the President which was under army influence). He obtained the President's signature to the decree without going through the State Secretariat, the regular channel for a Presidential decree. Even if the procedure for obtaining them was unorthodox, the decrees provided the LPKB with a more secure base than they had yet had. What had been established by Presidential decree could not be undone without a further decree by the President. The new governmental body was placed under the supervision of Roeslan Abdulgani, then Minister of Information. Perhaps because of the peculiar circumstances in which his new charge had appeared, he was slow to set it into motion. As a result, Sindhunatha relied upon the President's personal appointment of himself as acting head and began the conversion of private to state body on his own authority. But the administration and public understanding of the status of the LPKB were in confusion for several months; a confusion which Baperki leaders did nothing to alleviate.

Baperki had its own problems with these new developments. It was now constrained to accept usage of the word 'assimilation', but it pointed out that the President had not approved the term 'total assimilation' or assimilation by force. To demonstrate Baperki's opposition to 'exclusivism', Siauw Giok Tjhan presided over a ceremony in which 6 000 youths and students 'under Baperki co-ordination' were integrated into the left-wing youth and high school students' organisation IPPI.[124] On the other hand, it attacked the composition of the LPKB for not being in conformity with the President's formula of NASAKOM, since no Communists were represented in its leadership. This theme was touched upon in the President's 17 August speech. His only reference to LPKB was in the context of a diatribe against phobias of all kinds and in particular against Nasakom-phobia. Such phobias divided the nation, and it was to hasten Nationbuilding and Characterbuilding that he had formed LPKB, so he commissioned Roeslan Abdulgani to explain the error of these phobias.[125] It was a negative speech for LPKB; there was not a mention of 'exclusivism' or even of 'assimilation'.

LPKB's defence to attacks on its alleged Nasakom-phobia was to reply that since it was a government body it was thereby imbued with the spirit of Nasakom. It also moved slowly towards forming an advisory council on which all political parties and functional groups would be represented but argued that it was unnecessary to have a formal division of LPKB personnel among nationalists, religious people and communists. This was less than frank, since LPKB recruitment at the centre successfully sought to exclude Communists.

If LPKB's weaknesses at this time were evident enough, its successes must have given its leaders cold comfort. For example, they found themselves compelled by their commitment to assimilation to greet with pleasure the news that five leaders of the PPI (an 'exclusive' youth organisation affiliated with Baperki) had left it to join the PKI's youth organisation Pemuda Rakjat. They and their backers must have been

feeling uneasy that the visible consequences of their assimilationist programme were merely a strengthening of the leftist organisations. Although he cannot have felt the circumstances to be very favourable, in
November 1963 Sindhunatha sent a letter to leading cabinet ministers
asking that serious consideration be given to the position of Baperki. In
support of this request, he said that it was formed to cater for the needs
of the WNI Chinese and was exclusive; that, although not a political
party, it carried out policies which were parallel with those of certain
political parties; and that it was opposed in principle to assimilation,
thus hindering the national policy of promoting national unity.

Baperki's position was far too strong to be affected by this attack,
however. As if in answer to Sindhunatha's challenge, the Baperki vice-
chairman Oei Tjoe Tat (who was also a member of the Partindo central
board) was appointed a cabinet minister in December 1963. The President was not, it seems, concerned to maintain a balance between
Baperki and the LPKB.

The most severe blow to the LPKB leaders was the President's TAVIP
speech (*Tahun Vivere Pericoloso*—'The Year of Living Dangerously') on
17 August 1964.[126] In the previous month the LPKB at its working
conference at Cipayung had decided to try to promote national unity
and assimilation by means of tourism and co-operatives. The President
(in the speech as published) warned the LPKB not to meddle in these
matters which were not its field. Worse, he announced that he would
revise its structure by 'Nasakomising' the leadership. And he explained
that his dream of a nation in which all sukus, including peranakans and
those of foreign descent, would be united, should be achieved by means
of *both* integration and assimilation.

The LPKB leaders claimed that the speech published was not what
the President actually said. It was what appeared in the prepared text,
which, they said, they had persuaded the President to modify. They tried
to have later published versions altered to correspond with what they
said was the true version. In a publication of their own, which included
an extract from the TAVIP speech, the references to tourism, co-
operatives and Nasakomisation of the LPKB were omitted. For all their
textual quibbling, the LPKB leaders were on the run. After TAVIP,
they shifted to arguing that integration, properly speaking, was one of
three stages of assimilation (adaptation, integration and identification).
In this technical sense, the LPKB had no objection to the term and the
President must be understood to have used it in that sense. What the
LPKB objected to in the use of the term integration, it now said, was its
being used as a mask for continuing racial exclusivism.

The Baperki congress held immediately after the TAVIP speech
understandably welcomed the President's strictures on the LPKB. It
urged that the LPKB leadership should be Nasakomised and placed

directly under the President, with its day to day tasks handed over to the Cabinet Presidium. Baperki's position in the Indonesian political scene had been immensely strengthened. Its allies (the President, the PKI and Partindo) had the initiative over the rightist groups which were caught in the thickets of Sukarno's rhetoric. The relations between Jakarta and Peking were becoming increasingly cordial, contributing further to the strengthening of the Baperki position. Baperki had over the years added a number of indigenous Indonesians, mostly leftists, to its leadership, but its membership remained predominantly communal. By 1964, however, it was no longer, for the most part, stressing communal issues. Its pre-occupations were far more with general political issues, and as the threat from the LPKB and the racial riots receded, its attention to communal issues declined further.

In this way, therefore, the political potential of the assimilationists was neutralised before October 1965. Although the threatened Nasakomisation of the LPKB leadership did not take place, its activities slowed to a standstill and its publications lost their bite and even their distinctiveness. The LPKB was a spent force; it was saved from oblivion by the abortive coup of 1 October 1965.[127]

In the morning of 1 October 1965, the movement which styled itself 'the 30th September Movement' led by a Lt Col Untung kidnapped and (as it later appeared) killed six leading army generals, and took control of the Jakarta radio station, the tele-communications centre, and the President's palace.[128] The President himself went to Halim airbase in the Jakarta area (in circumstances which are to this day unclear) which was in the hands of the air force under the command of Air Vice Marshal Omar Dhani, who in the course of the day issued an order clearly supporting the 30 September Movement. In a broadcast message over Jakarta radio, Untung said that his movement had acted to forestall a coup which he alleged had been planned by a 'Council of Generals' sponsored by the CIA. He later announced the formation and composition of an Indonesian Revolution Council, of which he was chairman, which would 'constitute the source of all authority in the Republic of Indonesia'. The movement collapsed by the evening of the same day in Jakarta, following prompt and effective action by the commander of the army's strategic reserve, Major General Suharto. The military position in the capital was thus secured very quickly, but the political situation remained fluid and in doubt for a considerable time afterwards.

It was an agonising time for political organisations like Baperki and the LPKB. Sources of information were scanty. While Untung's troops were in control of Jakarta radio, there were several broadcast statements from the 30 September Movement which were reproduced with approval by several leftist Jakarta newspapers (notably by *Harian Rakjat*, the

PKI daily). Once Suharto's forces retook the radio station, its listeners were given quite a different picture, and recorded broadcasts from the President (now in his weekend palace at Bogor) followed. Every political organisation was faced with the necessity to define its own position publicly.

Neither LPKB nor Baperki released any statement before it was clear that the movement had been defeated in Jakarta, but each found it necessary to declare itself to some extent before the Cabinet meeting held at Bogor on 6 October. The first statement from LPKB (dated 2 October and published in the armed forces daily *Angkatan Bersendjata* on 4 October) was limited to an expression of gratitude that the President had been saved from the 'counter-revolutionary movement which calls itself the 30th September Movement'.[129] (In this, it followed the turn of phrase used by Suharto's forces after their capture of the radio station on 1 October.) Baperki, on the other hand, delayed its first statement until the President's strategy was disclosed in his broadcasts on 3 October (and the announcement by the commander of his palace guard at Bogor at midnight on 2 October).[130] The Baperki statement on 4 October followed the President's line closely.[131] In particular, it supported his appeal for 'the prompt creation of a calm and orderly atmosphere' so that he personally could bring about a political solution, and his commands 'to increase vigilance and preparedness in the frame-work of intensifying the implementation of *Dwikora*' (confrontation against Malaysia) and to 'steadfastly kindle the anti-*Nekolim* spirit'. ('*Nekolim*' was an acronym devised by President Sukarno to describe the forces of Neo-Colonialism and imperialism, in particular the Western powers headed by the USA.) It added that Siauw Giok Tjhan denied any knowledge of why the Indonesian Revolution Council announced by the Untung forces had included his name. The Baperki statement, like the President's, spoke of 'the 30 September affair' rather than of 'the 30 September movement' and avoided calling the movement 'counter-revolutionary'.

That very day the army recovered the bodies of its murdered generals, who were then given a heroes' burial in a blaze of publicity. Prominence was given in the army press to the role of members of PKI mass organisations in the killings and the PKI newspaper's approval of the movement. Anti-Communist political parties were already calling for the banning and dissolution of the PKI and its affiliated organisations. On 6 October the Cabinet met at Bogor, endorsing the President's call for national unity and harmony and 'strengthening the endurance of the Revolution.'[132] It was in just these terms that Baperki's central executive issued its second, brief, statement released on the following day.[133] The statement did not refer to the President's reported condemnation of the killing of the generals or disapproval of the formation of the Indonesian Revolution Council. LPKB's second press release did not appear until 12

October and, while supporting the President's appeal for the restoration of a calm and orderly atmosphere, it added that this had the 'aim of destroying the counter-revolutionary 30th September Movement down to its roots'.[134] In this, it again followed an army lead, that of the 5 October editorial of the army daily *Berita Yudha*.

The next day, after receiving a briefing from the staff of KOTI G-V (a new organisation, but a vehicle for the same military groups who had backed it since 1962) the LPKB issued a further statement which included a condemnation of the 30 September Movement and called on the masses of the people to take corrective action in a revolutionary way against bodies which supported the 30 September Movement and to weed out without fear or favour individuals and groups involved in the movement.[135] By this time, in fact, the army leadership had become impatient with the President's failure to produce his promised 'political solution'; the President, however, was in no hurry to disclose it, saying (on 14 October) that it would be based upon 'real facts' and not on the basis of inflammatory statements from whatever quarter.[136] Army headquarters that same day instructed local military commanders to ban activities of mass organisations or political parties whose leaders showed sufficient indications of involvement in the movement.[137] The LPKB central leadership at once notified its branches in the regions to publicise the LPKB's statements since the coup, to try to prevent any eruption of racism, and to purge themselves thoroughly of any elements of the movement.

Anti-Chinese feeling was certainly in the air. In Jakarta, Baperki's *Res Publica* University was burnt down, and the Chinese Commercial Counsellor's office was raided by Indonesian soldiers. Before the week was out, the LPKB leaders were writing to the President urging him to dissolve Baperki, and to have its schools placed in other hands so that they might be made non-exclusive. They said that Baperki, with a membership consisting almost entirely of WNI Chinese, by participating in politics was thereby encouraging political conflict to turn into racial conflict. This endangered the Revolution and the mass of Baperki's own members, who had only been attracted to it for social and educational reasons and now felt that they were caught in an unwanted situation.[138] There was no apparent response to this appeal from the President.

This letter, which was publicised, obtained, in the mounting anti-Chinese atmosphere, a response in a different quarter. The Krawang branch of Baperki dissolved itself and called for the dissolution of Baperki as a whole.[139] Once this appeal was taken up by Nahdatul Ulama leader H. A. Sjaichu early in November, the ground was prepared for a concerted drive against Baperki.[140] Military authorities and LPKB branches in different areas now co-operated to freeze Baperki activities and to encourage Baperki members to dissolve their own branches. Little encouragement was needed for many ordinary Baperki members who found themselves caught in an anti-leftist purge of gigantic proportions. So far as can be ascertained, few of them were victims of the killings which decimated the PKI and its mass organisations.[141] Many of the more prominent Baperki members, however, were jailed and numerous others lost their jobs as a result of the administrative purges. It was alleged that Baperki had financed the PKI in co-operation with the Chinese People's Republic, which was by now the target of constant fiery denunciation and retaliating by abusing the Indonesian government by way of Radio Peking and its newsagency. In their zeal to convert the rank and file Baperki members from the sins of 'exclusivism' and to have it dissolved, some LPKB activists played on fears of anti-Chinese violence which were only too easily aroused at that time. More constructively, they also tried to co-operate with local military and education department authorities in carrying out official army (KOTI G-V) policy for Baperki's schools and universities, which was aimed at securing the buildings, purging the staff and students of elements of the movement and reopening them on a non-exclusive basis as quickly as possible.[142] The policy was often difficult to enforce where other uses were found for the schools—for example, as places of detention for political suspects. A notable case where it was enforced was *Res Publica* University; the new *Trisakti* University was opened on its ruins on 29 November 1965, and was later rebuilt with voluntary labour from the students (and some financial aid from the Netherlands).[143]

THE CHINESE UNDER THE SUHARTO REGIME AND 'CUKONG' INFLUENCE

The full story of events as they affected the Indonesian Chinese in the next two years is too complex to relate here. Relations with the Peking government were stormy right up to the suspension of diplomatic relations in October 1967.[144] This was in part a cause and in part a consequence of an increase in publicly expressed anti-Chinese sentiment in Indonesia. Many Chinese, both citizen and alien, found themselves exposed to insult and violence. Extremist groups and newspapers demanded the expulsion of all alien Chinese and a review of the citizenship of all WNI Chinese. In an Indonesian political environment which was generally unstable, the risks of political activity for the Indonesian Chinese were evident enough.

In the two years before the attempted coup, the alien Chinese (other than those oriented toward Taiwan) had achieved a position of relative security. Although their position as aliens was in many ways less favourable than that of Indonesian citizens, they could at least console themselves that it seemed much more secure than that of other aliens, particularly the Dutch, British and Americans. If their economic activity was restricted in certain fields and areas, the restrictions could often be sidestepped, even legally, by transfer of a business to a relative who held Indonesian citizenship. Moreover, anti-imperialist actions could create business opportunities for some Chinese as well as government officials. The increasingly close relations between Jakarta and Peking and the increasing dominance of President Sukarno and the PKI seemed to assure Chinese generally of some governmental protection. The vehicles through which Chinese political expression had most naturally flowed in the past—the schools, the press and community organisations—remained intact. Although since 1957 Chinese-language education had not been open to Indonesian citizens and the Kuomintang schools had been closed, there were still over 600 Chinese-language schools catering for more than 270 000 children, who had access to tertiary education through Baperki's universities. Although the Chinese-language press was subject to some restriction—for example, the editors of newspapers had to be Indonesian citizens—there were still four Chinese dailies being published in Jakarta. Finally, the network of community organisations was able to function without hindrance and there were flourishing Indonesia-China Friendship Institutes.

The consequences of the changed political circumstances since the failure of the coup attempt have been radical for the alien Chinese, above all in the areas most closely related to political activity. The entire Chinese-language press was closed down on 2 October 1965, and the only Chinese-language newspaper now in existence is government-sponsored.[145] The Chinese language schools were all officially declared closed in May 1966 after many of them had been occupied by militant Indonesian youth and student organisations.[146] Many of the students attending these schools have been unable to continue their education, although the government later declared that they were eligible for admission to national schools (both private and government). In 1969 the first of a number of special project national schools was opened in Jakarta with the specific object of providing desks for some of these displaced alien children, subject to close governmental supervision. The funds for the schools were to come from the totok community, and alien children were guaranteed up to 40 per cent of the places. The language of instruction and the curriculum are Indonesian, however, and the government stipulated that a majority of the students in any class must be Indonesian citizens. Apart from providing school places for children who otherwise were dependent upon private tuition, the chief inducement for the Chinese to participate in these 'special project' schools was that the government undertook to allow the teaching of the Chinese language for a certain number of hours each week. By January 1971 there were three such schools in Jakarta and one in Palembang. Despite official requirements, the alien enrolment in at least two schools has exceeded 90 per cent.[147] Since the failure of the coup, the organisational network of the community has been torn apart. It is now the government's policy to prohibit all alien associations other than those specially permitted and supervised by it. Even these are restricted to such innocuous fields as health, religious, burial and sporting interests. Consequently, the disappearance of Chinese communal institutions (which among the WNI Chinese has been justified on the grounds of their 'exclusive' character) has also affected the aliens so that such venerable organisations as the Chinese chambers of commerce (*Siang Hwee*) and the regional and speech group associations as well as the federation of Chinese associations and the Indonesia-China Friendship Institutes, no longer exist. Quite a few of the leaders of these organisations, schoolteachers and journalists, have left Indonesia.[148]

Both the nationalist and integrationist patterns of Chinese political activity have been communal in inspiration. They have depended for their vigour upon a separate press (Chinese or Indonesian), a separate educational system (Chinese, Dutch or Indonesian) and separate associations representing Chinese interests in various fields. They have also required tolerance for their existence from governments in power. In present-day Indonesia, none of these conditions are met. If Chinese (whether alien or citizen) wish to participate in politics, their participation must take some other form.

Most of those who had been prominent before the coup attempt in political fields were unwilling or unable to participate now. Some, from frustration or fear, left the country. Others chafed at home (or in jail) in a political environment which, for the Chinese at least, had become less open than before. One such man, recalling the history of the nationalist awakening of the Chinese in Java and the movements which succeeded it, said to the writer: 'We have become a body without a voice.'

It is likely that as formal politics has become less open for the Chinese (and particularly the aliens) Chinese political influence has tended to move more in informal channels. This brings us to the sixth of the patterns outlined in this chapter, which has been postponed to this point although it is by no means confined to the period after the attempted coup. The pattern, here called 'cukong influence', is intended to refer to the political influence informally exercised on occasion by Chinese businessmen (or cukongs) who are in close contact with Indonesian power-holders.[149] The latter are as likely to be groups or agencies as individuals, thus including military units, political parties and government departmental cliques. What is being referred to here is not the practice of Chinese businessmen making gifts to government officials in the expectation of certain favours in return (which goes back to Dutch times), or the practice on the part of certain government officials of

requiring Chinese to make payments (or over-payments) in consideration of providing some licence or protection to which the Chinese concerned might or might not have some legal entitlement. These practices
have certainly become more common in recent years, indeed since the
middle fifties. It is possible that in such relationships (including the so-
called Ali-Baba relationship in which Ali, the Indonesian partner, is the
nominal principal but Baba, the Chinese partner, provides the capital
and skill under the counter) the Chinese party has been able to exercise
some political influence of the kind now under discussion. (If one
accepted the widely-touted allegation, for which affirmative evidence is
lacking, that Baperki was a principal financier of the PKI, it would be
arguable that the Chinese businessmen who backed Baperki were exercising 'cukong influence'; but this view overlooks Baperki's own overt
political role with its own ideology.) Another kind of relationship, which
has become more common since the attempted coup, is the Baba-Ali one
which has arisen where Chinese businessmen manage money held by
Indonesian powerholders or engage in joint commercial ventures with
them. It is widely known in Jakartan elite circles that certain Chinese
businessmen are closely associated with Indonesian government figures
at the very highest level, but details rarely appear in the press. One
might expect that in this kind of relationship the Chinese partner would
have more scope for the exercise of political influence. It is unclear
whether the influence so exercised is very great, whether it extends over
many issues, or to what extent the businessman concerned will wish to
influence policies in matters which go beyond his own personal or commercial interests. What does seem clear (in an area which by its nature
is bound to be obscure) is that members of the Chinese community who
wish to see certain policies implemented by the Indonesian government
or their application modified are far more likely today than earlier to try
to work through these cukongs both because of their greater prevalence
and because of the absence of effective alternative channels.

One alternative did emerge for the alien Chinese in the middle of 1967.
The Indonesian central government found itself compelled for the first
time to formulate and execute a co-ordinated Chinese policy after a
series of events which had culminated in April 1967 in a massive demonstration by alien Chinese in Jakarta which was followed two days later by
a violent Indonesian counter-demonstration. The violence, taking place
as it did in the capital, could not be hidden from diplomats and the
foreign press and indeed shocked many of the government's moderate
supporters in the outside world. One consequence of the rethinking
which followed these events was the formation of a Special Staff for
Chinese Affairs (*Staf Chusus Urusan Tjina*—SCUT) and the Contact
Body for Chinese Affairs (*Badan Kontak Urusan Tjina*—BKUT). It seems

not too unfair to view the SCUT and BKUT as functional equivalents of the *Kakyo Han* and the HCTH during the Japanese occupation discussed above (p. 39), with the important distinction that the latter were addressed to the entire Chinese population, whereas the newer bodies were concerned only with the alien and stateless Chinese.

SCUT, as originally formed, was a body consisting of army and government people placed directly under the Cabinet Presidium (later under the President). The BKUT, which included several members of the SCUT, consisted otherwise of 'four leaders or influential men' from the Hakka, Cantonese and Hokkien speech groups.[150] Its official function was to act as a channel of communication between the Chinese community and the government, so that the government could make known to the Chinese its requirements and demands and the Chinese could convey to the government, by way of SCUT, the feelings and desires of their community. Lt Kol Drs W. D. Sukisman, an army man who graduated from the Sinology department of the University of Indonesia and speaks and reads Chinese, doubled as the secretary of SCUT and the chairman of the BKUT. An official report by the SCUT to the government said that the choice of the Chinese members of BKUT was left 'as far as possible' to groups in the Chinese community itself 'which without doubt really knew just who would be suitable to represent them' in this linking role. The SCUT report was careful to note that, apart from its two-way communications function, the BKUT possessed '*no* executive authority whatever'. The SCUT-BKUT structure was meant to be reproduced at the provincial level, but the plan only came to fruition in a few regions.

There is a recurrent dilemma in this pattern of politics for both the government and the Chinese. For the Chinese, there is the risk of being labelled a 'collaborator' and betrayer of Chinese interests by his own community; for the government (in this case the SCUTs) there is the need to find Chinese who are both trustworthy and yet influential in the Chinese community. The resolution of these dilemmas, and an unsatisfactory one it has been, has meant that the persons favoured by the SCUT are Chinese who are Taiwan-oriented and were thus in eclipse in the Chinese community before the coup attempt.[151] In consequence, the BKUT has not seemed a particularly important body to much of the Chinese community. In June 1969 the SCUT itself was dissolved and its executive functions were taken over by BAKIN, the State Intelligence Organisation, and the BKUT came under the authority of the Department of Home Affairs. These moves undermined further the influence of the BKUT in the Chinese community. The SCUT, which had played an important part in the formulation of government policy on the Chinese, was now reduced to an arm of the security apparatus. The new

Special project national schools, which had been actively promoted by the SCUT and BKUT members, continued to develop after the dissolution of the SCUT.

The turbulence of the two years following the coup unsettled the national status of the Indonesian Chinese.[152] The continued implementation of the dual nationality treaty with China was frozen and later terminated, thus depriving some children now coming of age of the opportunity which the treaty provided of undoing the choice of nationality which their parents' action (or inaction) in the option periods had foisted upon them. Likewise, applications for naturalisation (which had never been processed with ease or in great numbers) were frozen for a time, but they have since been accepted again. In fact, the possibility of naturalisation is greater now than it has ever been (for the wealthy). The government resisted extremist demands for a wholesale review of the citizenship of the WNI Chinese, but many regional governments conducted 'check-ups' to try to detect those who had obtained citizenship by fraudulent or corrupt means (or to apply a squeeze on wealthier Chinese in the name of doing this).

In these unsettled times, when it was by no means clear that the government would maintain its restraint in the face of extremist demands, the LPKB clung to its central creed: 'There must be a clear line drawn between alien Chinese and WNI Chinese; and there must be no discrimination between indigenous and non-indigenous Indonesian citizens'. Unsympathetic observers read this as an attempt by WNI Chinese to deflect anti-Chinese feeling away from themselves and on to the aliens (a motivation present even when the assimilationist movement was first formed). This interpretation is given some support by the less guarded slogan sometimes used by LPKB people: 'WNI Chinese must be assimilated; alien Chinese must be discriminated (against)'. On the other hand, if the LPKB were to show too much concern for the alien Chinese, it would lay itself open to the charge of being a neo-Baperki which was only interested in the interests of the ethnic Chinese.

There were several concrete measures for which the LPKB pressed which could demonstrate the separateness of the alien and citizen Chinese. One was the adoption by the latter of Indonesian-sounding names. The local LPKB leaders in Sukabumi, in co-operation with local government officials, in June 1966 rushed almost the entire WNI Chinese community through a mass name-changing ceremony in which 6 662 people took part at two days' notice.[153] This 'pilot project' gave rise to many difficulties in practice and did not become the model for name-changing elsewhere. But in December 1966, the Cabinet Presidium took up the LPKB name-changing proposal, issuing a decree 'urging' WNI Chinese to change their names to Indonesian ones and providing a new procedure for doing so which was simpler and cheaper than under the existing law.[154] The decree expressed the belief of the assimilationists that the name-changing would hasten the assimilation of those concerned. The LPKB and its supporters assisted the government authorities responsible for the implementation of the decree by providing information and other assistance in a way curiously analogous to Baperki's role during the implementation of the dual nationality treaty. A Department of Justice spokesman announced in August 1969 that 232 882 WNI Chinese had used the new procedure to change their names.

As well as name-changing, the LPKB supported the moves in various regions to have signs erected which clearly distinguished the shops and houses which were owned or occupied by alien Chinese. In addition, it supported the calling of mass rallies of WNI Chinese in April 1966 which were designed to demonstrate their loyalty to Indonesia and their condemnation of Communist China. Another Cabinet Presidium instruction of December 1966 which resulted from LPKB representations abolished the old colonial distinction between Europeans, foreign orientals and natives for civil registration purposes and replaced it with a single distinction between aliens and citizens.[155] The LPKB also approached various government departments, with mixed success, requesting them to put an end to practices which discriminated against WNI Chinese. A major weakness of its policy of drawing a clear line to divide alien and citizen Chinese (which was adopted in principle by the government) was that in many individual instances there were families which, either from choice or necessity, found themselves divided by nationality.

With Baperki out of the way, the ambitions of LPKB leaders expanded. In May and June 1966, they joined forces with the KOGAM G-V staff (the continuation of KOTI G-V) to formulate policy recommendations for the Cabinet Presidium on the 'Chinese problem'—that is, on policy toward the alien and stateless Chinese. By July, they were beginning to make a case for a very substantial broadening in the scope of LPKB's functions and an increase in its powers. They argued that although it had so far confined itself to the Chinese problem, the original concept of the LPKB (as an institute for the promotion of national unity) had been much wider. It should, they said, become a key institution in Indonesia's modernisation process, a 'catalyst' of national unity which transcended divisions in society based upon ethnic minorities or sukus, regionalism, or 'groupism' (*golonganisme*). The problem of 'groupism', it was explained, encompassed political party groups, religious groups and others. The powers of this new body, which it was implied should be the LPKB, should match its scope. It should thus participate in government at every level in the policy-making and law-making process (from the nation-building aspect) and supervise the implementation of the policies and laws from that aspect. Its responsibilities did not end there, for it must also play a role in the community as well.

The basis of these grandiose dreams was said to be a resolution of the MPRS (Supreme Consultative Assembly) on the promotion of national unity which had been passed earlier in the month.[156] But it was another decision of the MPRS made in the same session which was to have a greater bearing upon the future of the LPKB. This was a decision to set up an ad hoc committee of the MPRS to re-examine the position of State institutes whose status under the 1945 Constitution was in doubt. As Roger Paget has pointed out, the 'purification of the implementation' of the 1945 Constitution was a prominent theme of the 1966 MPRS session.[157] The committee was placed under the chairmanship of NU leader Subchan, who was bound to be suspicious of a body like the LPKB with such far-reaching ambitions and in whose leadership Catholics were so strongly represented. Its report in February 1967 settled the question of the scope of the LPKB; its operations were to be confined to matters concerning Indonesian citizens of foreign descent. And although the LPKB was not, like some State bodies, listed for dissolution in the report, it was required to be placed within the ambit of the Department of Home Affairs.

The LPKB leadership continued until July 1967 to attempt to have its status redefined and regularised by law but it then gave up the struggle to maintain the LPKB as a separate governmental body, agreeing that it should actually be dissolved and its functions simply transferred to the Department of Home Affairs. To justify their capitulation, they proclaimed that the LPKB had in fact achieved the greatest possible result because the government had fully adopted its policies. Although in general terms this was true enough, if one looks at the wording of various statements of government policy and regulations, many discriminatory practices continue in various government departments. A continuing, if modest, role might well have been found for a separate body if the assimilationists had still been enthusiastic about having one. But it seems that their enthusiasm had abated by this time. Thus, although the circular letter which made known the decision to disband intimated that non-governmental organisations to promote assimilation might be formed, nothing substantial has ever come of the idea. The possibility of a role for the LPKB in the field of alien Chinese problems had really been out of court since the MPRS report in February 1967 but the LPKB leaders could salvage some pride by pointing out that the government had now appointed the high-level SCUT to deal with that area. In truth, the LPKB was scarcely qualified in that field; there were hardly any Chinese speakers in its central leadership. In November 1967 the decision of the LPKB leadership was implemented by Presidential decree and the LPKB was dissolved. Its supporting foundation, however, continued to assist various educational projects.

Some of the assimilationists have continued to be active in the political field but as practitioners of 'assimilated' rather than 'assimilationist' politics, particularly as members of the Catholic Party. The 'assimilated' pattern of political activity is in fact the only formal one now open for WNI Chinese. (The alien Chinese have had the BKUT as their sole formal channel.) However, because of the large number of Chinese Catholics, which has probably increased substantially since the attempted coup, there is a tendency for them to flock to the Catholic Party for protection, just as many former pupils of Baperki schools have flocked to Catholic schools. Seen as groups, there are some rather striking similarities between the WNI Chinese and the Catholics, even where these two categories do not overlap. In Java, at least, both are, by contrast with the population as a whole, disproportionately urban, well-educated, Westernised, and well-off, and have an extra-national focus of loyalty (which makes them something more than narrowly nationalist). Both tend to feel themselves beleaguered minorities in a potentially hostile Muslim sea. (These generalisations also apply, but to a lesser extent, to the Protestants; the convergence of interest with the Chinese is less striking than in the case of the Catholics because of the existence of separate Protestant denominations for the Chinese, the greater variety of the Protestants in class terms, and the fact that Protestants are more heavily represented outside Java. There is also less overlapping of the Protestant and Chinese minorities than is the case with Catholics and Chinese.) Another indication of the convergence and overlapping of Christian and Chinese minorities is the fact that, since the closure of the peranakan (Indonesian language Chinese) press, WNI Chinese opinion is almost exclusively found in that part of the national press which is Protestant or Catholic. The coincidence of interests which this analysis suggests also implies that both groups have an interest in 'centrist' politics, supporting President Suharto and his ruling group of *abangan* generals and technocrat intellectuals against the Muslims on the 'right' and the forces of social revolution (represented by the underground PKI) on the left. Muslim political leaders are understandably antagonistic toward such a strategy, particularly when it takes the form of association by some Chinese Catholics with certain military and intelligence elements (OPSUS) who are engaged in anti-Muslim politics of a cloak and dagger kind.[158] These Machiavellian anti-Muslims have been identified by one prominent journalist who has 'explained' their behaviour in terms of a theory about the characteristics of a 'double minority'.[159] The Chinese Catholics concerned have achieved a notoriety out of proportion to their numbers because of their close ties to a number of key generals. Many Chinese Catholics who support 'centrist' politics are critical of these OPSUS activists on the grounds that they are a potential danger to the Chinese.

CONCLUSION: ANALYSES AND PROSPECTS

The main concern of this chapter has been to demonstrate something of the changing extent and variety of political activity among the Indonesian Chinese since the turn of the century. The purpose of doing so has not been merely to demolish popular stereotypes on the subject but also to refine the more simplified analysis which appears even in scholarly writing.

In a recent book, Professor Lea Williams has argued that there has been a general trend among the Overseas Chinese in Southeast Asia toward 'political assimilation', which he defined as 'the participation of Chinese in the government and politics' of their overseas homelands.[160] The only alternatives open to them are 'to remain aloof from Southeast Asian politics... or to follow the path of communalism, including the Communist variety'.[161] He seems to assume that once political assimilation (as he defines it) is achieved, 'the major and most widespread minority problem of the area' will disappear.[162]

In fact, the 'political assimilation' which Professor Williams urges upon the Overseas Chinese includes three of the patterns of activity suggested in this chapter—the integrationist, the assimilationist, and the 'assimilated'. The exponents of the first two patterns (Baperki and the LPKB) were mutually opposed on two quite distinct fronts: one over the extent and kind of accommodation which the WNI Chinese should make to their Indonesian environment and the other over their attitude to the PKI. Because it ignores such important cleavages as these among the 'politically assimilated', Professor Williams's concept turns out to be too broad to be helpful.

Another shortcoming of his analysis in relation to the Indonesian scene is that it postulates a 'trend' toward political assimilation which is hard to discern. The picture is more one of fits and starts, and the trend, if there was one, has certainly suffered a setback since the coup. This setback, moreover, is to an important extent a result of the extensive mobilisation of WNI Chinese into Indonesian politics which Baperki had achieved (though it is also of course a product of the political alliances which its leadership entered into). His apparent surprise that 'even the fundamentally assimilationist Baperki experienced violence' after the coup[163] thus stems from too great a concentration upon the fact of 'political assimilation' with too little attention being paid to its nature and ideological direction. If the integrationist pattern represented by Baperki came to endanger the WNI Chinese, it should not be assumed that the 'assimilated' pattern (in my sense rather than Professor Williams's in this case) will prove to be their salvation. It has already been suggested that one form of 'assimilated' politics (the Catholic OPSUS one) may prove equally dangerous.[164] The truth of the matter is that the security of the Overseas Chinese and the solution of the minority problem which they represent cannot be assured solely by the form of political organisation which they adopt; that will depend upon a constellation of forces, not least government policies and majority attitudes.

Another attempt to generalise about the nature of Chinese political behaviour in Southeast Asia has been made by Professor Wang Gung-wu.[165] He has suggested that '*at all times* among the Overseas Chinese, three major groups can be distinguished by their political interests and activities'. His three groups are:

Group A, which is predominantly concerned with Chinese national politics and its international ramifications;
Group B, which is principally concerned with community politics wherever it may be;
Group C, which is drawn into the politics of non-Chinese hierarchies, whether indigenous or colonial or nationalist.

This classification, which is based upon the identification of the Chinese concerned, is immensely valuable. But it is drawn primarily from a Malayan model, and it encounters some problems when it is applied to the Indonesian scene, which may well have some peculiar features.

One of these is undoubtedly the importance which has been attached to nationality in Indonesia, coupled with the particular criteria which have been adopted to define Indonesian nationality. Thus, particularly in the last ten years, a large sector of the Indonesian Chinese has been compelled to make a public declaration of their identification as between Indonesia and China whereas those who did not get the choice and those who opted against Indonesian citizenship have been starkly identified as alien. Moreover, this division has been made exceptionally rigid in two senses. First, the possibility of a person whose status is clearly alien gaining Indonesian citizenship by naturalisation, although relaxed a little recently, has always been very slight. Secondly, Indonesian citizenship law treats the Indonesia-born children of alien or stateless Chinese as having the same nationality as that of their fathers.

Other peculiar features of the Indonesian scene which distinguish it from its immediate Southeast Asian neighbours have been the presence and activity (up to 1967) of Chinese Communist diplomatic personnel, the cleavage in Indonesian Chinese society between peranakan and totok, and the recent destruction of community institutions which form the very arena of 'community politics'. What are the consequences of these differences in applying Professor Wang's tripartite classification?

One is that the importance of Group B (those principally concerned with community politics) in Indonesia has been undermined by the public national identification forced upon the Indonesian Chinese so that community politics tended to become permeated by the national politics of either Indonesia or China. Even if the nationality issue had not been posed in so sharp a way, the division between totok and perana- kan would have led (as it did, in pre-war days) to Group B politics being split into two distinct halves corresponding to the two 'communities'. Further, the presence of an embassy and consulates representing the Chinese People's Republic which replaced earlier representation of Nationalist China probably injected a degree of Group A politicisation among the Chinese who were not Indonesian citizens, which was unusual in Southeast Asia. Among the peranakans who had become Indonesian citizens, on the other hand, the pressures to show themselves loyal Indonesians and against 'exclusivism' gave Group B politics in that community a defensive quality. The recent crushing of community institutions among both totoks and peranakans, in addition, has inhibited the development of either Group A or Group B politics.

A further problem in applying Professor Wang's categories to In- donesian conditions is that 'they rest on the premise that the Chinese do want to remain culturally distinguishable'. While this may cover the field of political behaviour among the Malayan Chinese, in Indonesia it excludes the assimilationists and at least some of the 'assimilated'.

The writer is conscious that his own way of looking at Chinese minority political behaviour also has its deficiencies; it probably has many more of which he is as yet unaware. One kind of intracommunal cleavage which is of great importance—that based upon class interest—has not been given any attention. This division is usually found in the context of integrationist politics. With the exception of the split between the CHH and the PTI in the 1930s (in which a class cleavage was com- pounded with one based upon national identification), this kind of intra- communal division has not been characteristic of Indonesian Chinese politics. In this respect, a striking contrast has been shown to exist in Sarawak, where the cleavages within the major ethnic groups (including the Chinese) have proved more deep-rooted than those between them.[166]

Other difficulties arise in applying the classifications adopted here to particular cases. The case of a person whose politics changes pattern over time presents little difficulty. A change like that of Liem Koen Hian from being a nationalist in the early 1920s to an integrationist in the early 1930s (in Professor Wang's terms a shift from Group A to Group C) is significant and should be noted. A more substantial difficulty is that some people engage in two styles of political activity simultaneously and that others who pretend to be engaged in one form of politics are actually engaged in another. The writer's only defence to this criticism is to acknowledge the difficulty and observe that it applies to Professor Wang's classification also; perhaps with greater force because of his greater reliance upon subjective, orientational factors, which are probably better suited to the more fluid political situation in Malaya.

In conclusion, it can be said that the policies implemented by the Indonesian government since the attempted coup in 1965 (regardless of whether they are good or prudent) have considerably reduced the extent and the variety of Chinese political behaviour in Indonesia. The Indonesian Chinese have been cut off from many of the influences from China to which they were previously exposed and their communal institutions among aliens and citizens have been fragmented.[167] These traumatic blows may be supplemented by slower-working social processes to bring about a radically different Indonesian Chinese society in the future. One factor of importance in this will be the availability of Indonesian citizenship by naturalisation to the alien and stateless Chinese. Another vital factor is the education of the alien Chinese children. If the alien children are exposed to an Indonesian language education with an Indonesian curriculum and the only access to learning Chinese is in the home, the old divisions between peranakans and totoks may well break down, as may the social barriers separating alien from citizen. The government is caught in a contradiction because it seeks to isolate the aliens from the WNI Chinese on the one hand but on the other hand proclaims its desire to ensure that WNI Chinese children are in a majority in totok-financed special project national schools. Since it was to be expected that many of the WNI children at such schools would be of Chinese descent (and usually from totok families), their assimilation to the Indonesian majority was likely to be impeded. But in practice, since the overwhelming majority of the students have been aliens, this has only occurred in a small number of cases.

It is in fact already possible to discern the process of disintegration of the totok and peranakan communities in Java.[168] By way of illustration, four groups can be distinguished. At one extreme, particularly in the older generation, are the old-style totoks, who are Chinese-speaking and Chinese-educated. Next come their children, who are Chinese-speaking at home, but increasingly Indonesian-educated, capable of mixing in a rather cosmopolitan way with both Indonesians and Chinese. They may, however, find greater difficulty in mixing with the older-style peranakans who, although not Chinese-speaking, often speak a mixture of Dutch and Indonesian and may paradoxically have a more strongly developed sense of Chineseness and separateness. At the other extreme, there are those in process of assimilation from peranakan to indigenous Indonesian society. These observations are highly impressionistic and do not derive from the careful sociological survey which would be required to substantiate them. But it seems that old-style totoks and old-style peranakans are disappearing, for different reasons. The totok way of life, once it ceased to be refreshed by new Chinese immigration in the thirties, was maintained by the Chinese schools, the

Chinese press, and the Chinese communal organisations. The only elements of these which the Indonesian government is prepared to tolerate are those which it sponsors itself, rather than those which spring autonomously from among the totoks. Consequently the Chinese content in the totok culture being transmitted to the younger generation is being watered down and the cohesiveness of totok society is being diminished. In addition, many wealthy totok parents are now sending their children overseas for further education, perhaps particularly to English-speaking countries. The old-style peranakans, however, many of whom enjoyed high status during the late colonial period, have now become a downwardly mobile group. Quite a number now believe that advancement for their children in Indonesia will depend upon their assimilation to Indonesian society. Those to whom this is unacceptable or who think it impracticable are often desperately having their children coached in Dutch or German with a view to their being educated and hopefully settling in Europe. Many prominent peranakan families already have at least one member settled in Europe. Another factor at work, in both totok and peranakan families, is a feeling among younger children that the life-styles of their parents are out of date. One pull among children of totok families comes from Singapore and Hong Kong: a kind of Overseas Chinese pop culture mediated through films, magazines, and entertainers. On the other hand, understanding of Chinese script has probably been declining rapidly since the closure of the Chinese schools, and Indonesian influences have probably gained some corresponding ground among the children. Among peranakan children, the closure of Baperki schools has led to a large influx of children entering schools run by church-affiliated boards which tend to be rather assimilation-conscious. This development, and the disappearance of 'exclusive' associations among peranakan students and in general, is almost certainly accelerating assimilation of young peranakans to Indonesian ways, particularly those of the Christian minority.

It would be rash to predict the shape of Indonesian Chinese political behaviour in the future, but it seems likely that it will be affected by these processes of social and cultural change.

3

ANTI-CHINESE OUTBREAKS IN INDONESIA, 1959–68

J. A. C. Mackie

Antagonism towards the Overseas Chinese, either latent or overt, can be found in most countries in Southeast Asia. Indonesia, however, has acquired an unfortunate reputation for particular hostility to them, largely because of the several episodes which are the subject of this chapter. These have been the most serious manifestations of anti-Chinese sentiment, although by no means the only ones. Government regulations embodying elements of discrimination against them have also provided evidence of such attitudes from time to time, as well as the behaviour and utterances of individuals or groups. Moreover, there have been occasional outbreaks of localised violence which have been effectively curbed by the authorities before they gave rise to more widespread hostility. And the Chinese have been vulnerable targets for looting or mistreatment at times when established authority has been shaken, such as at the end of the Japanese occupation and during the course of Indonesia's revolutionary struggle for independence against the Dutch (1945–49), when sporadic attacks on them occurred in various parts of the country.[1]

But the fact that outbreaks of violence have occurred more frequently in Indonesia than in the other plural societies of Southeast Asia may tell us more about the limitations of the government's authority in Indonesia in the turbulent aftermath of the revolution than it does about the intensity of anti-Chinese feelings there. It is noteworthy that such outbreaks have been much less frequent or serious at times when the authority of the government has been most securely established. (We should not forget, moreover, that many Indonesian leaders have been well aware of the danger of allowing racial antagonisms to become inflamed, some of them taking quite courageous stands against this.) It may be true the anti-Chinese feelings are more intense in Indonesia than in other parts of Southeast Asia, or it may not: the issue is not worth arguing here. What is more important is to notice that we lack the sort of data we would need to make confident judgements about such a complex question. It would be unwise to draw sweeping conclusions on the matter solely from the evidence provided by the outbreaks of violence. Yet many of the generalisations that have been made about anti-Chinese sentiment in Indonesia have been based on inferences drawn mainly from the overt manifestations of hostility, or their absence. It is as if we knew no more about an iceberg than we could see above the surface, without realising how much remained below. Little or no research in depth into racial attitudes in contemporary Indonesia has been undertaken by social psychologists, so writers on this subject have had little choice but to draw what conclusions they could from incidents such as we will outline here. Perhaps this has produced a somewhat distorted impression. At any rate, the results have not been very satisfactory and if we are ever to achieve a sound understanding of the social dynamics of racial tensions in Indonesia, we will need much more precise information, not only about the particular incidents which have given rise to violence, but also about the latent attitudes which underlie them and the factors which have operated to restrain hostile feelings at other times.

In the account which follows, the emphasis will be given primarily to the political factors which have either contributed to outbreaks of overt hostility or have helped to contain them. It has frequently been observed that anti-Chinese sentiment has generally been most prevalent on the right wing of the Indonesian political spectrum, among the strongly *santri* (devout) Muslims and their allies, whereas during the period under discussion the left wing was generally noted for its much more favourable attitudes to the Chinese. This polarisation of attitudes seemed readily explicable at the time, for it was the small shopkeepers and emergent businessmen of the right who were most frequently in competition with the Chinese (though in other respects it might have been thought that their class interests as embryo capitalists would coincide with those of the Chinese rather than conflict). On the left, however, the Indonesian Communist Party (PKI) had, as Ruth McVey put it,

> exhibited a notable tolerance of the Chinese minority, even at times when the advantages of taking up anti-Chinese positions far outweighed the advantages that might conceivably be gained from defending that minority. A principal factor in this abstention seems to have been the internationalist, anti-racist character of Marxist ideology; another the fact that anti-Chinese sentiment has always

been strongest on the right—on the part of the Indonesians com-
peting with or aspiring to replace the Chinese shopkeepers, merchants and moneylenders—and there has thus been a natural
tendency for the left to become involved in such defense as the
Chinese minority enjoys.[2]

The PKI's relatively favourable attitude toward the Indonesian Chinese
was not, contrary to a widespread misapprehension, due to the fact that
many of the latter were members of that party. In fact, quite the opposite
was the case; in the early fifties the PKI under Aidit's leadership had
quickly eliminated from its top ranks the only Chinese who had earlier
been at all prominent in it. Relations with the Chinese minority posed
delicate problems of strategy for the PKI, since its opponents were
always likely to interpret any lack of nationalist enthusiasm by the party
on anti-Chinese issues as a sign either of its servitude to Peking or of
opportunism dictated by the need for the funds which the PKI was said
to receive from Chinese businessmen. However, the party leaders consistently and courageously stood out against racialist attacks on the
Chinese, despite the political and even ideological problems this posed
at times. So also, it must be said to his credit, did President Sukarno—
for similar reasons which are more readily explicable in terms of the
alignment of political forces in Indonesia, as we shall see, than in terms
of abstract ideology or class analysis.

But while there is no great difficulty in explaining the attitude of
left-wing elements on the Indonesian scene in the period under consideration, the explanation of right-wing hostility to the Chinese poses a more
complex analytical problem. Economic competition certainly appears
to have been one causal factor, but so also has been the socio-cultural gulf
between the Chinese and the more devout Muslims.

> While anti-Chinese feeling is widespread in Indonesian society,
> it is most marked among Indonesian business groups determined
> to expand at the expense of the Chinese, and in ethnic communities
> like the Minangkabau and the Sundanese where business elements
> play a major role. Many of these entrepreneurial groups and com-
> munities adhere strongly to Islam, which provides a business ethic
> and often also a rationale for hostility to the Chinese, who are seen
> as heathens, pork eaters and tools of the Communist.[3]

How far it is economic competition that is the key variable in this
situation and how far it is something to do with fervent commitment to
Islam itself is a question which still requires investigation at a deeper
level. Competition has been singled out as the decisive factor by W. F.
Wertheim in one of the most authoritative discussions of anti-Chinese
outbreaks yet attempted, but he may have overstated his case to the

point of giving insufficient attention to other factors. Anti-Chinese outbreaks in Southeast Asia are not a new development, he argues, but they have recently been accompanied by violence and discrimination on a mass scale which is not comparable with the occasional riots and pogroms of past centuries.[4] This change has occurred because in the present transitional phase of social development of the newly independent societies of Southeast Asia, characterised by the breakdown of traditional society, 'competition on a group basis starts, enabling the newcomers [i.e. the challengers for entry into fields of activity formerly closed to them by colonial caste barriers] to enlist the support of a much broader following, and a tendency develops to align according to criteria which find their roots in the traditional structure of society'—i.e. along communal or primordial lines. Thus, according to Wertheim, the Indonesian small traders made use of Islam as a unifying ideology to fight their stronger Chinese competitors—and the 'national' ideology was used for the same purpose by the secular nationalists by branding the rivals as 'foreigners' who have failed to assimilate to their host society. Even class struggle motives could be utilised to enlist the peasantry against 'capitalist' exploiters and oppressors, he suggests. But he regards the nationalist and class struggle arguments more as a 'rationalisation than the real motive force' and draws the conclusion that

> it is not cultural diversity which is at the root of the tensions. The movements [Islam and nationalism] become virulent precisely at the moment when the cultural differences are waning to such an extent that competition becomes possible. Lack of assimilation is not the real motive force . . . It is a convenient rationalisation . . . an excuse to select a special group of 'foreigners' as the target . . . [The] basic aim is to oust them in order to supplant them in a position of economic power.[5]

But if cultural diversity is not at the root of the tensions, it is surely one causal factor and a ubiquitous one. Islam has been a very important variable in the equation, obscure though its influence may be. Wertheim seems determined to dismiss cultural diversity as a sufficient condition of the tensions he is seeking to explain in order to strengthen his case for looking for a more all-embracing cause at some deeper level of analysis of the social structure itself. However, by singling out as 'the basic aim' of the anti-Chinese groups the elimination of their commercial rivals, he commits himself to a logical strait-jacket which is neither necessary nor helpful to the explanation of hostility to the Chinese in Indonesia; in fact, it is a positive hindrance when we attempt to understand the different intensities of anti-Chinese feeling at different times and places in Indonesia. Certainly there is no straightforward correlation to be made between the outbreaks of racial violence and the intensity of economic rivalry. Other factors have to be taken into account also, particularly the political and socio-cultural background in each instance.

The apparent correlation between anti-Chinese sentiment and fervent commitment to Islam in Indonesia has been extensively discussed by The Siauw Giap in an article on the anti-Chinese riots in Kudus (1918) and Sukabumi (1963), both devout Muslim centres. He notes that strong adherence to Islam has been an important factor in both cases, but he goes on to argue, like Wertheim, that this element alone would not necessarily produce anti-Chinese disturbances or aggressive collective action, for no instances of anti-Chinese riots have been recorded in Madura, another militantly Muslim area. Hence he concludes that it must be the coincident growth of an Indonesian middle class in the more devout Muslim communities that is responsible for anti-Sinicism rather than Islam itself: 'it is economic competition between adjoining groups which lies at the root of the tension'.[6] (This would still leave some puzzles about the situation in Madura, however, for there are many Madurese businessmen.) Dr The goes on to advance an intriguing argument against the frequently stated proposition that Islam has in the past been a substantial barrier to the assimilation of the Chinese in Indonesia since few of them were willing to become Muslim—in contrast to the situation in Buddhist countries like Thailand, where Chinese embraced Theravada Buddhism much more readily and in large numbers.[7] Conversions and full assimilation to local society were quite frequent before 1900, he suggests, but since then there has been a breakdown of the older social structures which integrated members of the two racial groups and they have been replaced by structures which have been formed on a racial or religious basis; 'Islam proved to be a strong integrative force and personal quarrels between a Muslim and a non-Muslim could easily degenerate into group-conflict of greater or lesser scale'.

How far Dr The's interpretation is historically accurate is a question that deserves closer investigation. But for our purposes here of trying to understand the antagonisms that exist and the outbreaks of hostility that have occurred, his bald assertion that economic competition between Indonesian and Chinese businessmen is at the root of the tensions is of very direct relevance. By putting too much stress on this factor, important though it undoubtedly has been, The and Wertheim have tended to obscure other elements in the picture.

A more fruitful approach would be to isolate different aspects of the problem of inter-racial relations in Indonesia—the general causes of racial antagonisms in the first instance and then the particular causes of outbreaks of inter-group violence—and to recognise that a number of factors are likely to be involved, with complex patterns of interaction, without singling out any particular element as decisive. It would also be prudent to avoid drawing general conclusions about the causes of racial antagonisms from the evidence thrown up by overt manifestations of violence, which simply happen to be the most abundant and striking evidence about the phenomenon we have. We know far too little, for instance, about the nature and the intensity of the resentments towards the Chinese that are silently harboured in the breasts of non-*santri* Javanese engaged in non-commercial pursuits to warrant any confident generalisations about the correlation between intensity of Islamic fervour and anti-Sinicism or even business rivalry and anti-Sinicism.[8] One need not go as far in the other direction, however, as the semi-official Leknas report on the 1963 Sukabumi riots, which asserted that because Islam enjoins tolerance of other religions, Muslim fanaticism should not be blamed for the violence that occurred. It seems undeniable that Islamic fervour has been an important variable underlying the development of anti-Chinese hostility in Indonesia; but whether it has functioned as a fundamental cause of heightened antagonism, or as a catalytic factor which intensifies such feelings to the point of explosion we do not really know. This is an area where deeper research into the social psychology of racial tensions in Indonesia is badly needed. In the final section of this chapter, an impressionistic summary will be offered of the main factors to be considered in our search for explanations of these antagonisms and the outbreaks of violence that have occurred. But first we must look more closely at the particular episodes which help to illuminate our understanding of the problem.

THE 1959 BAN ON RETAIL TRADERS

A revealing example of the tangled mixture of emotions, motivations and political pressures involved in an outburst of anti-Sinicism is provided by the attempt in 1959–60 to ban alien-owned retail stores from rural areas. This episode brought about a sharp deterioration in Sino-Indonesian relations which contributed to the intensification of nationalist sentiment already stirred up by the issue. It gave the anti-Communists in Indonesia a convenient weapon with which to attack their opponents when the latter endeavoured to defend the Chinese, and it thereby helped to push the Chinese towards the Communists for protection. It also generated an atmosphere of considerable hostility towards the Overseas Chinese and created a sense of acute insecurity for all of them, whether Indonesian citizens or not. (Although the ban was officially directed only at alien Chinese and was not, despite initial fears, applied against WNI Chinese, the line of distinction between aliens and Indonesian citizens was apt to become blurred, particularly as it was not beyond question in many cases, for the Dual Nationality Agreement of 1955 was not ratified and brought into force until January 1960.)

The episode was the most alarming they had experienced since the Revolution, and it seemed to show that the Chinese had few friends at court in the newly reshaped power structure of Guided Democracy, hence that there would be few restraints on further anti-Chinese measures.[9] More than a hundred thousand Chinese left Indonesia during 1960 and many more are said to have considered leaving in the belief that there was no future for them in Indonesia.

Yet the intensity of feeling aroused by the episode and the fears it created among the Indonesian Chinese derived more from the political overtones of the whole affair than from the severity of the measures actually taken against them. While the ban undoubtedly caused severe hardships and loss of livelihood for many Chinese from the rural areas, its implementation was by no means as harsh or unrelenting as was generally feared at first, except in the one province of West Java where it was coupled with a ban on residence in rural areas. (In fact, the ban seems to have been widely disregarded in most provinces, including West Java, within a couple of years.) There was far less violence than might be inferred from Peking's lurid propaganda accounts of 'bloody crimes', 'cruel and inhuman treatment' and 'uncivilised behaviour' on the Indonesians' part. The only episode involving serious injury and death to Chinese occurred in the final stages of the affair, when two Chinese women were shot by an army unit at Cimahi in July 1963. More significantly, there appears to have been little or no mob violence against the Chinese, such as characterised by the 1963 and 1965–67 outbursts of anti-Sinicism. The measures taken in 1959 were deliberately ordered and executed by government instrumentalities, though not uniformly nor with the same degree of commitment to them by all government authorities. In the few cases where violence occurred, it resulted less from popular hostility than from confrontative situations between army or police units and Chinese who were resisting orders to leave their homes. It would be quite wrong, of course, to give the impression that popular resentment against the Chinese in general was not stirred up by the episode. It certainly was. But it was by no means the primary factor in the political dynamics that determined the course of the dispute, even though there was a strong element of economic nationalism behind the whole affair, as we shall see.

The ban

The political storm which arose over the ban in the last ten weeks of 1959 had a more complex set of causes than those which underlay the original decision of the Minister of Trade to promulgate the ban in the first place on 14 May. As initially formulated, it was a very brief, vague and general regulation declaring that the operating licences of 'small or retail trading businesses of an alien character (*jang bersifat asing*) outside the capitals of Kabupatens, Residencies, Municipalities and Provinces' would not be extended beyond 31 December 1959.[10] The words used, could have been interpreted in such a way as to apply to all Chinese businesses, not merely to those owned by aliens; but a more careful wording was used and several important modifications were made when the ban was finally promulgated under President Sukarno's authority in November as a Presidential Regulation (PP 10/1959, the form in which it is generally known). In the meantime, quite a tug-of-war had occurred between those who wanted the ban to be watered down and those who insisted that it be applied with maximum effect.

It was significant that the Minister of Trade who first announced the ban, Rachmat Muljomiseno, was a member of the Nahdatul Ulama (NU) and that he chose to make the announcement at a meeting of the 'national (i.e. indigenous) businessmen' who were business rivals of the Chinese traders and who had close ties with the Muslim political parties, NU, Masyumi and PSII. The timing and wording of his announcement were also significant, for it came at a moment when all private business-men in Indonesia were in low spirits and facing a bleak future because of the government's decision in April to exclude them from all but a small part of the lucrative field of import trade, of which the lion's share was now to be monopolised by State Enterprises, in accordance with the all-pervasive new ideology of 'Sosialisme à la Indonesia'. The preamble to the Ministerial Decision stated that the ban on alien retail shops in rural areas had been determined 'in connection with efforts to speed up the process of giving an appropriate place to national business-men in all fields of trade', which suggests that the Minister was trying to compensate them for the contraction of opportunities in one sphere by creating wider opportunities in another. The Muslim parties had been pressing strongly for measures to assist the 'economically weaker group' in business ever since the Assaat movement had popularised this phrase in 1956.[11] In the mood of heightened nationalism that accom-panied the nationalisation of all Dutch businesses in Indonesia in 1957–58, there was some speculation that Chinese businesses would be the next to go. But the national businessmen were also apprehensive that they too might suffer from the general ideological reaction against capitalism and private enterprise, whether foreign-owned or Indonesian, for the political climate was becoming increasingly chilly for them.[12] Thus the ban must be seen in the context of these two sets of forces pulling in opposite directions, on the one hand, a series of increasingly threatening anti-Chinese measures through the years 1956–58, urged mainly by right-wing parties, on the other hand a continued narrowing of the scope and prospects for private businessmen of all kinds in an economy now dominated by a large state sector and by an ideology of radical Socialism, urged mainly by the left.

The timing of Rachmat's announcement of the ban was interesting in two other respects. It came at a time when President Sukarno was out of the country and the Djuanda government was preoccupied with the party political manoeuvring that was necessary to ensure that the Constituent Assembly would accept the proposal to 'return to the 1945 Constitution.' The NU vote was of crucial importance for this purpose, but there were open differences of opinion between the party's ministers and its rank and file members about the appropriate political strategy for the party to adopt. Just where Rachmat stood in relation to the rank and file of his party, to his cabinet colleagues or to President Sukarno on these issues is not entirely clear. But if party members were pressing him to take action against Chinese businessmen, the moment to do so was most propitious—and unlikely to recur. It is hard to believe that Sukarno would have permitted such a drastic step to be taken on the authority of a single minister if he had known of it in advance. He is said to have been extremely angry with Rachmat later and dropped him from the new cabinet (a non-party cabinet, admittedly) that was formed in July after the return to a Presidential constitution. But not even Sukarno could by then afford to go back completely on a decision over which such strong nationalist feelings could be aroused, although he was later to soften the impact of the regulation in several respects.

In his first major policy statement on 17 August, later characterised as his Political Manifesto, Sukarno touched fleetingly on the problem of how to reconcile the demands of economic nationalism with the role of alien Chinese capitalists in the Indonesian economy by proclaiming that 'an appropriate place and opportunity' would be given to 'all funds and all forces which have proved to be progressive', including 'non-native funds and forces which have settled in Indonesia'. At the same time, he issued stern warnings against non-compliance with Indonesian laws and against 'foreign non-Dutch capital [which] illegally gives support to counter-revolution ... or carries out acts of economic sabotage'. These characteristically vague, ambiguous allusions to the problem may have been intended to signal his intention to persist with the ban (since he did not repudiate it), but they also carried an implication that he shared the favourable view taken of the Chinese traders by the PKI, whose terminology he had adopted, rather than their enemies on the right, who drew a sharp line between 'native' (*asli*) and 'foreign' (*asing*) capital.[13]

Nevertheless, Sukarno and other defenders of the Chinese, most notably the PKI, were in the awkward position of having to justify the continued existence of the most conspicuous group of capitalists in Indonesian society at a time when Socialism and 'national identity' were potent slogans. While it was easy to advance strong justification in their defence on pragmatic grounds (the valuable commercial role played by the Chinese shopkeepers, the weakness of the Indonesian co-operative movement as an alternative and the lack of working capital elsewhere in the economy to replace them), these arguments lacked the heady appeal of the prevailing ideological doctrines of that epoch. Consequently the issue provided an ideal opportunity for the anti-communists in the government, notably the army leaders, to outflank the PKI on a popular issue and cu ɔ· s growth. For the PKI had skilfully taken advantage of the ideological climate of the two preceding years to outstrip the other parties and was beginning to emerge as a major contender for political power in a three-sided relationship between itself, President Sukarno and the army.[14]

In this tense and rather fevered atmosphere (in which the draconian 'monetary purge' on 25 August plunged the entire economy and government administration into confusion), the military commanders of several regions where anti-Chinese sentiment was traditionally strong decided to go beyond the ban on Chinese traders and, on the basis of their martial law powers, ordered bans on residence by Chinese in the rural areas as well.[15] In some places the use of shop-signs in non-Roman lettering was also forbidden. Residence bans were announced in South Sulawesi on 7 August (operative as from 31 September) and in West Java on 28 August. At the end of August, an increasing amount of attention was given by the press and Trade Ministry to the preparations required for the implementation of the trade ban. There was considerable debate about whether the functions of the Chinese rural stores should or could be taken over by co-operatives or Indonesian capitalists. (Neither was likely to have anything like the capital or experience required.[16]) The alien traders were required to indicate by the end of October whether they intended to close down, sell or transfer their businesses to Indonesian citizens or move to the larger towns. Questionnaires were sent out to them by the provincial Trade Inspectorates, but toward the end of September it was admitted officially that very few replies had been received (less than 25 per cent) and in many cases the Chinese shopkeepers simply replied that they wished to stay in business where they were, which was not at all what they were asked.[17] There were also reports that many Chinese believed the Chinese Embassy would intervene to defend their interests, or that the regulation would not be put into effect—a view that had a good deal of prima facie plausibility in September 1959, when the Indonesian economy was virtually paralysed by the disastrous impact of the government's first major economic reform, the 'monetary purge' of 25 August, which decimated cash holdings and savings. The new cabinet decided in early September to uphold the ban, but at about the same time the Chinese government began to interest itself in the matter much more positively than before.

The diplomatic storm

There was little forewarning that the diplomatic storm that blew up over the trade ban would be as intense as it turned out to be. Indonesia's relations with the Peking government throughout the 1950s had been very cordial, especially in the years after the Bandung Conference and the Chou En-lai—Sunario Agreement which had opened the way for a solution of the dual nationality problem.[18] The success (from China's point of view) of Sukarno's visit to China in 1956, his increasingly anti-Western posture in world affairs and his success in isolating the leading anti-communist and anti-Chinese elements in Indonesian politics were all pointers to a steady convergence of political outlook and interests between the two governments. During the 1959 UN debates on China's actions in Tibet, the Indonesian government carefully avoided antagonising China. Exchange of the instruments of ratification of the Dual Nationality Treaty had been planned for September 1959, but this was postponed shortly beforehand. The vehemence of the Chinese government's reaction to the trade ban was something of a puzzle, therefore, since it seriously endangered the goodwill that had been fostered earlier. In fact, it proved to be disastrously counterproductive where its aim was to uphold the rights and interests of the Overseas Chinese, for its failure simply revealed how little China could do to defend them when it came to a showdown.

The clue to Peking's behaviour is probably to be found in the account given by David Mozingo, who explains its reaction in terms of two considerations.[19] One, the balance of advantages and disadvantages involved in standing up firmly for the rights of the Overseas Chinese against a government which they felt to be oppressing them; the other, an apparent strategy of trying to force President Sukarno to intervene against the Indonesian 'reactionaries' who were advocating the trade and residence bans to the detriment of Sino-Indonesian relations. Mozingo suggests that after the announcement of the trade and residence bans on the Chinese in Indonesia, 'each of the policy options open to Peking entailed an unavoidable sacrifice of some of its interests in Indonesia'. A vigorous defence of the Chinese was likely to produce a widespread anti-Chinese outburst there and a conflict with the forces of Indonesian nationalism; moreover, it would put the PKI in the embarrassing position of either turning its back on the Chinese minority or opposing the discriminatory measures and isolating the party from the mainstream of nationalism. On the other hand, a conciliatory response also entailed risks, since the Peking government's standing in the eyes of all the Overseas Chinese was at stake. Moreover, to do nothing might merely sharpen the appetites of the 'reactionaries' rather than satisfy them. Evidently the Chinese concluded that the arguments against conciliation were stronger than those for it. In any case, they were probably angered by the provocatively hasty implementation of the residence ban by the two provincial military authorities, which according to Mozingo they regarded as a much more reprehensible move than the trade ban *per se*.

Early in October, Indonesia's Foreign Minister, Dr Subandrio, visited Peking, at very short notice, for talks about the ban and the Dual Nationality Treaty. Instead of leading to the completion of the formalities of ratifying the Treaty, which Subandrio had mentioned as one of his aims in the visit, or producing closer understanding between the two governments on the problem of the Chinese traders, his visit had quite the reverse effect. He was allegedly subjected to heavy pressure for a withdrawal of the ban. The experience was hardly calculated to evoke a conciliatory response and Subandrio is said to have been deeply shaken by it.[20] But neither side initially revealed anything of this, though the joint communiqué signed by Subandrio and Foreign Minister Chen Yi on 11 October barely disguised the fact that the two sides had been unable to reach agreement. Its crucial paragraph on the trade ban read as follows:

> Both Foreign Ministers take cognisance of the fact that in the process towards economic development and stability in Indonesia, the economic position of the Chinese nationals residing there may be affected in some ways. Both the Foreign Ministers consider that an appropriate way should be sought for the solution of this question so that it will be in the interest of the economic development of Indonesia and that the proper rights and interests of the Chinese nationals will be respected. Both the Foreign Ministers agree that the economic resources of those Chinese nationals will still play a useful role in the economic development of Indonesia.[21]

This clause of the joint communiqué gave rise to consternation and controversy in the Indonesian press, for it seemed to imply that the ban might yet be withdrawn or modified, and it contained no acknowledgement by China of Indonesia's right as a sovereign state to implement the ban. Did this mean that the ban was not going to be upheld asked the NU newspaper. What did it mean by 'an appropriate way should be sought for the solution of the question' asked others. Most of the criticism came from the right wing, but even the official PNI paper expressed its dismay.[22] Dr Subandrio's several explanatory statements after he left Peking left the answer obscure, presumably because he himself was not yet sure what President Sukarno's response would be. He said nothing in public about the pressures to which he had been subjected in Peking, so as to avoid exacerbating an already delicate situation. But in the fortnight that elapsed before the President announced his decision on the matter, a controversy flared up in the Indonesian press over the question of whether (and how) the ban was to be implemented. The PKI daily, *Harian Rakjat*, accusing its enemies of treating the Subandrio-Chen Yi joint communiqué as 'purely a formality and not one to be implemented', claimed that 'the reactionaries are trying to imitate the Indian reactionaries in drawing smokescreens', but went on to warn them that the 'progressive potentials' in Indonesia were sufficient to develop an anti-Chinese agitation into an anti-capitalist one: 'we will gladly support government actions nationalising or "co-operativising" Chinese retail shops ... provided that British, Dutch and American capital be nationalised in advance'.[23] This approach was promptly attacked by the NU daily as 'trying to sidetrack the issue'. On the whole, the supporters of the ban had a much more popular case to argue than their opponents. They were able to charge the Chinese government with inconsistency in opposing Indonesia's efforts to 'nationalise' her economy (the ambiguity of the word being exploited deliberately) and to root out capitalist elements at the village level, especially as the capitalists were not only aliens but also notorious for their evasion of economic regulations. The opponents of the ban tried to meet such charges by quoting President Sukarno's endorsement of 'funds and forces proved to be progressive' or by relying on two other lines of argument; one, that no real plans had been laid to introduce a socialist or co-operative system of distribution in the village, the other that Indonesia must at all costs avoid a conflict with Peking, lest she find herself caught in a trap set by the 'reactionaries'.

At the beginning of November Sukarno threw his weight unequivocally on the side of maintaining the trade ban, even though he simultaneously ordered some important modifications, which may have been intended to mollify Peking as well as to soften the impact of the measures. The new regulation, which was now issued under the President's name, specifically mentioned that aliens affected by the trade ban were not required to leave their places of residence, except where the regional military authorities required it on grounds of the security situation—a qualification which left the decision in the hands of the military and so avoided a show-down with them, even though the clause implied an oblique rebuke. Supplementary regulations also exempted from the ban various service occupations in which the Chinese were extensively engaged, such as transportation, catering, dentistry, hairdressing, etc. The definitive formulation of the ban, Presidential Regulation (*Peraturan Presiden*), no. 10 of 1959, was issued on 16 November, some time after the cabinet session at which it was considered on 3 November.[24]

A tangled set of developments now brought the dispute to a higher level of intensity during November, from which it became harder for either government to back down without serious loss of face. The Military Commander for West Java issued a new decree early in November, advancing the date on which the residence ban applying to aliens in rural areas of that province would come into effect; whereas his earlier regulations on this matter had stated that the Chinese should move out of the villages by 29 December, the modified version said only that they should prepare to leave—and the military authorities immediately began to evacuate them forcibly, frequently on overnight notice.[25] A violent clash occurred at Cibadak, near Sukabumi, on 3 November, in the course of one of the earliest compulsory evictions; it was a relatively minor incident which did not involve loss of life, but wild stories about it were soon circulating in Jakarta.[26] Soon after this, Chinese Embassy officials began to intervene openly, instructing local Chinese organisations and Chinese nationals not to obey the army's orders and in some cases personally obstructing the evictions that were taking place. Tempers were now becoming inflamed on both sides. Matters were not helped by press reports that a pro-Peking newspaper in Hong Kong had published a letter from a Chinese in Indonesia calling upon all Chinese to 'rise and fight' the Indonesian government's action, nor by publication in *Nusantara* on 14 November of Dennis Bloodworth's London *Observer* article about Subandrio's experiences in Peking, embellished with comments about 'Han chauvinism', the inevitability of a Chinese drive to the south and the Chinese view of Indonesia as an 'inferior nation'. Subandrio publicly denied the Bloodworth story and his press secretary issued a plea to the Indonesian press to avoid exaggeration.[27] But the activities and attitudes of the Chinese diplomats now became a more immediate source of contention. After a meeting with the Chinese Ambassador, Huang Chen, on 17 November, Dr Subandrio announced that the former had promised to support the Indonesian government in implementing the ban, provided no further 'excesses' occurred. The Ambassador issued a public denial that he had agreed to such a proposition and the implication that Subandrio was a liar provoked demands in the Indonesian press for Huang Chen's recall.[28] At this stage, the West Java military authorities announced an order banning Chinese embassy personnel from entering or staying in West Java until further notice, but at least one case of Chinese officials defying this order was later reported and the press seized upon it eagerly. By the third week of November the dispute had hardened to a point of bitter confrontation. Only the PKI continued to oppose the ban in principle, whereas the PNI, with its characteristic sensitivity to prevailing winds, had come down firmly in favour of it.[29]

It has been suggested by David Mozingo that the main objective of the Chinese government's policy up to this stage was to force Sukarno's intervention in the crisis, since only he could overrule the generals.[30] If so, his endorsement of PP 10 should have been a clear indication that Peking had failed in this aim. After that, the actions of the Chinese Embassy personnel in attempting to obstruct the West Java evictions of Chinese during November simply played into the army's hands. Whatever the legal rights or wrongs of their behaviour may have been, the spectacle of Chinese consular officials defying the orders of the Indonesian army and claiming diplomatic privileges in order to obstruct the implementation of an official policy was bound to arouse the ire of most Indonesian nationalists.[31]

Peking reassesses her strategy
During December the Chinese government tried two new tactics of a carrots-and-sticks nature in order to induce the Indonesian government to reverse its policies. Chen Yi sent a letter to Subandrio on 9 December urging 'immediate consultations' towards an overall settlement of the questions at issue between them. On the following day Radio Peking began a series of broadcasts attacking the Indonesian government with unprecedented vehemence and calling upon the Overseas Chinese to return to 'the warm bosom of the motherland'. Mozingo suggests that the purpose of these broadcasts and the policy of repatriation they advocated may have been to 'punish Indonesia' by enticing home Chinese with special skills whose departure would do most damage to the Indonesian economy, but the aim may have been simply to add to the pressure on Sukarno and Subandrio to agree to an overall settlement of the dispute through compromises on both sides.[32] The fact that the broadcasts were stopped on 21 December, just as suddenly as they had started, suggests that the latter hypothesis is more likely, especially as there was a perceptible change in Peking's policy soon after. Inevitably, most of the Indonesian press seized upon the Radio Peking broadcasts as evidence of China's hostile and slanderous attitude, quoting phrases such as 'the methods of terror used by Hitler against the Jews would be repeated in Indonesia' and 'six hundred and fifty million Chinese will not remain passive in meeting unjust discrimination like that experienced by Chinese traders in Indonesia'. The anti-Communist press seized on the opportunity to implicate the PKI in the Chinese 'slander campaign', charging it with being a tool of an international ideology and unconcerned with Indonesia's national interests.[33] In this respect, as in its failure to pressure Sukarno into repudiating the army's residence ban, the Chinese move seems to have done more harm than good to any prospect there may ever have been of changing Indonesia's policy in the matter.

Chen Yi made it clear in his letter of 9 December that the Chinese government put the blame for the rift not on the Sukarno government but on 'the forces bent on sabotaging the friendship of our two countries', since a solution to the problem of the Chinese traders could easily have been found on the basis of the Subandrio-Chen Yi joint communiqué and Sukarno's formula about 'non-native funds and forces'. He did not explicitly call for the withdrawal of the trade ban as such, nor even of the residence ban, but he put forward three proposals as the basis for negotiations toward an overall settlement of the issues in dispute.[34] Subandrio's reply two days later showed that the Indonesian government was not in the least willing to sit down and negotiate an overall settlement (for it would presumably have found itself under pressure to trade concessions with Peking for the sake of the appearance of amity and the conclusion of the Dual Nationality Treaty), though it was anxious to complete the exchange of instruments of ratification of the Treaty, which China had been holding up, he said, 'for reasons not clear to the Indonesian government'. The greater part of Subandrio's reply was devoted to an elaboration of Indonesian grievances about Chinese interference in Indonesia's internal affairs and of the 'rather unpalatable attitude' of the Overseas Chinese toward the Indonesian people during and since the struggle for independence, his charges ranging from the part played by the *Pao An Tui* in 1947–49 to Chinese manipulation of the markets for gold and dried fish in the months just past. Chen Yi's second letter of 24 December was expressed in much less demanding tones and merely reiterated his earlier call for an overall settlement, but this time as if more in sorrow than in anger; it also announced that the way had been cleared for an immediate exchange of instruments of ratification of the Dual Nationality Treaty. However, Subandrio again flatly refused to be drawn into overall negotiations.

The 1960 aftermath

This was still not the end of the affair. Tensions remained high for many months after the trade ban came into effect at the end of 1959. Nearly 100 000 Chinese decided to take advantage of the opportunity provided by the Peking government to return to their homeland and their repatriation created a good deal of friction in the early part of the year. There were numerous allegations from the Chinese side of vindictive treatment and harassment of the returnees at the hands of customs officials; they were prohibited from taking more than token quantities of money and goods with them and cases were reported of bicycles being sawn in half, ostensibly to ensure that gold and precious stones were not being smuggled out. To make matters worse, it was a period when Chinese capital was already flowing out of Indonesia through the black market on an unprecedented scale, not only because of the trade ban, but also because the Chinese businessmen's confidence in the Indonesian economy had been so severely shaken by the 'monetary purge' of August 1959, which left business severely crippled for months afterwards. Prices and the black market rate of the Rupiah were again rising rapidly as the government resorted to inflationary deficit financing, with the result that hoarding of goods created acute shortages, which were also blamed on the Chinese, frequently with justification, sometimes without.[35] All these circumstances aggravated popular hostility to them which could easily be exploited for their own political purposes by groups opposed to the PKI or the President.

Several anti-Chinese incidents which occurred in the middle of 1960 reinforce the suspicion that some elements in the army were still deliberately trying to fan the flames of anti-Chinese sentiment. On this occasion, there was far less provocation from Peking than there had been in late 1959, but far stronger reasons of domestic politics, for Indonesia was now posed on the brink of a tense political crisis which was threatening to polarise the right and left wings of the political spectrum. The crisis arose out of Sukarno's action in suspending the Parliament in March after it had rejected his government's 1960 Budget and then proceeding to nominate a new one which would be subservient to his wishes. This provoked the formation of a new political grouping, the Democratic League (*Liga Demokrasi*), consisting of leading members of the anti-Sukarno and anti-Communist political parties, notably the Masyumi, PSI, Christian and Catholic parties.[36] Some maverick politicians from the PNI and NU were also sympathetic to the League because of their hostility to Sukarno, so that for a few weeks it seemed possible that the League might snowball into a broadly-based coalition of forces opposed to the President and his leftward-leaning policies. Some leaders also seemed to be sympathetic since it was inconceivable that the League would be allowed to operate without their approval. Nasution and his colleagues had been alarmed by Sukarno's willingness to elevate the PKI into prominence as one of the major political pillars of his regime, while denying office to the anti-Communist parties who were the army's strongest supporters; they were also apprehensive about the PKI's increasingly critical attitude towards certain ministers, as well as the political implications of Krushchev's barnstorming visit to Indonesia in February. Some army officers gave the League strong support, particularly in regions outside Java, and in general it was allowed a degree of freedom to organise which was quite abnormal under Guided Democracy. Sukarno was away on another of his world tours from April until June, at the time when the League's bandwagon began to roll. Perhaps it was not entirely coincidental that another wave of anti-Chinese incidents occurred about that time, although once again there were various factors responsible.

At the National People's Congress in Peking in early April Chou En-lai and Fang Fang, of the Overseas Chinese Commission, made sharply critical speeches which put the blame for China's difficulties with

Indonesia on 'bourgeois elements' attempting to 'undermine the patriotic democratic forces in their own country to pave the way for achieving military dictatorship'.[37] A strong protest note was sent by the Indonesian Embassy in Peking. More ominously, Chinese consuls were forcibly evicted later in the month from Samarinda in West Borneo and Selatpanjang (South Sumatra) for allegedly interfering in the army's handling of the repatriation of Overseas Chinese. The Indonesian Foreign Ministry now backed up the army commanders by demanding the withdrawal of Chinese consuls from Medan and Banjermasin, a move which provoked a strong protest from Peking, and, according to Mozingo, brought the two countries to the verge of an open diplomatic break in May.[38] Soon after, in late May, the West Java military authorities 'launched a second large-scale campaign of compulsory evacuation of Overseas Chinese by armed force' according to a later Chinese official protest note, resorting to 'arrest, interrogation, beating, cutting off supply of water and electricity to living quarters and sealing up houses and properties'. The timing of this drive appears to have been due to the fact that a six-month postponement granted earlier on the enforcement of the residence ban in West Java was due to expire in June. But the measures taken culminated in an incident at Cimahi on 3 July, in which two Chinese women were killed and two other Chinese wounded when Indonesian troops opened fire on a crowd in the course of forced evacuation in that town.[39]

After the Cimahi episode, however, the wave of anti-Chinese incidents suddenly ended. The fact that the forced removals were stopped, says Mozingo, could not have been the work of anyone else but Sukarno; the army leaders were rebuked in a subtle and characteristically Sukarno-esque fashion when Colonel Kosasih was transferred soon afterward to Sumatra and promoted. Not long after that Sukarno embarked upon a new diplomatic initiative to restore more cordial relations with Peking. Chen Yi visited Jakarta in April 1961 to sign the Dual Nationality Treaty and Sukarno paid a return visit to Peking later in that year. These moves paved the way towards the development of much closer relations between the two countries in the years 1963–65.

The abrupt ending of the 1959–60 conflict is itself revealing. Sukarno had returned to Jakarta from a world trip in June and moved with remarkable speed and self-confidence to re-establish his personal ascendency over the Indonesian political scene. The Democratic League collapsed like a pricked balloon and the wavering politicians of other parties quickly came to heel. Likewise, the army leaders came reluctantly into line, after Sukarno had banned the Masyumi and PSI, his most persistent opponents, although in August some regional commanders endeavoured to take action to curb the PKI similarly, in the strange episode known as the 'Three Souths Affair'. Sukarno was able to resist their efforts to push him into a choice between the army and the PKI, but he had to manoeuvre carefully to do so. The entire episode revealed how delicately the whole political structure was balanced, hence how little scope he had to simply override the army on an issue such as the position of the Overseas Chinese, on which popular sentiment was likely to favour his opponents.

Effects of the ban

The total number of Chinese businesses in rural areas subject to the trade ban was estimated at the time to be of the order of 20–25 000. About half of these were in Java (of which 5 000 were in East Java alone), according to Mary Somers. The total number of foreign enterprises in Indonesia at that time was estimated by the Parliamentary Committee on Foreign Capital to be around 167 000, of which 125 000 were involved in trade, 10 000 in transport, 2 250 in agriculture and 150 in banking. Presumably most of these, except the agricultural enterprises, were Chinese. Nearly 15 000 Chinese aliens were moved forcibly along with some hundreds of WNI.[40]

Approximately 136 000 Chinese left Indonesia in the course of 1960, compared with a normal annual figure of about 12 000. Not all of these were traders displaced from the rural areas. There seems to be little doubt that the Chinese consular officials responsible for the repatriation process also selected quite a large number of skilled artisans and did not confine themselves to Chinese citizens, but even encouraged some Indonesian citizens, including prominent peranakans, to leave. Many of the returnees were high-school and college students. Some had already suffered loss of a livelihood for quite other reasons and for them 'the alien ban was less a cause of a decision to go to China than an opportunity to do something they had been hoping to do but could not afford' because they would have had to pay for it.[41]

The Chinese government soon tired of the difficulties and cost of aiding the repatriation of the Indonesian Chinese. As early as April 1960 the Chinese Embassy stopped its recruiting activities and began to urge applicants to stay on in Indonesia. Many of those who returned to China were sent to large state farms in the southern provinces, which appear to have offered them a hard and frugal livelihood. Reports reaching the Indonesian Chinese from the returnees by the end of 1960 were, in general, discouraging. In the words of one peranakan community leader in Jakarta at that time, an elderly banker who was thoroughly critical of the Sukarno regime, 'When people ask me what they should do, I tell the young ones to go back to China and start a new life while they can. It will be hard, but they can adjust. But for us older people, there is no alternative but to stay and make the best we can of it'.

The regional variations in implementation of the ban provide a striking illustration of the extent to which the execution of a national policy varied according to local circumstances and the attitudes of regional military authorities. The contrast between the stringent application of both the trade and residence bans in West Java and the much milder implementation of the trade ban in Central and East Java, where no ban on residence was attempted, was most striking.[42] Yet there were many more alien Chinese scattered throughout the rural areas of East Java (44 000) than West (16 500) or Central Java (12 000). It is not surprising to find that relatively little anti-Chinese sentiment was aroused in Central Java, the heartland of the Javanese *priyayi* culture, based on an eclectic blend of religions, and of the two non-Muslim parties most closely supporting the President on this issue, PNI and PKI: it was also a region where rural *santri* influence was localised and relatively slight, the Chinese were few in numbers and long-established in the area. In East Java the situation was not quite so simple, for Islam was much stronger there and the Chinese much more numerous. On the other hand, there too the Chinese were relatively long-established and well acculturated to Javanese society, so that they had better links with the ruling elite, who were predominantly *priyayi*, as in Central Java.

West Java presented a rather special case in nearly all these respects. Chinese had not been permitted by the Dutch to settle into the interior there until well into the twentieth century, so they were by no means as well acculturated as the peranakans of Central and East Java. Among the various other factors that tended to retard acculturation and give rise to stronger anti-Chinese prejudice in West Java, Mary Somers has noted the strength of Islam in the region (and, in particular, the influential social position of the religious leaders, the *kiyais*, vis-à-vis the landowning and business elite of West Java); the unhappy legacy of the old Dutch system of 'private lands', many of which fell into Chinese hands, giving them quasi-seigneurial rights over the local population; the very uneven spatial distribution of the Chinese; and to some extent the weaker acculturative pull of Sundanese culture as compared with Javanese.[43]

Outside Java, we find that the ban on residence was applied in South Sulawesi and South Kalimantan, much of South Sumatra and Jambi and in North Sumatra military district, though there were relatively few alien Chinese living outside the towns in most parts of these regions. No attempt was made to enforce a residence ban in West Kalimantan, where there was a large and long-established Chinese rural population, although the ban on alien-owned retail stores was applied. In the province of Riau and the two tin-mining islands of Bangka and Belitung, where there were considerable numbers of Chinese, the situation was not entirely clear; in the former (a Navy-controlled area, very close to Singapore), the authorities admitted that implementation would be difficult, but the ban was applied in the latter and many Chinese tin-miners sought repatriation, although apparently they were also influenced by the decline of employment in the industry at that time. And as the account of the South Sumatra rubber traders in this volume indicates, the trade ban appears to have had little effect in driving the Chinese out of the rural areas, creating far less impact than the upheavals of 1965–67.

In general, it seems that in most places outside West Java it was not very difficult for the Chinese to reach an accommodation with the authorities. (From the press accounts, one is left with the impression that around Medan also, the pressure from local politicians and business-men in search of issues to exploit may have been more intense than elsewhere.) In theory the ban did not apply against Chinese who were Indonesian citizens; but because even the peranakan Chinese could not always produce documentary proof of their Indonesian nationality, many were little better off than aliens and were similarly vulnerable to extortion and harassment. Many Chinese were able to get around the trade ban by transferring their businesses either to relatives who were Indonesian citizens or to asli 'partners' or employees. There were many reports that bribery often helped to obtain exemption, even in West Java, and in some cases alien Chinese were even permitted to maintain their shops in rural areas, provided they resided in the towns and commuted daily.

As for the aim of hastening the development of the Indonesian traders in rural areas, if the ban did succeed in helping them, the evidence for it is so tenuous as to be almost imperceptible.

THE MAY 1963 RIOTS

The anti-Chinese riots which broke out in May 1963, mostly in West Java, stand in contrast with the other episodes examined here in that they were eruptions of popular sentiment which were strongly condemned by the government and (in theory, though not always in practice) by the local authorities: yet they showed very clearly that the ambivalence of the authorities on racial issues could easily be exploited if the circumstances were appropriate. The outbreaks were very destructive in terms of property, although fortunately there was relatively little bloodshed or loss of life. They were shortlived and confined to a fairly small number of towns, all in West or Central Java, apart from three or four minor outbreaks in East Java and Medan. They seem to have had their origins in both the social circumstances of the time—such as frustration, envy and discontent with economic conditions—and in the attempts by right-wing groups to manipulate these sentiments for political purposes. Because of this mixture of causes and because a valuable study has been made of the social background to the last and most serious of the series of riots at Sukabumi, an examination of the May riots provides an interesting supplement to our picture of the 1959–60 outbreak.[44]

The 1963 riots consisted of three distinct but inter-connected sets of events. First, there occurred a chain of about half a dozen minor incidents involving fights between Indonesian and Chinese in small towns of Java during the week following 29 March. Secondly, about a month later, another series of outbreaks occurred, culminating in the 10 May riots in Bandung, which precipitated a number of serious riots throughout the following week, mostly in West Java.[45] Thirdly, the Sukabumi outbreak of 18–20 May proved to be the longest and most destructive of them all; but it was also the last, for it brought about President Sukarno's open intervention, which finally led to firm action by the authorities to prevent any further outbursts.

In looking for the causes of these outbreaks, we must give due regard to the importance of local factors and such circumstances as the difficult economic conditions of that time—the price inflation, the shortages and frustrations resulting from the Sukarno government's disastrous economic policies and the widespread resentment of Chinese wealth in the midst of Indonesian poverty (and not only Chinese wealth, but that of the 'new rich' generally)—but it is equally necessary to take into account three features of the broader political situation prevailing in 1963 in order to appreciate how and why anti-Chinese sentiment was again being manipulated as part of the struggle for power between the right and left-wing forces in Indonesian national politics, just as in 1959–60. Once again, West Java was the main source of tension and once again the alignment was, broadly, between the Muslims and supporters of the banned political parties, Masyumi and PSI, on the anti-Chinese side, with support from Bandung student groups and some (or many) army officers; on the other side, Sukarno, the PKI and Baperki. Other parties were ranged indeterminately in between, as usual.

Relations between the Indonesian and Chinese governments were good in 1963, having improved dramatically from their nadir in 1960, after the end of the dispute over PP 10 and the implementation of the Dual Nationality Treaty in 1960–62. The visit to Indonesia of the Chinese Head of State, Liu Shao-Chi, in April 1963, symbolised the steady convergence of the two governments' interests and outlook on world problems at that time, as Sukarno's constant emphasis on anti-colonialism and anti-imperialism drew Indonesia increasingly towards an anti-Western position in world politics and into closer accordance with China's views.[46] As a result of the Sino-Soviet rift, the PKI had moved by 1963 from its earlier position of careful non-alignment between the two great Communist powers towards open identification with the Peking line on the politics of world revolution, although in its domestic policies it remained as cautious as ever. Through the PKI's influence on Sukarno, particularly on the issue of Malaysia and 'confrontation' which Sukarno had proclaimed at the beginning of 1963, Peking was apparently trying to draw Indonesia into deeper opposition to the Western bloc and, by weakening her ties with the 'imperialists', to strengthen the hand of the Communists there. To the anti-Communists in Indonesia, the implications of such a policy were alarming for they had seen in the 1961-62 struggle for West Irian how recklessly Sukarno was willing to gamble with the nation's economic stability and its good name overseas (both its credit-worthiness and its political reputation) for the sake of pursuing short-term foreign policy goals based on his increasingly radical foreign policy doctrines and his predilection for 'the thrill of a political surfride'. Hence their anxiety to prevent too cordial a rapprochement between Indonesia and China, even if it required the instigation of anti-Chinese outbreaks to do it.

A more pressing reason why the budding friendship with China posed dangers to the right-wing forces in Indonesia in early 1963 was that Sukarno's government was then hovering uneasily on the brink of committing itself to an economic stabilisation policy, backed by substantial funds from the USA, the IMF and a consortium of Western creditor countries, designed to remedy the damage to the Indonesian economy resulting from the disastrous inflation generated by the struggle to regain West Irian. The PKI was strongly opposed to the scheme, as also, presumably, was China; but on this occasion sheer economic necessity was inclining Sukarno towards reluctant acceptance of it, although the stringently anti-inflationary terms attached to the foreign aid being offered were extremely distasteful to him and bound to be politically unpopular. The PKI was trying to abort the stabilisation scheme during the early months of 1963, when delicate negotiations on the matter were being conducted with the IMF and Washington, by pushing Indonesia towards a more aggressive policy of opposition to Malaysia.[47] Thus the political balance in Jakarta was rather precariously poised until Sukarno finally committed himself on 26 May to the stabilisation scheme and a 'swing to the right' politically; meanwhile, both sides were attempting to draw him away from their opponents. It would be too simple to infer that the anti-Chinese outbreaks of 1963 were deliberately incited by anti-Communist elements just for that reason; insofar as they were responsible, their motives were probably far more tangled and diffuse —a matter of putting pressure on Sukarno or on pro-Communist officials in Jakarta or the regions to force them to choose between supporting or opposing a popular cause, or simply to generate (or demonstrate) local mass support to increase their own power, or else to force the PKI and its allies onto the defensive.

A further complication was that the State of Emergency (or martial law, as it was earlier called), which had been maintained for more than six years, was due to be lifted on 1 May, the day West Irian was to pass under full Indonesian control. Indonesia was now fully secure and at peace for the first time since independence. But the ending of martial law was not universally welcomed, even though it had not been popular and many people, perhaps most, were glad to see its end and a return to civilian rule. The PKI's opponents were worried at the opportunities that would now be opened up for that party which had been heavily shackled by the martial law authorities over the two previous years. Many army officers were not at all happy about the loss of their powers and were by no means averse to the prospect of seeing the civilian authorities in such difficulties that they would have to call in the military. It is sometimes said that certain army officers were aware that anti-Chinese demonstrations were likely to occur and welcomed them precisely because they would demonstrate that they were indispensable or would necessitate a restoration of their martial law powers. This may well have been the case, but it is in the nature of things extremely difficult to prove, even though anti-Communists were to talk almost boastfully after the 1965 coup about their part in sponsoring the Bandung riots. Similarly unprovable are allegations that LPKB men from within the Indonesian-Chinese community itself were partly responsible for pre-cipitating the riots through the manner in which they were bitterly attacking their Baperki rivals at that time over the assimilation issue, since they were said to be fanning Indonesian resentments against Chinese who were not prepared to assimilate fully.[48] That quarrel had more to do with the internal politics of the Chinese community than with national politics and it is doubtful that it had more than a marginal influence on the events of May, though in some places it may have been a significant background factor.

The first waves

The first in the chain of anti-Chinese incidents occurred at Cirebon on 27 March, arising out of a fight that developed between Indonesian and ethnic Chinese students after a court case involving an Indonesian high-school student who had been involved in a traffic accident in which a young Chinese was killed. The fight developed into a retaliatory attack by a larger Indonesian group on houses and shops in the Chinese quarter of the town, where extensive damage was done, but order was restored in about half an hour.[49] The outbreak triggered off a series of similar incidents over the next few days in small towns near by in West Java, as well as a few in East Java. None of these seems to have been parti-cularly serious, fortunately, and throughout most of April no further troubles of this kind occurred.

Between the first wave of riots and the second, several significant developments occurred in national politics. The visit of the Chinese Head of State, Liu Shao-chi, in April signified a step towards closer Chinese-Indonesian relations which was regarded with some apprehension by the right wing. Martial law formally came to an end on 1 May, inaugurating a new and somewhat unpredictable phase in Indonesian political life. Thirdly, the political implications of Sukarno's 'Economic Declaration' of 25 March became a matter of intense speculation: a few hints emerged that the President was moving tentatively away from the excessive regulations of the 'Sosialisme a la Indonesia' phase, but he continued to veil his intentions in riddles and euphemisms. The political atmosphere was abnormally expectant and highly charged with a sense that Indonesia was approaching a crossroad, attention being focused on the second MPRS session due in Bandung in the third week of May, at which some clear indication of the President's political course (towards the right or the left) was expected.

In this rather tense situation another anti-Chinese outbreak at Tegal on 5 May (continuing over several days) precipitated a second and much more serious wave of actions. Tegal is a major trading town of 90 000 people on the north coast of Java, not far to the east of Cirebon, in the province of Central Java. Here the trouble began with a fight between an Indonesian labourer and his Chinese employer, which spread in due course to become a mass attack on Chinese properties in the town. A distinctive feature of the episode, however, was that attacks were also directed against rich Indonesians and government warehouses, including an ammunition dump and oil depot.[50] Shouts of 'After the Chinese, the important people' were reported. According to an official statement, there were indications that the mobs were organised, although the evidence for this does not seem to have been much more than cries of '*Siap ... Serbu ...*' ('Ready ... Attack ...') and '*Jangan ambil barang*' ('Don't take goods'). There were strong rumours afterwards that PKI members had also been involved in this episode, for which various explanations have been put forward. One theory saw it as the work of a pro-Russian group in the PKI, another as a stratagem to provoke and discredit the right wing. The most plausible, in view of later admissions of ill-disciplined PKI involvement by the party's leaders, was that it came as a spontaneous move by PKI rank and file members who were impatient with their leadership's policies of collaboration with the 'bourgeois' government and parties and who wanted more revolutionary action.

Soon afterwards occurred the Bandung riots of 10 May, which were in many respects the most significant of the entire series because of the political involvement of the university students there, who played a key role in instigating them and, later, in sparking off other anti-Chinese outbreaks in towns in West Java. Again the affair began with a fight, this time amongst students at the Bandung Institute of Technology, which started around 8 a.m. and then snowballed into more general attacks on Chinese cars and other property. Processions developed in three columns down the main roads to the heart of Bandung, where the shops in Jalan Braga and the near-by area were utterly wrecked. During the procession down Jalan Dago, cars belonging to the Chinese were overturned and set on fire. But the main rioting seems to have centred in Jalan Braga, where it continued throughout most of the day (and, later, in North Bandung, well into the night), the students now being vastly outnumbered by the *rakyat* generally, including *becak* drivers, unemployed labourers, etc. Accounts differ on the question of whether the origin of the outbreak was organised or spontaneous, but there seems little doubt that it was deliberately fanned into mass violence. Some Indonesians who were involved in the affair have claimed (even boasted) that they and the Siliwangi division intelligence officers knew in advance that something of the kind was about to happen.[51]

According to newsagency reports, 125 shops and 69 cars were damaged on this occasion.[52] The reports conflict as to the amount of plundering. Some mention that there was a good deal of looting, others say that this occurred only on the second day and stress that at the outset the student leaders, in particular, strictly forbade looting. A story illustrating the puritanical mood of the students was later told about a Chinese businessman who begged the rioters not to burn his Mercedes and offered them Rp. 6 million to spare it; they accepted the money, then stuffed it in the boot and burnt it along with the car. It is quite possible that all these stories contain some degree of truth.

The role of the governmental apparatus during the entire affair is not entirely clear. Policemen were said to have been at the head of the procession down towards the centre of the city, but they made no serious effort to stop it—perhaps because they would have been simply unable to do so, or because they were afraid to, or because they rationalised their role so as merely to ensure that there would be no bloodshed and to maintain what degree of restraint they could.[53] Evidently there was no serious attempt to disperse or check the rioters until 4 p.m. when the Governor of West Java himself came out to address one of the columns of rioters which had gathered outside his residence. But by this stage, according to some critics, the situation was thoroughly out of hand and his efforts were rather ineffectual. He was welcomed enthusiastically by the students who chaired him on their shoulders cheering '*Hidup Pak Mashudi*', implying that he was on their side, which made it much harder for him to castigate them firmly.[54] The Governor also used the radio to broadcast warnings that stern measures would be taken and he imposed a curfew from 9 p.m. till dawn. Some reports refer to truckloads of troops firing into the air to disperse the crowd. Two demonstrators were killed when they were struck by a falling power line which had been hit by bullets. Next day the army established road blocks on the main outlets from Bandung to prevent students leaving for Jakarta and other towns to extend the actions. These road blocks seem not to have been very effective, however, since students went travelling by bus to other towns in West Java in the week following to incite high school students elsewhere to further riots—although this seems not to have been at all well organised and was not solely anti-Chinese in inspiration, but directed against the government and OKB ('*orang kaya baru*'—the nouveaux riches) generally.

In the week following the Bandung riots, similar (but less destructive) affrays flared up, despite a series of official statements condemning them, at near-by Sumedang on the following day, at Bogor on 15–16 May and at Cipayung, Tasikmalaya, Garut and Singaparna (all in West Java), as well as in Solo, Surabaya, Malang and Medan. Last of all came the most serious outbreak at Sukabumi and near-by Cibadak on 18–19 May.

It is noteworthy that the troubles did not spread to Jakarta, apart from a few sporadic incidents; Chinese shops were closed and boarded up, the town was very heavily guarded by troops, and some student leaders were detained. Sukarno summoned the leaders of the main student organisations to the palace to warn them against any repetition of the riots. He was not entirely successful. The students at the University of Indonesia were being taunted by those in Bandung, who sent them gifts of lipstick, and on several occasions the former set out to start trouble, but were checked before they were able to, once by the personal intervention of the Rektor of the University, Sjarief Thajeb. (In Surabaya, similarly, the university authorities took a firm stand, threatening to expel any students who started trouble.) A number of official statements were made condemning the riots during this week, but few of them at all forthright or confident and it is hardly surprising that they were widely disregarded.[55]

The Sukabumi riots

The rioting in Sukabumi was inspired in large part by the events which preceded it in West Java, but there had also been a prologue some months before which has been emphasised by the authors of the *Leknas* report for the light it throws on the prevailing mood and the relations between the strongly Muslim population of the Sukabumi region and the Chinese.[56]

In February the main Chinese and Indonesian festivals of the year had occurred within a short time of each other. The Chinese festival, *cap go meh*, was traditionally celebrated with a carnival atmosphere of music, fireworks and a procession of the *barongsai*, amidst general gaiety and dancing. Although it fell in the Muslims' fasting month (*Ramadhan*) in 1963, this was not considered an obstacle to its observance, as it had been traditionally celebrated in Sukabumi, and the occasion passed without untoward incidents; in fact many Indonesians joined in the procession. Ten days later the Indonesians celebrated the end of their fasting month (*Lebaran*) with similar festivities. These, too, were bigger and better than usual, for Indonesia's victory in the struggle for West Irian and the coming relaxation of martial law were grounds for cele-bration. It was customary in some of the neighbouring villages to mark the approach of Lebaran with prolonged beating of mosque drums (*dulag*); in fact, the villages used to hold contests to see who could continue the longest. Normally, this lasted only one night, but on this occasion the *dulag* went on for several days, interspersed with pro-cessions through the main streets of Sukabumi, which were lined with Chinese shops. After the first night, however, the mood changed from a carnival atmosphere to one which was overtly anti-Chinese and threatening. There were far more people and more drums from the mosque than ever before, 500 of them. 'It was as if the Indonesians wanted to outdo the festivities of the Chinese.'[57] Many of the participants were masked and carried chopping-knives, torches and fire-crackers made of bamboo filled with petrol which they exploded right outside the Chinese shops. Wild shouting drowned the recitation of Koranic prayers as the procession wound through the city streets. The whole affair became intensely alarming to the Chinese, although no violence actually occurred. On the third day of the *dulag*, the military authorities summoned the youths who were leading it and imposed a degree of control, so that the disturbance to law and order was minimised there-after.

During early May tension was again mounting in Sukabumi as the menace of racial clashes reared its head in more and more neighbouring towns. The local authorities (*Catur Tunggal*) summoned leaders of both the alien and WNI Chinese to meetings on the 11th and 13th, at which they were urged to remain calm, as the local government guaranteed that law and order could be maintained. The Chinese were advised not to resist should rioting occur. Moreover, it was suggested that they should not risk provoking the Indonesian community by displaying so openly their worldly goods. The local judiciary head even suggested that responsibility rested with the Chinese to see that no violence occurred, as they were 'like guests' (*seakan-akan tamu*) in Indonesia. Wealthy Chinese who were not reassured entrusted their valuables and cars to Indonesian friends as a precautionary measure. Some even parked their vehicles in the grounds of the Police Training School. Others engaged uniformed armed guards and posted them openly in front of their houses. Rumours abounded that Chinese were bribing members of the *Catur Tunggal* so that peace might be maintained, and likewise teachers of government schools that they would influence their pupils to reject anti-Chinese doctrines.[58]

For three days (13–16 May) stones were thrown intermittently at Chinese-owned buildings in Sukabumi. Then, on the 16th a funeral service was held at Sukaraja, a village three kilometres from Sukabumi, for an Indonesian student who had been fatally stabbed by a Chinese. Speakers at the burial urged students of Sukabumi to initiate anti-Chinese activities. In the last few days before the riots chain letters circulated and placards were posted calling on Indonesians to unite against the Chinese ('a yellow danger for Indonesia')—and oppose them with force ('let's declare war on them'). University students visited Sukabumi, cajoling and threatening high school students there to agree to an anti-Chinese demonstration. (The hesitant were warned that failure to participate might result in difficulty in gaining admission to the universities of Bandung and Jakarta.) They also spread rumours that Sukarno's son was staying at the Police School in order to plan riots for Sukabumi.

Actual rioting in Sukabumi broke out on Saturday, 18 May, at about 3.30 p.m., led by youths from Sukaraja. Truckloads of students from outside Sukabumi were brought into the town in the course of the afternoon. The damaging of Chinese property began in the main street, which was lined with Chinese shophouses in the manner of so many Indonesian towns. Students went in groups to Chinese residences, explained their intentions and began systematically to break windows and burn cars. There was apparently little or no plundering or molesting of persons at this stage, neither was there any resistance on the part of the Chinese. By 5 p.m. the rioting had spread over the whole town and many members of the public had joined in. Their actions were wilder than the student-perpetrated measures. Finally, when the head of the Police School became aware that there were Chinese cars parked in the school grounds, he ordered them to be pushed outside, whereupon they were promptly burned by the rioters. At about 6.30 p.m. the rioting began to subside, and the Mayor proclaimed a curfew from 8 p.m. until 6 a.m.

Rioting commenced again at about 8 a.m. on the Sunday morning. This time it was the masses who took the leading role and the course of events seems to have altered somewhat. Whereas only luxury cars and motorcycles were burned on the 18th, buses, trucks and even *becaks* were destroyed on the following day. At about 1 p.m. the market complex was burnt out and Chinese houses in near-by streets suffered a similar fate. Much more looting now occurred. Some people claimed to have seen police and troops plundering houses evacuated by Chinese: and there was said to be no sign of fire-damaged goods finding their way to the market subsequently.

Because of the recent lifting of martial law on 1 May, there seems to have been an excessively literal attitude among the civil and military authorities on the question of just who was responsible for the maintenance of law and order; hence a power vacuum developed. After the outbreak of violence on the 18th, the police posted guards to various parts of the town. They fired warning shots into the air, but these went unheeded. Several young men were arrested and interrogated concerning the riots, but under pressure from gangs of youths they were released with a warning to cease lawless action. When the riots erupted, there were only about 150 army men in the town, the remainder being deployed on operations elsewhere. Troops justified their inaction on the grounds that children were in the vanguard of the rioters and that they did not want to shed blood. Furthermore, the Mayor, who was formally responsible for whatever action was to be taken, had not requested their aid.

At noon the Mayor officially requested the help of the army by telephone. Military authorities demanded a written request, but the Mayor replied that there was no time for it. The Mayor considered the request had been received; the army did not. Neither was able to make contact with the provincial authorities, so, having no instructions from above, the local military authorities declined to make any move. However, at about 2 p.m. placards appeared calling for the rioting to cease and threatening prosecution for those who disobeyed the policy or military. These were signed by the Mayor, the local army commander and a youth representative. At about 4 p.m. the army authorities decided to take matters into their own hands, following the arrival of Mobile Brigade units from Bogor: soon afterwards all rioting subsided and a curfew was imposed.

Four people were killed and eight wounded during the riots. Damage to property was very extensive—75 shops and houses and 24 market stalls were burnt to the ground, while 42 factories and 738 shops and houses were damaged, according to the *Leknas* Report, and 69 cars destroyed.[59] Relief measures were undertaken through a 'Committee to Assist Victims of Counter-Revolutionary Activities', but appear to have been of relatively slight practical significance.

The Government's response

The Sukabumi outbreak was the last of the May riots except for some mild disturbances at Yogjakarta a few days later. Their ending happened to coincide with the only public statement on the matter by President Sukarno on the 19th, in which he accused counter-revolutionary elements of the PSI, Masyumi and PRRI-Permesta groups, as well as 'foreign subversive elements', of having instigated the disturbances.[60] Their aim, he said, was to undermine the reputation of the Indonesian government and, ultimately, the good name of the President himself (which the MPRS had just upheld by creating him President for life). The riots were directed against him since he was a danger to the imperialists because of his domestic policies and because he had broadened Afro-Asian solidarity into the doctrine of the New Emerging Forces. Socialism, he said, could not be achieved through acts of terrorism: but he also reminded the Chinese that the nation must be built on the unity of the Chinese citizens and the asli Indonesians.

It would be naive to assume that this statement was in itself a very significant factor in bringing the riots to an end. The general attitude of the government, and Sukarno's endorsement of it, had been quite clear throughout the week, but the local authorities had been reluctant to act firmly against the rioters. In fact, one of the most curious aspects of the whole episode was the lack of a forthright response by the President or any of his senior ministers at a much earlier stage. Their reaction to the whole chain of riots was strikingly hesitant and euphemistic throughout.

The first official statement after the Bandung riots came from the Police Department on 11 May concerning the 'undesirable incidents' at Cirebon, Tegal, Bandung, etc., in which 'material damage was suffered by certain groups of the community'. It continued in the circumlocutory vein that was generally used in these situations: 'An urgent appeal is made to the community for co-operation and understanding for the best solution of these undesirable incidents by avoiding matters or deeds that may involve legal prosecution'.[61] On the same day, Roeslan Abdulgani, the Minister for Information and Deputy First Minister for Special Affairs, issued a statement after conferring by telephone with the President, in which he called on all student organisations to be vigilant (*waspada*, 'on the alert') so that there might be no repetition of riots such as those at Bandung.[62] Presumably their purpose at this stage was to exercise restraint over the student activists mainly through the student organisations and their leaders, not by heavy-handed methods.

The same note of appeal rather than firmness was expressed two days later in a statement issued by the Federation of Indonesian Student Organisations (PPMI) executive after a meeting with the National Front.[63] It branded the riots in Bandung, Cirebon, etc., as efforts to undermine the unity of the nation and to distract the people's attention away from the real enemies of the Indonesian Revolution, which were imperialism and feudalism; its economic programme was being sabotaged in order to destroy the nation's unity. The PPMI appealed to all students to 'beware the trap set in connection with the Tegal and

Bandung destructive actions'. But it also called on 'a certain section of society with a privileged, strong and better economic position, particularly foreigners . . . to adjust themselves to the national aspirations of the Indonesian people'.

Statements on 13 May by the Governor of West Java and both the Governor and Chief of Police of Central Java were more forthright in condemning the riots and warning of stern measures if fresh outbreaks occurred—although they were not sufficient to stop them. But the few political leaders who spoke on the subject still did so in euphemistic or convoluted terms, apart from those on the left who characterised the outbreaks as 'counter-revolutionary terror' for which they blamed the USA and its 'accomplices' in Indonesia.[64] Chairul Saleh made a very general call for national unity at a gathering of the 1945 Generation (*Angkatan '45*) in Bandung on 14 May, just before the opening of the MPRS session there. (Later that week, when driving back to Jakarta to convey formally to President Sukarno the decision of the MPRS that Sukarno should become President for the term of his life, Chairul Saleh was held up at Cianjur by an anti-Chinese demonstration for over an hour.) Subandrio told newsmen that he and Sukarno had discussed the riots on 14 and 15 May, their discussion being centred on the question of whether the outbreaks were related or merely isolated incidents. He lamented that young people should fall into such counter-revolutionary plots—but he also went on to say, according to *Duta Masjarakat*, the NU newspaper, that there were grounds for discontent with minorities who had not shared the burdens of the Revolution or the struggle to liberate West Irian.[65] Among the Armed Forces leadership, only the Air Force chief, Omar Dhani, issued any strongly critical comment; the silence of the others may have been intended to convey that this was not a matter for which they now bore any responsibility, but the discomfiture of the PKI and the President was probably not unwelcome to them, either.

From these statements and those made by the political party leaders or their newspapers, it is clear that at a time of great political uncertainty and confusion about what was happening, men spoke in terms of the clichés and stereotypes which came most naturally to their minds, without much regard for the real facts. On the PKI side, the riots were condemned as the work of counter-revolutionaries and racists who were trying to smash national unity at a time when a concentration of the nation's powers was essential. Racism was a colonial legacy which the reactionaries were now exploiting, commented *Bintang Timur*—though this was evidently a message which some youthful Communists had not yet grasped, to judge from allegations that some of them had participated in the rioting. *Harian Rakjat* made much of rumours that Americans from the Peace Corps (predominantly athletics coaches, at the time) and the Malaria Eradication Units of AID were involved in the spreading of anti-Chinese propaganda around Sukabumi. On the other side of the spectrum, we find the Muslim groups giving an anti-Chinese slant to their stories, implying that the blame lay largely with the Chinese. For example, the PPMI statement condemning the riots on 13 May added that in order to achieve the completion of the Revolution, exclusivism, isolation and capitalism must also be abolished. When the NU finally got round to issuing a statement on the riots at the end of May, in which it condemned the riots and blamed the counter-revolutionaries for them, it also launched into the traditional complaint against the Chinese:

> While the People are suffering economic privation, there is one group in the community which is sometimes even increasing the People's sufferings through such steps as abusing its position in their distributive network, apart from hurting the People's feelings with its conspicuously luxurious living. Therefore the Executive of the NU recommends that these groups, notably foreigners and citizens of foreign descent, consider this problem and work together with the People toward attaining a just and prosperous society.[66]

One of the most striking features of the 1963 riots was the prominent part played by students in starting them. In the more serious outbreaks, 'the masses' joined in also and the riots became far more violent. Commenting in the *Leknas* Report on the Bandung riots, Hartanto drew a distinction between three classes of rioters: the spontaneous, the organised and those who just 'went along'.[67] The spontaneous rioters were generally swept in by feelings of solidarity with their comrades because they would feel ashamed at not standing by them in a tense situation. The organised groups were exemplified by a force of veterans of the struggle for independence mobilised by ex-Major Buntaran, who played a part in the Bandung riots; they had been organised during the West Irian campaign and struck heavily at former members of the hated *Pao An Tui*, a Chinese organisation formed to provide protection against Indonesian attacks during the Revolution, who were deemed to be pro-Dutch. Those who 'just went along', in Hartanto's categorisation, were *becak*-drivers and the urban unemployed, who joined in for the excitement or the looting. This classification is useful in drawing attention to the variety of motivations of the participants, but there may be even more variants to be incorporated—for example, the students (apparently semi-organised, at least) who travelled from Bandung to Sukabumi and other towns in West Java after 10 May inciting other student groups to take action against the Chinese and the *'orang kaya baru'* (the nouveaux riches) in some cases virtually threatening them to do so. The fact that the distinction between the nouveaux riches and the Chinese was not sharply drawn in some cases should not be overlooked, even though the racial aspect of the outbreaks usually overshadowed the class aspect.

But were the students merely the puppets of more sinister elements manipulating them from behind the scenes? Many Indonesians were quick to draw such a conclusion. And one could certainly not argue that the entire series of outbreaks was spontaneous. But it is difficult to assess how much was manipulated and how much simply spontaneous. It is equally difficult to discern who were the manipulators, if any. What part did members of the banned political parties, Masyumi and PSI, play behind the scenes? Or other anti-Sukarno and anti-PKI elements, including army officers? Or Muslim businessmen who wanted to eliminate their Chinese rivals?

There are no clear-cut answers to these questions, except perhaps the last. The *Leknas* researchers concluded that economic rivalry was not a sufficient factor to generate an aggressive movement and it does seem likely that political and psychological aspects were more important.[68] The role of the army, as we have seen, was ambiguous. Because of uncertain consequences attending the abolition of martial law, senior officers were by no means as vigorous in moving against the rioters and may in some cases have welcomed the discomfiture of their civilian counterparts. Some middle-ranking officers of the Siliwangi Division (said to be traditionally more anti-Chinese than most others) may have known before 10 May that something was brewing among the Bandung students. But beyond that there is little indication of army involvement. The role of Masyumi-PSI and other anti-Sukarno elements is even more cloudy. The *Leknas* researchers commented that no evidence had been produced by the government to substantiate the allegations of Masyumi-PSI involvement in the Sukabumi riots. On the other hand it seems probable that some of the student leaders involved in the Bandung affray had connections with these parties. And the fact that the riots occurred in areas where the Masyumi had been strong before it was banned points towards a possibility that supporters of those parties, being deprived of political outlets through legal channels, were eager to exploit local discontents for their own purposes. It has been suggested also that local leaders of these parties may have encouraged anti-Chinese actions as a means of conveying a warning to President Sukarno on the eve of the MPRS session that he could not disregard them with impunity, that they could mobilise mass actions as effectively as the PKI if it became necessary for them.[69] All these factors probably contributed in some degree to the tensions of May 1963, but there is no way of assessing precisely which had the greatest influence in precipitating the riots.

THE 1965-67 CRISIS

Anti-Chinese sentiment was surprisingly muted during the last two years of Guided Democracy, despite the serious aggravation of social tensions in many spheres of life and the economic deterioration resulting from continuous inflation. With the collapse of President Sukarno's almost autocratic power, however, as a consequence of the abortive coup attempt of 1 October 1965 and its savage aftermath of reprisals against the Communists, anti-Chinese hostility again welled up to the surface.[70] The two years that followed were a period of frightening insecurity for most of the Indonesian Chinese, whether WNI or aliens. The fierce backlash of hostility toward the Communists and their former allies which now swept over the whole country was bound to affect them in some measure, even though Indonesians rather than Chinese were the primary victims of the massacres. The sharp deterioration of relations between the Jakarta and the Peking governments also had adverse effects for them. They saw their former friends and protectors overthrown from power throughout Indonesia and many whom they regarded as their old adversaries, in the army and the Muslim parties, emerge as the victors. Many of them suffered considerably from harassment, intimidation, threats and loss or destruction of their property through mob attacks or uncontrolled extortion. The ability and willingness of the Jakarta authorities to curb mass demonstrations and outbursts of popular hostility to the Chinese seemed to be extremely uncertain, particularly in the earlier stages of the struggle for power that was being waged both in Jakarta and the provinces, at a time when the government's control over its own supporters was still very uncertain.

The extreme instability of the entire political situation in Indonesia during the next two years should perhaps be regarded as the most important element common to the various outbursts of anti-Chinese hostility in that period. It is significant that the outbreaks died down soon after the new Suharto government succeeded in consolidating its power during 1967-68. For the sake of clarity, however, the various anti-Chinese actions of 1965-67 are best seen as falling into six phases forming a chain of loosely connected episodes, each with its own distinctive dynamics. But while this analytical device is convenient for the purpose of emphasising the variations in intensity of anti-Chinese sentiment from place to place and from one period to another during those troubled years, it is necessary to remember that only the overt manifestations of hostility are being recorded here. The other side of the story is almost impossible to document. For many of the Chinese in Indonesia, no matter whether WNI or alien, one of the most disturbing aspects of life at that period was the constant sense of insecurity and vulnerability to harassment, against which there seemed to be little certainty of obtaining protection until such time as the authority of the government was re-established on a more secure basis, which seemed a remote prospect in 1965–66. When an army sergeant walked into one's house and ominously deposited a machine-gun on the table before asking for money, it was risky to deny it to him. To complain to his superiors was not likely to achieve much (if one happened to have access to them and if they were disposed to listen sympathetically) since the army was notoriously underpaid at that time of acute inflation, so it was dependent on 'unconventional finances' for the very livelihood of its soldiers. The Chinese were not only the obvious targets for extortionate demands for money because they were all presumed to be much richer than Indonesians, but they were an easy prey because the authorities were unlikely to take the political risk of incurring unpopularity for the sake of defending them at a time when the struggle for power was still unsettled.

October 1965 to March 1966

Almost immediately after the coup, the anti-Communists began to take action against the PKI and its allies of a kind that they would not have dared to attempt before 1 October, when President Sukarno's authority was still beyond challenge. One of the first such moves was the burning of Baperki's university in Jakarta, coupled with a demonstration against the Chinese Commercial Attaché's office by a mob of 800 Muslim youths on 15 October, barely a week after the first of the snowballing attacks on PKI offices. Sukarno condemned these actions, but he was now powerless to stop them, for it was obvious that the army leaders were not prepared to take action to defend the PKI, which they wanted to ban and which was still entrenched strongly enough in Central and East Java to plunge the country into civil war. Attacks on China's Embassy and consulates served the anti-Communists' purpose of either forcing Sukarno to yield to their pressure or revealing his inability to resist it. Baperki was banned and several of its leaders arrested for their PKI affiliations during these early weeks.

At first, the hostility of the anti-Communists was directed not so much against the Indonesian Chinese as such as against China's diplomatic representatives and the PKI. But as potential scapegoats the Chinese were highly vulnerable to politicians who wanted to stir up popular feelings with the aim of either precipitating a rift between Jakarta and Peking or simply of mobilising a personal following.[71] Some attacks on Chinese shops and property occurred in these early months, but in general, with three or four exceptions, order seems to have been maintained fairly effectively in the towns, where most Chinese resided. It was the uncertainty of their position at a time when the country was hovering on the brink of civil war and their lack of redress against political pressures or harassment that was most alarming at that stage.

In the general reaction against the Communists, demands for the breaking of diplomatic relations with the Peking government were soon being put forward by anti-Communist organisations in the same breath as demands for the dissolution of the PKI. Sukarno's eager espousal of a 'Jakarta-Peking axis' had aroused much apprehension among his enemies during the previous year and they now seized upon the issue as a weapon against him and Dr Subandrio in order to embarrass and isolate them politically. Wild rumours about Peking's behind-the-scenes role in the affair were soon circulating, based on allegations of foreknowledge by Sukarno's Chinese doctors of an imminent collapse in his health and assertions that the Chinese were smuggling arms into Indonesia for the PKI. It is, in fact, highly doubtful that Peking had any part in the coup attempt—just as there is strong reason to doubt that the PKI itself was involved to anything like the degree that the army version of the coup has depicted. But in the crisis-laden atmosphere of October 1965, it was not the facts which mattered so much as what people wanted to believe. In the third week of October, Muslim youth organisations were beginning to demand the breaking of diplomatic ties with Peking; a week later, a rally outside the Department of Foreign Affairs made the same demand, linking it with a call for Subandrio's resignation. Sukarno resisted both demands stubbornly, with the result that his opponents took matters into their own hands in order to create a *fait accompli* in both respects.

Peking did not take long to change its tune also. On 19 October Hsinhua News Agency attacked the group of 'right-wing generals' at the helm in Jakarta, accusing them of mounting a 'campaign of terror' in Indonesia. The Chinese Embassy had earlier antagonised the army leaders by refusing to fly its flag at half-mast on the day of the funeral of the officers who had been killed in the coup attempt, an action which aroused much angry comment. Although the Chinese Ambassador met Dr Subandrio for a 'cordial discussion' on 20 October, the flow of Chinese protest notes against attacks on consular buildings soon began to increase.[72] The rift between the two countries was made very clear at a meeting of the Standing Committee of the postponed Second Afro-Asian Conference (previously scheduled for June at Algiers), when Indonesia made no move to support China's terms for a resumption of the conference in striking contrast to the close co-operation between them at the earlier meeting.[73]

The Chinese press was initially rather guarded in its comments on developments in Indonesia, pending the outcome of the struggle for power there, but it soon threw off its restraints and embarked on a campaign of abuse against the army and the right wing. Charges and counter-charges proliferated on both sides during the next two years. Summarising them later, Coppel remarked that the Chinese campaign had four main themes:

> Protests over the treatment of Chinese diplomatic buildings and staff, accusations about the treatment of PKI members and supporters, protests over the persecution of the Indonesian Chinese, and exposures of a Westward shift in Indonesian foreign policy . . . There was a countercampaign from the Indonesian side, rather muted at government level, but strident in certain Jakarta newspapers and organisations, which continually urged the government to take strong steps against the alien Chinese. They complained that China was interfering in Indonesia's internal affairs, that her diplomats were misbehaving in Indonesia, that Indonesia's leaders and international reputation were being insulted, that China was harbouring Indonesian traitors, and finally that the Indonesian diplomats and embassy in Peking were being mistreated.[74]

Many of the charges made by both sides were so lurid that one might have wondered that diplomatic relations were maintained for so long, were it not for the obvious reluctance of both governments to take the final step of breaking or suspending them.

Sukarno was still speaking in mid-November as if the Jakarta-Peking axis remained intact and insisting that Indonesia was still a 'leftist' nation.[75] But the pretence was becoming increasingly threadbare, even though he seemed to be re-establishing his position at the head of the government a little more securely in the last weeks of 1965. While protesting impotently at the fact that the PKI was being banned and its members gaoled or killed in scores of thousands throughout the country at the behest of regional military commanders, against his orders but with the obvious approval of Generals Nasution and Suharto, he taunted his critics to launch an open challenge to his authority. That would have been a risky gamble for either of the generals; however, at a time of dangerous tensions within the army as well as throughout the country. But during January, army-backed student demonstrations in Jakarta, now directed quite openly at the PKI and President Sukarno's policy of defending them, began to reveal just how hollow was Sukarno's power if the army refused to support him. It is noteworthy that these demonstrations were not directed specifically against the Overseas Chinese. In fact, some WNI Chinese student leaders played a prominent part in spearheading the opposition to Sukarno.

In February the President made a determined effort to reassert his authority against the student demonstrators. On 21 February he reshuffled his cabinet and dismissed General Nasution as Defence Minister, at the same time calling for an intensification of the dwindling 'confrontation' campaign against Malaysia and announcing that relations with China must be repaired. It was this move that precipitated the second round of student demonstrations which finally resulted in his overthrow on 11 March, when Lt General Suharto decided to assume control in Jakarta and demanded full executive authority. Although Sukarno remained titular President for another twelve months and Suharto assumed the full style and title of President only gradually over the next two years, there was little doubt thereafter that the 'Old Order' had been overthrown.

Prior to this point, the most serious incident involving violence to the Chinese had been one which occurred in Medan on 10 December. During a demonstration outside the Chinese consulate there, shots were allegedly fired against the demonstrators from the consulate. The incensed crowd then marched to the Chinese business area of the town and proceeded to burn, wreck and kill in a terrifying bout of destructiveness. Peking claimed in its protest Note that 300 Chinese had been killed in the affray.[76] There were also reports of violence on a smaller scale in Banjarmasin, Bali, Lombok, Sumbawa and Aceh. Estimates of the total number of Chinese killed during this first stage of the upheaval range up to about one thousand, which is not a particularly high figure by comparison with the estimates of between 300 000 and 500 000 Indonesians who were slain at that time. The very scale of all this violence tends to numb one's sensibilities about such matters, but it is necessary to stress, in view of the widespread misconceptions on this point, that it was Indonesian Communists and not primarily Chinese who were the main victims of the outburst of hostility which followed the abortive coup.

March–May 1966
In the weeks immediately after Suharto's assumption of power, anti-Chinese actions took on a different character. The momentum of the recently mobilised 'action fronts' which had toppled Sukarno now became directed against other targets, such as the Chinese government's representatives and the Chinese school system, to a point where it became doubtful whether the new and still very insecure Suharto government would be able to curb their passions. Sweeping anti-Chinese threats and slogans were uttered, in reply to which Radio Peking's attacks on Indonesia's 'military fascist' regime became more strident than ever— all of which led in turn to widespread demands in Indonesia for the breaking of diplomatic relations. The Suharto government gave way to the pressure from New Order activists on the schools question and also ordered the closure of the New China News Agency and some Chinese consulates; but it resisted demands for more extreme measures

and even endeavoured to exercise some restraint on anti-Chinese sentiments, apparently wishing to avoid an open breach of diplomatic relations with Peking. The degree of pressure to which the Chinese were
subjected at this time appears to have varied greatly from one province
to another. In some regions, notably Aceh and North Sumatra, terrorisation and harassment of the Chinese forced thousands to flee elsewhere
for safety and ultimately to seek repatriation to China. Elsewhere conditions were less oppressive. Local factors played an important part in
shaping the course of events, but news of what was happening in one
part of the country had an effect in other parts too.

During March and April KAPPI demonstrators seized Chinese-
language schools in a snowballing series of actions in various cities and
towns, justifying their actions on the grounds that the schools had been
centres of Communist indoctrination. These takeovers were almost
always followed by decisions of the local military commander to close
the schools, sometimes also to ban Chinese social organisations. Very
few Chinese-language schools remained open by the end of April and
in May the government regularised the *fait accompli* by announcing a
ban on all foreign-run schools, other than embassy schools for the families
of diplomatic staff.[77] In a move intended to demonstrate their loyalty
to Indonesia and the new regime, WNI Chinese organised a mass rally
in Jakarta on 15 April, at which resolutions supporting the closure of
Chinese schools were passed, and also one calling for the breaking of
diplomatic ties with Peking. Some of the demonstrators became involved
in a scuffle with officials at the Chinese Embassy and a Chinese diplomat
was shot in the course of the mêlée.

The propaganda war began to intensify on both sides around this
time. Peking had earlier demanded that Chinese nationals be permitted
to return to China immediately, calling for simplified emigration procedures and the provision of ships by the Indonesian government to
make it possible. Jakarta replied that alien Chinese were entirely free
to leave, but only after complying with the prevailing emigration procedures, adding that it was not Indonesia's responsibility to facilitate
their return home. China announced on 18 May that she would send
her own ships to bring home Chinese nationals who wished to return,
repeating her demand for simplified emigration procedures and calling
for joint consultations on the matter. But these 'consultations' between
Chinese and Indonesian officials dragged on until September before
agreement was finally reached on the arrangements for a Chinese ship
to begin the slow process of repatriating a few thousand from Medan.[78]

In Jakarta, an NU leader declared that the sooner Chinese citizens
in Indonesia went home the better, because they were only interested
in making profits and did not want to understand the aspirations and
national interests of Indonesia. There had been a good deal of public

comment in this vein, along with demands that departing Chinese should not be allowed to take any property with them (a sore point at a time when inflation was still spiralling uncontrollably and the nation's foreign exchange reserves were negligible) and that PP10 should be reactivated in areas where it had been allowed to lapse. Adam Malik, the new Indonesian Foreign Minister, repeatedly urged restraint: a Foreign Ministry statement of 26 April used the time-honoured formula that while the government 'was able to understand the people's anger' it could not condone wild and destructive attacks on foreign embassies. Many Chinese were endeavouring to leave the country by that time, although there were very few countries which were willing to accept them in any significant numbers. The problem was most acute in Medan, where many thousands of refugees from Aceh were congregated in emergency camps with no source of livelihood, awaiting repatriation to China.

Aceh and North Sumatra were the regions where the Chinese suffered most heavily during 1966. Just what happened to the Chinese in Aceh (never a very numerous group) is not entirely clear, apart from the fact that several waves of terrorisation occurred, one after the coup and one in April 1966. Houses and shops were ransacked, community leaders and teachers are said to have been tortured, some hundreds killed and slogans were scribbled on walls threatening 'Drive Out the Chinese now' and 'You will be beheaded if you don't leave'. The military commander ordered on 8 May that all foreign Chinese would have to be out of Aceh by Independence Day (17 August). However, some of them appear to have been allowed to remain.[79] More than 7 000 Chinese refugees from Aceh were crowded into temporary refugee camps around Medan in dreadful conditions by September and hundreds more were said to be arriving daily. This aggravated the tensions in and around Medan, which were already bad enough after the December 1965 outbreaks there.[80]

Demonstrations by KAMI and KAPPI student organisations occurred in Medan during March and April, directed against the Chinese consulate and Chinese-language schools. In June they seized the consulate building itself. Pressure on the municipal and North Sumatran provincial authorities was maintained by the student organisations, with demands for the expulsion of all Chinese nationals by the end of the year and calls for the withdrawal by the Ministry of Trade of the trading licences of all Chinese nationals throughout the country. Although these demands were not met, special regional regulations restricting the rights of Chinese citizens to move freely or engage in certain commercial transactions were applied in North Sumatra. Throughout the second half of 1966 the authorities seem to have been very much on the defensive against the student militants of the ethnically heterogeneous and hard-boiled city of Medan, who found it easy to exploit the tensions aroused by the presence of Chinese refugees in the camps on the outskirts of the town. Incidents occurred every time the Chinese refugee ship, *Kuang Hua*, called at Medan to pick up refugees. For some time shops in the Chinese section of the city were closed, except for short periods each day, and an uneasy atmosphere prevailed. The military commander tried to calm students in October by telling them that anti-Chinese demonstrations would not break the Chinese control over the economy and urging instead that they should boycott and picket Chinese shops, buying and selling elsewhere. After a serious incident on 9 November in which 80 Chinese were attacked and robbed by a mob of armed Indonesians, Major General Mokoginta, the All-Sumatra Territory Commander, issued a much sterner threat of action against 'actions aimed at disturbing society', insisting that Chinese desiring repatriation should not be hampered and that 'demands for the repatriation of foreign Chinese should be made through legal channels'. The warning does not seem to have had much effect, however. Anti-Chinese incidents persisted well into 1967 in Medan, although they gradually became less frequent after the cessation of the *Kuang Hua's* visits. In May 1967 the government appointed Brig. General Sarwo Edhie, the ex-RPKAD (paratroop) commander who had been something of a hero to the KAMI and KAPPI students in Jakarta because of his role in the overthrow of the PKI and Sukarno, to be the military commander in North Sumatra. Although he made some efforts to restrain the students in their anti-Chinese actions, incidents continued to occur in North Sumatra throughout most of 1967, for he also took a very tough attitude towards the refugees in the camps, who defiantly insisted on celebrating China's national day by singing the Chinese national anthem and hoisting the Chinese flag, contrary to his orders.[81] The situation did not settle down there until 1968.

June–December 1966

During the second half of 1966 the pressures upon the Chinese became slightly less heavy than they had been in most parts of Indonesia, except in North Sumatra. The central government seemed to be trying to keep anti-Sinicism in check, but it had a difficult course to steer. On the one hand, it could not afford to appear to be giving in to Peking in the various diplomatic wrangles which arose over the repatriation question and on the other hand it had to deal carefully with its own supporters, many of whom were still clamouring for much more drastic action against 'Old Order' supporters and the Chinese. There were various indications that the government was not anxious to encourage a large-scale exodus of Chinese, if only because it was beginning to address itself at that time to the critically important task of curbing inflation and restoring the flow of trade, which had been seriously disrupted during the previous year.[82] It was now working in close conjunction with the assimilationist WNI Chinese of the LPKB in order to make use of those Chinese whose loyalty to Indonesia and the 'New Order' were unquestioned. General Suharto expressed his government's policy towards the Chinese in a major statement on 15 September, in which he deplored 'racialist excesses' as contrary to the *Panca Sila* (putting the blame, however, on Chinese actions to which they were a response) and stated that 'the Indonesian government will always attempt with all the resources at its disposal to protect all of its residents, Indonesian or foreign, as long as they respect the prevailing laws ... and are able to adjust themselves to the way of life of the community in which they live'.[83] In general, however, government's efforts to keep anti-Sinicism in check were still only partially successful. The adoption of the pejorative term '*Tjina*' for China or Chinese, instead of the former '*Tiongkok*' and '*Tionghoa*' seemed to be an ominous sign that the government could not stand up to its supporters on this sort of issue.[84] Subordinate officials and military commanders continued to make regulations on their own initiative which diverged from the policies applying elsewhere.

Examples of these variations were to be found not only in Aceh and North Sumatra, but also in West Java and South Sulawesi. While there were fewer manifestations of anti-Chinese sentiment in West Java than one might have expected in the light of its earlier record, some tough measures were taken by the regional authorities. All organisations of Chinese nationals were banned and shortly afterwards all 'committee members and activists' were required to register for purposes of arranging their repatriation. Chinese nationals were forbidden to transfer their assets. In several smaller towns (Garut, Cirebon and Sukabumi) harassment was severe, Chinese citizens being required to hang out signboards indicating their nationality and forbidden to change their place of residence; there were also student-organised boycotts of their shops in one instance, while in Sukabumi all WNI Chinese were ordered to change their names to Indonesian ones within 24 hours. The latter episode led the way towards a nationwide campaign in favour of name-changing, to which the government gave its backing.

Not much has been written about the impact of all these measures on the lives of the Indonesian Chinese or about the extent of the harassment that accompanied them. Many may have been able to purchase a degree of immunity by bribing officials. Others lay low until the storm passed, as political and economic conditions gradually settled down. Relatively few Chinese seem to have left or been expelled from Indonesia at this time, as was feared earlier in the year when talk of a mass exodus and large-scale repatriation was running rife; in fact, probably fewer left than in 1959–60.[85] And on the whole, WNI Chinese seem to have escaped at least the worst of the storms of this period, although there was undoubtedly some spillover of anti-Chinese prejudice which adversely affected them. In this respect at least, the legal distinction between Chinese who were Indonesian citizens and those who were aliens had come to acquire greater significance by the latter half of the 1960s than it had had in the 1950s, when the citizenship status of so many was still uncertain.

January–April 1967
The relative tranquillity that seemed to be developing in the latter part of 1966 was abruptly shattered early in the following year, after a series of far-reaching measures against the Chinese in East Java was promulgated on 31 December by the regional military commander, Major General Sumitro. These included a head tax of Rp. 2 500 (approximately US$320 at the free market rate) on Chinese nationals, a ban on their operations as wholesale traders throughout the entire province, their exclusion from intermediary trade in any part of the province except the city of Surabaya, and from retail trade in two of the seven residencies.[86] In addition, the use of Chinese characters and language in economic or financial matters or tele-communications was also banned. Altogether, this unprecedentedly radical attack on the Chinese businesses of East Java seemed to be tantamount to an attempt to drive them completely from the province—and it provoked an unprecedentedly violent reaction from them.

These measures, coming as they did at a time of acute monetary stringency and business uncertainty, proved to be extremely disruptive for trade in the province. The prices farmers received for agricultural produce fell sharply, but market prices of manufactured goods in the towns shot up and business remained very slack for months.[87] This dismayed the central government considerably (or at least its economic planners who were just getting to grips with the tangled problems of economic stabilisation), since its plans to restore trade and production were likely to collapse if regional commanders went their own way in such a fashion.[88]

In fact, the implementation of Sumitro's measures appears to have been patchy from the outset and to have been quietly abandoned within the course of the year. (He himself was transferred soon afterwards.) In some cases the regulations appear to have been harshly enforced, in others they were modified to some degree. Cases were reported of alien Chinese signing over their capital and functions to WNI Chinese, or doing deals with army officers, or switching over from trade into still permitted industrial undertakings.[89] But one general consequence was to increase the informal pressures upon the Chinese, including WNI Chinese, whose documents testifying to their citizenship were frequently queried, leaving them highly vulnerable to blackmail and harassment.

The reasons for the introduction of these drastic measures illustrates how important local and personal factors can be in such a fluid situation. Major General Sumitro himself had a reputation for being strongly anti-Chinese, but this alone hardly seems sufficient to account for a move so radically out of line with the general trend of the central government's policy at the time—and so contrary to the previous record of relatively slight hostility to the Chinese in East Java. (The Brawijaya division did not have the same anti-Chinese reputation as West Java's Siliwangi division.) Sumitro may have suspected that the Chinese were a potential source of financial support to the supporters of President Sukarno, who were still resisting the moves being made by 'New Order' elements to oust him and against whom Sumitro had been taking very tough measures throughout the previous year. Not until well into 1967 was the threat of a Sukarnoist resurgence in East Java reduced to insignificance.

Another factor prompting Sumitro's anti-Chinese measures may have been the demonstration effect of similar actions elsewhere, although on a less sweeping scale. In South Sulawesi, a regulation was issued in December 1966 barring aliens from trading in the nine staple commodities of everyday commerce (rice, kerosene, sugar, salt, etc., the essential goods sold by every Chinese *warong*). The same province was declared 'closed' to newcomers who were alien Chinese. From West Kalimantan, also, there were reports that the military commander had ordered a more rigorous application of PP 10.[90]

In East Java, the Chinese reaction to Sumitro's regulations was dramatic. Two massive protest demonstrations by Chinese in Malang and Kediri, one of them a funeral procession, provided the unprecedented example of a gesture of defiance verging on provocation on the part of the Chinese. A rash of similar demonstrations followed in other parts of East Java. It was as if the Chinese there had become desperate in the face of the harassment and victimisation to which they had been subjected and had decided to abandon their traditional low posture of acquiescence, restraint, and patience in order to stand up openly at last against their persecutors. Reports of Maoist slogans being shouted during these disturbances point to a new factor in the situation, also, the inspiration of the Cultural Revolution which was then reaching its most tumultuous stage in China.

The incident in Malang started after the army closed down the shop of an old Chinese peanut-paste processor who had transferred ownership of his firm to his daughter, who was an Indonesian citizen; this was the beginning of a train of events which ended in his death from a heart attack. His funeral on 11 March was then made the occasion for a major demonstration by the Chinese community of Malang. A large procession developed, estimated to be between 4000 and 10000 people, even though most of the Chinese nationals in Malang were confined to their boarded-up shop-houses. When army men tried to stop the procession, shooting at the tyres of the car bearing the old man's body, the effect was merely to increase the mourner-demonstrators' determination, until they finally reached the cemetery. Shouts of 'Long Live Mao Tse-tung' were said to have been heard during the speeches at the graveside and charges were later made that Chinese Embassy officials were involved in inciting the Chinese of East Java to fight back.[91]

In Kediri a thousand Chinese had earlier marched in columns to the police station on 3 March to demand the release of 33 Chinese who had been arrested. About three weeks later, the local authorities arrested over 60 Chinese for failure to pay the head-tax and 29 for refusing to hand over their businesses. One of these committed suicide by jumping down a well. Guards at the gaol prevented would-be rescuers from reaching him. As the news of this episode spread through the city, hundreds of Chinese swarmed to the gaol and broke in to seize the body and take care of it. A struggle with several truckloads of troops ensued, but it was eventually agreed that the body would be put in a casket and taken to an undertaker, after which the demonstrators left the gaol.

Other Chinese demonstrations of a less dramatic nature occurred in Pasuruan and Probolinggo on the day after the Malang funeral, followed by more violent outbreaks in early April in Bondowoso, Situbondo and other towns at the eastern end of Java. In Bondowoso one Chinese was killed and several were injured when police opened fire on an anti-government demonstration, after Chinese demonstrators attacked police amidst shouts of 'Long Live Mao Tse-tung'. In Situbondo, anti-Chinese rioting broke out after troops opened fire on a group of Chinese who were protesting at the refusal of the district commander to meet them to discuss the earlier arrest of 24 Chinese there. Mob attacks on the Chinese then followed, under the leadership of anti-Communist action groups. Houses, shops and cars were damaged and ransacked, amidst cries demanding the revocation of citizenship for 'chameleon Indonesian citizens'. Thousands of Indonesian youths were involved, beating up any Chinese in sight and burning a Chinese-owned factory. The rioting and looting spread to near-by Panarukan and Besuki over the next few days. Thereafter it seems to have been curbed by the authorities, except for an isolated outbreak of similar character at Lumajang toward the end of May. By that time, the tensions throughout the province were beginning to subside and WNI Chinese felt free to return to the villages, so that gradually the flow of credit and trade revived again.

April–October 1967

The flare-up of anti-Chinese hostility which occurred in Jakarta in April was probably attributable in part to the earlier outbreaks in East Java, although no reports of them appeared in the Jakarta press for several weeks. But the series of violent demonstrations and verbal wrangles between Jakarta and Peking which continued from then until October had quite different dynamics, as anti-Communist organisations in Jakarta strove to exploit the situation in order to force a diplomatic rift between the two countries.

On 20 April a huge funeral procession in Jakarta, involving 30 000 Chinese and lasting for more than four hours, brought anti-Chinese feelings in the capital to a new peak of intensity. It resulted in a violent Indonesian demonstration two days later, which was followed by demonstrations against the Indonesian Embassy in Peking by Red Guards, and then by counter-measures and counter-charges against the Chinese Embassy in Jakarta. The man whose funeral triggered off this train of events was a prominent merchant and leader of the Chinese community in Jakarta, a Chinese national who had lived in Indonesia for about thirty years. He had been arrested early in April on a charge of involvement in subversive activities. The Chinese Embassy asserted in a protest note that he was tortured to death, but according to the Indonesian version he committed suicide in order to avoid revealing the network of subversion he was involved in. The Chinese who joined in his funeral procession out of Jakarta's Chinatown were in an angry mood and behaved provocatively toward bystanders, waving bicycle chains at Indonesians, brandishing pistols and scuffling with policemen and KAPPI students at several points. (An interesting sidelight is that pro-Sukarnoist Marines, who were the traditional enemies of the pro-government paratroopers and the KAPPI activists, were protecting the Chinese and this is said to have led to retaliation by their rivals.) Although little serious violence occurred during the procession, tension increased sharply in Jakarta.

Two days later, a much more violent Indonesian counter-demonstration occurred. The numbers involved were not large, less than a thousand, but the participants apparently belonged to organised groups, some of them Muslim youth organisations, while others were involved with the Jakarta underworld. They have been described as a very tough lot who behaved in a most bloodthirsty way as they ran riot through the Chinese sections of the city, stabbing people, slashing them with chains, throwing them into canals and cutting their bellies open. Scattered violence continued in Jakarta over the weekend, despite various calls for order from national leaders; but in general the attempt to prevent the demonstrations from spreading was successful. KAMI leaders and several prominent supporters of the 'New Order' spoke out courageously against further violence. If anything, the excesses perpetrated during that riot alarmed members of the smaller ethnic minorities in Jakarta, such as the Christian Menadonese, and emphasised the opportunities for trouble-making inherent in outbreaks of racial hostility.

This increase in tension at the end of April and early May brought the problem of what to do about the Overseas Chinese right to the forefront of the government's attention. Relations with China took a sharp turn for the worse at that time, after anti-Indonesian demonstrations by Red Guards in Peking which were followed, inevitably, by further demonstrations against the Chinese Embassy in Jakarta by Indonesian youth groups and retaliatory actions by both governments against the other's diplomats.[92] But the army maintained a heavy guard over the Chinese area of Jakarta and warned student leaders against further violence. The Foreign Minister, Adam Malik, called for restraint, arguing that Peking was trying to provoke the Indonesians into racist actions in order to blacken her good name internationally. Some supporters of the regime, while also urging moderation, called upon the government for an 'orderly but radical solution' of the Chinese problem, including the severing of diplomatic relations with Peking and accelerated repatriation of Chinese citizens. Most important of all, a State Committee was set up by the government at the end of April with instructions to report to the Cabinet Presidium on an overall policy for dealing with the problems of the Overseas Chinese.[93] Its recommendations can be seen, in retrospect, as something of a landmark in the development of Indonesian policy in this sphere, but they did not give Adam Malik much help with his immediate problem of deflecting political pressures for a break with Peking. The intensity of these pressures was revealed by demands in parliament in June for a severance of diplomatic relations, the repatriation of Chinese aliens, and firm measures against Chinese aliens found guilty of subversion.[94]

Although the Suharto government resisted the pressures upon it for a break with Peking as long as it felt able to (including the efforts of the Taiwan government, applied mainly through a group of generals with whom it had established commercial contacts), its room for manoeuvre was being steadily restricted from both sides, until little choice remained but to accept a break as inevitable. The issue was brought to a head between August and October by two mob attacks on the Chinese Embassy in Jakarta which again provoked retaliatory action by Peking that made it still harder for Adam Malik to resist demands for a severance of relations. There are indications, nevertheless, that both governments were still seeking to avoid being driven to take the final step (or were trying to make the other one bear the responsibility for it), but events were gradually slipping beyond their control and neither could do much to reverse the trend.[95] The first of the two attacks on the Chinese Embassy on 5 August was precipitated by a relatively small group of about 300 youths from the Panca Sila Youth Front, who broke into the Embassy grounds and set fire to several buildings. Shots were fired, and several people on both sides were allegedly injured in what seems to have been a confused mêlée, although the violence did not go any further on that occasion. (The reason given for this attack was a grotesquely trivial one: the Embassy's wall slightly exceeded a height limit that had just been promulgated by the municipal authorities.) Counter-demonstrations were then launched against the Indonesian Embassy in Peking by the 'revolutionary masses' and restrictions were imposed on the freedom of movement of Indonesian diplomatic personnel there; these created a situation in which Malik had to take some retaliatory action, in the face of renewed Indonesian demands to sever diplomatic relations. Yet another attack on the Chinese Embassy in Jakarta occurred on 1 October, this time a much more substantial affray, far more destructive and backed by a broad range of the student action groups, ostensibly in protest against the treatment of Indonesian diplomats in Peking. Anti-Chinese feeling was again running high in Jakarta and it was clear that if the government yielded in the face of Peking's protest Notes, it would find itself in open conflict with its own supporters. And so on 9 October, the Indonesian cabinet decided upon a suspension (but not a formal severance) of diplomatic relations between the two countries, through the complete withdrawal of the diplomatic representatives of both sides.[96]

It should be emphasised that relatively little violence was directed against the Indonesian Chinese generally in Jakarta during those last few months of intense agitation, although there was apparently still a good deal of spill-over of hostility and extortion at the individual level.[97] The primary purpose of the demonstration seems to have been a political one and once the political objective was achieved, the issue of relations with China was no longer amenable to exploitation in the ways it had been. The anti-Chinese sentiments which had been aroused during the previous two years gradually began to subside, although further outbreaks of violence occurred in Jakarta in February 1968 and in Surabaya in October.[98] There was also a terrible epilogue in West Kalimantan at the end of 1967, to which we must shortly turn. The diminution of anti-Chinese actions after the end of 1967 was probably due in part to the closing of the Chinese Embassy, as it had provided both an irritant and an issue for those elements which were seeking to arouse hostility to China and the Chinese, but in part also to the fact that the Suharto government was by that time much more firmly in the saddle, much more prepared to act firmly against demonstrators and dissentients, and better able to control its regional military commanders than it had been earlier.

October–November 1967: West Kalimantan
The last and most horrifying of the major anti-Chinese outbursts occurred at the end of 1967 in West Kalimantan. It arose out of the unique
local circumstances created by the presence of many pro-communist
Chinese guerrillas from Sarawak, who had come to Indonesia for refuge
and military training during Confrontation, in combination with the
problems created by a substantial Chinese population in the rural areas
between Pontianak and the border, among whom the guerrillas were
able to find shelter and supplies. The rift between Jakarta and Peking
may have aggravated the anti-Chinese actions which broke out, but it
is improbable that this was a very important factor in precipitating the
outbreaks. It is also noteworthy that on this occasion the assault came
not from Muslims, but from the Dayaks, who are mostly animists (or
in some cases Christians).

After the ending of hostilities between Indonesia and Malaysia in
1966, the left-wing Sarawak guerrillas of the PGRS (*Pasukan Geriljawan
Rakjat Sarawak*—Sarawak People's Guerrilla Force), mostly young Chinese who had been receiving aid and succour from the Indonesian
authorities in West Kalimantan, regrouped in the jungle near the
frontier, where they now found themselves hunted by the armies of
both countries.[99] It is unlikely there were many Indonesian Chinese
from West Kalimantan (or elsewhere) among them, for the latter had
not been recruited as irregulars in the struggle against Malaysia. Some
members of Indonesian army units of known left-wing sympathies are
said to have fled to the jungle after the coup, but few of these seem to
have linked up with the essentially Chinese PGRS.

Early in 1967 an attempt was made by Brig. Gen. Riyacudu, the
regional military commander for West Kalimantan, to bring about the
resettlement of rural Chinese in his area through the reactivation of the
PP 10. This appears to have been unsuccessful, since the urban authorities were in no position to feed or accommodate newcomers, so most of
the Chinese drifted back into their villages. On 2 July the guerrillas
launched a major attack on the airfield at Sanggauledo, near Singkawang, in which a number of government troops were killed and a large
quantity of arms and ammunition captured.[100] This led to a considerable
reinforcement of the airfield and local military command by crack units
of all branches of the armed forces, which were placed under a unified
command. Co-operation with Malaysian forces across the border was
also stepped up at about that time. PGRS activities seem to have been
intensified in the third quarter of 1967, with the killing of Dayaks in
several places, including village leaders, and a destructive attack on the
village of Uduk in mid-October.

At the end of October, the Dayaks struck back against the Chinese
in a devastating series of raids throughout the region. Just how far their

attacks were instigated or approved by the authorities is not clear. It was reported that they had asked the government for a mandate to retaliate against the PGRS raiders before the Uduk raid and that soon after it papers were issued to the Dayak leaders authorising them to take action. But their attacks spread far beyond the border areas and were not confined to the guerrillas.

The stories of these attacks are blood-curdling, for the Dayaks swept down on their victims, brandishing their long knives and shouting their ancient war cries. Indonesian press and radio accounts spoke of 'declaration of war' by the Dayaks against the PGRS through a 'traditional ceremony' that involved ritual drinking from a bowl of blood. The attacks occurred at widely separated points, mainly in the last week of October. The pattern generally seems to have been that they descended on the Chinese villages, took their food and put the Chinese to flight: if this was not enough, the houses were burnt and any Chinese left behind were killed.[101]

By mid-November at least 300 Chinese had been killed and over 45 000 Chinese had fled from the inland areas of West Borneo to seek refuge in the main towns near the coast, about half to Pontianak, the remainder in Singkawang, Mempawah and Bengkayang. A few were able to find accommodation with relatives, but the vast majority were in camps, schools, church-yards, Chinese factories and storehouses, all of which were used as temporary accommodation centres. The pressure of 20 000 refugees was particularly acute in Singkawang, whose normal population was only twice that number. There were severe problems of providing sufficient food and medical supplies for them and the mortality rate among children in the camps was high. A Jakarta newspaper report in April 1968 estimated that 1 500 children aged between one and eight had died in the camps.[102] The Indonesian Red Cross did what it could to provide a minimal ration of food (initially 400 grammes of rice a day), but its supplies soon ran out. The government sent some rice to the area, but the disaster occurred at a time of acute rice shortage and rocketing prices throughout Indonesia, which greatly hindered its efforts to provide relief.

The Dayak attacks simmered down slowly during November. An order went out from Jakarta to the West Kalimantan authorities on 17 November to stop all Dayak actions and send the members of raiding parties home. But ten days later an attack occurred on the town of Tebas by 700 Dayak tribesmen armed with daggers, which resulted in the looting of shops and the eviction of both civilians—and, significantly, military officials—and 400 Chinese. No further Dayak attacks were reported after that and the actions against the PGRS guerrillas, which continued at a rather low level throughout the next three years, were conducted thereafter by the army units.

The attitude of the authorities to the Dayak actions appears to have been ambivalent, at least at the outset. Obviously, the Dayaks were achieving through terror the strategic objective of 'resettlement' which the army had failed to achieve through more orderly means, by cleaning nearly all the Chinese out of the border areas and so depriving the PGRS guerrillas of sources of supply, information or refuge. Herbert Feith wrote at the time that 'an apparently dominant group of staff officers at the military headquarters in Pontianak took the view that the guerrilla fish could best be caught if the water (of the people, in this case the Chinese people), in which he swam . . . was drained off'.[103] The regional commander, Witono, was not himself anti-Chinese, but he was apparently unable to keep control over the course of events. Major Gusti Usman Idris, the *bupati* of Pontianak, was reported as justifying the Dayak's deeds as a 'people's demonstration' which would have the effect of destroying the guerrillas' bases and killing former members of the Communist-led *Barisan Tani*, although at the same time he spoke about 'excesses' which were to be deplored.[104] How far the army leaders positively encouraged the Dayaks to take action against the Chinese in the first place is not known, but they do seem to have been reluctant to take any action to restrain them. Officials in Pontianak claimed that they were under orders not to shoot unless the Dayaks descended on the provincial capital itself and it was not until mid-November that the Jakarta authorities ordered a halt to the actions. By then, the ferocity of the Dayak attacks was creating other problems for the government, not merely the economic disruption of an important rubber-exporting region (which was a serious matter at that time, for the government's economic programme was still threatened by foreign exchange problems), but also the unfavourable publicity it gave Indonesia at a time when she badly needed to present an image of stability and orderliness to the outside world.

The pressures on the Chinese in West Kalimantan diminished after the end of 1967 and many apparently returned to their villages despite an attempt at compulsory resettlement in a belt of cleared jungle near Pontianak, the cost of which was imposed upon those Chinese who were not willing to accommodate or employ the refugees.

Guerrilla activity continued, but no longer at a dangerous level. Three years later the military authorities introduced another scheme for the 'voluntary resettlement' of 17000 Chinese from the northeastern part of the province, between the Kapuas River and the border, following increased activity by guerrillas there. Again, the aim was to clear them away from the border, down toward new settlements along the Kapuas. But on this occasion no serious violence occurred.[105] The predicament of the Chinese in West Kalimantan, however, remained far more uncertain than in most other parts of Indonesia.

EXPLANATIONS: A PROLEGOMENON

The diversity of causal factors behind the outbreaks of anti-Chinese violence has been one of the most striking features of this survey. Is there any coherent pattern of explanation to be discerned there? The inadequacies of over-generalised explanations in terms of one or two dominant features of the relationship between Indonesians and Chinese have already been mentioned. It may be more fruitful to approach the problem in terms of the threefold categorisation mentioned earlier, identifying factors which create a predisposition towards group antagonisms, those which operate to restrain the expression of hostility, and those which seem likely to precipitate violence in situations of acute tension.[106]

A Predisposing factors

In a plural society such as Indonesia's, the sources of antagonisms between different racial groups are complex, deriving from experiences deeply rooted in the history and social development of the various communities. Why are ethnic differences so explosive in some cases but not in others? One can answer this in large part by showing how differences of race coincide with other differences (of religion, social status, income level, political affiliation etc.) and exacerbate tensions arising out of resentment or prejudice or the sense of injustice on either side of these overlapping lines of social cleavage. This will not tell us the whole story, however, for there may well be significant differences from region to region in the mechanisms by which the attitudes of individual Indonesians toward the Chinese they know personally become transmuted into more general stereotypes about the Chinese as a whole— and in more extreme cases into racial prejudice toward them. We can list some of the elements involved, but there is a great deal more we need to know about the way they combine to create, in some circumstances, a predisposition toward violent hostility.

1   The simple facts of racial difference and socio-cultural separateness must constitute our starting-point. These need not necessarily give rise to antagonism except where differences of wealth, economic roles, educational levels and social status have tinged the sense of separateness with bitterness, envy or hostility: in many circumstances of Indonesian-Chinese contact they have not done so, for it is not the fact of difference and separateness that counts so much as the subjective feeling that these things are important. Not all Chinese are richer or better educated than all Indonesians, of course, though in general they tend to be. Nor should we think in terms of one single homogeneous group of Indonesians or of Chinese in Indonesia; both categories are strikingly heterogeneous. But the sense of a deep-seated ethnic difference exists and is easily inflamed and exploited.

2 The socio-cultural differences between Chinese and Indonesians were aggravated in most unfortunate ways by development in the colonial period—by the physical isolation of the Chinese in special 'quarters' of the towns, by policies debarring them from certain rural areas and classifying them for legal purposes in a special category as 'Foreign Orientals' with a higher status than the 'natives'.[107] The tendency of the peranakan Chinese elite to assimilate towards the Dutch community and to strive for legal, political and social equality with the ruling caste rather than identifying with the Indonesians whom they tended to despise, also intensified the sense of racial, cultural and social difference between the two racial groups. The awareness of racial differences was intensified by the growth of Indonesian and Chinese nationalism (as we call the various movements making appeals of a nationalist character in the hope of overcoming primordial particularisms) in the early twentieth century, for race and nationalism often seemed to be two sides of the same coin.[108]

3 The attitudes of many Chinese in Indonesia towards the Indonesian independence movement and Indonesian nationalism in the years before 1949 also tended to deepen the gulf between them, by aggravating Indonesian hostility and suspicion toward the Chinese and reinforcing a stereotyped view of all Chinese as unsympathetic to Indonesian aspirations. Uncertainties about the citizenship status of the Chinese after independence was achieved (which persisted until 1962) and doubts on the Indonesian side about the sincerity even of those Chinese who opted for Indonesian nationality tended to perpetuate the view that the racial difference between Indonesians and Chinese went deeper than the legal distinction between citizens, including WNI Chinese, and non-citizens.

4 The feeling of resentment between the 'haves' and the 'have-nots' has certainly been an important part, perhaps the most important part, of the prevailing Indonesian stereotype of the differences between the two ethnic groups during this century. It was probably a less significant element before 1900. But we know little about the intensity of this sentiment at different levels of society. Do the poorest Indonesians feel the strongest resentment against the Chinese—or is it found among the wealthy, or among struggling Indonesian businessmen? Or among the intellectuals and politicians who need to rationalise their people's relative poverty or to exploit easily fanned passions for their own political purposes?

5 Related to this feeling is the widespread Indonesian belief in Chinese 'economic domination' of their country through a tight and allegedly impenetrable network of credit and personal ties, which give them enormous advantages over Indonesians in such matters as access to capital, trading contacts and market information. In its more extreme form, this kind of belief seems to be a fairly recent element in the anti-

Chinese syndrome, insofar as the Dutch were the more obvious villains of the piece down to 1958. But the spread of the Chinese retail trade network was already a serious obstacle to Indonesian businessmen even in colonial times and the myth that the Chinese had some mysterious ingrained advantages or aptitudes in commercial activities has long since contributed to a sense of inadequacy, resentment and need to over-compensate among Indonesians.

6   Competition between Chinese and Indonesian businessmen has undoubtedly been one of the factors creating unfavourable predispositions toward the Chinese among an influential group within Indonesian society, even to the point where economic discrimination against the Chinese has been advocated on the grounds of an essentially racial difference. It is no coincidence that some of the most vehement anti-Chinese sentiments have emanated from those groups in Indonesian society which have a strong commercial orientation and constitute an embryonic trading class, in competition with the Chinese. They are also, in general, the strongest devotees of Islam, which has served as the ideological driving force of the major commercial communities. But the question of whether the correlation between anti-Sinicism and the 'Islamic-entrepreneurial pole' of Indonesian socio-political life is due primarily to economic competition or to some more complex interaction of social structure and social ideology is, as we have already seen, one which requires further investigation.

7   The xenophobic aspect of intense nationalism nurtures complex negative attitudes towards other peoples which tend to reinforce the sense of group separateness on both sides—distrust, envy, fear and hostility among many Indonesians (not all, it should be emphasised); cultural arrogance, contempt or condescension towards Indonesians among some Chinese, particularly the more chauvinist of them. An overlapping and complicating factor has been the historic importance of Islam as one of the constituent ideological elements in the nationalist amalgam in Indonesia (and Malaysia), so that fervent Muslims claim to be good nationalists by virtue of their Islamic credentials and seek to demonstrate the strength of their convictions by fulminating against non-believers (and renegades). Some nationalists, such as Sukarno, would deny that there is an intrinsic connection between Islam and nationalism, but the more fanatical Muslims would hardly be convinced by arguments based on nationalism at the expense of religion.

8   Insofar as the Overseas Chinese have been regarded as an offshoot of a great power that looms threateningly over Indonesia, hence as a potential 'fifth column' in the event of conflict in Southeast Asia, the sense of apprehension about them and of suspicion about the distinction between WNI Chinese and aliens has been heightened.[104] Fears of this kind, whether rational or unrealistic, reinforce primordial attitudes and

obstruct the growth of more mature civic sentiments. Moreover, such fears were most prevalent among anti-Communists who increasingly came to identify Communism with China during the late Sukarno era and feared that his policies were delivering their country into China's power; hence they were not inclined to draw a fine distinction between aliens and Indonesian citizens of Chinese descent who might have been perfectly loyal to the Republic and by no means pro-Communist. On the whole, the Indonesian left-wing parties took a less alarmist and more defensible view of this matter—but the very fact of their doing so was likely to intensify the suspicions of the extreme anti-Communists. In the later years of Guided Democracy, apprehensions of this kind contributed greatly to the heightening of the tensions which exploded in 1965–67.

B   Restraining factors

While the factors mentioned above have created varying degrees of pre-disposition toward antagonism to the Chinese, other elements have operated to constrain the expression of overt hostility or discrimination, either constantly or occasionally.

1   The desire of most members of the Indonesian elite to present a non-racialist image before the eyes of the world must be mentioned first and foremost. Moreover, their traditional beliefs and value-systems incline them toward doctrines of harmony and tolerance, although there are exceptions to such a generalisation, Islam in particular being highly ambivalent in this respect. The inclination toward a self-image as reasonable, civilised, tolerant people, free from the taint of racialism, extends (with differing degrees of comprehension) widely among the elite and well beyond it. The official rhetoric of slogans about a 'Panca Sila state' with its call for humanitarianism and internationalism reinforces this, as also the stress put upon the tolerance of Islam and the respect accorded to all religions in Indonesia. Even those who seek to discriminate against the Chinese try to provide acceptable justifications for their policies, such as the argument that the 'economically weaker group' (the Indonesian asli) must be protected or assisted against the greedy, monopolistic 'economically stronger group'. Proclaimed values do not always determine action—and they differ greatly in different segments of Indonesian society—but they are frequently an important influence on it.

2   The doctrine of legal equality for all citizens of Indonesia, regardless of their racial ancestry, which is embodied in laws, regulations and the proclaimed principles of the new Republic serves to deny legitimacy to blatantly anti-Chinese measures, even if it is not always upheld effectively. Progress towards a single framework of laws and regulations which distinguishes only between citizens and aliens has been slow; retrograde steps such as the economic regulations giving preference to

asli businessmen have sometimes violated the principle of equality, and the law has not been a very effective source of protection for individuals in circumstances where administrative decisions have often been arbitrary.[110] But at least in theory the principle of legal equality among all citizens has become accepted since 1968 and it can be appealed to with some hope of success on occasions, even if not always.

3 A desire to maintain good relations with China has inclined most Indonesian governments since 1950 (including the Suharto government) to try to avoid tensions over the Overseas Chinese, although there have been some politicians who have not shared this desire and have sought to gain political advantage by promoting hostility toward China. There have been various reasons for wanting cordial relations with Peking which have waxed and waned in importance from time to time—the need for her co-operation in dealing with the dual nationality question and the sheer administrative problems posed by the presence of over a million ethnic Chinese who were not Indonesian citizens; the desirability of having her support and friendship in the councils of Afro-Asian nations; the value, at one stage, of her backing in the struggle to mobilise the New Emerging Forces against US and British 'neo-colonialism and imperialism'; not least the disadvantages entailed in incurring her hostility, because of the influence she might be able to exert through the PKI or the Overseas Chinese, if she chose to cause difficulties for the government.

4 An awareness of the need to minimise the economic costs of disrupting Indonesia's distributive network by harassing the Chinese has operated as a restraint on some Indonesians in positions of authority, even some who were by no means unsympathetic to 'indigenisation pressures'. Vice-President Hatta and Ir. Djuanda might be cited as outstanding examples. In 1959–60 this restraint did not operate (although in some areas, such as East and Central Java, it may have softened the implementation of the ban on rural storekeepers) and the results were extremely costly. In 1966–67, it was clearly a very important consideration influencing government policy toward the Indonesian Chinese, although not always a decisive one—and it was utterly ignored by several regional commanders for brief periods. The Suharto government's recognition of the need to make optimal use of the capital and skills of the Chinese, both foreigners and WNI, has probably been the most important single factor in the improvement of their social and economic situation in the years since 1967.

5 Related to this concern to utilise what Sukarno called the 'funds and forces' of the Chinese has been the realisation by some Indonesian leaders that a favourable business climate would have to be maintained to attract foreign investors, that violent attacks on Chinese shops and factories, or looting and threats to private property, were a bad example

which might encourage attacks against others. During the Sukarno era this constraint was a notably weak one, except perhaps in 1963 when his government was seeking foreign aid from the West rather desperately. By 1967–68 it had become a very important consideration which apparently became accepted by most of Indonesia's senior military men responsible for maintaining law and order, many of whom were now acquiring a direct interest in not frightening off either foreign capital or domestic Chinese capitalists.

6   The growth of connections between Chinese businessmen and many generals and top people in the Indonesian government (the so-called *cukong* relationship) can also be considered a restraining factor of some significance, varying greatly in influence from place to place and time to time. It could, however, prove counterproductive if the unpopularity of the officials were to give rise to popular antagonism toward their Chinese associates—and it would be naive to assume that because some (or even many) high officials have such relationships with a few wealthy Chinese they would feel a strong commitment to restraining anti-Chinese sentiments in general. The politics of manipulation can be a very dirty game. Nevertheless it is probably better for the Indonesian Chinese, in general, that the men who run the country should be accessible and amenable to the representations of the Chinese community leaders than that they should be hostile or indifferent to them.

7   A general reassertion of the need for constraints upon the overt expression of anti-Chinese feelings may sometimes be made by the central government because a regional official or military commander has on his own initiative gone beyond the limits intended by government policy in taking anti-Chinese measures (as in the 1959 West Java situation or 1967 in East Java), so that the government has had to assert its authority in the matter and in doing so come down more firmly against such measures than it might otherwise have done. Similarly, the regional authorities had to assert their authority in May 1963, as much to maintain their control in a highly explosive situation as because they had especially tender feelings towards the Chinese.

8   Sometimes the government will yield a little on one issue in the face of strong anti-Chinese sentiment in order to allow some particular objective to be achieved without bearing direct responsibility for it, then step in as an advocate of restraint to prevent matters being pushed too far. The adoption of the word *Tjina* (*Cina*) in 1966 and the government's attitude to name-changing were to some extent examples of such a strategy. While this may be deemed a rather convoluted form of restraint, it makes some sense in situations where the government is simply not strong enough to stand up to anti-Chinese activists forthrightly.

C   Precipitating factors

The factors which have played a part in actually precipitating anti-Chinese outbursts in recent years can be grouped together under seven general headings:

1   The general political situation in Indonesia has been a major influence where it has affected the stability of the government, its capacity to uphold the legal rights of the Chinese and the extent to which opposition to the government could be expressed in the form of anti-Chinese activities, when these have forced the government either to accede to 'the demands of the people' (thus reducing its moral authority) or to take an unpopular stand against such demands. The government's ability to exercise effective control over its subordinates in the regions has been a related factor. In general, it can be expected that anti-Chinese actions are more likely to be attempted in periods when the central government is weak or unsettled than when it is securely in the saddle.

2   The general state of relations with China can have an important bearing on anti-Chinese sentiments, particularly if Peking's reaction is one which Indonesians regard as provocative, threatening or interfering, as her response in 1959-60 and 1965-67 was seen to be. In May 1963, however, the fact that relations between the two governments were becoming closer was an important consideration, even though Peking said and did nothing to embarrass the Sukarno government; one of the motives of some instigators of the anti-Chinese riots in Bandung and elsewhere seems to have been to damage relations with China and prevent a further rapprochement between the two countries.

3   The state of the economy has been a factor of considerable significance in generating anti-Chinese sentiments, in that discontent with rising prices, shortages and hoarding have frequently been blamed upon the Chinese. Moreover, inflation has generally burdened the poor most heavily while benefiting the rich with windfall profits, thus aggravating the sense of cleavage between 'haves' and 'have-nots' which tends to be seen as a division between Chinese and Indonesians. But there is no simple correlation between economic hardship and anti-Sinicism, even though many Chinese themselves believe that when the price of rice soars, they will be made the scapegoats. Economic troubles seem to have been one of the contributing factors in the 1963 riots; the months of crisis over PP 10 in 1959-60 also coincided with acute economic dislocation, as also did the 1965-67 troubles. But in none of these cases could the economic factor be regarded as the sole or dominant precipitant. In some respects we should categorise economic distress as a predisposing rather than a precipitating factor to anti-Chinese outbursts, though not in the same sense as we have used that term previously. It

is also worth noting that one of the major complaints against Chinese businessmen during the period of inflation, that they were heavily engaged in smuggling, black-market operations and the bribing of officials, has had much less force (except, perhaps, on the last score, and even that is arguable) since the economy became stabilised in 1968–69.[111]

4   The general security situation is also relevant in much the same way as the economic situation as an important background consideration, though not an immediate sole precipitant of trouble. The 1963 riots coincided with the ending of martial law and a period of confusion about who was now responsible for law and order. In 1965–67 also the Suharto government's precarious hold over the country was a crucially important factor. Similarly, the anti-KMT measures of 1958–59 were quite directly related to the fact that Taiwan had openly sided with the PRRI-Permesta rebels against Sukarno's government at a time when the security situation was felt to be precarious.

5   Incidents that involve or symbolise racial antagonisms between Chinese and Indonesians or Malays, either inside or outside the country, are likely to arouse anti-Chinese hostility in some degree. For instance, the hanging of four Indonesian marines by the Singapore government in October 1968 provoked riots in Surabaya, although they were soon brought under control. One might expect a similar triggering effect if, for instance, an uprising of Chinese Muslims were forcibly repressed at a time when relations between the two countries were bad. On the other hand, it is noteworthy that the May 1969 race riots in Kuala Lumpur did not spark any reaction in Indonesia; in fact the Indonesian government is said to have counselled restraint to hotheads in Malaya who were advocating Malay-Indonesian solidarity against the Chinese.

6   Going further down the scale of possible triggering mechanisms, we may categorise various types of actions which entail the open expression or flaunting of cultural and ethnic differences. Processions have been the most provocative such occurrences; e.g. the *barongsai* procession before the Sukabumi riots (several months before them, it should be noted) and the funeral processions in East Java and Jakarta in April 1967. Perhaps even the symbolism of the high Chinese embassy wall had a similar significance in August 1967. At times of acute tension, the public demonstration or assertion of Chineseness *on Indonesian soil* is likely to be seen as an affront to Indonesian nationalism, arousing sentiments which have previously been dormant. Crowd scenes are particularly likely to engender such reactions.

7   In a slightly different category, we might list the flaunting of wealth by the Chinese as a triggering mechanism—said to have been a significant factor behind the May 1963 riots, since it highlighted the distinction between the 'haves' and 'have-nots' at a time when this was

likely to cause acute grievance among the latter group for other reasons. But in cases like this, how do we distinguish between precipitating and predisposing factors?

It could hardly be claimed that this list of elements which have played a part in producing explosions of racial violence between Indonesians and Chinese is exhaustive, nor that on the basis of it we will find any set of formulae to explain which combinations of factors are most likely to produce such explosions. The analogy with chemistry cannot be carried very far because of the high degree of indeterminacy of social processes. Outbreaks of violence probably will continue to occur from time to time, sometimes in quite unforeseeable circumstances. If we are to understand their causes, it is toward the unseen mass of the iceberg of racial antagonism, to the unexpressed attitudes and dimly recognised roots of racial hostility that we need to direct our future research, using much more precise analytical tools than have yet been employed in this task.

Postscript

Further serious outbreaks of anti-Chinese violence occurred in Bandung on 5 August 1973 and in Jakarta on 15–16 January 1974, the latter arising out of the anti-Japanese demonstrations which occurred during the visit of Prime Minister Tanaka to Indonesia. The complex political and social background to the latter cannot be sketched with any confidence at this stage (March 1974). It is sufficient to say that the element of anti-Chinese feeling was in this case probably little more than an extension of generalised antagonism towards Japanese 'economic imperialists' and the wealthy groups in the Indonesian community in general, an outbreak of hostility by the frustrated, 'have not' elements of Jakarta society against the most conspicuous symbols of wealth and high living among the Indonesian elite, the Chinese and foreigners. It was not predominantly an anti-Chinese outbreak.[112]

The Bandung riots arose after an incident in which an Indonesian horsecart driver was beaten up by the Chinese driver of a Volkswagen with which it had had a minor collision. Shortly afterwards an attack on the Chinese by Indonesian *becak* drivers and others from the urban poor quickly snowballed into very widespread destruction and looting of Chinese (and some Indonesian) property in the Jalan Braga shopping area and parts of the Chinese residential quarter. The destruction continued from 6.30 p.m. until far into the night. Police and army units were slow to take action, but the following day, apparently on orders from Jakarta, security measures were intensified in Bandung and other cities, and no further violence occurred. The authorities were quick to blame the whole affair upon pro-Communist elements, though the evidence for this is unconvincing.

The episode was reminiscent of the 10 May 1963 riots in Bandung in its origins and the immediate reaction of the security forces, although the authorities seem to have moved rather more promptly and effectively to check the rioting on this occasion. There was again a strong note of protest by the Indonesian poor against wealthy Chinese and the high-living Indonesians, but this time stemming less from student groups than from the urban poor and lower-ranking soldiers. There were again rumours that the rioting was organised and had a political background—that it represented a power play or threat by an anti-Suharto faction in the army against the regime's close association with wealthy Chinese cukongs. It is impossible to summarise the available evidence for and against these allegations here. But it is important to relate the outburst to the change in the national mood towards the Indonesian Chinese during the five years between 1968 and 1973.

Between 1968 and about 1971 conditions improved considerably for the Chinese in most parts of the country and there were no serious anti-Chinese outbreaks after the Surabaya episode in October 1968. They were among the prime beneficiaries of the economic stabilisation and boom that the Suharto regime brought about in those years; and many wealthy Chinese individuals and firms established close connections with key military officers (cukong relationships) which ensured political protection to them and considerable wealth to the generals. This situation aroused intermittent hostility from the traditionally anti-Chinese groups among Indonesians (the editor of *Nusantara* was sentenced to gaol in 1971 for a series of inflammatory articles against cukongs), but the security authorities prevented any attempts to exploit or fan these sentiments for political purposes. Unlike the pre-1965 situation, the Chinese were now looking for protection to the right wing of the political spectrum, including some of their old enemies, rather than the left; and it began to seem as if this might prove a better guarantee of security for them. But some Indonesian Chinese were growing apprehensive by 1971–72 that too close an association with the leading generals around Suharto might be creating dangers for the community, in the event of outbursts of popular hostility to the regime. The generals could not be relied upon to risk their political power to defend the Chinese; in fact some might even be tempted to manipulate and exploit anti-Chinese sentiments if it proved expedient. Wealthy and well-connected Chinese *towkays* might be able to assure their own protection, but what of the poorer Chinese without connections if things went wrong? The trial in 1972–73 of Robbie Tjahjadi, a Chinese arrested in connection with a notorious scandal involving highly placed Indonesian officials over the smuggling of luxury cars, seemed to underline this point. Moreover, the prominence of several young Catholic Chinese political intellectuals as aides to key members of President Sukarto's personal staff had aroused a good deal of criticism, particularly among Muslim politicians and student critics of the regime. In short, the Chinese were becoming uncomfortably vulnerable again by 1972–73, despite their prosperity and the country's outward calm. The dangers implicit in an outbreak such as the August incident were all too obvious in the potentially explosive political atmosphere.

4

THE CHINESE IN THE SOUTH SUMATRAN RUBBER INDUSTRY: A CASE STUDY IN ECONOMIC NATIONALISM

K. D. Thomas and J. Panglaykim

Chinese entrepreneurs have been involved in the rubber industry throughout the Indonesian archipelago since seeds were first brought into the country from Malaya in the first decade of the present century. Along with the pilgrims returning from Mecca, Chinese traders were active in distributing seeds in what are now the major rubber areas in Indonesia. Prohibited from owning land in the Netherlands Indies under the Agrarian Law of 1870, the Chinese were largely confined to trading and processing a variety of agricultural products including smallholder rubber. Largely through their efforts, to the amazement of the Dutch colonial government officials, Indonesian smallholders eagerly adopted the new plant into their cultivation cycle, seeing it as a welcome source of cash income to supplement their rather low yields from shifting cultivation.

Rubber production and exports expanded considerably between 1920–41, and in spite of restriction on planting and production in the 1930s, rubber was by 1940 Indonesia's major agricultural export; smallholder rubber accounted for almost half of the total.[1] The Chinese had come to dominate both trade and processing of smallholder rubber by that time in the whole of Indonesia.

This essay is largely concerned with the development of the industry in South Sumatra[2] in the post-war period, but certain trends in the colonial period are of interest because of the light they throw on issues which have become prominent since independence. After an introduction on developments in smallholder rubber and the role of the Chinese in the growth of the industry in the colonial period, the essay considers in more detail the post-war situation. The story of the South Sumatran

Chinese since independence has been, from their point of view, one of constant adjustments to a variety of changes in the political power structure as it affected their business of getting rubber from the villages on to the ships for export. Throughout the post-war period they have been under constant attack by economic nationalists with a variety of motives, attacks to which they were particularly vulnerable because of the way in which they were obliged to conduct their business under conditions of economic deterioration. Whereas they had been pioneers in developing a good quality product in the colonial period, the Chinese were now charged with malpractices detrimental to the rubber trade, to the state's foreign exchange earnings and to the rubber grower's income. The predicament of the Chinese becomes apparent as we trace the history of the industry from colonial times into the 1950s and 1960s.

THE COLONIAL PERIOD

The beginnings

Many of the problems which have plagued the industry in the post-war period can only be fully understood in the context of its development during the colonial period. This section emphasises the role which the Chinese played in the early days of the industry and touches on some of the difficulties they faced after independence when certain trends in the industry were reversed as a result of adverse economic and political conditions. These matters will then be considered in depth in later sections.

Rubber began to be exported from Palembang in the 1920s and by 1940 it had become South Sumatra's major agricultural export, with the Chinese playing an important role in trading and processing. But Palembang's history as a great trading centre did not begin with rubber, nor were the Chinese newcomers to trade in the region. Palembang was the capital of the Sriwijaya empire in the seventh century and a major port in the China-India-Mediterranean trade. With the decay of the empire, Palembang fell into Chinese hands and remained thus for about two hundred years. Purcell writes that it 'was one of the earliest places in Southeast Asia where the Chinese settled in any numbers'[3] and with the fall of the empire it became a stronghold of Chinese pirates.

Palembang and the Chinese were also important in the pepper trade during the time of the Dutch East India Company. Towards the end of the last century *robusta* coffee was introduced into South Sumatra and, together with pepper, became an important export of the region. The Chinese traded in both products. The Chinese population in the area was fairly small at that time. It is reported that in 1912 the Chinese in South Sumatra numbered some 11 600 out of a total population of about 1.1 million.[4] In Palembang alone, the Chinese accounted for 11 per cent of the population of 61 000 in 1915. If these data are correct only about 4 600 Chinese were resident outside the city. By 1930 a remarkable change had taken place; out of a total population of 1.8 million, the Chinese numbered 41 000 of whom 16 000 were living in Palembang, then a city of 109 000. Chinese residing outside the city totalled 25 000, an increase of 440 per cent compared with an increase in the numbers of Chinese in the whole region of some 243 per cent.[5]

Parallel with the increase in the Chinese population living in the region were the growth in rubber exports, the expansion of the petroleum industry and the construction of the rail network in South Sumatra. Our concern here is with the rubber industry, but it is important to note at this stage that, although it is possible to trace the growing involvement of the Chinese in rubber, data are not available to indicate the extent to which the Chinese were also employed in the petroleum industry and on the construction of the railway. A mere 58 tonnes of rubber was exported from South Sumatra in 1921, all from Palembang. By 1927 rubber exports through Palembang had risen to 15 000 tonnes; by 1928 rubber exports were second in value only to coffee, having just edged out pepper from that position.[6]

By residency, rubber was important only in Palembang, coffee in both Palembang and Bengkulu, and pepper was exported almost entirely from Lampung. By 1940 rubber had moved into first place for the South Sumatran region as a whole, with exports for that year, all through the port of Palembang, valued at fl. 38 million for a total volume of 58 000 tonnes.

No data are available on the numbers of Chinese engaged in the industry at that time, but as traders and industrialists they had come to dominate the industry, as we shall see, at all levels outside the village.

There are indications that in the early days of smallholder rubber in South Sumatra indigenous (*pribumi*) traders played an important role in channelling rubber from the village to Palembang. Boeke notes that in Palembang and elsewhere 'intermediary trade by the late twenties of the century had already passed almost entirely into the hands of the Malays'.[7] As production increased throughout the 1920s, so too did the role of the Chinese. The pribumi were not strong enough financially to handle the rapid increase. Slowly but surely, the Chinese came to dominate the trading sector and gradually to process the rubber as well. Much of this processed rubber still went to Singapore for re-export, but by the end of the 1930s some of the Chinese in Palembang were beginning to export direct to Western Europe and the United States.

By virtue of their financial strength and trading experience, the Chinese maintained control over the marketing and processing of the rubber in the post-war period, although both citizen and alien Chinese[8] were subjected to a variety of pressures to make room for the indigenous businessman in the industry. Although the Chinese continued to process the rubber, the tendency towards better quality begun in the late 1930s was reversed and the part played by Singapore, instead of diminishing (as it had for a few years before the war), grew in importance. Pressures on the Chinese arose partly from the decline in quality and partly from the increasingly important role of Singapore; on both issues they came under increasing criticism by economic nationalists.

In spite of considerable Indonesian opposition to their dominant position in the industry between 1950 and 1965, the Chinese retained control. A new phase began after 1966 as the government of President Suharto seemed more inclined than the previous government to encourage both the citizen and alien Chinese to invest in the industry and to assist in the country's development in general. The character of Indonesian economic nationalism seemed to be changing and a more conciliatory attitude towards all groups of Chinese began to replace the more restrictive atmosphere of the earlier period.

The development of a processing industry

In the first decade of this century rubber cultivation began to spread into the hinterland around the ports of Palembang, Jambi and Belawan in Sumatra, and Pontianak and Banjarmasin in Kalimantan. In the early days smallholders in the villages sold their rubber in the form of *slabs*, made by pouring the latex, collected in a cup attached to the tree below the tapping cut, into a wooden box or trench in the ground. When with the help of a chemical agent the latex had coagulated, the slab was tipped onto the ground to make way for the next lot of fresh latex the following day. In most cases, slabs were purchased by Chinese who owned small retail stores (*warong*) in the villages. Their function in the trade was not confined to the purchase of rubber: they sold daily necessities to the farmers who brought their rubber to the store and often extended credit to these farmers.

Slabs were sent from the Indonesian port to Chinese-owned remilling factories in Singapore.[9] Gradually remilling factories were set up in the main ports of Indonesia, for the most part owned by Chinese resident in Indonesia, although some of them were established by Singapore Chinese, Japanese interests and a Dutch syndicate. Later, 'sheet' production of higher quality than slabs was developed, for which the producer in the village required access to mangles.[10]

Chinese traders brought the mangles in, and in many cases it was the Chinese warong owner who purchased them. The Indonesian smallholder then rented the mangle and produced his own sheets or sold the latex to the warong owner who ran a small rubber factory on the side. The sheets were either smoked in towns close to the village, or sent to the ports for smoking.[11] After being passed along trading channels controlled by the Chinese, the unsmoked sheets were finally bought by smokehouse owners who were also, for the most part, Chinese. In short, the Chinese played a crucial role at vital stages in pioneering a new technology which resulted in an improvement in rubber qualities. Palembang was the last region to make the transition to sheet production: in 1930 only slabs were exported while other main ports exported both blankets and sheets. By 1941 the transition to blankets in Palembang was far advanced, and in addition some 30 per cent was already being exported in the form of smoked sheets.

Immediately before the Second World War, the ethnic division of labour in the rubber industry was fairly clear-cut. Tapping and production of slabs and unsmoked sheets were done by Indonesian smallholders, but only rarely did Indonesian smallholders have smokehouses. The rubber then passed through a marketing system manned and financed by Chinese. Capital was largely concentrated in Chinese hands in the main rubber ports in Indonesia or in Singapore and in both cases the Chinese were usually operating remilling factories and/or smokehouses. Working capital was often provided by these industrialists in the form of an advance to the rubber traders who used the money to purchase daily necessities which they exchanged for rubber in the interior (usually at the Chinese-owned warong). At the same time, part of the capital used by the trader was also provided by Chinese wholesalers in such items as textiles, salt, agricultural implements and so on. The farmers benefited by obtaining not only foodstuffs on credit, but also medicines in times of sickness and loans for the education of their children.[12]

In the post-war period the ethnic division of labour and the organisational pattern established in the colonial period has remained substantially unchanged, except that a further division of labour between alien and WNI Chinese has emerged; but the industry has operated against a background of growing resentment against the Chinese, reflected partly in the burgeoning of Indonesian economic nationalism. The antipathy toward the Chinese was generally of local origin, but at times central government measures also discriminated against the Chinese in favour of the pribumi. Even so, in spite of minor differences which we will be examining, the ethnic division of labour in 1969 was still more or less the same as in the pre-independence period.

Internal marketing structure

The marketing organisation in the Palembang residency of South Sumatra in the colonial period was a six-tiered structure, reaching from the *talang* (temporary settlement) at the base to the exporter in the city of Palembang at the apex. In regional terminology traders in the interior were and still are designated according to the level at which they operate: *talang, dusun, pucuk* (Diagram 1).

Diagram 1

Some of the links at the various levels in the marketing channel for slabs in South Sumatra*

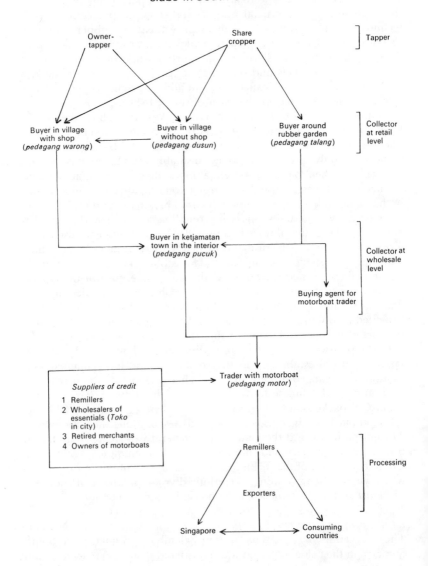

*This schematic presentation applies only to rubber entering the city of Palembang by river, mainly along the Musi River system. For Panjang remillers, transport by rail is the norm.

Under the shifting cultivation system, the village (*dusun*) can be permanent or can shift, as the farmer clears new areas of forest. In South Sumatra the village is usually a permanent settlement. As the land around the village was used and abandoned in the cultivation cycle, the farmers tended to move further and further away from the village in search of new land to clear for one or two rice crops, before moving on again. To avoid walking long distances, a temporary settlement (*talang*) was established where the farmer and his family lived during peak working periods in the rice cycle. Rubber trees were often planted in the rice fields around the talang,[13] so that today a farmer may have rubber trees as far away from the dusun as 30 kilometres. When tapping the rubber at such distances from his home, the farmer continued the talang pattern of rice cultivation and often lived for weeks in the temporary settlement, a system still practised today.

Talang were scattered throughout South Sumatra and those who worked as share tappers usually sold their rubber to traders (*pedagang*) who, with their bullock carts, travelled around from talang to talang. These *pedagang talang* sold their slabs to the traders in the villages, the *pedagang dusun*, who also bought directly from owner-tappers. The pedagang talang was usually pribumi, whereas the pedagang dusun generally Chinese, a warong owner in addition to trading in rubber.[14]

Trading at the next stage took place in the capital of the sub-district (*kecamatan*). The dusun trader brought the slabs by river or road to the kecamatan town, usually situated along a river, and sold them either to a *pedagang pucuk* (retail trader) or to a trader who had come up-river from Palembang in his motor driven houseboat (*pedagang motor*). Throughout the 1950s both the pedagang pucuk and pedagang motor were ethnic Chinese, whereas after 1959 small numbers of Palembang pribumi entered this part of the business.[15]

The slabs were then taken by the pedagang motor to Palembang and sold to remillers. After processing them into blankets, the remiller either exported directly or sold to an exporter. In both these sectors of the industry, the Chinese have tended to dominate. Although some indigenous Indonesians were to be found in the exporting business, as well as in the rural end of the industry, they rarely entered the remilling sector which remained predominantly Chinese.

The village inhabitants of South Sumatra required a considerable amount of imported goods, most of which came into the area through Palembang. As in most other parts of Indonesia, trade both in domestic and imported goods was largely controlled by Chinese: the village warong was often run by Chinese with Indonesian assistants, while the actual movement of goods was in the hands of Chinese traders. In the city, importers included both the Dutch (especially the Borsumij company, one of the 'Big Ten' trading firms in colonial times) and Chinese;

both of these groups financed trading in the interior either directly through loans to itinerant traders, or indirectly by providing credit to warong owners through the traders.

Just as the smallholder cultivation cycle was adapted to rubber, so too were traders' operations. The trader in the city, with little capital of his own, sought to establish a close relationship with the remiller. Once a bond of mutual trust (*kepercayaan*) was established, the remiller would advance credit to the trader for purchase of a stock of daily essentials such as salt, fish, kerosene, textiles and so on for sale to the warong owners. These goods were brought from city stores (*toko*) run predominantly by Chinese in Palembang.[16] Toko owners also advanced credit to traders, enabling them to expand their scale of operations. Thus many of the traders, generally Chinese until the 1960s, became customers (*langganan*) of the remillers and the system operated to the advantage of both parties.

Communication with the interior was mainly along the river Musi and its tributaries, road transport being rarely used, and the railway not being well patronised either.[17] The major form of transportation, one well-suited to the trade, was the large motorised houseboat with storage space both for essential commodities needed by the peasants and also for rubber brought in from the interior.

The trader tended to establish links between himself and certain pedagang pucuk along the route similar to the relationship between remiller and trader. A town might have several warong, but each travelling trader selected one or two of these as his own agents. The bond between the two was cemented by ties of credit patterned by the nature of the trade itself. The houseboat trader would leave goods on credit with the warong owner on his way up the river and on his way back the warong owner would settle his account, partly in the form of rubber. Any excess would be paid in cash.

A similar relationship was forged between the pedagang pucuk and the lower level traders at the warong level. Likewise the smallholder might also depend on the warong owner for the use of a mangle. In all cases, transactions involved a calculation of the relevant prices of the daily necessities and the rubber. Sometimes the smallholder would take both cash and goods, at other times he might go into debt.

The whole network was built upon mutual trust. This is far from saying that each party to every transaction entered the arena on an equal footing, for as a general rule the smallholder was at a disadvantage in his relations with the buyer. At all levels, the buyer was the dominant partner. And while there was trust there was also suspicion. Slabs when first made are dirty and contain a certain amount of water. Sale is by weight with allowance for dirt and water. The peasant tended to distrust the weights used by the buyer and he also questioned the calculation of

Table 1
Palembang: Smallholder Rubber Exports by Quality, 1930–41
('000 tonnes, dry rubber content) [a]

	Blankets	*Sheets*	*Slabs*	*Total* [b]
1930	3.1		6.6	10.4
1931	2.6		7.5	10.5
1932	1.4		3.9	5.2
1933	—		13.8	14.2
1934	1.4		29.9	32.7
1935	4.7	0.5	15.1	21.1
1936	9.4	1.6	10.4	21.4
1937	11.8	9.8	13.7	35.7
1938	17.1	5.8	1.1	24.0
1939	21.7	9.5	1.1	32.5
1940	35.8	16.5	5.3	57.8
1941	46.8	31.6	7.0	85.4

a From 1934, all figures are given in dry rubber content. Before that year, exports of slabs (and scraps and earth rubber) were given in terms of wet rubber with two totals, one of which was in terms of dry rubber content (d.r.c.). A conversion percentage was given for the years 1930–34 inclusive, i.e., 74 per cent, 71.9 per cent and 69.5 per cent respectively. Using those percentages, we converted slab exports into d.r.c. figures. For 1932 this calculation gives a total for blankets/sheets plus slabs in excess of the total d.r.c. amount. Fortunately the discrepancy is not large.

b The difference between total exports and the sum of the three qualities listed is accounted for by scraps and earth rubber.

Source: Mededeelingen van het Centraal Kantoor voor de Statistik, *De Landbouwexport-gewassen van Nederlandsch-Indie, 1930–1940.* The figures for 1941 were taken from an internal report of the Smallholder Rubber Office in Jakarta.

water content. To offset the 'faulty' scales, the peasant took to putting stones, iron bars and the like into the centre of the slab. There was little he could do about the water content.

As sheet production became more common in the late 1930s, those remillers who also dealt in sheets set up depots in the interior. But this did not drive the traders out of business: they continued to operate as multi-purpose functionaries earning a living as sellers of essential goods, buyers of rubber, providers of credit, transport operators and so on.

The Chinese in Palembang

Rubber came to the Palembang area later than to most other rubber producing regions, although the seeds were brought in by the same types of person. At the end of the 1920s the Palembang residency ranked sixth among the major producing areas and was exporting the lowest quality of rubber (slabs), with Singapore as the sole destination. Five remilling factories had already been set up in Palembang by 1928, but their total export was 2 296 tonnes out of a total of 17 917 tonnes of blankets for the Netherlands Indies. The changes brought about in the industry in the next decade were remarkable.[18] By 1940 Palembang was at the top of the list of exporters of smallholder rubber, with a total of 58 000 tonnes (Table 1).[19] Quality improvements were also noticeable in the 1930s, beginning with remilled products in the early part of the decade, followed by sheets in the closing years. While Indonesian smallholders were responsible for the increase in acreage under rubber which underlay the increase in production it was the Chinese who stimulated quality upgrading.

Instrumental in the establishment of remilling factories in Palembang were the two largest Chinese firms, Kian Gwan and Hok Tong.[20] Kian Gwan was a Java-based company which had its origins in the sugar industry. Early in the 1930s the head of the company decided to invest in rubber and in 1933 rented a Dutch-built remilling factory in Palembang.[21] Hok Tong, based in Singapore, moved into the remilling business in Palembang at about the same time. These two played a major role in pioneering the transformation of rubber exports from slabs to blankets and by 1936 almost half of Palembang's rubber exports were blankets. It was at this stage that Kian Gwan decided to switch to sheet production and to set up collecting agencies in the interior. Since hand mangles were essential to the production of smallholder sheet rubber, the company also encouraged their import and distribution, selling them mainly to the warong owners. Others, probably including Hok Tong, must have made a similar move because in 1941 a total of 31 000 tonnes of sheet rubber (36 per cent of exports) went out from Palembang.

Kian Gwan was also moving to break the dominance of Singapore as the major importer of Indonesian smallholder rubber at that time. When the Indonesian industry began the transition to blanket rubber, Singapore kept its grip on the trade by serving as an entrepot centre. Although the volume of sheet rubber exports increased, Singapore purchasers still attempted to continue to act as intermediaries between Indonesia and the consuming countries.[22] As Kian Gwan increased its production of blankets (and later of sheets), it also began to export direct to the United States, under special concessions from the Dutch shipping line KPM.

Summarising the colonial experience in the smallholder rubber industry in the Palembang residency, we find that the indigenous population quickly took up the cultivation of rubber, producing slabs at first and unsmoked sheets later. Trade in slabs between the village and the port of Palembang came under the control of the Chinese, those at the end of the marketing chain exporting the slabs for processing in Singapore. Close ties between the traders at the various levels in the marketing structure developed as the industry expanded, and the smallholder in the village became involved in this closely-knit network based on credit and mutual trust. These ties remained as a small group of Chinese in the city of Palembang set up remilling factories in competition with Chinese remillers in Singapore or financed by them. The next stage came in the mid-1930s with the gradual transition from slab production at the village level to the production of sheet rubber, using hand mangles imported into the region by the five remilling companies. Remillers at the end of the marketing chain purchased both slabs and sheets, remilling the one and smoking the other.

The ethnic division of labour was thus clear-cut at the end of the colonial period. The pribumi were, for the most part, confined to the production of slabs or unsmoked sheets at the village level, the latter in co-operation with a Chinese warong owner who had purchased a set of hand mangles.[23] The relationship between the trader and smallholder contained elements of both trust and suspicion, but in the colonial setting the latter element did not become a source of political tension. More important was the antagonism engendered by the Rubber Restriction Scheme (1934) for restricting production. We have not emphasised this issue because our main concern has been to bring out the ethnic character of the pyramidal structure of the industry, with tens of thousands of pribumi smallholders forming the base of the pyramid and the five Chinese remillers–smoke-house owners at the apex, towards which the numerous Chinese traders, at various levels from the village to the city, channelled the rubber for processing. It was this structure and the relations between the pribumi and the Chinese which became the focus of attack by economic nationalists in the independence period.

THE ECONOMICS OF THE INDUSTRY IN THE POST-WAR PERIOD

When the Dutch withdrew from Indonesia in December 1949, the five pre-war remilling factories in Palembang, which had been badly damaged during the early fighting, had already been re-established. Four years later the old group faced strong competition for slabs both internally and externally. Rubber was being exported from both Palembang and Panjang, a South Sumatran town on the southern tip of the island. In Palembang itself, seven new remilling factories had been set up, mostly by Chinese, and in Panjang also the Chinese had entered the remilling industry. The expansion of the number of factories in the region so soon after the end of the revolution set the pattern for the future. Whereas the colonial government had adopted a policy of strict control over remilling enterprises, the Indonesian government was more flexible, for reasons that were largely political rather than economic in origin.

A more serious threat to the position of both the old established remillers and the newcomers came from Singapore-based remilling interests. A large proportion of the slabs produced in South Sumatra were still being exported to Singapore for remilling. The expanded remilling capacity owned by Chinese domiciled in Indonesia was likely to remain under-utilised in the face of competition for raw materials from Singapore Chinese. Recovery and expansion of the South Sumatran remilling industry was not paralleled by a revival of sheet production and export. The trend towards sheet exports and away from blankets, pioneered by the pre-war remilling group, was reversed in the independence period and sheet exports have been negligible since 1950.

In this section we focus attention on certain aspects of the economics of the industry. Our first concern is with the steps taken to eliminate the Singapore competition in the market for slabs and with the changes in the internal market structure resulting from the withdrawal of a major competitor. In particular, it is necessary to discuss the extent to which the local remillers presented what was often regarded as a united front in their dealings with the producers in the village, operating in effect as a monopsonistic group.

Our second theme centres on the effects of the remilling industry on the quality of rubber produced and on farmers' income from rubber. In view of the criticisms made by economic nationalists of the role of remillers and traders, mainly Chinese, in their relations with the farmers, an analysis of the market structure and its alleged effects on quality and farmers' income is illuminating. To some extent there is an overlap between the points raised in this and in the subsequent section. But an understanding of the position of the economic nationalists is facilitated by filling in the background of the economics of the industry. The dilemma of the Chinese and of the economic nationalists becomes evident in the succeeding discussion: both were victims of an environment over which they had little control.

South Sumatran remillers and Singapore
In the post-independence period Palembang rubber exports are no longer synonymous with South Sumatran exports. Exports from the city of Panjang in Lampung residency have accounted for some 20 per cent to 30 per cent of South Sumatra's exports since 1950, first in the form of slabs, and later as blankets. Our major interest is in the Palembang residency, but when necessary reference will be made to developments in Lampung.

Table 2
South Sumatran Smallholder Rubber Exports
by Port of Origin and Quality, 1950–57 ('000 tonnes)

	Palembang		Panjang		Total	
	Slabs	Blankets	Slabs	Blankets	Slabs	Blankets
1950	n.a.	n.a.	n.a.	n.a.	67.2	58.5
1951	n.a.	n.a.	n.a.	n.a.	95.4	49.5
1952	30.6	43.6	37.7	0.3	75.0	46.5
1953	44.4	41.8	17.3	—	62.6	42.2
1954	44.4	40.3	30.6	2.2	76.4	43.5
1955	nil	82.4	7.2	14.1	7.2	96.5
1956	nil	75.3	9.2	19.8	9.2	84.5
1957	nil	84.1	4.5	24.5	4.5	108.7

Source: Smallholder Rubber Office (DKR).

NOTE: We have accepted the convention that production and exports of smallholder rubber are the same in all the tables in this paper. This convention is probably reliable for annual data but not for monthly data.

At the apex of the pyramid we find that in 1950 the remilling industry in Palembang was being hindered in its expansionary drive by severe competition from rival remillers in Singapore. The remilling factories in Palembang had been destroyed in the early days of the struggle for independence. But the Dutch government, which controlled the area during most of the revolutionary period, was very active in encouraging the reconstruction of the industry. Several of the remillers also attempted to revive the trade in unsmoked sheets by building smokehouses in addition to their remilling factory, but their efforts in this direction failed.[24] The changing situation in the years 1950–57 can be seen from the table of rubber exports, classified according to quality (Table 2), which shows the position of the Palembang remillers vis-à-vis their rivals in Panjang and Singapore, the sole destination of South Sumatra's slabs. In 1952 Panjang's remilling industry was negligible compared to that of Palembang, while exports of slabs from both ports exceeded the blanket exports of Palembang remillers. By 1954 although the number of remilling factories in Palembang had risen to thirteen, the Palembang remillers controlled a smaller percentage of the slab market than they had done two years previously, although for South Sumatra as a whole slab exports as a percentage of total exports remained unchanged.

Singapore industrialists were apparently providing severe competition for the remillers in Palembang (and in Panjang also, it seems).

For the most part this meant a struggle of Chinese versus Chinese, in which the Singapore group seemed to be the stronger. During the 1930s Singapore businessmen had been hard hit by the growth of the Indonesian rubber processing industry, first by the expansion of remilling capacity, secondly by the transition to sheet production and finally by the tendency for direct export to consumer countries. The effects of the rise of a domestic remilling industry were particularly disastrous for the Singapore processors, except for those who were astute enough to move their operations to the region, either by renting a factory or establishing their own. Total purchases of slabs by the remilling industry in the British colony were a mere 8 000 tonnes in 1940 compared with 131 000 tonnes in 1934. Slab exports from Palembang fell from 15 091 tonnes in 1935 to 5 322 tonnes in 1940, by which time Palembang was the major source of slabs for Singapore. Remilling factories in both cities were destroyed during the upheavals of the 1940s, but the Singapore factories were rebuilt at least as rapidly as those in Palembang. And in Palembang, the Singapore factories were regaining the ground they lost as slab buyers after 1934.

Indonesians in business and government frequently alleged that the competition between the remillers in Palembang and Singapore was bogus and that the Palembang remilling industry was controlled financially from Singapore. As far as we can judge from the evidence of the 1963 takeover of what were called 'ex-Malaysia' remilling factories, five of the thirteen remilling factories in Palembang in 1955 were owned by alien Chinese based in Singapore or Malaya. Of the rest, four were owned by WNI Chinese and four were owned by pribumi. In 1955, when the export of slabs was prohibited, the five 'ex-Malaysia' firms controlled 61 per cent of blanket exports, the Chinese-Indonesian firms accounted for 37 per cent and the pribumi group a mere 3 per cent.

The dominant position of the alien group is not evidence in itself that control of these companies came from outside. At least one of the five 'ex-Malaysia' firms became independent of its parent company in the 1950s; but it is not possible at this stage to gauge the exact nature of the new relationship to meet the charge that in this one instance, at least, Singapore finance remained a powerful factor. For the rest, we have no data at all to assess the real importance of Singapore finance in Palembang remilling between 1954 and 1965.

In spite of the expansion of remilling capacity in Palembang, Singapore remillers were gaining ground by 1954. Local remilling capacity in that year was sufficient to remill all of the slabs in the residency, if we include the factories in Lampung. In fact, there was a tendency towards over-capacity. In self-defence, the Palembang remillers organised themselves into the *Persatuan Pengusaha Penggiling Para Palembang* and pressed the Nationalist Party government of Ali Sastroamidjojo to prohibit the export of slabs in order to enable them to operate at higher capacity. This in itself would seem to indicate that the interests of the alien Chinese remillers were not identical with those of Singapore.

Elimination of Singapore as a market for Palembang slabs was favoured by the regional Nationalist Party (PNI) branch which had strong roots in the area. The reasons for the PNI attitude stemmed partly from an ideological bias against the middleman role of Singapore, but just as importantly from a need for financial support from the remillers. Another pressure group within the bureaucratic hierarchy was also anxious to ban slab exports as a step towards increasing production of sheet rubber, with the avowed aim of ensuring a 'better deal' for the farmer. The proponents of this view were centred in the Smallholder Rubber Office (*Djawatan Karet Rakjat* or DKR).

In the debate on the move to prohibit slab exports, the DKR group expressed the view that elimination of the Singapore buyers would merely improve the position of the local remillers and not raise the income of the smallholders in the villages. The most extreme form of this criticism was couched in terms of the increase of the 'monopsony' power of the remillers, arguing that the remillers acted together and not as separate units in purchasing slabs. Suggestions were made that the Department of Trade could redress any unfavourable consequences for the producers in the village by fixing a minimum price for slabs. It was also recommended that a special organisation be set up to supervise both the minimum price and the market structure in general.

Palembang remillers and N.V.Karet

When the export of slabs was prohibited in September 1954, a Price Committee was set up in the Department of Trade in Palembang with instructions to fix the minimum price of slabs of 100 per cent dry rubber content (d.r.c.). Since most slabs tend to vary between 40–60 per cent d.r.c. when brought in by traders, the government established the Rubber Corporation (N.V.Karet),[25] one of whose functions would be to arbitrate on the gradings.

The government held 51 per cent of the company's shares (transferred to the regional government in 1957); the rest were to be held by private individuals who were, for the most part, remillers. The main function of the company at the outset was to act as an intermediary between the remillers and the traders. Inspectors were to make spot checks on the grading of rubber and were to be called in whenever there were disputes. Grading was crucial because the minimum price was set for 100 per cent d.r.c. For its service N.V.Karet was to receive a 2 per cent commission without handling the rubber at any stage.

N.V.Karet was not, in the long run, to be restricted to overseeing the minimum price. On the contrary, article 2 of the company's statute indicates that the government saw its functions as open-ended. It was to

> co-operate with the government in trying to stabilise the produc-
> tion and prices of smallholder rubber, taking care that the small-
> holder should receive a reasonable price for his rubber. Attention
> was also to be directed toward the interests of the government,
> owners of the remilling factories and smokehouses, rubber traders
> and labourers.

As if the reconciliation of these conflicting interests were not enough,
the company was also directed to 'try in the field of production, taken
in its widest sense, to include the processing of the rubber and the buying
and selling of the rubber, (in short) to do everything related to rubber,
both directly and indirectly'.

Implicit in the articles of the new company was a desire to reorganise
the rubber industry in the region and, in doing so, to weaken the position
of the Chinese remillers vis-à-vis both the traders and the peasants in
the village. Devoting itself to action on the minimum price set in the
city was only a first step towards an all-pervasive role as mediator and
regulator within the industry. Operating exclusively in the city was no
guarantee of protection to the farmers at the village level. To be effective
in ensuring that a minimum price was being maintained in the interior,
N.V.Karet was eventually to set up branches in the interior to compete
with traders at village level, according to one key official in the Ministry
of Economic Affairs.[26] Besides trading rubber, the N.V.Karet depots
would also handle rice, salt, kerosene, textiles and other daily necessities
required by the peasant. The government recognised that the traders
performed many functions at that time and at least one official argued
that the peasants were paying too high a price for their essential goods,
even taking into account the cost of transportation. But to see a problem
is one thing, to solve it another. At no stage did the government even
make available the amount of capital, far in excess of the allocated
Rp. 50 million,[27] which would have been required to operate in competition with the existing traders.

Had N.V.Karet operated as envisaged by its statutes as a trader in
the interior, an important competitive element would have been injected into the industry at least in those villages where it acted as buyer.
In reality it was never in a position to do so and never went beyond an
attempt at policing the price set by the Department of Trade, but even
here it was ineffectual.

N.V.Karet was also required to assist the government at a later stage
to encourage the peasants to plant or replant rubber with high yielding
strains. Such assistance was to be mainly in the form of finance, the
extension work to be done by the Smallholder Rubber Office. But a rift

soon developed between that body and N.V.Karet, making co-operation impossible.[28] For the immediate future, the company was instructed to promote the production of sheet rubber.

N.V.Karet was supposed to act as an intermediary between the trader and the remiller, especially in cases where there was disagreement over the dry rubber content of the slabs. But since most of the traders were clients (*langganan*) of the remillers, the whole notion of an arbiter in case of disputes was ludicrous. At this level, N.V.Karet offered no challenge or threat to the position of the remiller. Expansion to the interior and direct purchase from the peasants might have provided some competition to increase the price paid to the peasant, but only if N.V.Karet had entered the field on a large scale, with the aim of reducing intermediate costs; yet this it never did. In fact, the original aims of N.V.Karet were subverted because of its political relationship with the elite in Palembang, an issue discussed more fully in the section on economic nationalism.

Officials of the Smallholder Rubber Office were strong advocates of sheet production and saw in the remillers a barrier to achieving this goal. But our study of the trends in the 1930s shows that it was the remillers themselves who pioneered the transition to sheets. It is therefore necessary to consider the problem of rubber qualities and compare the post-war and colonial environments within which the Chinese traders and remillers operated. *A priori*, there seems no reason why the Chinese should not have continued where they left off in 1940, completing the transformation of their own function from that of processing slabs to that of producing smoked sheets out of the unsmoked sheets made by the farmers in the interior. The improvement in qualities before the war was a result of decisions in the private sector with little encouragement by the government.[29] We will see in due course why a similar process did not occur after 1950.

The remillers and rubber qualities
Controversies about rubber quality have recurred constantly in rubber politics of South Sumatra since 1950. N.V.Karet was set up partly to improve the quality of South Sumatran rubber by encouraging sheet production by Indonesian growers. The dispute evolved into a two-sided struggle as far as the Smallholder Rubber Office (DKR) was concerned which, in its view, represented the interests of the producer in the village, in contrast to the remillers. At issue was the question of which product *should* be produced by the farmer. The DKR argued that an increase in the production of sheet rubber would benefit both the farmer and the state, as sheet rubber brings a higher price on the world market than blankets. The nation's People's Consultative Assembly (MPRS) supported the advocates of sheet rubber when it ratified the blueprint

for the Eight Year Plan in 1960. A target was fixed for the relative proportions of the two categories so that by 1968 sheet production would account for 70 per cent of the total output. Production of sheet rubber in South Sumatra was negligible in 1960. Annual targets were set for the region in the expectation that by 1968 sheet production would total 105 000 tonnes, compared with 45 000 tonnes of blankets. But to some extent, the advocates of sheet rubber in South Sumatra, and later in the MPRS, were understating the value of blanket rubber and at the same time misrepresenting the real situation with regard to rubber qualities throughout the whole of Indonesia. (See Tables 3 and 4.)

In 1964 the fact that high-grade blankets, i.e. blankets C and above, were equivalent to high-grade ribbed smoked sheets, i.e. RSS III and above, was accepted by the government. In the South Sumatran region the recognition that production of such blankets would represent an improvement in quality meant that the remillers were not seen as playing a pariah role, but were regarded as respectable and useful once again. Even so, it is of interest to pose the question why only South Sumatra— of all the regions in Indonesia which produced smallholder rubber— happened to concentrate on blankets and not sheets. The role of the Chinese as remillers was unique to South Sumatra, although they played a dominant role in the marketing and processing of rubber everywhere. The remillers claimed that in South Sumatra the farmer was lazy, could not wait for his money and preferred to produce slabs. If this were true, it would put the farmer in the position of decision-maker in determining qualities; and yet the same remillers pointed with pride to the fact that in the pre-war period it was they who had pioneered the switch from slabs to unsmoked sheets in the village.

At the time of the 1955 prohibition of slab exports from Palembang and Panjang, the remillers had already re-established themselves. And the Minister for Trade in the first cabinet of Ali Sastroamidjojo encouraged the remillers in the region to expand their capacity, regardless of their licensed output. So, when the Smallholder Rubber Office (DKR) advocated strict adherence to N.V.Karet's policy of encouraging sheet production, the bulk of South Sumatran production was already in the form of blankets. The DKR argued that it was in the interests of the remillers to produce low-grade blankets and export them to Singapore for up-grading for sale on the world market. Insofar as blankets dominated until the end of the 1950s, South Sumatran rubber qualities were, in fact, higher than in other provinces, where low-grade sheets were of major importance. The trend towards lower grades began earlier in other regions than South Sumatra, if we can trust the statistics. And in the other regions the Chinese were also blamed for their role in this trend, with emphasis being put on their ability to 'manipulate' their transactions (the euphemism normally applied to illegal practices in

Table 3
Indonesia : Exports of Sheet and Remilled Rubber
in Selected Years (percentages)*

	1952	1956	1960	1964
SHEETS:	40.7	37.6	33.3	42.5
of which				
RSS II	0.9	0.1	—	—
RSS III	10.3	1.9	2.0	3.9
RSS IV	11.8	10.0	6.6	11.0
RSS V and below	17.6	25.3	24.7	27.6
BLANKETS:	14.6	32.0	34.4	38.0
of which				
BLANKET C	9.9	17.9	18.4	7.4
D and under	4.3	14.1	16.0	30.6
FLAT BARK	4.4	8.0	7.5	12.7

Source : Central Bureau of Statistics, *Ekspor Karet.* 1952, 1956, 1960 and 1964.

NOTE: Table 3 shows the breakdown of sheet and remilled rubber exports for specified years between 1952 and 1964. Both categories are further subdivided and, in the case of the remilled products, flat bark crepe is listed as a category distinct from blankets. By 1964 remilled rubber accounted for 50.7 per cent of rubber exports compared with 42.5 per cent for sheets; in 1956 the figures were 40 per cent and 37.6 per cent.

Critics of slab production in Palembang continually argued that sheet rubber brought a higher price on the world market than the remilled product. More specifically, they noted that prices quoted for RSS III were invariably higher than for Blanket C, the equivalent grade; but little notice was taken of the fact that the price differential fluctuated considerably during the 1950s and 1960s. In any case, in using the RSS III—Blanket C price differential, the advocates of sheet production were to some extent begging the question. The breakdown of sheet and remilled rubber into sub-categories, as shown in this table, indicates that from as early as 1956 RSS IV and lower grades dominated the former group, whereas Blanket C accounted for almost 50 per cent of blanket production to the early 1960s. Until 1960 therefore, the proportion of Blanket C to total output was greater than that of RSS III. Those who favoured a shift to sheet rubber failed to point out that this would only be an improvement if higher grade sheets were produced. Government recognition of the similarity between the higher grades of both sheet rubber and blankets was finally acknowledged when a new classification for smallholders' rubber was introduced in 1964; Blanket C and above were included in the higher grade along with RSS I to IV. By that time, however, a trend towards lower qualities in the remilled rubber was under way.

* Blankets and flat bark are both products of the remilling process, the latter being the lowest grade produced in this way. Theoretically, flat bark production should be a constant 5 per cent of blanket production because it is a by-product. But this has not been the case, indicating a great falsification of export documents.

Indonesia) in relation to Singapore, mainly by falsifying export documents.

Table 4
Palembang—Panjang:
Qualities of Remilled Rubber Exports in Selected Years (tonnes and percentages)

	1952*	1956	1960	1964	1968
A. PALEMBANG					
BLANKET C	32 851 (75)	61 084 (81)	59 851 (78)	20 364 (31)	4 990 (5)
D	10 669 (25)	14 169 (19)	16 398 (22)	43 344 (67)	101 149 (95)
E	—	—	127 (—)	—	—
FLAT BARK	74 (—)	63 (—)	132 (—)	1 250 (2)	845 (—)
	43 594 (100)	75 316 (100)	76 508 (100)	64 958 (100)	106 984 (100)
B. PANJANG					
BLANKET C	310 (93)	3 015 (15)	3 349 (11)	2 329 (5)	663 (2)
D	18 (5)	16 784 (84)	25 903 (81)	20 747 (43)	21 472 (50)
E	—	10 (—)	2 717 (8)	14 968 (31)	64 (—)
FLAT BARK	3 (—)	33 (—)	96 (—)	9 906 (21)	20 697 (48)
	331 (100)	19 842 (100)	32 065 (100)	47 950 (100)	42 896 (100)

Source: Central Bureau of Statistics.

NOTE: This table reveals that Blanket C was the most important product exported from Palembang between 1952 and 1960, but that by 1964 Blanket D exports predominated. The Panjang figures show the peculiar prominence of flat bark after 1963, which should in principle have been only 5 per cent of the total volume. This is presumably a further indication of under-invoicing, which supports the proposition that the alleged trend towards lower qualities was greatly exaggerated by the statistics. (The statistics of flat bark exports from Panjang fluctuated wildly after 1964.) It was widely acknowledged in the trade that Panjang remillers paid higher prices for slabs than those in Palembang: they were probably able to do this because they enjoyed higher profit margins than their Palembang rivals by understating the quality of their exports to a greater degree.

* Exports of slabs from both Palembang and Panjang were high in 1952

The apparent decline in quality of remilled rubber gave point to allegations that the exporters were largely responsible. For Chinese were involved in the trade (and 'manipulation') at both ends. The DKR therefore argued that export qualities could be improved if only the grip of the Chinese could be broken—it would then be possible to export directly to the consuming countries. Singapore would be eliminated as an entrepôt and Indonesian foreign exchange earnings would be increased. No-one mentioned the fact that such a transformation had been under way in the 1930s, along with a tendency to sever the tie with Singapore, or that South Sumatran Chinese remillers had been in the forefront of that transition, as they divided their activities between remilling and the smoking of sheet rubber. If a policy of encouraging sheet production were to have been adopted in the 1950s, it would have meant a gradual reduction in the role of the Chinese as remillers, but they could still have remained in the industry by switching their activities to sheet rubber. And a glance at the functions of N.V. Karet is sufficient to indicate that it was indeed the Chinese remillers who were expected to finance the production of sheets.

The advocates of sheet production were caught in a cleft stick, insofar as they were also anti-Chinese. Chinese capital was the foundation of the rubber industry. To eliminate the Chinese altogether would require almost complete government finance. Such finance was never made available to those opposing the position of the Chinese.

It is pertinent at this point to consider why the trend of the 1930s towards better qualities was not resumed after the war. Since the remillers themselves had pioneered the earlier transition to sheet rubber, why was it necessary to establish a semi-governmental body to oblige them to do so in the 1950s? Opponents of the remillers argued that it was the remillers' substantial investment which led them to insist that the farmer produce slabs. For some reason, it would appear that it was more profitable for the remillers, both Chinese and pribumi, to take slabs and export blankets of a quality which was tending to decline by the early 1960s. In part, lack of sufficient raw materials and equipment for the remilling factories explains the deterioration in quality over the years, but it must be admitted that there were ways of getting such material if it had been profitable to do so.[30]

In the face of a steady decline in the economic rationality of government policies, businessmen did what they could to keep the rubber moving—and to make a profit, of course. Rupiah earnings became less important than earnings in foreign exchange as the black market value of the rupiah fell. Under-invoicing of rubber was one of numerous ways of earning foreign currency overseas, a practice which partly 'explains' the decline in qualities mentioned above. Similarly, the existence of the price disparity was an outward sign of what the businessmen were obliged to do in order to continue operating.[31] Disparity is defined as the excess of the rupiah costs of export products to exporters over the rupiah receipts they can obtain by converting their foreign exchange receipts at *legally* permitted rates. The existence of such a disparity seemed to imply that exporters could only sell at a loss. But the rupiah price paid by exporters on the local market was presumably. a price which they were prepared to pay because they could make a profit from exports. The explanation of the apparent paradox is of course that some exporters, if not all, found illegal ways of making the operation profitable.

Businessmen in general became involved in a wide variety of illegal practices, while corruption became rife under a system which would have been unworkable had the rules been adhered to. In the process, those Chinese who were engaged in the rubber industry were an obvious target for both the sincere and less sincere economic nationalists. And the link between the Chinese and remillers and Singapore was seen as having sinister overtones of economic domination and manipulation.

Conflict between N.V.Karet and the DKR was apparently inevitable and insoluble. The former had been set up to prevent the emergence of what some termed a 'single buyer' policy of the remillers. The DKR and its supporters were soon to point out that in this respect N.V.Karet had failed. Instead, they alleged, it had become a 'tool of the remillers', a monopsony institution in the purchase of slabs.[32] And from its position as 'single buyer' the Corporation, together with its remilling allies, prevented the farmers from producing sheets. In reality, the marketing structure was oligopsonistic rather than monopsonistic. Agents of the remillers had, as we have seen, their own customers at the level of the retail shop (pedagang pucuk). There was probably an unwritten agreement dividing up the market at this level in the interior. At the same time, there seems to have been no attempt by the larger companies to drive out the smaller ones. Having received their licences from the government and entered the market for slabs, those already in the industry adopted a policy of 'live and let live'. It is not the philosophy of the Chinese to destroy each other in business. On the contrary, a closer examination of the various groupings which the ethnic minority had established reveals that the Chinese were more inclined to expand their businesses through informal associations (*kongsi*). These kongsi are even established for the purpose of assisting business associates who are in temporary financial difficulties. This is neither a case of pure competition nor of monopsony. In the remilling industry, entry remained restricted after 1954 for political and not economic reasons. Until 1959 the thirteen remillers in Palembang and their rivals in Panjang operated in an environment where, as a group, they were protected by the political strength of the PNI. It was only after the re-adoption of the 1945 con-

Table 5
Breakdown of Palembang Remilling Production
by Ethnic Ownership of Factories, 1954–68 (Percentages)

	Pribumi	WNI Chinese	Alien Chinese	Total Output (in '000 tonnes)
1954	5 (2)	28 (5)	67 (5)	40.5
1955	3 (2)	37 (5)	61 (5)	82.2
1956	5 (2)	35 (5)	60 (5)	75.8
1957	5 (3)	34 (5)	61 (5)	85.9
1958	5 (3)	32 (5)	63 (5)	94.1
1959	6 (3)	33 (5)	61 (5)	94.1
1960	7 (3)	30 (5)	63 (5)	76.3
1961	11 (5)[1]	37 (5)	52 (4)[2]	71.4
1962	10 (5)	38 (8)	53 (5)	82.5
1963	10 (5)	39 (11)	50 (5)[3]	69.6
1964	12 (5)	49 (13)	40 (5)	68.3
1965	7 (5)	66 (17)	27 (5)	71.5
1966	8 (5)	66 (18)	26 (5)	78.0
1967	10 (5)	65 (19)	25 (5)	78.2
1968	11 (5)	71 (19)	19 (4)[4]	89.4

(Figures in parentheses refer to the number of factories in each group active during the year.)

NOTES:
1 In 1961 the WNI Chinese firm Kian Gwan was taken over by the government and became P.T.Radjawali. We have included this firm in the pribumi group from 1961.
2 One alien Chinese firm was non-active in 1961.
3 After the refusal to recognise the new state of Malaysia, these five firms were 'taken over' by the government. Their position is discussed in the section on economic nationalism pp. 178 ff.
4 One alien Chinese firm was non-active in 1968 (not the same one as in 1961).

Source: Information from remillers.

stitution and the drive towards a 'guided democracy' that the power of the PNI in the region began to weaken. The way was then open for the emergence of a group of newcomers, a trend described in more detail below.

In considering the extent of competition among the remillers in an oligopsonistic structure, it is possible to discern some variations from year to year in the percentage of the market controlled by each (Table 5). Only a detailed study of the operations of the buyers in the interior would reveal the reasons for the shifts in allegiance of the pedagang pucuk. Ties of credit and mutual confidence would tend to stabilise relationships. A period of considerable instability began in 1961, largely as a result of changes in the power structure in the region and at the centre. These changes will be analysed in the section on the Chinese, the rubber industry and the new order, below.

Political and economic instability were endemic throughout the period 1950–65, but were particularly severe after 1961. Given the overall economic malaise of these years, attempts to improve the rubber grades were futile,[33] especially where part of the apparent decline in quality was attributable merely to falsification of customs documents. The environment was not conducive to a continuation of the trend of the 1930s towards better qualities. But as the Chinese remillers who had pioneered the improvements in the industry in the colonial period adjusted their trading practices to cope with the drift towards economic chaos, they were severely attacked for instigating the trend toward lower grades and market manipulation. Whether under more normal conditions the Chinese would again foster upgrading was open to question. Economic stability remained elusive in the Sukarno period; it was not until Suharto's period that general economic conditions improved. By that time, a new process to replace remilling had been developed and the old problem took on a new guise.

Another issue which requires clarification here is the alleged effect of the single buyer system on the price of rubber and on farmers' incomes in South Sumatra.

Rubber prices and farmers' incomes
Underlying most attacks on remillers for the low qualities produced was the allegation that slab production meant both low prices and low income for the farmer—and that this situation was the fault of the remillers. Once again the ardent economic nationalist and the not-so-principled opponents of the Chinese trading community had a weapon at hand to use in their campaign to wrest the marketing and processing functions from the well-entrenched ethnic minority. In the literature available on this issue little is said about the changes that were taking place in the trading sector and the remilling industry. From a cursory glance through the material it seems that the attack was usually directed against the middleman role of the Chinese, from the early 1950s on. By the early 1960s the pribumi position in trade had improved and after 1963 the government had control over the bulk of the remilling capacity; an opportunity was thus available for the opponents of the ethnic minority to do something about it if they were serious in their charge.

To understand the nature of the complaint concerning the low incomes received by the farmer, it is necessary to elaborate a little on the method of slab production and trading at the village level. The low quality of rubber is reflected in low prices which therefore influence the smallholder's *money* income. Since the remillers required slabs rather than blankets or sheets, they were held responsible for the low income received by the farmer. There was some truth in this allegation, especially after the prohibition on slab exports in November 1954, as the remillers occupied a key position at the apex of the marketing structure with N.V.Karet as an intermediary. Had it been in the interests of the remillers to switch to sheet rubber, they could no doubt have persuaded the farmers to produce sheets. That they did not do so gave rise to the suspicion that it was not in their interest to do so, hence not in their interest to see the peasants' incomes raised by a shift away from slabs to sheets.

In the production of high quality blankets and sheets the most important factor is that the rubber should be free of impurities. But slabs produced by smallholders contain not only rubber and water, but also a lot of twigs, leaves, dirt and stones; yet the price is based upon the estimated dry rubber content of the slab and its actual weight.[34] Allowance can be made for the dry rubber content by estimating the water content, but it is the buyer who has discretion in making this assessment. The farmer is well aware of this and he may also suspect the buyer of tampering with the scales, so his practice of mixing dirt in the slabs is his way of retaliation—he hopes to gain on weight what he loses on the estimate of water content.[35] Each party to the transaction takes precautions to offset the underhand practices of the other. No matter who comes out best, there is no doubt that low quality slabs are the end result.

In the early 1920s regional administrators issued regulations limiting the thickness of a slab to 3 centimetres to minimise adulteration. The regulations were backed by legal sanctions and the record of court cases indicates that some attempt was made to enforce the law. In the early 1950s when slabs were still being exported the 'thickness' regulation was still in operation. In 1954, when slab exports were prohibited, it was again emphasised by the regional government that slabs in excess of 3 cm should not be accepted. N.V.Karet was supposed to ensure that this requirement was upheld, but with no personnel in the interior this proved impossible. Although the regulation was repeatedly 're-introduced' between 1954 and 1965, it was never enforced. In our own fieldwork in both 1963 and 1969 we saw slabs 10 cm thick. To offset their lower weight the better quality slabs should bring higher prices per kg or the farmer will have no incentive to produce them. The farmers say that no attempt is made by the buyer to make such a distinction between slabs, grading being based largely on the age of the slab when brought to the market (*mingguan*—weekly, *bulanan*—monthly) rather than on thickness. For his part, the remiller says he accepts low quality slabs because the peasants will not take the trouble to produce higher grades.

Internal prices of rubber are partly determined by world prices, but not entirely so, as our brief discussion of the price disparity phenomenon has indicated. In addition, if we concentrate our attention on the farmer's income, it is important to distinguish between real and money income. It is not enough to consider the price the farmer receives from the warong for his rubber: this covers only one aspect of the socio-economic relationship between the peasant and the warong owner. Attempts to assess trends in the farmer's real income are often confined to the price he receives for his rubber or, at the most, relate this price to the purchasing power of rubber in terms of rice. Inclusion of a terms of trade analysis confined to rice is not enough: trends in real income can only be obtained by taking into account the total economic relationship between the buyer and seller.

The stereotyped notion of the relationship between the farmer and the Chinese (sometimes also pribumi) warong owner tends to emphasise the exploitative nature of the contact. Studies on the trading sector in a variety of countries in recent years have pointed out that little data exist to prove the point, and that where studies have been undertaken *the profit margins of the traders do not seem to be excessive.*[36]

The questionable practices of the trading community have a long history in both European and Asian history and the 'evil' nature of the trading function has often been associated with the role of an ethnic minority. Clearly the study of the rubber industry and the role of the trade and processing sectors is further complicated by the ethnic division of labour. In Palembang the Chinese dominate the market structure and processing while the indigenous population is concentrated at the village level. Exploitation of the farmer is therefore depicted in terms of the ethnic division as well as in terms of economic function. It would be difficult enough to assess the degree of exploitation by collecting data on all transactions between the farmer and the warong owner over a long period of time; but when a political dispute centring on the exploitative role of the trader is also an element, it is understandable that little data have been readily available.[37] The rapid rate of inflation in Indonesia, the annual changes in exchange rate systems and so on would have required that data be collected over a considerable period of time in order to assess the real income of the farmers under constantly changing conditions.[38]

Ever since we began our research into the rubber industry in 1955, the political tensions in the Palembang area have made the collection of data difficult. Not only was the ethnic issue involved, bound up as it was with the increasing trend towards economic nationalism, but so also was the question of corruption in the wake of increasing inflationary pressures. The hidden taxes referred to above relate partly to the attempts made by civil and military personnel to hold their real incomes constant against rising prices and low salaries. Myrdal has complained that economists do not study the economics of corruption.[39] He might have added that some economists do not attempt to delve too deeply into the operations of the determination of market prices. The reasons should be obvious: such matters involve the livelihood of many people and are tainted not only with corrupt practices in times of economic decay, but also involve matters which are political dynamite.

The complex relationships between trends in quality, prices, farmers' incomes and the part played by the Chinese in the rubber industry provided the economic nationalists, sincere or otherwise, with a great deal of ammunition in the period 1950–65. But in spite of considerable pressure, the Chinese remained the controlling group in the remilling industry, although, for a variety of reasons, they tended to move out of the trade in the interior, particularly after the late 1950s. It is crucial to stress, however, that the composition of the group changed, even at the top, and that a dominant section of the industry came into the hands of newcomers after 1962.

Those who attacked the ethnic minority's control over the industry made little headway. Trade remained in private hands, although the pribumi element came increasingly to the fore toward the end of the Sukarno period. Behind the new pribumi traders, however, was the finance of the Chinese. As for the growth of co-operatives, little progress was made.

We have argued that the decline in quality was determined more by the overall economic situation than by any inherent preference within the industry for low grades.[40] Low grades did tend to give the farmer lower incomes and we have little doubt that in his relationship with the rubber buyer the farmer was in a weak bargaining position. The tendency for the opponents of the remillers and the trading structure as a whole was to advocate radical measures which would bring about the elimination of the role of the ethnic Chinese. If our analysis is valid, implementation of such a policy would have accomplished little without a simultaneous improvement in the economic environment. And from the point of view of the farmer, an increase in money income would have been no guarantee of a higher real income in the face of shortages of essentials and rapid price increases. The farmer's terms of trade could have been improved as much by lowering the price of rice as by increasing the price of rubber. On the other hand, the position of the farmer would probably improve automatically in a situation where the region was being opened up by the improvement of the transportation network, where economic conditions were conducive to the emergence of institutions which would tend to a division of labour in the provision of the many needs of the farmer, instead of perpetuating the concentration of a variety of roles in the hands of the warong owner.

ECONOMIC NATIONALISM AND CHALLENGES TO THE ECONOMIC POSITION OF THE CHINESE

Even after Indonesia had achieved political independence the 'commanding heights' of the economy remained in foreign, mainly Dutch, hands. In effect, the modern industrial-commercial-agricultural sector was dominated by Europeans with the Chinese controlling most of the intermediate trade, including the collection and processing of agricultural products (especially smallholder rubber). During the so-called liberal period (1950–57) a dominant theme in the attempt to create an economic system was the struggle between those who attempted to pursue policies within the framework of the 1949 settlement and those who sought to weaken foreign control.[41] Both sides appealed to the national ideology embodied in the Constitution, particularly Article 33 which provides for the organisation of the state on a 'co-operative basis'.

Economic nationalism was a complex phenomenon in this and subsequent periods. Its protagonists fell into two major groups, one which sought to replace foreign control by a form of socialism or state enterprise economy, the other hoping for an enlargement of the private sector in pribumi hands, either by transfer of existing foreign enterprise to indigenous hands or by the creation of entirely new companies. Development of an indigenous private sector was seen as leading to an Indonesian-dominated capitalist system no better than colonial capitalism. Creation of such an indigenous capitalist system would require government finance and such a use of funds was strongly opposed by the anti-capitalist group. The widespread antipathy toward capitalism and the tendency to link it with colonialism obliged even the proponents of a strong private sector to couch their arguments in vaguely socialistic terms.

Two main issues bearing on the new regional rubber policy are taken up in this section: the establishment of N.V.Karet, which represented one of the first threats to the economic position of the Chinese by the economic nationalists; and the 1959 ban on alien traders in rural areas. By 1959 the Dutch economic enterprises had been nationalised and the modern sector of the economy was largely in the control of the government.[42] This was the beginning of the period of 'Guided Economy' which was to last until the emergence of the New Order in the mid-1960s.

The conversion of the Dutch companies into state enterprises was to satisfy those who favoured increased state control over the economy, while the replacement of alien traders by private pribumi traders was intended to pacify those to whom economic nationalism meant domination by indigenous capitalists. Later, the government announced that it expected that the role of the alien traders would be taken over by co-operatives. This move represented a swing towards the anti-capitalist side of economic nationalism. As we shall see, the end result favoured neither group.

A dominant theme in the concept of Guided Economy was increased government control. Even so, the period saw a swing toward liberalism in 1963 with the Economic Declaration (*Dekon*) and the May Regulations. The Economic Declaration was made by President Sukarno in March 1963 and represented a compromise among the major political forces at that time, including the Communist Party. As such, it was capable of a variety of interpretations, one of which was contained in the government's May Regulations.[43] These regulations emphasised the liberal interpretation of the Declaration, favouring more autonomy for state enterprises and a greater reliance on the price mechanism. This policy aroused a storm of protest, the outcome of which was still undecided when it was abruptly terminated by Confrontation.

It was during this so-called liberal phase that the South Sumatran legislature began discussing a rubber policy for the region. Some groups in South Sumatra appealed to the spirit of the Economic Declaration in their efforts to weaken the power of the Chinese remillers and traders. Their object was to increase the strength of the pribumi private entrepreneurs at the expense of the ethnic minority, so they presented their local interpretation of the national ideology in defence of regional action.

The debate on a new rubber policy in the region merged into the last years of the period of Guided Economy which, in theory at least, emphasised more government control. The apparent drift towards a so-called liberalism in 1963 stood out in sharp contrast to the increasing tendency to talk in terms of enlarging the government's activities which was so much in evidence after September 1963. But as far as the position of the private remillers was concerned, the result was contrary to what one would have expected from speeches made at the time. As late as 1965 the private remilling sector was as strong as ever and there were more remillers than when the rubber policy was first made a matter of debate early in 1963.

This divergence between stated objectives and practice is a common feature of the issues discussed in this section. The remilling industry remained under the control of the Chinese ethnic minority in spite of the efforts made by one group in the region to bring it under government control. Pribumi participation in the industry did increase, but as part of a gradual process rather than as the result of direct assaults on the position of the Chinese (as represented by the ban on alien traders, for example).

In considering these three major issues in detail it is interesting to note that attempts to enlarge the private indigenous sector were confined to the trading side of the rubber industry only, not the processing. Those economic nationalists who resented the position of the Chinese remillers were more concerned with increasing controls over the remillers rather than their replacement by pribumi industrialists.

N.V.Karet: economic nationalism backfires?

It might have been expected that N.V.Karet, as a semi-government rubber corporation, would pose an immediate threat to the dominance of the Chinese ethnic minority in both the remilling and trading institutions in the Palembang rubber industry. Its functions were broad enough to enable it to participate actively in all aspects of the industry. Prohibition of slab exports tended to strengthen the remillers, but N.V.Karet was supposed to act as a countervailing power to protect the interests of the pribumi vis-à-vis the Chinese.

So much for the theory. In practice, the Palembang remillers as a group benefited from the elimination of Singapore competition. There is little evidence, however, that N.V.Karet benefited the peasants, as anticipated, nor did it provide the remiller-trader combination with effective competition in the interior. Economically, it lacked the finance; politically, it was biased against such a move.

Palembang was a stronghold of the Nationalist Party (PNI), and N.V.Karet was to a great extent the brain-child of a prominent PNI politician, Dr Isa, who became its first President Director. Its two other directors were also PNI men, one of them being Mr Lim Tjong Hian, a prominent lawyer in Palembang, head of the local remillers' association and a member of the Baperki. The PNI dominance lent support to the claim that the creation of N.V.Karet was part of the same overall PNI policy of granting licences to the business community in return for funds for the coming general elections.

At no stage did N.V.Karet ever emerge as a threat or competitor to the existing marketing and processing structure in Palembang. From the beginning, the company was attacked by the Palembang Smallholder Rubber Office as a 'tool of the remillers'. According to its statute, N.V.Karet was given the impossible task of reconciling conflicting interests in the industry, especially with regard to the pricing of slabs, and at a later stage it was supposed to act as a competitor of the remillers without becoming their liquidators. Not only were the directors of the corporation unlikely to pursue such a policy, but the very fact that the remillers themselves held the bulk of the shares in the company made such a task impossible. Had the national and regional governments been serious in their intentions, a wholly government-financed and operated company would have been necessary.

Only government pressure could have obliged the Corporation to adhere to its original programme, a policy which would have required the government itself to be more consistent in its overall approach to economic matters than was ever apparent. Given the conditions under which it operated, the Corporation was inevitably more of a political than an economic institution. The PNI continued to dominate regional politics and there was little change in the role of the company when all of its shares passed into the hands of the regional legislature in 1957. The remillers and the PNI had been able to neutralise the competitive element in the Corporation's statutes while benefiting from the withdrawal of Singapore as a major purchaser of slabs. The PNI acted as protector to the remillers in a generally unstable political environment, and it was a relationship advantageous to both groups.

From 1954 to 1966, when the Rubber Corporation was disbanded, the attacks by the Smallholder Rubber Office on the company and the remillers did not cease. Even in 1965 a rubber study in South Sumatra by a team from the Agricultural Institute in Bogor referred to the company and the remillers in terms of their single buyer position.[44] The fieldwork for that report had been carried out in 1963, by which time the combination of the remillers, PNI and N.V.Karet, was being undermined by the emergence of a new political constellation in the region and in Indonesia as a whole, based largely on the increasing importance of the armed forces. Power was slipping away from the PNI supporters of the old-established remillers as the trend toward 'Guided Economy' intensified.

The ironic results of the weakening of PNI control over the region and its outcome for 'Guided Economy' are considered in more detail below. Here we need only note that long before the PNI was discredited in South Sumatra in the aftermath of the abortive coup, its ability to protect the positions of the old-established remillers had vanished. The disbanding of the Rubber Corporation in 1966 was a symbolic gesture, its usefulness for that group having long since ended. As originally conceived, it had never lived up to the expectations of the Smallholder Rubber Office and, insofar as it was a protector of the remillers, that role had been better played by the PNI, which was the real power behind the façade of the Rubber Corporation. Once the PNI's power began to wane the way was open for the emergence of a new, if inexperienced, group of remillers. This change began in the early 1960s, several years before the final demise of both the PNI (at least temporarily) and N.V.Karet. As we shall see, the new group mainly consisted of WNI Chinese, who gradually became a major challenge to the old-established remillers; at the same time they also demonstrated the power to survive not only of the Chinese, but also of the system of private enterprise, during a period of outwardly intense hostility to both. Throughout all of these changes the position of the Smallholder Rubber Office remained weak. For a brief period in 1963 it appeared to come into its own, as we shall see; but the economic environment was no more to its advantage than it was to those attempts by others in the industry to improve the situation either by raising qualities or by replanting with high-yielding plant material.

Before tracing the role of the Smallholder Rubber Office in the debate on a new rubber policy for the region in 1963, we will consider the impact on the industry of the ban on alien traders in rural areas introduced in 1959.

The ban on retail traders

The aim of the 1959 ban on alien traders in rural areas, as formulated in the 14 May announcement by the Minister of Trade, was to widen the scope for national businessmen by breaking the grip of the Chinese over retail trade. Later, however, the expressed objective was reformulated to conform more closely to the prevailing notions of Indonesian Socialism by stressing the opportunity for co-operatives to take over the functions of retail traders.[45] Substituting co-operatives for national businessmen was no easy solution to the problem of taking over the role of the alien firms. The co-operative movement was weak and could not by itself muster the necessary capital (estimated at Rp. 17 billion by the Secretary of the Co-operative Department). The government was also in no position to provide such financing. Apparently no-one had considered the extent to which the indigenous traders would require assistance, especially bank credit, to replace the alien traders. Political considerations simply took precedence over economic considerations.

Little detailed information is available on the extent to which the regulation was actually implemented. It seemed at the time that business transfers to co-operatives or national enterprises were rare or were arranged privately in such a way as to minimise dislocation, although experience varied from region to region. In the case of the rubber trade, the complex system of trading which had been built up over the years would have been unable to withstand the drastic reorganisation implied in the regulation at such short notice. Even so, PP 10 seems to have had some effect on the trading structure. While there was no clear-cut break in the personnel involved in the Palembang rubber trade as required by the regulation, the Chinese did begin 'to give ground' to indigenous traders in numerous ways, not always those expected by the top decision-makers.

In the absence of statistical data on the citizenship status of those involved in the rubber trade, we have been forced to rely on the understandably vague comments of those engaged in the trade itself for an assessment of the regulation's impact. Although it was emphasised that only alien traders were to be affected by the regulation and Chinese who were already Indonesian citizens were exempt, the unsatisfactory situation regarding citizenship rights gave an air of uncertainty to the implementation of the ban. It was common to find in one family both types of citizenship. But because the onus of proof of citizenship rested upon the individual concerned, there were numerous reports of the difficulties faced by those who claimed that they were in fact citizens, but were unable to satisfy the officials dealing with the matter. Such a situation lent itself to a wide range of malpractices.

Where, for example, the father was an alien and the son an Indonesian citizen, the father could merely transfer the business to his son. Mention was also made of the special licences issued by the Governor of South Sumatra to enable aliens to continue trading in the rural areas. (Apparently this 'loophole' was more prevalent in West Kalimantan where the Chinese were more numerous.) A third possibility modified to some extent the rather widespread impression that the relationships between the Chinese, either alien or citizen, and the indigenous Palembanger were based on distrust and animosity. Indigenous Indonesians often worked for Chinese traders as clerks, scale operators and so on. After PP 10 some businesses were transferred to pribumi and the former employer-employee relationship was transformed into a business partnership. With the formal change-over, the alien trader merely left his capital in the business and let his former employee manage the enterprise.

A comparison of the effects of PP 10 on the position of the Chinese in South Sumatra with those which arose as a result of the abortive coup of October 1965 is most revealing. Most of those whom we interviewed agreed that PP 10 did not represent a sharp break with the past as far as the position of the Chinese role in the rubber trade was concerned. Pribumi traders were already moving into the trade before 1959 and the trend was not sharply accelerated after 1959. After the 1965 coup, however, anti-Chinese feeling ran high. It was at this stage that the Chinese, both aliens and citizens, moved out of the rural areas in large numbers, and even the Chinese who operated along the river in motor boats and houseboats declined to continue working in the interior.[46] But to demonstrate this from the trade statistics is not simple. It would seem reasonable to expect that the volume of rubber flowing into both Palembang and Panjang, to be processed and then exported, continued more or less uninterrupted after PP 10, whereas there would be a breakdown in trade for a considerable period after 1 October 1965. In fact, the statistics seem to point not to such a conclusion, but to the opposite. Closer investigation modifies this impression, however, although the problems of interpreting the figures are complex, and we do not feel that our generalisations about the effect of PP 10 and the 1965 events are invalidated by the statistical evidence.

To summarise the latter, it appears that total Indonesian production of smallholder rubber in 1960 was about 21 per cent below the 1959 level, but the latter was an exceptionally good year when prices were high. Compared with 1958, which was a more 'normal' year, 1960 production was only 7 per cent down. In Palembang, however, production in 1960 was 18 per cent below the 1958 level and 23 per cent below in 1961—but this decline was partly offset by an increase in exports from Panjang. For reasons which are not entirely clear, Palembang's exports of rubber remained below 'normal' until 1962. But before we jump to the conclusion that this was due to the impact of PP 10, we must take account of the fact that exports from Panjang, Jambi and Pontianak did not decline, although the Chinese were playing a crucially important role there also.

It is equally difficult to assess the consequences of the abortive coup and the anti-Chinese campaign that followed it. Once again we must emphasise the numerous local factors influencing the exports of rubber, some of which are discussed in the next section. Production of rubber in Palembang continued in a depressed state through to 1968, with a slight recovery in 1967. Panjang on the other hand performed well, exceptionally so in 1965, in spite of the alleged disruption in international communications immediately following the abortive coup itself. One reason for the differences between the two ports was the impact of Confrontation, which, as we shall see, appears to have affected Palembang more than Panjang. Palembang was, therefore, in a depressed state before the abortive coup and any impact on production of rubber consequent on the possible withdrawal of Chinese traders would have been merely one of several adverse factors affecting the industry. Panjang seemed to be unaffected by whatever factors were depressing Palembang's production, and it may well have been that its competitive strength vis-à-vis Palembang at that time was one of the factors responsible for Palembang's decline. Jambi also absorbed the impact of the coup with apparent ease, for exports from both Jambi and Panjang were well above 1958 levels (see Table 6). In West Kalimantan, it is likely that Pontianak's exports declined in 1967 precisely because of the anti-Chinese outbursts. One other region which was the scene of severe anti-Chinese reaction was Medan, and there too rubber exports declined sharply in 1967.

After 1965, from all accounts, the Chinese traders ceased their activities in the rural areas as traders and moved into the cities. For ports such as Panjang and Jambi it was done with relatively little dislocation to the industry. In all cases, the pribumi strengthened their position at the expense of both the alien Chinese and the WNI. Several of those interviewed estimated that 70 per cent of motor boat or *tongkang* (river barge) traders in Palembang were, by 1969, pribumi, with a somewhat higher figure for warong traders.[47] As the pribumi moved into positions in the Palembang marketing structure closer to the village and the farmer-

Table 6

Exports from Indonesia, Palembang, Panjang, Jambi, Medan and Pontianak,[a] 1958–68 ('000 tonnes)

	Indonesia	*Palembang*	*Panjang*	*Jambi*	*Medan*[b]	*Pontianak*[c]
1958	424.5	94.1	23.5	31.0	38.7	64.8
1959	479.8	96.5	36.7	50.4	45.6	59.6
1960	378.0	76.7	32.4	43.6	38.4	43.3
1961	429.7	72.2	40.9	50.8	30.1	62.2
1962	466.2	82.4	43.4	63.8	32.2	62.3
1963	359.3	70.7	36.8	45.3	33.2	51.3
1964	409.8	65.6	45.2	50.2	64.1	80.1
1965	483.8	77.5	51.3	66.6	77.3	91.3
1966	429.5	73.1	42.3	60.6	72.2	80.4
1967	437.7	85.6	36.6	75.1	61.9	50.5
1968	522.9	109.0	44.5	82.1	66.8	74.7

Source: Central Bureau of Statistics. There is a slight difference between the production figures for Palembang presented in Table 5 and the figures presented above, but since, the discrepancy is small we have not attempted a reconciliation of the figures even assuming this were possible. For 1968 the figures show a considerable difference, but we are not able to indicate the reason.

a Besides the ports listed, the group of nine in the Riau archipelago are the most important.

b For Medan it may be of interest to consider the sharp rise in exports after 1963. Our preliminary investigations led us to the conclusion that rubber from the Riau group of ports went out through Medan during the confrontation period and probably after. Moreover, whereas before 1963 rubber from the Riau group was exported in the form of slabs and unsmoked sheets, after that time very little rubber of these qualities was exported from Indonesia at all. Again, our tentative conclusion is that the slabs and unsmoked sheets from the Riau ports were processed in Medan into blankets and smoked sheet respectively before being exported. This is another important issue of the confrontation period which deserves further study.

For Pontianak, the rise in exports after 1964 may be due to factors similar to those noted in the case of Medan, i.e. a movement of rubber from ports close to Pontianak. If such shifts actually took place it is evidence of an ability to operate under conditions of extreme difficulty, in this case in spite of an allegedly poor communications network.

producer, the Chinese tended to concentrate in positions closer to the city end of the trade. Basically, the strength of the Chinese lay not only in their experience in the trade (which a pribumi could acquire in time), but also in their possession of financial resources or their ability to attract finance for trading. Legislation to increase the role of the pribumi in the trade could not work unless the pribumi were supported financially and unless they had the experience. The ban on alien traders may well have expressed the feelings of antipathy of some of the pribumi towards Chinese in business, but legislation emanating from such antipathy was a poor substitute for the slow process of indigenisation which was actually taking place at some levels in the trading structure. Regulations of the PP 10 type attempt to bring about change overnight without preparation in advance, and are of more harm than good to the very cause they espouse, including an alleged attempt to get a better price for the farmer.[48] Working arrangements between pribumi and the Chinese had been developing gradually since independence, the Chinese spurred on no doubt by an awareness of their precarious positions as a result of forces favouring nationals. Slow change of this nature may be preferable to such ill-prepared efforts as PP 10.

By 1969 the pribumi in Palembang residency had come to dominate the lower levels of the trading structure, but at the same time were working closely with the Chinese in the industry in a variety of combinations. The remillers were still mostly Chinese and the owners of the large toko (stores) in Palembang city were also Chinese. Both groups continued to finance the rubber trade and a system of mutual confidence between pribumi and the Chinese was emerging.

The Regional Assembly and the debates on rubber policy
The Extension Service for Smallholder Rubber (a division of the Smallholder Rubber Office) continued its struggle against N.V.Karet and the remillers between 1963 and 1968. Early in 1963, at the time of Confrontation, it seemed to be at last making headway, when its policy was favoured by the DPRD-GR (regional assembly) in its debates on a regional rubber policy. But this victory was more apparent than real. Although the position of the various groups within the remilling faction changed considerably in the years that followed, the remilling industry remained as powerful as ever and the Extension Service was still struggling to correct the balance. Early in 1963 an ad hoc Committee was set up by the South Sumatran regional legislature (DPRD-GR), to formulate a policy for the rubber industry. The DPRD-GR argued that government action was necessary to increase rubber production by formulating a more progressive policy which would require in particular that the farmer be given a more direct incentive to increase his income from rubber and thereby indirectly increase the income of the State.

A document was tabled in the DPRD-GR on 21 April 1963, composed of an overall review of the rubber industry and proposals for improvement suggested by the committee. Appended to the views of the committee as a group were additions submitted for consideration by the Smallholder Rubber Office and by N.V.Karet.

Government and traders and remillers were criticised by the committee. Specific points in the document included the allegation that the farmer was not getting enough for his rubber, partly because there were too many links in the marketing organisation. N.V.Karet was regarded as ineffective in protecting the producer in the village because it had insufficient capital. Government policies were criticised as inadequate in their attempts to co-ordinate the activities of the various departments involved in the rubber industry.[49] As a result of a wide range of deficiencies in the way in which the industry was organised, the farmer was getting little whereas others were making considerable profits.

In the preamble to the committee's report, reference was made to the President's recent Economic Declaration of 26 March 1963 which had promised an economy 'without exploitation of man by man' and the creation of an Indonesian socialist society; Article 33 (1) of the Constitution was also mentioned to the effect that the 'national economy shall be organised on a co-operative basis'.[50] But the committee did not confine itself to vague pronouncements on principle. It proposed that the 1960 decision of the MPRS be implemented to ensure that within the region the ratio of sheets to blankets be 70:30 by 1968. Projects for encouraging sheet production were recommended, with the government taking the necessary steps to prevent delay in such projects. Farmers producing sheets should, the committee argued, be able to sell their product quickly and receive payment immediately, thus eliminating the possibilities for the *'ijon* system'.[51] To protect the farmer vis-à-vis the trader in the determination of the dry rubber content of the slab, it was recommended that an organisation be set up to be responsible for quality standards, although nothing specific was mentioned about how this body would be organised. The committee also urged that the farmer be supplied with inputs at reasonable prices and in suitable locations. An awareness of non-monetary incentives was indicated by the proposal that attention should be focused on adequate supplies of essentials at the village level, such as rice, fish, kerosene, coconut oil, etc. None of these proposals were new; they all harked back to what was said when N.V.Karet was established in 1954.

These proposals clearly indicated a dissatisfaction with the way in which the traders operated, particularly concerning supplies of inputs for sheet production and adequate supplies of essential goods at the village level. Efficient marketing was also a prime concern of the committee and its specific recommendations included the creation of a strong co-operative structure to replace the private enterprise system currently in operation. In the village, primary co-operatives (*PRIKA-Primer Koperasi Pertanian Rakjat*) were to be set up, with membership consisting of both owners of rubber gardens and tappers. At each district (*kabupaten*) level a central (*pusat*) co-operative would be required to organise incentives for the PRIKA concerning quality, value and so on. Where co-operatives were not likely to be set up in the short run, it was proposed that auctions should be introduced as a way of inducing the farmer to produce better quality.

The committee put forward alternative suggestions for action, in addition to those recommended by the committee as a whole. Most important of these were the recommendations made by Sukarmin of the Extension Service and by Mr Lim of N.V.Karet. Sukarmin wanted a central buying agency to be created in the first level (provincial) district, which would control all buying and selling of rubber. Such an organisation should be under the regional government and the remillers should operate solely as processing units on contract. The remillers would thus obtain their rubber from the central buying agency, return it when processed, leaving it to the buying agency to arrange export. N.V.Karet would no longer be required and could be dissolved.

Finance for the new organisation was expected to come from the regional government, private businessmen (including the remillers or N.V.Karet), rubber producers and tappers and from those State Enterprises involved in the rubber industry. Of interest here is Sukarmin's distinction between the remillers and the Corporation as such and the impression he gives that the Corporation was independent of the regional government. If a new agency were to be set up, the assets of the corporation would probably have been transferred to it in the process of dissolution of the old organisation.

Sukarmin's proposals went into many other aspects of the industry; in most cases he regarded the role of the government as paramount. In transport by road and rail, the government was to be the regulatory body, though whether he envisaged a continued role for private enterprise on a contract basis is not clear. Exports were to be shipped direct to consumer countries, with the central government acting as agent, so as to get the highest price. This method of sale would reduce dependence on Singapore, which at the time still performed the role of an entrepôt for Palembang rubber. Processing equipment and raw materials should be controlled by the government, presumably with an emphasis on import control.

Mr Lim's set of proposals on behalf of N.V.Karet can be considered in most respects as counter-proposals to Sukarmin's. Lim wanted to increase the capital of the corporation to enable it to operate actively in the purchase of slabs in the interior; at the same time he saw this addition to capital as giving it an opportunity to encourage sheet production. Second level districts were to have shares in the corporation and government agencies were to be requested to play an active part in its operations (a role which they should have been playing in any case). And as co-operatives developed, the corporation was to work with them to reduce the links in the marketing organisation.

More control over quality was also advocated by Mr Lim. In an oblique defence of the remillers, both alien and WNI Chinese, he referred to the 'all funds and forces' slogan of President Sukarno,[52] urging that the remillers should be allowed to continue buying slabs on their own account, to process them and then export the blankets directly or sell them on the local market, as they preferred. The price fixing policy was to be improved by allowing the pricing committee to announce estimates for the minimum price of slabs at the village level. This could be done, said Mr Lim, by using the price set in the city and making allowances for transport costs, reduction of water content in transit,[53] and including a reasonable profit for the traders.

Mr Lim stressed the need to pay more attention to the problems of transportation. In agreement with Sukarmin, he argued for government control over water transport (the railways were already owned by the State) and he urged that roads be improved throughout the region. Apart from his comments on transportation, Mr Lim also favoured government control over the sale of the raw materials used in the industry (again with special reference to imports).

In many instances, the only conflict between Mr Lim and Sukarmin related to the position of N.V.Karet. But it is possible that in those cases where they were in agreement Mr Lim really doubted the efficacy of many of his own proposals. At a time of 'Guided Economy' Mr Lim could well have been bowing to what he felt to be inevitable, regardless of practicability. The most important point to make in this respect concerns his proposals for N.V.Karet. Much of what he said related to an expansion of its activities which, to be effective, would have required that branches be set up in the interior. These activities were already envisaged in the Corporation's statutes, but had remained dormant from the outset. Did Mr Lim really think anything could be done at so late a stage? It is most unlikely. As for the suggestion that the pricing committee fix the price of slabs for the village as well as the city, he must have realised that this could be done only if the committee had inspectors operating in the interior with powers of enforcement. And if the trade was conducted as we have indicated, with close ties between buyer and seller based partly on financial obligations, how could an inspector police such transactions? As we shall point out later, much would have had to be done to the regional economy before many of Mr Lim's suggestions could become a reality.

The ad hoc committee assessed the proposals of Sukarmin, Mr Lim and others, and their final views on the reorganisation of the marketing structure were very close to the ideas expressed by Sukarmin. A new

Central Buying Agency was to replace N.V.Karet and the remillers were to be obliged to process slabs for the agency and were excluded from buying slabs from traders or from selling blankets overseas or on the local market. Exporters would be able to buy blankets and sheets from the central agency and from no-one else. Finance for the new organisation was to come from the group listed by Sukarmin, with the exception of N.V.Karet. The regional government was to control and determine the rubber policy of South Sumatra in the future.

We have seen no evidence that this document was actually adopted by the regional assembly. But as we trace the events following confrontation after 15 September 1963, we find that attempts were made to implement some of the proposals. On the other hand, in spite of the internal confrontation between the remillers and the Extension Service, the position of the remillers was as strong as it had ever been when Confrontation came to an end.

Confrontation and its ironies

On 15 September 1963 the new Federation of Malaysia was formed; President Sukarno refused to recognise the new state, diplomatic relations were suspended and on 20 September Indonesia broke off all diplomatic and trade ties with Malaysia. Of crucial importance for South Sumatra was the sudden ending of the role that Singapore had played as a buyer of the region's rubber. Singapore could no longer act as an outlet for Palembang's rubber and, as for most of the other ports exporting smallholder rubber, the true significance of Singapore now became apparent. Palembang was not situated on international trading routes, but Singapore had hidden the importance of this fact. With the elimination of Singapore, disadvantages of location hit the industry severely. The remillers and exporters in Palembang faced a difficult problem of readjustment in the months following the loss of the Singapore market. On top of that came the action of the government against what were called 'Malaysian' firms. It was decided on 29 October 1963 that the government should take over (*kuasai*)[54] all remilling factories and smoke houses which were partly or fully owned by citizens of Malaysia or whose owners were resident in that country.

Five remilling factories, *Sunan*, *Hok Tong*, *Remco*, *Remifa* and *Sumatra Rubber*, were affected in Palembang, although there was some doubt as to the validity of the government's claim that all should be categorised as Malaysia owned. These five factories accounted for 53 per cent of Palembang's output in 1962 (44 191 tonnes out of 83 522 tonnes) (Table 7). *Remifa* was leased to Rahman Tamin, the pribumi textile manufacturer; *Remco* was leased on contract to a new company *P.T.Peksin*;[55] while *Sunan* came under the management of the WNI-Chinese remilling company *Metro*. *Hok Tong* remained in the hands of the government, to

Table 7
Palembang: Production of the Five 'Ex-Malaysian' Remillers
1962–68 ('000 tonnes)

	1962	1963	1964	1965	1966	1967	1968
HOK TONG	16.4	10.5	8.5	4.1	3.1	1.9	2.5
REMIFA	7.5	5.8	5.0	5.6	6.2	6.1	4.8
REMCO	6.2	6.7	5.1	3.2	3.1	3.3	2.7
SUMATRA RUBBER	2.0	2.0	1.2	0.7	1.0	nil	0.6
SUNAN	12.0	10.2	7.9	5.5	7.2	8.5	6.6
TOTAL	44.2	35.2	27.7	19.2	20.6	19.8	17.1
PERCENTAGE OF PALEMBANG PRODUCTION	53	50	40	27	26	25	19

Source: Information from remillers.

be managed by *PPN Karet*. *Sumatra Rubber* became the subject of a controversy between the regional and central governments, although it was at first leased to *P.T.Peksin*.

The leasing of three of the firms to private enterprise was clear indication that the government itself lacked trained personnel to manage the companies. It was also evidence of a pragmatic accommodation to circumstances. At the same time, the leasing of *Sunan* to the WNI-Chinese owned *Metro* represented an additional accommodation to realism considering that a great deal of tension in the region was based on ethnic divisions, particularly centring on the Chinese control of the remilling industry. In fact, the period from 1963 to 1966 illustrated a clear difference between the central government and the regional government in tempering action to fit the circumstances, regardless of the content of official statements.

Hok Tong and *Sumatra Rubber* remained under government management and, where the remillers could be blamed for the low qualities of rubber and the low incomes of the farmers, the government opponents of the remillers now appeared to have an opportunity to do something constructive to improve the situation. Presumably the new managers of the two companies were responsible to the central government. Some of the new personnel in *Hok Tong* came from the Smallholder Rubber Office (by then called *Dinas Karet*, although it soon changed its name once again) and the top managers, all Chinese, had been removed. (In the companies leased to private enterprise, the old management was permitted to remain.) In the case of *Sumatra Rubber*, a struggle for control ensued between the central government, represented by *P.T.Peksin*, and the regional government. Both companies were seriously affected by the changes which took place, although the others were not spared the effects of disruption. *Hok Tong* was not involved in such disputes and from the beginning was in a position to offer some competition to the Chinese and also to try to implement some of the policies which the regional opponents of N.V.Karet claimed were the responsibility of the Corporation itself. *Hok Tong* was also well placed to introduce some of the policy recommendations of the ad hoc committee on rubber. But subsequent events revealed the political weaknesses of the opponents of the remillers. In spite of the opportunity offered by the takeover, no alternative to the present marketing system was given a trial.

The performance of the five firms was disastrous, as can be seen in Table 7 which shows their output between 1962 and 1968. The causes of their failure during the period under review are still obscure. The years 1963–65 were a period of low output compared with 1962, which was a good year, with a production of 82 000 tonnes, although it was below the performance of 1958, the base year used in our discussion of PP 10. Recovery was under way by 1966 and 1968 was another outstanding year. So, in spite of the decline of the five firms which had dominated the industry in 1962, remilling output for the industry withstood the shock. The manner in which this was accomplished is considered below. Here we merely mention that production by new entrants to the industry offset the fall in production of the 'ex-Malaysia' firms and that the newcomers were WNI-Chinese.

The immediate effect of Confrontation and the break with Malaysia was stagnation for Palembang's remilling industry. Considerable consternation prevailed among the farmers. Their attitude was shared by the remillers in Palembang and for a time confusion reigned. A slowdown in production was to be expected, of course, because Singapore had been Palembang's major outlet and the closing of the entrepôt to Indonesian business forced exporters to look for new trading partners. This adjustment inevitably cost time and money. During the early months of the changeover the remillers were obliged to cut down on slab purchases, so that the whole of the industry was affected.

One interesting consequence of the difficulties created by the crisis was the reaction of the regional government, which tended to blame the remillers in part for the stagnation in production. This attitude could have had serious implications for the Chinese remillers because of the identification of Singapore Chinese with the new Federation : fortunately this did not have any serious effects for the Chinese in Indonesia. But the local government in Palembang did take some action against the remillers. A regulation was introduced obliging all remillers to process slabs for three outside organisations on a cost-and-fee basis determined by the regional government.[56] This *'wajib giling'* (compulsory remilling) regulation designated the Rubber Cooperative (*GAKKA—Gabungan Koperasi Karet*) of South Sumatra,[57] the State Trading Companies and 'bona fide and progressive private businessmen', as the groups permitted to contract their slabs for processing to the remilling factories. During rapid inflation, a fixed cost for remilling would operate to the benefit of those sub-contracting to remillers. Even if the contracting costs were periodically adjusted to allow for inflation, there would be a sufficient time lag to enable windfall profits to be earned by the sub-contractors at the expense of the remillers.

A later regulation considerably strengthened the tide (on paper at least) against the predominantly Chinese remillers. The regional authorities, this time under the imposing title of the Governor/Assistant to the Chief of Staff/Deputy Head of the Economic Command (*KOTOE— Komando Tertinggi Operasi Ekonomi*) in South Sumatra,[58] instructed the remillers to make 50 per cent of their capacity available to the three organisations mentioned as from 1 May 1964. Regardless of the practicability of the Instruction, some leading officials were clearly in favour of dealing with the industry in a manner similar to that advocated by the ad hoc committee in 1963. Even so, the threat to the position of the remillers turned out to be more apparent than real.

In practice, the three newcomers (brought into prominence in the trading sector of the industry as a result of the wajib giling policy) were in no position to purchase slabs. They lacked finance and personnel in the city, towns and at the village level. Yet the challenge implicit in the wajib giling instruction continued even after a regulation prohibiting compulsory remilling was issued by the central government on 16 December 1964 through Deputy First Minister Leimena in his capacity as Supreme Economic Commander.

A report by a team from the Bogor Agricultural Faculty claimed that after Leimena's regulation there were no further problems connected with wajib giling.[59] In fact, it was only the beginning of the dispute between the central and regional governments on this issue. The central government decided to transfer *Sumatra Rubber* to the provincial Governor in return for an end to the wajib giling contracts. This new regulation was issued on 15 July 1965, some six months after Leimena's order. Under the July regulation the Governor was to leave the operations of the company to the Rubber Co-operative (GAKKA) and the factory was to obtain its working capital from the Central Bank.

That was not the end of the story. Although the transfer of *Sumatra Rubber* to regional control was a quid pro quo for ending the wajib giling operation, the Governor was, in fact, still issuing contracts for the three groups as late as November 1965. Clearly there was a conflict of authority between the central and regional governments, with opponents of the remillers supporting the Governor. The real situation was even more complex, for in spite of these signs of pressure, a new group of remillers was emerging, probably with the support of at least some elements among the regional elite. This complication will be considered after we have assessed briefly the economic aspects of the period.

The economic situation in those years was as obscure as the political. Remilling operations in Palembang continued at reduced levels in 1964 and 1965, and recovered in 1966 to reach a peak in 1968. The pattern for Indonesia as a whole was similar for 1963–65, indicating that Confrontation and the elimination of the Singapore entrepôt must have required a period of adjustment for all areas.[60] The recovery in Palembang was complicated by attempts to enforce the wajib giling instruction and by the strength of a group of WNI Chinese firms which only commenced operations during and after 1961. Although lists were issued regularly to the remillers notifying them how much tonnage they were to allocate to the designated 'third parties' under the wajib giling scheme, in practice these groups were able to utilise little if any of their allocation, according to our informants. On the other hand, the appearance of a group of newcomers to the remilling industry indicated that the PNI had begun to lose ground in Palembang early in the 1960s. With the decline of the PNI, N.V.Karet also became weaker, but the influence of the Extension Service did not show any relative increase. On the contrary, it was the up-and-coming WNI Chinese remillers who emerged successfully—although only for a short while, since the advent of a new method of processing slabs was ushering in a new chapter in the development of the rubber industry.

To say that the years between 1962 and 1968 constituted a period of great stress for the rubber industry—as they did for Indonesia as a whole—would be a considerable understatement. The old-established remillers of Palembang had to contend with a hostile regional government which was attempting to take advantage of Confrontation to impose its wajib giling regulations; they had to adjust to the 'takeover' of the five 'ex-Malaysia' firms and to accommodate to the entry of a group of newcomers into the remilling industry; the abortive coup of October 1965 was followed by an anti-Chinese campaign, although this was less severe in Palembang than in Medan and Pontianak. Throughout these eventful years inflationary pressures mounted alarmingly and not until 1968 did the new Suharto government begin to bring the spiralling prices under control. Yet rubber production in South Sumatra showed no tendency to decline and Palembang's share in the regional total remained roughly constant, except in 1964–65.

Aggregate statistics for Palembang remilling production, however, conceal some significant changes which were taking place within the industry itself, changes which affected both the relative shares of the individual firms in the city and the number of producing units. The companies which had been operating in 1955 when the export of slabs to Singapore was first prohibited still dominated the industry in 1962, accounting for 88 per cent of production. But compared with the situation in 1955, production of the old-established WNI firms and of the alien Chinese group had fallen. By contrast, output of the indigenous group had doubled, a fact which could be accounted for by the transfer of *Kian Gwan* from WNI-Chinese control to the government in 1961 and also by the opening of a new pribumi firm in 1958. There were five newcomers to the industry by 1962, four of them in the hands of WNI Chinese, accounting for 7 per cent of total Palembang output.

The major transformation in the industry occurred between 1962 and 1968, involving a shift in the relative position of the WNI Chinese firms between the old-established and the new-comers, as well as a decline in the importance of the role of the alien Chinese. These are hardly the changes one would have expected of a government committed to a 'Guided Economy' with strong nationalist overtones. But reality was at a variance with theory in many spheres at that time and the course of events in the South Sumatran rubber industry reflected not only a significant change in the regional power structure but also a weakening of the control of the government in Jakarta. The division of the industry by ethnic group into pribumi, WNI and alien Chinese remained, although four of the five 'ex-Malaysia' firms had come under indigenous management in 1963 (the remaining firm in the group had been transferred for a WNI firm to operate). The 'ex-Malaysia' group of remilling companies suffered the most during the 1962–68 period, their production falling from 44 000 tonnes to 17 000 tonnes. The major beneficiaries were those companies belonging to WNI Chinese (Table 8).

There was a sharp increase in the number of firms in the newcomer group from 1961 onwards. In 1962 there had been only five, whereas by 1968 nineteen were listed, of which thirteen were in operation, all but one of them owned by WNI Chinese. And in that latter year, they accounted for 61 per cent of remilling output in Palembang, compared with 19 per cent (of a lower output) in 1962 (Table 9).

Our discussion of the period 1962–65 has centred on the ideological trend towards more central government control and on the rather bitter attacks against that part of the private sector of the economy dominated by the Chinese (WNI or alien) in South Sumatra. These attacks were not always supported by the central government, although the regional opponents of the remillers often used statements made by the national leaders to substantiate their claims that they were acting in accordance with current ideology. The anti-Chinese sentiment was, if anything, heightened after 1965. Yet we do not find this sentiment reflected in the

Table 8

New Firms Operating in Palembang between 1961 and 1968
and Their Contribution to Remilling Production in Specified Years
(production in '000 tonnes)

	1963	1964	1965	1968
commenced operating				
1961–63				
Pribumi	1.9 (1)	1.6 (1)	1.0 (1)	1.6 (1)
WNI Chinese	5.3 (6)	10.0 (6)	11.7 (8)	13.1 (5)
1964–65				
WNI Chinese	—	2.9 (2)	9.6 (6)	22.9 (5)
after 1965				
WNI Chinese	—	—	—	—

Figures in parentheses denote number of firms in operation.

pattern of control over the remilling industry in South Sumatra. Not only did the position of the WNI Chinese improve, but ironically another trend was gathering momentum with the rise of an outside group of WNI challenging the position of both the old WNI group and the 'ex-Malaysia' firms by then in Indonesian hands. Evidently this is to be explained in terms of the beginnings of a change in the power structure in the region in the early 1960s, reflected in the weakening of the role of the Governor and the increasing power of the army. This shift in power led to a movement of patronage away from the old-established firms relying on the PNI in the direction of the newcomers.

Our analysis of production trends in the factories taken over by the government during Confrontation shows that neither the government nor private enterprise companies (indigenous or WNI) proved capable of maintaining 1962 output levels absolutely, or their share of the market relatively. Perhaps the transition period was too short. Failure of the 'ex-Malaysia' firms tended to shroud the extent of the real increase in remilling capacity. By 1968 licensed capacity in Palembang was 172 300 tonnes. Had the 'ex-Malaysia' firms maintained their 1962 levels of output, the competition for slabs would have been intense. Admittedly data on capacity must be treated with caution,[61] but it is more than likely that licences were issued to the new group of WNI Chinese firms without considering the possible consequences in terms of increased competition for slabs. The failure of the 'ex-Malaysia' firms was merely a fortuitous event which concealed weaknesses in the system of granting licences.

An unexpected increase in slab production tended to reduce the intensity of competition among the remillers just as the failure of the 'ex-Malaysia' firms had done. Remilled rubber exports from South Sumatra and Lampung of 150 000 tonnes in 1968 were the highest since 1955; Palembang remilling production rose by some 7 000 tonnes between 1962 and 1968, compared with a rise of 1 000 tonnes for Panjang. Relations between the newcomers and the old-established firms, WNI and indigenous (both government and private), must have been strained as the former succeeded in obtaining licences to set up their remilling factories. Both the regional and central governments claimed the authority to issue new remilling licences and there is no indication that there was any co-ordination between the two. If their relations on other matters concerning policy on rubber in the region are any indication, the contrary was probably the case.

The 'Guided Democracy' antipathy toward private enterprise and the local feeling against the Chinese might have been expected to check an increase in remilling licences to the private sector, particularly in the hands of newcomers who were not only private but also Chinese, albeit WNI. It was not to be.

Falling production of the 'ex-Malaysia' firms tended to reduce the competition for slabs, which would otherwise have intensified as a consequence of the emergence of the WNI newcomers. Better management of the 'ex-Malaysia' firms during the period 1962–68 might well have brought to the surface the latent problems of excess capacity. Detailed information on the way in which the one group was able to enter the market for slabs as the other withdrew is not available, so we can only sketch in outline the possible sequence of events. With a total remilling output for the South Sumatran region as a whole fluctuating around a maximum of 129 000 tonnes up to 1967, the newcomers would have to capture a share of the market from the others and the struggle had to centre around control over some or all of the links in the marketing channels: *warong/pedagang dusun, pedagang pucuk, pedagang motor*. It might have been possible for a new remiller to assist a trader set up in business as a pedagang motor, but less likely for the pedagang motor to be instrumental in establishing a new pedagang pucuk or the latter a new pedagang dusun. An alternative would have been to attract the traders of a rival firm to transfer their rubber dealings to a newcomer. Such a process would have tended to break the old links based on mutual trust and the more substantial bonds of credit which had grown up between the parties to the trade at all levels in the market structure. Panjang remillers had been able to 'capture' Palembang rubber during the early 1950s, but it is impossible to discover which levels in the structure they were able to enter. Even though the decline in importance of the 'ex-Malaysia' firms enabled the new WNI Chinese firms to break into

Table 9

Palembang: Remilling Production by Ethnic Origin of Individual Firms: 1960–68 ('000 tonnes)

	Licensed Capacity	1960	1961	1962	1963	1964	1965	1966	1967	1968
I. FIRMS IN OPERATION BEFORE 1959										
(a) Pribumi										
1. Familidin	4.0	2.6	3.3	3.0	2.4	3.2	2.5	3.1	3.7	4.4
2. Soleh	4.0	2.1	2.7	2.0	2.3	2.4	1.5	1.6	1.4	2.3
3. M. Ali	4.8	0.6	0.7	0.6	0.7	1.2	0.9	1.0	0.6	0.8
4. Kian Gwan[1] (P.T.Radjawali)	3.8	1.9	0.8	2.4	2.6	2.8	1.9	2.1	1.7	2.8
(b) WNI Chinese										
1. Sun Kie (Suar Karya)	15.0	11.0	11.4	10.9	10.7	7.1	14.0	12.6	13.6	13.4
2. Ong Bun Tjit (Nirawan Indah)	6.0	7.0	7.3	6.7	4.4	4.3	4.0	3.4	0.6	nil
3. Metro/Gandus	6.3	4.5	4.8	6.0	4.0	4.5	3.5	3.2	2.3	4.1
(c) Alien Chinese ('Ex-Malaysia')										
1. Hok Tong	15.0	14.5	17.8	16.4	10.5	8.5	4.1	3.1	1.9	2.5
2. Remifa	7.5	7.9	7.0	7.5	5.8	5.0	5.6	6.2	6.1	4.8
3. Sunan	6.0	13.9	13.0	12.0	10.2	8.0	5.5	7.2	8.5	6.6
4. Remco	4.5	8.6	—	6.2	6.7	5.1	3.2	3.1	3.3	2.7
5. N.V.Sumatra	2.0	1.7	0.9	2.0	2.0	1.2	0.7	1.0	nil	0.6
Group I (c) as % of total				(53)	(50)	(40)	(27)	(26)	(25)	(19)

II. FIRMS IN OPERATION FROM 1959

(a) *Pribumi*

1. A. Abubakar

(b) *WNI Chinese*

Firm										
1. A. Abubakar	3.6			1.2	0.6	0.4	0.7	0.4	0.8	0.5
1. Muara Klingi	10.0		0.4	0.5	0.7	1.9	2.2	3.3	2.1	3.8
2. Tjeq Ebeq	3.6			1.2	0.6	0.4	0.7	0.4	0.8	0.5
3. Empat Tunggal	5.0			1.5	1.8	2.2	3.4	2.5	3.5	3.7
4. Niamco	2.0				0.1	1.4	1.7	2.4	0.8	0.9
5. Muharsu	5.0		1.3	2.4	2.6	4.3	4.7	4.3	4.6	5.8
6. Sungai Selintjah	6.0				0.2	1.4	0.8	1.3	1.0	2.4
7. Dewi Seri	0.6				0.1	0.2	0.4	0.2	nil	nil
8. Djasa Musi	7.5					2.7	4.9	5.7	5.5	5.6
9. Pegangan Baru	2.5					0.1	1.9	1.6	1.7	1.8
10. Air Saling	2.4						1.6	1.8	1.8	2.5
11. Ganda Muara	5.0						0.3	1.1	0.5	nil
12. Nilakandi	12.0						0.6	2.7	4.2	6.7
13. Tjeq Oong	7.2						0.2	2.5	4.6	6.3
14. Djaja Marga	2.0							0.2	nil	nil
15. Kemala Raya	9.6								1.1	1.9
16. Dian Sari	2.5								1.5	2.0
17. Para	2.0									
18. Murai	2.0									
19. Lingga Djaja	2.0									
	171.4	76.3	71.4	82.5	69.0	68.3	71.5	78.0	78.2	89.4

1 Kian Gwan has been included in I(a) in 1960 for convenience only.

Source: Information from remillers.

the market more easily, there must have been some repetition of the Panjang situation. Again it is not possible to ascertain where the competition was most intense. But wherever traders of the new remillers did appear, the rather stable relations built up on the principle of customer-client ties (*langganan*) must have been transformed radically.[62]

Coincidental with the rise in importance of the new WNI remilling group were the upheavals caused by Confrontation and the abortive coup. As mentioned earlier, the anti-Chinese sentiment after the abortive coup was sufficient to induce the Chinese from the small retail stores (*warong*) and those who were traders in the *kecamatan* towns (the *pedagang pucuk*) to move into Palembang. We assume that their roles were taken over by indigenous traders who were able to establish financial links with both remillers and wholesalers in Palembang. This new element tended to compound any confusion which may have been caused by the intrusion of a group of new traders in the interior consequent upon the emergence of the new WNI Chinese remillers. In spite of all these changes, 1963 stands out as the only year in which there was a serious setback in production for South Sumatra as a whole, if we assume that production in excess of 110 000 tonnes can be considered reasonable. This is a rather remarkable fact under the circumstances.

THE CHINESE, THE RUBBER INDUSTRY AND THE NEW ORDER

A new phase in the role of the Chinese in the rubber industry gradually evolved after 30 September 1965. The Suharto administration promised to give top priority to economic matters, but until inflation had been brought under control (in the middle of 1968) little could be done.

For the Chinese community, the aftermath of the coup was a period of crisis. Some were accused of involvement in the coup and anti-Chinese campaigns developed in various parts of the country. South Sumatra was relatively untouched by such incidents during the period when General Suharto was establishing his authority. At the time of the coup, the Chinese still played a vital role in the South Sumatran rubber industry, despite the considerable local opposition they had been subjected to previously. However, up to 1967, they remained at the upper levels of the industry.

In the months following the coup the Nationalist Party (PNI) was under extreme pressure from its political opponents. In Palembang the party was banned by the local authorities, and with its political backing removed N.V.Karet was soon disbanded. As a result of the policy on licences, a new group of WNI Chinese remillers emerged between 1962 and 1965 and in spite of the political turmoil soon dominated the industry.

But the future of the Chinese was precarious, though more so in Medan and Pontianak than in Palembang. Rubber exports fell sharply in both the former areas in 1967, whereas for South Sumatra the decline was insignificant.

The re-opening of diplomatic ties with Malaysia in August 1966 and the enactment of a new Foreign Investment Law at the end of the same year can, in retrospect, be viewed as steps along the way to a change in attitude toward the 'ex-Malaysia' remilling factories. And, at about the same time, the removal of President Sukarno made it possible for the new government to reverse the steps that had been taken during his heyday toward some form of nationalisation of British, American and 'ex-Malaysia' firms. Foreign Minister Malik and other influential members of the Cabinet did what they could to quell the anti-Chinese sentiments at the same time as they re-opened diplomatic relations with Malaysia and Singapore and began negotiations for the return of the 'ex-Malaysia' remilling factories. Formal talks on the latter began in August 1967, and continued until April 1968 when the Department of Agriculture transferred control over the 'ex-Malaysia' rubber factories to their former owners.

So, even as the Chinese remillers were being deprived of their old protectors in the form of the PNI and N.V.Karet, the Suharto government was cautiously adopting policies which would eventually ensure welcome both to foreign investors and to domestic investors, including WNI Chinese as well as pribumi. Future investment was to be regulated by the provisions of the Foreign or Domestic Investment Laws, while rehabilitation and reinvestment were conditions of the return of the factories to their original owners.

With the return of the 'ex-Malaysia' factories to their alien Chinese owners, the way was open for them to try to regain their old position in Palembang. But their return coincided with the government's interest in the new 'crumb rubber' method of processing (discovered in Malaysia in 1964), which added a new element to the situation. Protected as they were by the Foreign Investment Law and assisted by its favourable conditions, the alien Chinese (and foreign investors in general) seemed to have considerable advantages compared to both the pribumi groups and the WNI Chinese. Criticism of the government on these grounds was bitter, but a Domestic Investment Law passed in August 1968 remedied this shortcoming. With the passage of this law, just four months after the official return of the ex-Malaysia factories, the WNI Chinese and pribumi could compete with the alien investor on more equal terms. But what were they expected to invest in?

One answer to that question was provided by the new technology of crumb rubber, the development of which happened to coincide with the gradual transfer of power from Sukarno to General Suharto. The new process involves cutting the wet coagulum into small pieces which can be rapidly and efficiently dried in minutes rather than hours. The rubber is then compacted into uniform, polythene wrapped bales. There were numerous processes available by 1968 and the Indonesian government was negotiating with the British company, Guthrie & Co., for credit facilities for the import of the process developed by Guthrie's.[63]

General Suharto was engaged in his long-protracted struggle for power against Sukarno as Malaysia was pressing ahead with crumb rubber. His government inherited the problems of rehabilitating a rubber industry which, in the case of the smallholder section, had an almost negligible acreage under high-yielding trees and an industry which lacked the backing of an efficient research organisation. If the new government was going to continue to rely on rubber as an important foreign exchange earner, it was quite clear that it must devise a new and replanting scheme and encourage investment in the new rubber.

General Suharto's advisers were obviously influenced by Malaysia's progress with crumb rubber when they included a clause in the transfer agreements with the 'ex-Malaysia' firms requiring them to invest in crumb rubber processing units. With the enactment of the Domestic Investment Law, the government also offered inducements to both WNI Chinese and pribumi with capital to invest in the new rubber. This new emphasis on crumb rubber, found also in the Five Year Plan (1969–74), could have important consequences for the role of the Chinese in the industry. A Dutch consultant on agriculture, E. de Vries, foresaw a role for 'some foreign capital (joint enterprise)'[64] but it seems more likely that, apart from investment by the 'ex-Malaysia' firms, the WNI Chinese will take the lead in pioneering the transition in Palembang. Foreign capital, other than that from Singapore, will probably hesitate to enter an industry which has been in Chinese hands for so long. For the industrial buyers it is more economical to purchase rubber on the world market than to invest in its production. They do not have to fear a monopsony situation because they can always buy natural rubber from Malaysia. Entering the industry as processors would involve them in all the problems and uncertainties connected with the smallholder sector.[65] Foreign investors might also be reluctant to enter an industry in which they too could be in a vulnerable position and open to the criticism of exploiting the farmer. Joint ventures may attract some, but the government may find it more attractive to accept loans from the foreign companies to assist pribumi to set up their own crumb rubber factories. Up to the beginning of 1970 most of the applicants for licences for crumb rubber factories in Palembang were WNI Chinese, the only exceptions being two applications from pribumi.

Most of the firms are to be located in Palembang, although de Vries favoured locating the new factories in the interior. His suggestion had explicit implications for competition in the industry. It was claimed that if the remilling factories were situated closer to the village more fierce competition would be assured, and thus the income to the farmer would be increased significantly.[66] According to this argument, the crumb rubber industry would serve as a means to end the imperfect competition for slabs; but it would also tend to concentrate those efforts to improve the real income of the farmer on what happens in the rubber industry alone, and especially on the price of rubber. Yet real incomes can be increased in a variety of ways, particularly by improving the terms of trade for rubber compared to those for essential goods. Increased educational and employment opportunities and better medical facilities would also assist the farmer and his family.

Under a government giving priority to economic issues, it is once again appropriate to consider the rubber industry and those who participate in it within the context of the possibilities of overall regional development.

The economic nationalist faces a real dilemma in the new circumstances. Even with the advent of crumb rubber, the processing is likely to remain in the hands of the WNI Chinese. And, despite de Vries's recommendation, most of the applications for crumb rubber licences have specified Palembang as the location. The socio-economic requirements of the new process favour the city, although transportation of slabs to Palembang does involve the cost of carrying a lot of water (some 50 per cent of the weight of the slab being made up of water). The bales of crumb rubber must be treated with care to keep them clean. Under present conditions of transporting rubber from the interior to Palembang it is highly unlikely that such a condition can be satisfied. Roads are very bad and almost impassable in the wet season. Transportation of bales wrapped in polythene would most certainly require a new type of vehicle to replace the *tongkang* (barge) and house boat. Each crumb rubber bale is now $28'' \times 14'' \times 6''$ (previously $27'' \times 13'' \times 6''$) and thirty such bales are packed in a wooden crate giving a total weight of one tonne (each block is $33\frac{1}{3}$ kilograms). As well as a new type of river transport, new handling equipment is necessary because of the weight of the crates and because crumb rubber cannot be handled as roughly as slabs. Considered by itself, the transportation requirement would favour a city location for the crumb rubber factories. The crumb rubber plants in Malaysia can use latex because the road network is far superior to Indonesia's and the crumb rubber plants can be situated inland because the roads are good and river transport is not used. In Indonesia's case, therefore, inland location would require finance in addition to that needed for the plant alone,[67] merely to develop the transportation system. For the factory itself, there are several other shortcomings in the infrastructure to consider. It would not be easy to find towns inland which have adequate facilities for a crumb rubber plant, including a steady supply of clean water, electric power and so on.

Probably more important than the economic factors are the social ones. Compared with a remilling factory, a crumb rubber plant requires only about 30 per cent of the labour force of a remilling factory. Given the strict technical specifications imposed by a Standard Indonesian Rubber type scheme, a technically trained staff is vital. Palembang, even though itself isolated, does offer a satisfying social life. How many highly trained men would be prepared to live in the much more isolated towns of the interior? Shell Oil Company formerly had installations at Prabumulih some 130 kilometres from Palembang, but its personnel lived in a wired-off compound, a self-contained enclave.[68] Crumb rubber factories, if independently owned, could hardly treat their staff in a like manner. So Palembang would seem a logical choice. And because crumb rubber samples have to be chemically tested, an easily accessible location would be preferable.

Encouraging a switch to crumb rubber in factories located in Palembang still does not provide a solution to one deep-seated problem which has plagued the industry since the early 1950s: dirty slabs.

The crumb rubber process will not turn dirty slabs into high grade crumb rubber. So the old problem of ensuring a maximum thickness of 3 cm for slabs still remains. The farmer must be offered sufficient inducement to produce high-grade slabs and the buyer must provide a market for scraps, tree lace and earth rubber, otherwise all three will end up in the slabs.

Probably the government will have to assist the private sector in ensuring that the quality of the slabs is improved. As it is, the trader already has the government to thank for bringing inflation under control and, under conditions of stability, it is now possible for the trader to offer the farmer better prices for his rubber. If a regulation on 3 cm slabs can be enforced, a higher money income to the farmer can now be translated into a higher real income.

But can an efficient industry be revitalised when there is still excess capacity?

In the past the remilling factories' capacity was in excess of slab production. In such a situation competition should have bid up the price of slabs to the benefit of the farmer, at least in terms of money income; yet many have argued that competition among the remillers did not operate to the advantage of the farmer. De Vries accepts the findings of the Agro-Economic Survey along these lines when he refers to the 'imperfect competition' in the slab market, but he gives no reasons why locating the crumb rubber factories in the interior would ensure competition and a higher price to the farmer.[69]

Even if crumb rubber factories were set up in Palembang, the problem of over-capacity in the remilling industry might persist and intensify, as the crumb rubber producers enter the market for slabs. But the tendency for the demand for slabs to increase would be eased somewhat if firms with licences to establish crumb rubber factories were also remillers, since they would presumably phase out their remilling operations gradually.

For the rest, the free market may decide their fate. Reports from Malaysia indicate that consuming countries will prefer the technically specified rubber and that they will eventually replace the older grades. But this may take time, and in the transition period there may be excess capacity in both the remilling and the crumb rubber plants. A programme of planned phasing-out of remilling would be preferable to this eventuality, since the capital equipment for the crumb rubber units would represent a waste of foreign exchange to the extent that machines were standing idle.

But what of the trading sector and the issue of the real income of the farmer? The Domestic Investment Law was partly designed to redress the imbalance created by the Foreign Investment Law by offering Indonesians (pribumi and WNI) inducements to invest similar to those offered to foreigners. In addition, the law permits aliens who have accumulated capital from their operations in Indonesia, i.e. aliens with *domestic capital*, to invest such capital in Indonesia. The Domestic Investment Law also covered investment in trading enterprises and once again the government's objectives were twofold: incentives to Indonesian citizens and safeguards to aliens with 'domestic capital' to invest in trading. By the time the law had been enacted in 1968, the changes which had already occurred in the rubber trade meant that its provisions were applicable to only a minority in the business. The large stores (toko) in Palembang which offered goods on credit to traders who went inland for rubber were owned either by WNI or alien Chinese. Under the new law those owned by alien Chinese had to cease operation by 31 December 1977.[70] The other levels in the marketing structure were controlled either by WNI Chinese or pribumi and the law does not distinguish between them.

The trading community has a vital role to play in offering inducements to the farmer to produce better quality slabs. Whatever form these incentives take, the objective is the processing of high quality crumb rubber.

Both the farmer and the country as a whole are the intended beneficiaries. The farmer is expected to get his reward in the form of higher prices. The gains to the country must be seen in the context of the world market situation. A downward trend in rubber prices commenced in 1961 when, for the first time, the production of synthetic rubber exceeded natural rubber.[74] The trend was interrupted between February 1968 and

September 1969, but by April 1970 the price of RRS I was back on the trend line and stood at US 21.7 cents per lb. The introduction of crumb rubber may not stop the downward trend but it may slow it down, as technically specified natural rubber is in a much better position to hold its own against synthetic.[72]

Since the government is relying on rubber as a foreign exchange earner, it is in its own interest to encourage the production of high quality rubber (and more specifically, crumb rubber). The present policy of welcoming investment from both indigenous and foreign entrepreneurs in crumb rubber by offering inducements under both the Domestic and Foreign Capital Laws is adequate evidence of its attitude to those who process rubber for export.

The farmer's real income depends on the prices of the goods he buys, as well as on the price of what he sells. If it is in the national interest to encourage the farmer to produce and invest in rubber it may be necessary to subsidise the prices of essentials and/or the price of rubber at the village level. This can be done without interfering directly with the marketing structure.

To summarise, the present trends indicate a processing industry controlled by the WNI Chinese with a small number of pribumi on the fringe. This pattern of ethnic division of labour could be altered by a government more disposed toward the pribumi group and prepared to finance their entry into crumb rubber processing. But such a policy would be unjustifiably costly in circumstances of excess capacity. An alternative would be to encourage economic diversification outside rubber in the region to create new opportunities for the pribumi.

The industrial sector in Palembang is small. This fact alone is enough to explain why economic nationalists have focused their attacks on the remilling industry.[73] There has been no other comparable industry to lay hands on. Enlarging the industrial sector would tend to increase opportunities for all groups in the South Sumatran community and should diminish existing and potential areas of friction between ethnic groups.

Regional development could also ease the pressures on the Chinese traders at all levels. Opening up the region would require improved communications. This in turn would encourage rural industry, and the government itself could offer inducements to the expansion of that sector. Specialist transport companies could emerge, responsible for moving a variety of products, including rubber. Entrepreneurs would be encouraged to enter the retail trade as the movement of goods by road, rail and river improved. Banking institutions would follow. The rubber producer might then be able to choose between a number of buyers for his rubber, choose the institution from which to borrow, buy his essential goods from a number of warong and so on.

It seems that as late as 2 May 1968 the regional government was still thinking along the old lines of bringing about major changes in the structure of the industry. It proposed that crumb rubber units be joint ventures between the rubber producers organised in co-operatives and either government or private capital. Its policy in the marketing of rubber tended toward a cooperative type structure at all levels: collecting, transportation, distribution (*sic*).

Our discussion has been directed to showing the rubber industry in the context of overall regional development. The Suharto government does not seem to display any ideological preference for an economy organised along co-operative lines, although there is certainly room for co-operative ventures of the type suggested by the regional government. But there is no economic reason to justify the belief that the rubber producer will benefit only from an economy organised co-operatively. There is room for co-operatives alongside other types of enterprise, all of which can be of benefit to the farmer in the village.

If overall regional development takes place, we would expect the regional government to design its rubber policies accordingly. Our contention is that only if such a development takes place will the pressure on the Chinese community be eased. Rubber will cease to be the focal point of conflict. Tolerance of the ethnic minority may thus increase, although it would be unwise to conclude that the path will be smooth, as recent experience in Malaysia under much more favourable economic circumstances has tragically shown.

CONCLUSION: A PERSPECTIVE ON DEVELOPMENT: THE RUBBER INDUSTRY AND THE ROLE OF THE CHINESE

In our discussion of the role of the alien and citizen Chinese in the South Sumatran rubber industry we have traced the changes which took place in the ethnic division of labour within the industry up to the eve of the introduction of the crumb rubber process. There is a real possibility that the introduction of crumb rubber will mark a turning point in the position of the ethnic minority in more ways than one.

Our study of the industry up to 1968 dealt with the way the Chinese minority accommodated to the demands of economic nationalism in what was, essentially, a stagnating economy. The pribumi gradually moved into positions in the marketing structure, especially as traders with shops (pedagang warong) and as traders along the rivers with motor-powered boats (pedagang motor). It was largely an evolutionary process marked by two distinct watersheds: PP 10 of 1959 and the abortive coup of 1965. WNI Chinese continued as traders at various levels and, as the pribumi trading group grew, WNI Chinese financed them from positions as remillers or owners of toko supplying essential goods on credit to facilitate the rubber trade.

The accommodation of both WNI and alien Chinese to changing circumstances in South Sumatra was a matter of survival for a group whose expertise lay mainly in the rubber trade; it was a case of adjust or perish. And until 1968, with the wealth of the region concentrated in the rubber industry, the economic nationalists had little choice but to demand greater participation for the pribumi at all levels in that industry.

It is possible to argue that staying in business between 1950 and 1965 inevitably led those involved to engage in smuggling, under-invoicing of exports and other such manipulations in the foreign exchange market. In this process, the remillers and traders were accused of lowering the quality of rubber exported and of paying low prices to the farmer.

There may be some truth in these allegations, but it is equally true that the government failed to implement policies introduced to stimulate farmers to plant high yielding rubber seeds, in spite of the fact that the tax levied on rubber exports was intended to finance planting programmes—a burden that was undoubtedly passed on to the farmer.[74] As the rate of inflation increased, unauthorised taxes as well were imposed by both civil and military personnel. The economic survival of the Chinese community in these circumstances depended very much on political patronage, at least until 1966. The alignment of the Chinese with a political party more concerned with raising funds for the party (and the pockets of certain individuals) was definitely not in the interests of the rubber industry or the economy as a whole. The Chinese were obliged to accommodate themselves to the dominant political groupings in the region and to the central government bureaucracy. Refusal to participate in this type of activity could have had serious consequences for their chances of continuing in business. In the process, the Chinese no doubt made adequate profits; but with the entry of newcomers into the industry demonstrated that they were not a homogeneous group dedicated to the elimination of competition.

Pressures on the position of the Chinese in the rubber industry inevitably increased as the general economic situation deteriorated. The region showed no signs of diversifying its economic base and the rubber industry remained the focus of a wide range of manipulations as various regional groups sought a share in the spoils. As Indonesia stagnated, so too did South Sumatra.

The advent of a government dedicated to growth should lessen the dependence of the Chinese on political patronage. If the South Sumatran economy can be diversified, there should be more scope for pribumi participation in a variety of economic occupations. Both the Foreign and Domestic Investment Laws encourage Chinese investment and much of this investment in South Sumatra will flow into crumb rubber processing. Such investment will be of major benefit to the country if the government is also successful in following the lead of Malaysia with a planting and replanting programme.[75]

There were already signs of interest by the Chinese in investing in crumb rubber factories early in 1969 and this interest has continued. But the warning given by Soedjatmoko on the future of foreign investment in Indonesia is very pertinent; he stresses the importance of involving local business in some spin-off activities, and the necessity of avoiding the danger that foreign firms become 'an alien enclave in a stagnant and increasingly hostile environment,' concluding that 'ultimately, the protection of foreign private investment lies in the rapid development of an indigenous commercial and entrepreneurial middle class and the development of a community of business interests between them and foreign enterprises in their country'.[76]

Many of the pribumi who entered the rubber trade between 1950 and 1965 did so with the backing of Chinese. But they did so in an economy which itself was not expanding. And there is little evidence that they gained a foothold in other sectors. It is to be hoped that in the future more pribumi will become involved in an expanding rubber industry and that others will enter new fields. As the economy expands, communications will improve and many of the functions now concentrated in the hands of the rubber trader may be taken over by specialist institutions. Specialisation and improved communications may lower costs and improve the real income of the farmer who should also benefit from the lower costs of tapping high yielding rubber trees. Adequate supplies of such essentials as rice will also curb inflationary price increases to the benefit of the farmer.[77] Instead of a frontal attack on the many dissensions within the rubber industry, exacerbated as they were by the ethnic element, overall development may provide much-needed relief.[78]

The Chinese minority engaged in the South Sumatran rubber industry showed remarkable resilience in the pre-1965 period. But insecurity and uncertainty was a high price for them to pay, both as businessmen and as individuals with families. The rights of the WNI Chinese are more likely to be safeguarded under conditions of economic development wherein the pribumi shares in the expansion of the economy than in circumstances where the ethnic minority has to rely on political patronage.

The conditions for a secure existence for the WNI Chinese are similar to those spelled out for the foreign investor by Soedjatmoko. As a group, the WNI have everything to gain by supporting the Suharto government in achieving its economic objectives—in fact, more than the foreigner, because the WNI Chinese have nowhere else to go. The Chinese have shown that under favourable circumstances, even during the difficult years of the depression, they can co-operate with farmers in producing good quality rubber, either sheets or blankets. There is no reason why they should not pioneer the establishment of crumb rubber factories in Palembang and throughout the rubber growing areas of Indonesia if the political climate and economic conditions are conducive to such a transformation of the industry on a long-term basis.

The Chinese have a history as innovators in the industry. Only in the independence period have they participated in practices which were detrimental to the industry as a whole, insofar as it weakened the competitive strength of natural against synthetic rubber. At the same time, the government suffered in terms of lower foreign exchange earnings as a result of a trend toward lower qualities, whether this was real or merely a reflection of under-invoicing. Such practices were distasteful to many Chinese businessmen, but economic survival dictated their business methods to some extent.

Taking up their former role as innovators in a developing regional economy could well ease the pressure on the Chinese coming from economic nationalists intent on increasing pribumi participation in the economy. If they play a role in Indonesian development, they may continue to survive and even to flourish. In the long run, it is easier to envisage a brighter future for the WNI Chinese in Indonesia than in Malaysia, insofar as hostility toward the Chinese is based on their economic roles. Economic development will bring more and more pribumi into important positions either in the private or government sector, including decision-making posts. It is to be hoped that as South Sumatra develops the Chinese will become a less 'conspicuous' feature in the economic landscape and that hostility toward them will decline accordingly. Perhaps the same will also happen in due course throughout the whole of Indonesia.[79]

5

'ARE INDONESIAN CHINESE UNIQUE?': SOME OBSERVATIONS

Wang Gungwu

The question of uniqueness was asked of me some years ago by a WNI Chinese who was inclined to believe that the answer was 'Yes'. Although I was interested in his question and had been reading various studies on the Indonesian Chinese, I was not prepared to comment on his catalogue of facts and problems which he thought was peculiar to these Chinese. Now that I am reminded of his catalogue by many of the points brought out in his volume, I have been tempted to reconsider the question. There is obviously presumption on my part in taking up the question, since I do not have equal knowledge of Chinese everywhere and no one can be sure that all groups of Chinese are comparable, especially over different periods. There is also the difficult word 'unique', especially the danger of saying 'more or less unique' and the question-begging idea that parts of some phenomena are unique while others are not. But after reading the three essays, re-reading other pioneer studies on Overseas Chinese and recollecting encounters with Chinese communities on five continents over a period of twenty-five years, I feel one ought to begin somewhere, and where else better than in Indonesia, the largest country in the world with a Chinese problem.

It is not possible to cover all aspects of the question in this short essay. The areas obviously least comparable have to be excluded; at one extreme China, Taiwan and Hong Kong-Macao, and, at the other, those countries in the Americas, Africa, Europe, Oceania and other parts of Asia where the Chinese are well under one per cent of the total population.[1] This leaves us mainly with the countries in Southeast Asia where the Chinese constitute 3–10 per cent of the total population. Within the region, Malaysia with 35 per cent of its population Chinese and Singapore with over 75 per cent are clearly different in demographic structure, but they are comparable for other reasons: proximity to Indonesia, related Muslim and Malay communities, and the fact that the Chinese communities in all three countries have been in close contact with one another. Also, there are many facets of Indonesian Chinese life and society which have been studied during the past few decades. It is not feasible to explore all of these here, and I shall therefore confine myself to the main points raised in our three essays and my observations must, therefore, be read in conjunction with them. The article is not a critique of the essays mentioned, but an attempt to see how the latest research on the Indonesian Chinese has identified their special characteristics.

Let me begin with Coppel's 'patterns of political activity'. He begins by contrasting the Indonesian patterns with those political attitudes which I discerned in Malaysia and extended to other parts of Southeast Asia.[2] He has approached the subject more historically than I have and has therefore listed patterns dominant at different stages in the history of the Netherlands East Indies and independent Indonesia. His six patterns, in other words, do not occur simultaneously, although three or four of them may be prominent at about the same time and others may overlap. Since he has concentrated on 'activity' where I have talked about 'attitudes', our categories are not directly comparable. It would be possible to trace political attitudes among Indonesian Chinese very similar to those in Malaysia, just as it is possible to take some of Coppel's patterns and follow them closely among Malaysian Chinese at different periods of history.

This is really by way of saying that the initial impression, that Malaysian and Indonesian Chinese are quite different, as derived from the ways the two of us have chosen to describe their politics, may be a misleading one. Indeed, what is so useful about Coppel's patterns of political activity is that they are so much easier to compare with the external patterns found in other countries in Southeast Asia than are the internal attitudes I had chosen to emphasise. Provided we are clear that we are comparing similar stages in history and do not treat each pattern of politics as having the same weight wherever and whenever it is found, comparisons can be made.

For example, the traditional officer system and one of its modern variants, the one during the Japanese occupation, can be found with local modifications throughout Southeast Asia up to about 1945. This system was a loosely structured affair and was originally evolved when there were no distinctions of nationality among the Asian peoples. It gradually declined throughout the region during the first decades of the twentieth century when China appointed consular officials to act on behalf of Overseas Chinese. Since 1945, with diplomatic relations established between most of the new nations and either China or Taiwan (the exceptions were Malaysia and Singapore), the traditional system was never really effective even where it has survived. But when nationality alone seemed inadequate to solve the 'Chinese problem', especially in Indonesia, a method of having local *Chinese* views represented within modern political institutions was used. This could be seen as a modified form of the officer system which would remain useful until the Chinese are totally assimilated. Such a system should cease to be necessary when citizens of Chinese descent are totally indistinguishable from all other citizens and the only Chinese in the country are aliens represented by their embassies and consulates.

The officer system and its variants have been based on certain assumptions: that, for the time being, the rulers did not expect or wish the Chinese to integrate or assimilate and the Chinese themselves agreed that they either might not or could not do so. There are two ways of looking at the system. First, that it was one imposed from above and set the limits on what the Chinese might or might not aspire to. From this point of view, the system determined patterns of behaviour different from the 'nationalist' and the three 'integration-assimilation' patterns[3] which imply that the Chinese took some initiatives in political affairs. The other is that, granted that the Chinese wanted to stay essentially Chinese and were, in any case, most useful to colonial and national governments when they were recognisably so and behaved according to certain given norms, then some kind of officer system could ensure that there were less ambiguities and misunderstandings about Chinese status, rights and obligations. During periods when the Chinese were uninterested in being anything but Chinese, this system was eminently workable and it is no wonder that it was used everywhere by indigenous rulers, colonial successors and Japanese conquerors, and it should not be surprising that a modified form of the system survives or re-appears even in post-colonial Southeast Asia.[4]

A similar comparison may be made for the 'nationalist' pattern, where politics was primarily the extension of China politics. Again, with little local variation, such a pattern of political activity may be found throughout Southeast Asia from about the beginning of the twentieth century until at least the 1950s and, in some areas, until the present day. Here was a pattern partly rooted in the Chinese communities themselves and partly directed and moulded by politicians, government officials, educators and journalists from China. Throughout this century, we can observe in every country in the region traditional, colonial and nationalist governments trying to intervene to break the tensions created between the Chinese overseas and their mentors in China.[5] Some governments have been more successful than others in containing such political activities. And indeed the methods employed in doing so vary considerably from country to country and from time to time. Here, it seems to me, is a crucial point. Where the Chinese exercised their initiatives, the different reactions of various governments and various indigenous leaders created totally different conditions for the Chinese to live and act in. With the officer system largely imposed from above, Chinese political activity within that system was severely limited, but with attempts to open up new 'nationalist' patterns on their own, the Chinese found themselves being hemmed in by different and often unexpected laws and measures which were increasingly to differentiate the levels of political activity at which they could operate as Chinese. In short, while the 'nationalist' pattern of activities may be similar everywhere (largely because of norms determined in China), the local consequences could be strikingly different.

Before we look at the three 'integration-assimilation' patterns which are so vital to Coppel's investigations, let me bring forward his sixth patterns. 'Cukong influence' cannot by definition be found outside In-this as a separate pattern. My own understanding of 'cukong influence' leads me to believe that this may be a temporary state, part of a kind of political anarchy, which is a prelude to either the re-institutionalisation of a kind of officer system or to the merging into 'integration-assimilation' patterns. 'Cukong influence' cannot by definition be found outside In-donesia where there are no cukong, but I believe that there are comparable cukong types elsewhere in Southeast Asia and that the major reason why the cukong seem distinctive is due to the present unstable condition of Indonesian national politics rather than the special nature of Chinese political activity in Indonesia. This is a point I shall return to later.

I now come to Coppel's main contribution to our understanding of Indonesian Chinese politics: the distinction he makes between 'integrationist' and two varieties of 'assimilation' patterns and the further distinction between 'assimilationist' and 'assimilated' patterns. Here at last is where peculiarly Indonesian factors, whether among the politically-conscious pribumi or the Chinese, have underlined the Chinese 'problem' for the Indonesian government and the parameters of Chinese activity in local politics. I have grouped the three together here because I believe they are closely related and represent three stages of political change for the Chinese, a steady narrowing down of choices as Indonesian nationalism becomes more tightly defined, a moving in at each stage from the outer circles into the inner nationalist centre as the outer positions become untenable. The inward movement takes over forty years, starting from the 1920s and reaching a climax just before the 1965 coup. It seems to have run its course and perhaps there is left now only the final stage of predominantly 'assimilated' politics accompanied by a revival of an officer system (or the cukong 'non-officer' transitional stage) and some residual 'nationalist' politics within sections of the Chinese communities connected with either China or Taiwan.

The three 'integration-assimilation' patterns outlined by Coppel are not, of course, unknown elsewhere in Southeast Asia. Some kind of 'assimilated' pattern can be found in local and national politics in nineteenth century Thailand and Philippines.[6] But the important difference is that these others were at different stages of history and served the Chinese quite differently from the way the 'assimilated' pattern was to affect the Indonesian Chinese during the past two decades. In post-colonial Malaysia, the Indonesian experience may eventually influence developments towards assimilation, but, with the much larger Chinese communities there, it is doubtful whether their politics will narrow down much beyond the 'integrationist' pattern, and it may well be that a modified officer system hinged onto modern political institutions there will be found to be more satisfactory for the majority of the Chinese. As for Singapore, the struggle still continues as to whether future Singaporeans will be mainly 'Westernised', 'Sinicised' or 'Malayo-Indonesian'.

From looking at Coppel's 'integration-assimilation' patterns, it is strikingly clear that the group which established these patterns and thus distinguished the Indonesian Chinese from other Southeast Asian Chinese was the peranakan Chinese of Java. There were equivalent groups in parts of Sumatra and Eastern Indonesia, in Malacca, Penang, Singapore and the Malay States, but nowhere else were they so politically active and enterprising. Also, nowhere else did such long-settled Chinese groups successfully resist, on the one hand, the pressure to assimilate totally as in Thailand and the Philippines and, on the other, the pressure to re-sinicise as in Sumatra and Malaya. It can, of course, be argued that both pressures were weaker in Java for a number of well-known historical reasons, but the fact of their separate and most articulate existence in the first decades of the twentieth century provided the hard cast from which some unique patterns of political activity were to emerge.[7]

A final point on Coppel's patterns needs to be made. While his historical analysis suggests how much weight we might give to each of the patterns, he is less explicit about their long-term significance. There is certainly a kind of finality for the Chinese about the 'assimilated' pattern which seems to 'presuppose the desirability of their ultimate assimilation', but he is right to point out the modern variants of the traditional officer system (including his mention of the cukong stage) and to hint at the remnants of 'integrationist' patterns which may still be of importance. This leads me to suggest that, of the six patterns proposed, the first, the officer system kind of politics, may be the most fundamental to our Asian multi-ethnic situation. It has persisted for centuries as a means of achieving stability and security for minority peoples and still seems to have some life in it. As compared with it, the other patterns seem related to it, or are much too ephemeral or represent some kind of final solution. If the 'integrationist' position survives its leaders will probably be taken into some form of officer system. If the 'nationalist' pattern can be contained and tamed, its leaders, too, could be fitted into the officer system. If such alien 'nationalists' cannot be contained, they will be crushed and sent to China or Taiwan or elsewhere and the solution is final. Similarly, the 'assimilated' pattern is also final insofar as there would eventually be no Chinese left. The 'assimilationist' pattern seems quite ephemeral, its protagonists having had to move towards 'assimilated' finality or drift around waiting for the new type of officers to emerge. This is true also for the cukong who, if they do not soon become officers themselves, will surely depart with their fortunes or be forced to assimilate totally in order to save their money or their lives, both positions being of some finality where the 'Chinese problem' is concerned.

These suggestions are made not to detract from the usefulness of Coppel's contributions, but to relate them to the question asked about the uniqueness of Indonesian Chinese. The Indonesian Chinese perceptions of 'integration-assimilation' and the kind of politics that developed are certainly unique, but neither the kinds of final solutions that might follow nor the survival of some form of officer system for the Chinese minority would distinguish the Indonesian Chinese position from those of Chinese elsewhere in Southeast Asia.

I now take my question to the next stage, the stage when politics fails and people resort to violence or when politics is stretched and nourished by violence, and look at Mackie's analysis of anti-Chinese actions during the years 1959–68. This is a very sensitive treatment of the subject and has added much to my understanding of Indonesia and, perhaps unjustifiably, to my courage in tackling the question of Indonesian Chinese uniqueness. Certainly the events and the range of Indonesian Chinese fears and sufferings during those years are unique. For whatever understandable reasons, nowhere have more Overseas Chinese been killed or wounded, run away or been chased away, and been so insecure during the past twenty years than in Indonesia. On this point alone one could make a strong case for the unique position of the Indonesian Chinese and many WNI Chinese would agree that their post-war experiences are unprecedented. But there is need to enquire further whether what is unique here is rooted more in Indonesian history and society than in the Chinese communities there. The two are, of course, not always separable, but as Mackie himself shows in his thorough efforts to explain the violence against the Chinese in the 1959–68 period, some distinctions can be identified. His 'prolegomenon' serves as a valuable starting point for this attempt to sort out the contributions to the events of 1959–68 which reveal the special features of Indonesian Chinese society.

First, let me point to the factors which are clearly peculiar to Indonesia as a new nation and an underdeveloped country. Among the 'predisposing factors', we can point to the twists and turns of the anti-colonial movement against Dutch rule and the aspects of that nationalism which were associated with fanatical Muslim groups and had long affected business competition between the pribumi and the Chinese. Of the 'restraining factors', the absence of relations with China is closer to the norm for the region, but the pre-1966 anxieties over relations with China did arise from special features of Indonesian anti-imperialist politics. And such relations created special problems of Chinese nationality which have never ceased to arouse Indonesian fears of the alien Chinese. Also the cukong relationship, central-regional tensions within the country and the yielding to anti-Chinese sentiments from time to time are different aspects of the weakness of central government. Long years of instability and ineffectual administration mark out Indonesia somewhat from the rest, although the records of countries like Burma, Cambodia, South Vietnam or even the Philippines are themselves poor. This may be a difference in degree, but because Indonesia is much larger than the others the difference is significant. As for the 'precipitating factors', five of the seven Mackie lists are clearly peculiar to Indonesia. They stem from political and economic instability on a scale no other Southeast Asian nation experienced and the consequences of long periods of instability on international and inter-ethnic relations are fairly obvious. But all such differences mark out the uniqueness of Indonesia rather than that of the Indonesian Chinese. They suggest that what the Indonesian Chinese are and what they do in response to their environment appear unique only because that environment is not found anywhere else.

Secondly, we should consider the factors deriving from either Chinese activities or the nature of Indonesian Chinese society which may be generally found elsewhere in the region. This is not as easy as it might appear. For example, 'the simple facts of racial difference and sociocultural separateness' may be said to be common to all countries with Chinese minorities; as might the resentment which non-Chinese 'have-nots' feel about Chinese 'haves' and the feeling that the Chinese dominate economically because of the sinister and immoral methods they are willing to employ. Yet the perceptions of race and sociocultural difference do vary, for example, between Muslim Malays and Buddhist Thais and between Chinese attitudes towards Malays and towards Thais.[8] Similarly, the resentment of 'have-nots' may vary in intensity according to whether political and economic conditions are stable or not and whether local politicians need to exploit these resentments for their own ends. Thus there are many qualitative elements in such factors which would need to be taken into account, and it may well be a case of the general similarities being obvious while the subtle differences are vital.

All the same, it is worth attempting to separate those factors in Indonesian Chinese society and in their activities which most closely resemble those among Chinese elsewhere from those which do not. It would then be clear that the socio-cultural separateness, the fact of 'having', the appearance of dominating the economy by dubious means and unfair advantages, are part of the image of Chinese everywhere in Southeast Asia. Similarly, there is Mackie's eighth 'predisposing factor', the Chinese appearing to represent the interests of a great power and seeming ready to subvert the new nation on behalf of an expansionist international communism, which also occurs throughout the region (with the possible exception of North Vietnam).[9] Also, among the 're-straining factors', the value to the national economy of Chinese business activities is also widely recognised and, in most countries, this weighs heavily in government plans and policies. The persistent fact of Chinese usefulness accompanied by the embarrassment of having the ubiquitous Chinese around in fairly obvious places are both common to the region. As for the 'precipitating factors', the flaunting of ethnic differences and the extent of conspicuous consumption among the Chinese are again repeatedly commented upon in every country in the region.

What then remains which is peculiar to the Indonesian Chinese themselves? From what Mackie has discovered, it would appear that what is distinctive is rooted in the new nation of Indonesia and its rich and manifold history, and what is Indonesian Chinese is really common to all Chinese in the region. Does this then lead to the view that there is something unusual about the country and its pribumi which makes the position of the Chinese in Indonesia, with their tragic sacrifices and deep insecurity, so unique since 1945? On the whole, I should say yes, though we should bear in mind that Mackie, in seeking mainly to explain Indonesian behaviour, was understandably general about the Chinese he described and carefully analytical and particularistic about Indonesian pribumi.

But one major feature of the Chinese communities in Indonesia should, I believe, be given more prominence. I return to the large peranakan community, mainly in Java, whose political and other activities Coppel and several others before him had described and emphasised. That this was already a large community in 1900, that it grew steadily larger through the century, that it became increasingly active in public and professional affairs and especially in journalism and politics —and that it did so without being either assimilated or re-sinicised— this had no equivalent counterpart anywhere else in Southeast Asia.[10] It is possible to show that their relations with the totok Chinese as well as with local Javanese or Sundanese or other smaller communities else-where had been unique at each stage of Indonesian history over the past century. It is possible to argue that they contributed independently (that is separately from other Chinese) and significantly towards political stability or instability in the country and towards economic growth and educational progress in ways which no other Chinese group in the region was able to do. Furthermore, if we should separate the peranakan when studying anti-Chinese actions both before and after 1959, we may expect distinctive roles for them in determining 'predisposing', 'restraining' and 'precipitating' factors behind anti-Chinese violence. Most obviously, they helped in strengthening 'restraining' factors like the Indonesian self-image of tolerance, anti-racialism and legality which must have salvaged many a dangerous situation for the Chinese. Similarly, their relative aloofness from China, their image of being westernised, if not Christian, their ability to communicate freely with Dutch and 'natives', with pribumi nationalists and local loyalists alike, were reassuring if not directly restraining factors. The peranakan effect on 'predisposing' factors is less prominent and certainly smaller than that of the totok; racially less 'pure' than the totok and culturally less distant and objec-tionable to the pribumi, their main negative role lay in the extent they had adopted Dutch ways and attitudes and saw themselves as having a higher status than the pribumi.[11] As for 'precipitating' factors, the peranakan were least responsible except where the political activities of a party like the Baperki were assertive, if not recognisably leftist, at a time when Chinese and Communists had a dangerous prominence.[12]

This is not to suggest that the existence of the peranakan Chinese reduced tensions and prevented more violence; this would, in any case, be very difficult to prove one way or the other. What needs emphasis is their uniqueness in Southeast Asia as an articulate, semi-assimilated group of Chinese who played an historic role before Indonesian in-dependence but whose failure to adapt as a group to nationalism since 1945 may have helped to open all Chinese to greater insecurity than need have occurred. This failure to adapt helps to explain why, for the period 1959–68, Mackie no longer finds it appropriate to distinguish their role in his analysis. And it is perhaps not surprising that, in 1959–68, Indonesian Chinese as a recognisable group have much more in common with other Southeast Asian Chinese. Their most distinctive group, the peranakan, was about to lose the fight to survive distinctively.

The erosion of the peranakan position since 1945 is not easy to explain. Certainly they failed to adapt as a group to the new conditions, their relatively high social status was removed, their political ambitions steadily crushed by rapidly changing events, and not least, their economic superiority which had been diminishing since the 1920s suffered further as new Chinese competitors found more favour with the nationalist elites. This last theme of new competitors and increasing pressures from other classes of Chinese may be found in most parts of Southeast Asia, but the Thomas-Panglaykim study of the rubber industry in South Sumatra before and after the war and before and after the 1965 coup shows how important such competition may be under conditions of great instability. The third essay in this volume does not tell us directly about peranakan losses since the republic was founded, nor who the new competitors have been. In South Sumatra, peranakan Chinese were less significant as a group, and close relations with Singapore, Malaysia and other parts of Sumatra where the Chinese have been predominantly totok had been conducive to competition and socio-economic mobility.

The point to note is that competition has always been a major factor, and is usually regarded as a normal and healthy feature among Chinese businessmen. What is striking in South Sumatra was that unstable political conditions speeded up the turnover of successful Chinese without the Chinese losing control over the key parts of the rubber industry. Also, it seems likely that the new men at each turn were totoks, WNI totoks or local-born totoks, most of whom had identified themselves with the destiny of Indonesia. Therefore, it is perhaps less significant whether they were Hokkiens, Cantonese, Hakkas or Hokchias and whether the industry was ever dominated by one dialect group, say, Hokkiens, and the competition was among the Hokkiens themselves.[13] If the new men depend less on their family and their dialect group and more on party affiliation, on local influence among the pribumi, on connections with the national bureaucracy and international contacts (whether with other Chinese or not), then a great step forward towards rational economic behaviour has been taken and a new age is near. If this is indeed so, then what prevents this step forward from leading to the end of the 'Chinese problem' in Indonesia is not so much traditional prejudice and ethnic jealousy as continued political instability and stagnation in certain sectors of the economy.

It is not possible here to enter satisfactorily into the large question of successful Chinese entrepreneurship. The case study of South Sumatra confirms that the Chinese have not lost any of their traditional skills and have acquired some new ones and may be becoming more innovative both in technology and capital accumulation. But this is the general picture throughout Southeast Asia and tells us little about the changes that are significant among the Indonesian Chinese themselves. In order to pursue the question of uniqueness, let me relate this economic competition to the issues discussed earlier about political patterns and conditions less conducive to anti-Chinese actions.

Insofar as a Chinese-dominated industry remains Chinese-dominated after intensive competition under extremely insecure conditions, the

Indonesian Chinese entrepreneurs have certainly had a unique experience. What is the secret of their success? Thomas and Panglaykim have mentioned 'assimilated' patterns of politics being employed to compensate for the lack of security, as with membership in the PNI. For the situation after 1965 Coppel's 'cukong influence' pattern is there to serve in a transitional period, and this is perhaps no less effective as a means of protecting life and profits. And, in addition, the major 'restraining factors' Mackie mentions which protect minorities, affirm legal equality, protect property to encourage foreign investment and encourage productivity in the national interest have been increasingly effective since 1968. As long as the Chinese—and so vital have they become to the nation's economic goals that they may be totok or peranakan, WNI Chinese or even alien—appear to be increasing the country's GNP, the 'restraining factors' are operative. And so long as the competition is fiercest between Chinese capitalists themselves and between various 'Ali-Baba' organisations,[14] racial tensions need not increase. And, if the assimilation process may actually be slowed down by the spectacular successes of Chinese capitalists, there are older political patterns, like that of the officer system, which can be revived and modified to control what may be 'integrationist' groups of Chinese.

There is, in short, a new sense of direction, a new confidence that the Chinese are manageable and can be made useful to the nation even when they have not assimilated. And here, the Indonesian Chinese are finally losing all claims to uniqueness, for their assigned role here is increasingly similar to the roles determined for them elsewhere in the region. This role is principally one of being an instrument of economic growth without either political ambition or social respectability,[15] and will remain their role until they are totally assimilated and, therefore, no longer Chinese.

I must emphasise that there is no intrinsic value in being unique and no special shame in having a similar role to play as other Chinese in Southeast Asia have. There are, in any case, other compensations. If the Chinese want to remain Chinese and find it possible to do so, they would remain markedly different from other Indonesians. If they wish to assimilate and succeed in doing that, they would identify wholly with Indonesia, and Indonesia certainly has much that deserves to be called unique. If, on the other hand, they are accepted as an Indonesian *suku* called 'Tjina' or 'Tionghoa', or some such name,[16] which is neither recognisably Chinese nor qualifies as pribumi, but is indubitably Indonesian, then that would indeed be unique.

The latest research in our three essays suggests that the prospects of such an Indonesian suku are now very slim. There is the medium-range possibility of officer-controlled Chinese and the long-range alternative of total assimilation. The two need not be contradictory, the former becoming some kind of staging station for the slow progress of the latter. If this can be recognised, then it would be easier to reduce the tensions which threaten harmonious race relations and even easier to fit the yet-unassimilated Chinese for valuable tasks which would consolidate and improve the nation's economic health. It remains to be said, however, that an Indonesian suku called 'Tionghoa' might well have come about. The nucleus of.this was the peranakan, and the only chance they really had to achieve their own suku status were the years 1945–65. For a time, they nearly made it. Had they done so, they would have created something no other group of Chinese in the region even thought of creating. My question thus has led me to appreciate how close the Indonesian Chinese were to uniqueness. Why they got that far and why they failed deserves a full story that has yet to be told.

Notes

PREFACE

1   The word *asli*, which had broader connotations of 'genuine' or 'real', has been replaced in official parlance since 1966 by the less contentious term *pribumi* ('son of the soil') to designate citizens of Indonesian descent.
2   Donald E. Wilmott, *The National Status of the Chinese in Indonesia 1900–1958*, p. x.

1   A PRELIMINARY SURVEY

1   The estimate of 3 million Chinese is based upon G. W. Skinner's calculation that in 1961 the total was 2 450 000 to which we have added an assumed annual increase since then of $2\frac{1}{2}$ per cent, with total net emigration between 1961–70 assumed to be within the range of 100–200 000. See G. W. Skinner, 'The Chinese Minority' in Ruth McVey (ed.), *Indonesia* (New Haven, 1963), ch. 3.
2   *Ibid.*, pp. 97–108: cf. also Tien Ju-Kang, *The Chinese of Sarawak* (London, 1953), and Victor Purcell, *The Chinese in Southeast Asia* (London, 2nd ed., 1965), *passim*.
3   Lea Williams, *The Future of the Overseas Chinese in Southeast Asia* (New York, 1966), see especially pp. 86–9 and 126.
4   See Coughlin's review of Lea Williams in *Journal of Asian Studies*, vol. 27, no. 1, 1968, pp. 175–7.
5   See C. P. Fitzgerald, *The Third China* (Melbourne, 1965), for a strongly sinophile statement of the view that Southeast Asia's Chinese will and can cling together in a hostile world, looking toward Hong Kong or Singapore for leadership and commercial backing. The view that Peking looks upon the Overseas Chinese as a potential 'fifth column' and has sought to win their allegiance is persuasively refuted by Stephen Fitzgerald in 'China's Overseas Chinese Policy: the "Fifth Column" as seen from Peking',

China Quarterly, no. 44, Oct.–Dec. 1970. Coughlin argues in *Double Identity. The Chinese in Modern Thailand* (Hong Kong, 1960), pp. 205–6, that 'we have been so conditioned to think of the inevitable assimilation of an immigrant minority group by the host society that we overlook too easily the likelihood of the host society itself being overwhelmed, demographically and culturally, by its giant neighbour'. His argument is debatable even for Thailand—let alone the radically different circumstances of Indonesia—but the broad geo-political line of thinking is wide-spread.

6   J. S. Furnivall, *Netherlands India* (Cambridge, 1944), pp. 408–9.

7   Purcell, *op. cit.*, ch. 47: J. L. Vleming, *Het Chineesche Zakenleven in Nederlandsch Indie* (Batavia, 1926).

8   These two terms have been used, not always consistently, in three different ways. 'The term peranakan, which implies mixed racial descent, is used in contradiction (read contradistinction) to totok, or full-blooded Chinese; it is also used to distinguish Indies-born Chinese from totok, or immigrant Chinese; and to distinguish a particular culture and society which developed, especially in Java, among the Indies-born Chinese from the totok, or purer, Chinese culture and society which developed among the new immigrants and to which, under the influence of twentieth-century Chinese nationalism, appreciable numbers of the Indies-born Chinese were attracted.' Coppel and Suryadinata, 'The Use of the terms "Tjina" and "Tionghoa" in Indonesia: An historical survey', *Papers on Far Eastern History*, no. 2, September 1970, p. 99. It is the last of these pairs of meanings which is adopted here.

9   For the best description of the diversity of Chinese society in Indonesia, see Skinner, 'The Chinese Minority', *op. cit.*, pp. 97–108. On Chinese of Java generally, and especially on the failure of the peranakans to assimilate to indigenous society, see G. W. Skinner, 'The Chinese of Java' in Morton H. Fried (ed.), *Colloquium on Overseas Chinese* (New York, 1958); 'Change and Persistence in Chinese Culture Overseas', *Journal of the South Seas Society*, vol. 16, 1960, pp. 86–100; 'Java's Chinese Minority: Continuity and Change', *Journal of Asian Studies*, 20/3, May 1961, pp. 353–62. See also The Siauw Giap, 'Religion and Overseas Chinese Assimilation in Southeast Asian Countries', *Revue du Sudest Asiatique*, vol. 1, 1965, pp. 67–84.

10   Tan Giok-lan, *The Chinese of Sukabumi* (Ithaca, 1963), pp. 4–11.

11   For distribution of the Chinese population, see the 1920 Census and the 1930 Census (vol. VII, ch. 2). For detailed studies of Chinese communities in Java, see Tan Giok-lan, *op. cit.* (Sukabumi, a town in the Priangan); Donald Willmott, *The Chinese of Semarang* (Ithaca, 1960), (Semarang, a north coast town in Central Java); Edward Ryan, The value system of a Chinese community in Java (unpublished dissertation, Harvard, 1961), ('Modjokuto', an inland East Javanese town); and Go Gien Tjwan, *Eenheid en verscheidenheid in een Indonesisch dorp* (Amsterdam, 1966), (a village in the Tanggerang district west of Jakarta). On the Agrarian Law of 1870, see Leo Suryadinata, The Three Major Streams in Peranakan Chinese Politics in Java 1917–1942 (unpublished MA thesis, Monash

University, 1969), pp. 167–9. On Chinese population growth, see 1930 Census, vol. VII, ch. 4.

12 1930 Census, vol. VII, pp. 22–3.

13 For a detailed examination of language usage among the Chinese in Indonesia in 1920, see Charles A. Coppel, 'Mapping the peranakan Chinese in Indonesia', *Papers on Far Eastern History*, 8 (September 1973). In Java, it is estimated on the basis of 1920 Census data that the main language of daily intercourse (*dagelijksche taal*) was distributed among the Chinese population in the following percentages: Malay 51.1, Chinese 30.1, Javanese 14.5, Sundanese 3.5, and Madurese 0.7. The proportion of those whose language of daily use was Chinese varied widely by region, ranging from 84.7 per cent in Yogyakarta to 6.1 per cent in Cirebon.

14 See 1930 Census, vol. VII, ch. 10, and Cator, *The Economic Position of the Chinese in the Netherlands Indies* (Oxford, 1936), pp. 103–4.

15 Furnivall, *Netherlands India*, p. 348, and Kahin, *Nationalism and Revolution in Indonesia* (Ithaca, 1952), p. 36; Kahin points out, however, that income of Indonesians from native agriculture is not shown in the assessment of incomes because it was subject to land tax rather than income tax, and that comprehensive land tax statistics do not exist. Most Europeans received incomes falling within the highest income brackets, most Indonesians received incomes falling within the lowest income bracket, while most Chinese received incomes which were neither in the highest income brackets nor the lowest. Figures on brick houses and motor cars are taken from 1920 Census, Table XI, and 1930 Census, vol. VII, ch. 7, and Furnivall, *op. cit.*, p. 348.

16 Anyone writing about the Indonesian Chinese outside Java is treading on dangerous ground because of the lack of detailed studies comparable to those already made for Java and because it is clear that Chinese society outside Java is more diversified. Valuable material may be found in the following sources: the Censuses of 1920 and especially 1930, vol. VII; Cator, *op. cit.*, pp. 127–251; de Groot, *Het kongsiwezen van Borneo* (The Hague, 1885); Skinner, 'The Chinese Minority', *op. cit.*, pp. 101–5; Somers, Mary F., Peranakan Chinese Politics in Indonesia (unpublished Ph.D. dissertation, Cornell, 1965).

17 See Cator, *op. cit.*, pp. 198–211 (Bangka), 138–80 (West Kalimantan), 239–40; pp. 247–51; also 1920 Census, Table VIII (for language spoken); 1930 Census, vol. VII, chs 3, 8 and 10 (for speech group, occupations and place of birth); and Skinner, 'The Chinese Minority', *op. cit.* (on acculturation).

18 See Cator, *op. cit.*, pp. 180–98 (Billiton), 211–17 (Bagan Siapiapi), 217–25 (*panglongs* of Riau and East coast of Sumatra), and 225–38 (East coast of Sumatra); 1920 Census, Table VIII (for language spoken); 1930 Census, vol. VII, ch. 3 (for place of birth).

19 Data in this paragraph are taken from 1930 Census, vol. VII, pp. 12–13 and ch. 8.

20 On population growth and immigration, see 1930 Census, vol. VII, p. 49 and ch. 4 generally; see also Statistical Pocketbooks issued regularly by the Central Bureau of Statistics in Jakarta.

21   These proportions are based upon the arguments put forward by Skinner in 'Java's Chinese Minority', *op. cit.*, pp. 356–8, and in his 'The Chinese Minority', *op. cit.*, pp. 103–5.

22   1930 Census, vol. VII, p. 129 and ch. 10 generally.

23   Donald E. Willmott, *The National Status of the Chinese in Indonesia 1900–1958* (Ithaca, rev. ed. 1961), chs 2–3.

24   *Ibid.*, pp. 14–15.

25   For brief accounts of the predicament of the Chinese during the Revolution, see Purcell, *op. cit.*, ch. 49, and Mary F. Somers, Peranakan Chinese Politics in Indonesia (Ithaca, unpublished Ph.D. thesis, Cornell University, 1965).

26   Willmott, *op. cit.*, pp. 40–3 and 118–30 (for text of 1958 Citizenship Law).

27   *Ibid.*, ch. 4 and pp. 130–9 (for text and elucidation of Dual Nationality Treaty).

28   These are the figures cited by Mary F. Somers in her Interim Report on *Peranakan Chinese Politics in Indonesia* (Ithaca, 1964), p. 34; Skinner, 'The Chinese Minority', cites an estimate by Mozingo that of the 2.45 million ethnic Chinese in Indonesia in 1961–2, approximately one million had been born outside Indonesia, about 200 000 had rejected Indonesian citizenship in 1945–51 and perhaps 50 000 were Indonesian-born but were children of Chinese-citizen parents; thus approximately 1.25 million were unequivocally aliens, mostly citizens of the CPR. Of the remainder, approximately one million had dual nationality and there were about 200 000 teenagers and young adults whose parents had earlier rejected Indonesian nationality.

29   The events which led to the abrogation of the Dual Nationality Treaty in 1969 are summarised in Charles Coppel, 'The National Status of the Chinese in Indonesia', *Papers in Far Eastern History* (Canberra), no. 1, March 1970.

30   Skinner, 'The Chinese Minority', p. 112.

31   See pages 98–9.

32   For the situation in the early years of independence, see Ralph Anspach, 'Indonesia', in Golay, Anspach, Dayal and Pfanner, *Economic Nationalism and Underdevelopment in Southeast Asia* (Ithaca, 1969); John Suttor, *Indonesianisasi* (Ithaca, 1959); G. C. Allen and Audrey Donnithorne, *Western Enterprise in Indonesia and Malaya* (London, 1957); and J. A. C. Mackie, 'The Indonesian Economy, 1950–1963' in *Studien zur Entwicklung in Süd- und Ostasien*, Neue Folg, Teil 3, Band XVI (Institut für Asienkunde in Hamburg, 1964), republished in Bruce Glassburner (ed.), *Studies in Indonesian Economics* (Ithaca, 1971). On the pre-war role of the Chinese in the economy, see Cator, *op. cit.* and other works cited in the Bibliography, Section VIII.

33   Anspach, *op. cit.*, p. 127, Skinner, 'The Chinese Minority', p. 113, and Willmott, *op. cit.*, pp. 87–90. It should be noticed that the word *asli* connotes not merely 'indigenous', but also 'genuine, authentic', so that there is an implication that those who are not *orang Indonesia asli*, i.e. even WNI Chinese, are not 'real' Indonesians. During the 1950s the term 'national businessmen' (*pengusaha nasional*) was also used in the sense of

excluding all Chinese businessmen, even WNI.

34 This point was emphasised by Hans O. Schmitt in his *Foreign Capital and Social Conflict in Indonesia 1950–58* (University of Wisconsin, Social Systems Research Institute, 1961).

35 Herbert Feith, *The Decline of Constitutional Democracy in Indonesia* (Ithaca, 1962), p. 481.

36 For a succinct account of the economic structure in 1959–60, see Douglas S. Paauw, 'From Colonial to Guided Economy', in R. McVey (ed.), *Indonesia* (New Haven, 1963), pp. 206–14; see also Lance Castles, 'Socialism and Private Business: the Latest Phase', *Bulletin of Indonesian Economic Studies*, no. 1, June 1965, pp. 13–45 (republished in Glassburner, *op. cit.*).

37 Skinner, 'The Chinese Minority', p. 114.

38 *Ibid.*, p. 115; cf. Willmott, *op. cit.*, p. 95—'If an anti-democratic and anti-Communist regime should ever come to power in Indonesia, drastic measures against the Chinese might be taken or allowed by the Government'.

39 Anspach, *op. cit.*, p. 193.

40 David Mozingo, *Sino-Indonesian Relations: An Overview, 1955–65* (Santa Monica, Rand Corporation, 1965).

41 See pages 97–110.

42 An excellent study of both the coup and the preceding relationship between the PKI and China is given by Ruth McVey, 'Indonesian Communism and China', in Tang Tsou (ed.), *China's Policy in Asia and America's Alternatives* (University of Chicago, 1968), vol. II.

43 See pages 124–5 and Charles A. Coppel, 'Indonesia: Freezing Relations with China', *Australia's Neighbours*, March–April 1968.

2 PATTERNS OF CHINESE POLITICAL ACTIVITY IN INDONESIA

1 The most valuable example of the quaint *Chinoiseries* is J. Moerman, *In en om de Chineesche Kamp* (Batavia, 1929). For the colonial administration of the Chinese and early Chinese officers, see L. H. W. van Sandick, *Chineezen buiten China* (The Hague, 1909), and articles by B. Hoetink which appeared in *Bijdragen tot de Taal—Land en Volkenkunde van Nederlandsch Indie* in 1917, 1918 and 1922. On contacts between China and Southeast Asia, see W. P. Groeneveldt, *Historical notes on Indonesia and Malaya, compiled from Chinese sources* (Djakarta, 1960). The most important economic and sociological studies include W. J. Cator, *The Economic Position of the Chinese in the Netherlands Indies* (Oxford, 1936); Ong Eng Die, *Chineezen in Nederlandsch-Indie* (Assen, 1943); Donald E. Willmott, *The Chinese of Semarang* (Ithaca, 1960); E. J. Ryan, The Value System of a Chinese community in Java (unpublished dissertation, Harvard, 1961); Tan Giok-lan, *The Chinese of Sukabumi* (Ithaca, 1963); and Go Gien Tjwan, *Eenheid en verscheidenheid in een Indonesisch dorp* (Amsterdam, 1966).

2 Donald Willmott, *The National Status of the Chinese in Indonesia, 1900–1958* (Ithaca, 1961), esp. pp. 101 ff.; Lea Williams, *Overseas Chinese Nationalism* (Glencoe, 1961); Mary F. Somers, *Peranakan Chinese Politics in Indonesia* (Ithaca, 1964), and her unpublished Ph.D. dissertation of the same title (Cornell, 1965); Leo Suryadinata (Liauw Kian Djoe), The Three Major

Streams in Peranakan Chinese Politics in Java 1917–1942 (unpublished MA thesis, Monash University, 1969).

3   Wang Gungwu, 'Chinese Politics in Malaya', *China Quarterly*, no. 43, July/Sept. 1970, pp. 1–30; and 'Political Chinese: an aspect of their contribution to modern Southeast Asian history', in Bernard Grossman (ed.), *Southeast Asia in the Modern World* (Hamburg, 1973), pp. 115–28.

4   Victor Purcell, *The Chinese in Southeast Asia* (London, 1965, 2nd ed.), p. 462.

5   J. S. Furnivall, *Netherlands India* (Cambridge, 1944), pp. 36 and 89 (emphasis added).

6   Williams, *op. cit.*, p. 8.

7   This paragraph follows G. Irwin, *Nineteenth Century Borneo: A Study in Diplomatic Rivalry* (The Hague, 1955), pp. 22, 165–74. The word '*kongsi*' is here used of political institutions said to have been modelled on village community organisation in south China, and not of commercial companies ('trading kongsi') which is the more common usage; see J. L. Vleming (ed.), *Het Chineesche Zakenleven in Nederlandsch Indie* (Batavia, 1926), p. 56.

8   The critics were de Groot and Schlegel—see Purcell, *op. cit.*, p. 425; also van Sandick, *Chineezen buiten China* (The Hague, 1909), p. 454.

9   Willmott, *The Chinese of Semarang*, pp. 148–50.

10 Williams, *op. cit.*, p. 125.

11 *Ibid.*, p. 38.

12 Willmott, *The Chinese of Semarang*, pp. 147–8.

13 Williams, *op. cit.*, pp. 131–2.

14 *Ibid.*, p. 126.

15 Williams, *loc. cit.*, and see also his 'The Ethical Program and the Chinese of Indonesia', *Journal of Southeast Asian History*, II/2 (1961), pp. 35–42.

16 Williams, *Overseas Chinese Nationalism*, pp. 127–8: van Sandick, *op. cit.*, p. 204.

17 Williams, *Overseas Chinese Nationalism*, pp. 125–6, 128–9.

18 On the Chinese nationalist awakening the major study is Williams, *Overseas Chinese Nationalism*; other valuable sources are Kwee Tek Hway, *The Origins of the Modern Chinese Movement in Indonesia* (trans. Williams, Ithaca, 1969); Fromberg, *Verspreide Geschriften* (Leiden, 1926), esp. pp. 405–47; Kwee Hing Tjiat, *Doea Kapala Batoe* (Berlin 1921); and Tjoe Bou San, *Pergerakan Tionghoa di Hindia Olanda* (Batavia, 1921).

19 Williams, *Overseas Chinese Nationalism*, pp. 27–36, and his 'The Ethical Program . . .', *op cit.*

20 Much of the material in this paragraph is based on Williams, *op. cit.*, ch. 3.

21 On the 'Tiong Hoa Hwe Koan', see Nio Joe Lan's fascinating fortieth anniversary history of the Batavia THHK, *Riwajat 40 Taon dari Tiong Hoa Hwe Koan—Batavia* (Batavia, 1940).

22 Of course, the Chinese their ancestors had spoken was almost invariably not the Mandarin they were to learn in school, but one of the Southern Chinese speech groups or dialects—in the case of the Chinese of Java, this was usually Hokkien. On the Malay language press, see Leo Suryadinata, *The Pre-World War II Peranakan Chinese Press of Java: A Preliminary Survey* (Athens, Ohio, 1971).

23 See the fortieth anniversary publication of the Batavia chamber, *Peringetan*

Tiong Hoa Siang Hwee Batavia Berdiri 40 Taon 1908–1948 (Batavia, 1948), cited in Suryadinata, The Three Major Streams ..., *op. cit.*, p. 6. On the political and quasi-consular functions of the chambers of commerce, see Willmott, *National Status* ..., p. 6, citing the thirtieth anniversary publication of the Semarang chamber, *Boekoe Peringetan 1907–1937 Tiong Hwa Siang Hwee Semarang* (Semarang, 1937).

24   Suryadinata, The Three Major Streams ..., p. 7.

25   Willmott, *National Status* ..., p. 14; cf. E. Ryan's review of Willmott, *Journal of Asian Studies*, vol. 21, May 1962, p. 415.

26   Cf. Skinner, 'Java's Chinese Minority ...', pp. 358–9—'... the Indies government accepted the challenge and joined battle for the peranakan soul'.

27   In 1893 there were only 28 Chinese in Java who had been admitted to European legal status (by the process of *gelijkstelling*)—Suryadinata, The Three Major Streams ..., p. 3; by 1940 some 16500 people had been admitted to the European group in this way (although it is not clear how many of these were Chinese)—Gouw Giok Siong, *Warga Negara dan Orang Asing* (Djakarta, 1960, 2nd ed.), p. 33.

28   Willmott, *National Status* ..., ch. 2; Suryadinata, The Three Major Streams ..., pp. 31–3.

29   Fartsan T. Sung, 'A brief historical sketch of the Chinese consulate general at Batavia, Java', *Sin Po Jubileum-Nummer 1910–1935*, (Batavia, 1935).

30   The requirement that Chinese should appear before native courts in criminal matters was abolished in 1914; the quarter system was abolished in 1917 and the pass system in 1918: Suryadinata, The Three Major Streams ..., p. 13.

31   On the Semarang conference of 1917, see Suryadinata, *ibid.*, pp. 17–24; for a description by a participant, see Kwee Hing Tjiat, *op. cit.*, ch. 5.

32   This section is largely drawn from Tjoe Bou San, *Pergerakan Tionghoa di Hindia Olanda*, esp. pp. 121–35, 168–78, 205–35. The book consists of a series of articles (including translations into Indonesian of several of Fromberg's essays on the Indies Chinese) which originally appeared in the newspaper *Sin Po* between 1918 and 1921; see also Suryadinata, *ibid.*, pp. 42–5.

33   Ruth T. McVey, 'Indonesian Communism and China' in Tsou Tang (ed.), *China in Crisis II. China's Policies in Asia and America's Alternatives* (Chicago, 1968), p. 359: 'The new immigrants among the totok working class had frequently absorbed revolutionary ideas—Kuomintang and, in the 1920s, Communist—in their South China homeland ...'

34   See Suryadinata, The Three Major Streams ..., pp. 128–30.

35   *Ibid.*, pp. 86–7, 197–8; McVey, *op cit.*, p. 357.

36   Skinner, 'Java's Chinese Minority', p. 358.

37   Suryadinata, The Three Major Streams ..., pp. 23, 27 and 37.

38   *Ibid.*, p. 7.

39   *Ibid.*, pp. 121–3.

40   *Ibid.*, pp. 38 and 126–8.

41   *Ibid.*, pp. 78, 108, 130 and 166.

42   Willmott, *National Status* ..., p. 9.

43   *Ibid.*, p. 17.
44   Suryadinata, The Three Major Streams . . . , p. 70.
45   *Ibid.*, p. 150.
46   Wang Gungwu, 'Chinese Politics in Malaya', *loc. cit.*
47   Suryadinata, The Three Major Streams . . . , p. 117.
48   *Ibid.*, ch. 3. The papers delivered at the first Semarang Congress were published under the title *Chung Hwa Congress (praeadviezen)*.
49   *Ibid.*, pp. 49–54.
50   *Ibid.*, pp. 169–70, 183–4. Chung Hwa Hui's claim for European status was made to the Visman Commission in 1940–41.
51   *Ibid.*, pp. 75, 117, 119–20, 151–2, 176, 178 and 182.
52   *Ibid.*, p. 112. I do not have access to figures giving the size of party membership, but it possibly numbered hundreds rather than thousands, with its main strength in Central Java.
53   *Ibid.*, pp. 170–2.
54   *Ibid.*, pp. 166–7.
55   *Ibid.*, p. 184; Ko Kwat Tiong was a co-author of the pamphlet *Indonesie Zelfstandig* (Batavia, 1937).
56   *Ibid.*, ch. 4.
57   In the 1935 Volksraad elections, the PTI formed an alliance with representatives of the Cigarette Merchants Association and Politiek Economische Bond—*ibid.*, pp. 118–19; for another example, see *ibid.*, pp. 178–9.
58   The PTI's base was in East Java, particularly in Surabaya; *ibid.*, p. 110. Precise membership figures are unavailable.
59   *Ibid.*, p. 210.
60   *Ibid.*, pp. 108 and 173. The PTI school itself probably promoted assimilation of a rather special kind—that of a few indigenous Indonesians into Dutch-educated peranakan circles—and acculturation of a special kind too—to Dutch rather than Indonesian culture. This was in fact also true of the Dutch system of education, since some indigenous pupils attended HCS, and at the secondary level (HBS) schools there were both Chinese and indigenous pupils. For a breakdown of Dutch school enrolments, see Mary Somers's dissertation, *op. cit.*, ch. 2.
61   Kwee Hing Tjiat's Chinese nationalist phase is well illustrated by his book *Doea Kapala Batoe*. For a biographical sketch of Kwee, see Suryadinata, The Three Major Streams . . . , pp. 138–41.
62   Kwee's *Mata Hari* campaign and the responses to it are reproduced in *Djawa Tengah Review* (August, 1934). I am indebted to Mr Suryadinata for this reference and the text of the issue.
63   Here and elsewhere in this chapter, the 'socio-cultural assimilation' is used as a shorthand (and oversimplified) expression to denote a variety of processes, which in practice may take place in varying degrees. These processes include acculturation (in which cultural patterns among the Chinese change to resemble those of Indonesian society), structural assimilation (in which Chinese enter the societal network of groups and institutions of Indonesian society), intermarriage of Chinese with Indonesians, and the development by Chinese of a sense of Indonesian identity.

For a valuable discussion of the term assimilation, see Milton M. Gordon, *Assimilation in American Life* (New York, 1964), pp. 68–71. These processes are not necessarily either one-way or continuous. For example, the peranakans of Java, whose culture at the turn of this century showed a significant degree of acculturation to Javanese and Sundanese culture, turned in some cases to Chinese culture (the so-called resinification process) and in others to Western styles of life (especially Dutch). There have also been cases in which indigenous Indonesians have assimilated to Chinese society (e.g. where Chinese have married indigenous wives and the children have been brought up as Chinese or at least as peranakan Chinese) and where elements of Chinese culture have become part of indigenous culture (e.g. the introduction into Indonesian diet of bean-shoots and bean curd—the Indonesian names for these two basic items of the diet derive from the Hokkien). Nevertheless, in this chapter references to socio-cultural assimilation will ordinarily refer to a process by which the Chinese move toward Indonesian society and culture.

64   The concepts 'political, cultural and racial nationalism' are taken from Willmott, *National Status* ..., p. 100; but where Willmott applied them to Indonesian Chinese, here they are being applied to indigenous Indonesian nationalism.

65   See Leo Suryadinata, 'Pre-war Indonesian nationalism and the Peranakan Chinese', *Indonesia*, no. 11 (April 1971), pp. 86–7, 91–2.

66   McVey, *op. cit.*, p. 359.

67   On Gerindo, see Suryadinata, 'Pre-war Indonesian nationalism ...', pp. 92–3.

68   The fullest account of the Chinese in Indonesia during the Japanese occupation is to be found in the dissertation by Mary F. Somers, to which the treatment here is heavily indebted. Nio Joe Lan described his experiences of internment by the Japanese in *Dalem Tawanan Djepang* (Djakarta, 1946); Kwee Kek Beng's experience in hiding during the occupation is described in his memoir *Doea Poeloe Lima Tahon Sebagi Wartawan* (Batavia, 1948), chs 11 and 12.

69   The 'Triple A' Movement (the three A's came from the slogan 'Japan the Leader of Asia, Japan the Protector of Asia, and Japan the Light of Asia') was an attempt to mobilise support for the Japanese war effort without working through Indonesian nationalism: Kahin, *op. cit.*, p. 103. H. H. Kan addressed a meeting supporting the Triple A Movement (Somers's dissertation, p. 106, citing Hong Po, 6 June 1942) but was later interned.

70   Somers's dissertation, p. 108.

71   *Ibid.*, p. 107; Willmott, *National Status* ..., p. 19.

72   Somers's dissertation, pp. 104–5.

73   *Ibid.*, p. 109.

74   For the period between the Japanese surrender and the transfer of sovereignty at the end of 1949, see the Somers's dissertation, pp. 112–34, and Willmott, *National Status* ..., pp. 19–29.

75   Willmott, pp. 19, 21. Chinese cabinet ministers in the Republican government were Tan Po Goan (1946–47), Siauw Giok Tjhan (1947–48), and Ong Eng Die (1947–48).

76 Somers's dissertation, pp. 124–5.

77 Somers's dissertation, pp. 112 ff, gives a careful analysis and description of the Tanggerang incidents and formation of *Pao An Tui*. See also Willmott, *National Status* . . . , p. 22. Although the idea seems to have been first mooted in Batavia, the Pao An Tui was first formed in Medan, North Sumatra. The Pao An Tui anthem, in its Indonesian language version, expressly stated that it was neither for nor against Indonesia, but was intended to guarantee the security of the Chinese who had been violated by the 'Laskars' of the independent Republic: they were 'burning, killing and slaughtering the Chinese people'—*Soeara Boeroeh*, 15 October 1947.

78 Somers's dissertation, pp. 125–7. Although van Mook's official title was Lt Governor General, there was no Governor General appointed after the war, and his position was virtually that of de facto Governor General—Kahin, *op. cit.*, p. 348, n. 38.

79 *Pangkal Pinang Werkelijkheidszin der Minderheden* (Batavia, 1946), p. 100: for Loa Sek Hie's views, see pp. 20–1.

80 Somers's dissertation, p. 130; and see the Sin Ming Hui tenth anniversary publication, *10 Tahun Sin Ming Hui—1946–1956* (Djakarta, 1956) pp. 14–27. (A similar development occurred in Makassar early in 1946 with the formation of the peranakan organisation *Pertip*.)

81 For names of PT leaders, see Somers's dissertation, p. 131; on aims of the PT, see L.G.S., 'Persatuan Tionghoa sebagai partai politiek', in *Kongres 1950 Persatuan Tionghoa* (Djakarta, 1950), pp. 49–51.

82 Although the broad outlines of the Communist v. KMT struggle among China-oriented totoks are common knowledge among both the leftist and rightist activists of the totok community, published studies are few and skimpy. But see G. W. Skinner, *Report on the Chinese in Southeast Asia*, December 1950 (Southeast Asian Program, Department of Far Eastern Studies, Cornell University, 1951, mimeo.) especially pp. 69–71; Skinner, 'The Chinese Minority', pp. 115–16; and, for the climax of the struggle, in 1957–58, see V. Hanssens, 'The Campaign against Nationalist Chinese in Indonesia', in B.H.M. Vlekke (ed.), *Indonesia's Struggle 1957–1958* (The Hague, 1959), pp. 56–76.

83 D. Mozingo, 'The Sino-Indonesian Dual Nationality Treaty', *Asian Survey* (December 1961), pp. 25 and 30, n. 3. On Liem Koen Hian, see Suryadinata, The Three Major Streams . . . , p. 161, n. 69.

84 *Berita PDTI*, no. 1, 15 October 1953, pp. 3–4 ('Dua Aliran').

85 When parliament was formed after the transfer of sovereignty, there were eight Chinese members, of whom the PDTI claimed four as members of PT (now PDTI). By 1951, one of these four (Yap Tjwan Bing) was conceded by PDTI to be a PNI representative; the other three were contested by PDTI and other parties, viz. Tan Boen An (PSI), Tjoa Sie Hwie (PNI) and Tjoeng Tin Jan (Catholic Party). See *Kepartaian di Indonesia* (Ministry of Information, 1951); *Kepartaian dan Parlementaria Indonesia* (Ministry of Information, 1954) and *Berita PDTI*, no. 2, 15 November 1953, pp. 4–5.

86 Willmott, *National Status* . . . , pp. 74–6, 87–90, and Somers's dissertation, pp. 136–40.

87 On the electoral law and minority representation: Somers's dissertation, pp. 141–2; and *Berita PDTI*, no. 1, 15 October 1953, pp. 1–3; no. 2, 15 November 1953, pp. 4–5; and no. 3, 15 December 1953, pp. 1–2.

88 Perwitt was formally established in Surabaya in January 1953. In its first anniversary publication *Perwitt Persatuan Warga Negara Indonesia Turunan Tionghoa Ulang Tahun ke-1 20-2-1954* (Surabaja, 1954), it claimed 750 families (or about 1500 people) as members, and to have four branches in East Java, three in Sumatra, and one in North Sulawesi. It stressed loyalty to Indonesia and the right of Indonesian citizens to be treated equally without discrimination. Pertip was confined to South Sulawesi, and particularly Makassar; it was formed much earlier, in 1946.

89 *Berita PDTI*, no. 3, 15 December 1953, pp. 3–5; no. 5, 15 February 1954, p. 4; and no. 6, 13 March 1954, pp. 1, 5; see also *Star Weekly*, 27 February 1954, pp. 1–2. On formation of Baperki generally, see Somers's dissertation, pp. 143 ff, and her monograph, *op. cit.*, ch. 1. Such characteristics as 'mass organisation', 'limited aims', and 'ideological non-alignment' were quite clearly spelled out in Baperki's original constitution.

90 *Pedoman Kampanje Perdjoangan Baperki dalam Pemilihan Umum* (Djakarta, n.d.).

91 *Berita Baperki Nomor Kongres Se-Indonesia ke III* (Djakarta, n.d.), pp. 17–18.

92 Somers's dissertation, p. 152.

93 *Ibid.*, pp. 149–50, *Berita Baperki*, 7 October 1955.

94 Somers's dissertation, pp. 157 ff.

95 Siauw Giok Tjhan had been a member of the PTI and a member of the editorial board of the Semarang daily *Mata Hari*; he was in hiding in East Java during the Japanese occupation and actively supported the Republican side after the Japanese surrender, becoming a cabinet minister in 1947. See Somers's monograph, p. 11; McVey, *op. cit.*, pp. 360–1; and *Purnama*, 5 March 1955, pp. 3–4.

96 This statement needs some qualification. The Masyumi and the PSI (representing the 'right') were heavily discredited in many quarters after some of their leaders took part in the 1958 Sumatran rebellion and they were dissolved in 1960. The rhetoric of politics became increasingly leftist in this period, particularly as enunciated by President Sukarno, whose public utterance became progressively more authoritative among the political public. But the 'right-wing' forces continued to have some influence and to receive protection, particularly in army circles.

97 Interview, Jakarta, and unpublished speech by Yap to the 1960 Baperki Congress in Semarang ('Dasar sempit, terbatas kontra dasar luas, tak terbatas'—mimeo, 24 December 1960).

98 For a published version of the central leadership viewpoint, see Siauw Giok Tjhan, *Gotong Rojong Nasakom Untuk Melaksanakan Ampera* (Djakarta, n.d. 1963?) esp. pp. 62 ff.

99 Willmott, *National Status . . .*, p. 89. On the Assaat Movement see Somers's monograph, pp. 16–18.

100 Somers's monograph, pp. 14–16, 29–35.

101 One of the seven appointed Chinese members of the parliament (Ang

Tjiang Liat) and three of the thirteen appointed to the constituent assembly were from a list submitted by Baperki—Somers's dissertation, pp. 152–3.

102 Somers's monograph, pp. 22–3.

103 But Siauw was not solicitous of the interests of the 'stateless' followers of the Kuomintang!

104 For an early example of Siauw Giok Tjhan's thinking on the economy, see his 'Membangun ekonomi nasional' in *Nomor Istimewa Berita Baperki* (December 1954?), pp. 10–29. On Ang Tjiang Liat and alien head tax: *Republik*, 20 July 1957.

105 V. Hanssens, *op. cit.*

106 Mistakenly, in my view: cf. pp. 35–7 above.

107 On UPBA and assimilation, see M. Tabrani, *Soal Minoriteit dalam Indonesia Merdeka* (Djakarta, 1950), pp. 40, 57, 98, 100–1; *Berita PDTI* (No. 3, 15 December 1953), p. 1; Willmott, *National Status* . . ., p. 78. For General Nasution's proclamation, Willmott, *National Status* . . ., p. 78, citing *Sin Po*, 17 April 1958.

108 This body should not be confused with the pre-war political party Chung Hwa Hui. The student body, formed in Leiden in 1911, did have a connection with the party, however, in that its former members who had returned to Indonesia were active in the formation of the party. See Suryadinata, The Three Major Streams . . ., pp. 49–51. My account of the 1952 move is based upon an interview in Jakarta with Junus Jahja (Lauw Chuan Tho, a participant) in December 1968, and the following sources: *De Noodzakelijke ontbinding van de Chung Hua Hui* (November 1952); and *Statement* (by former office-bearers of the CHH-Netherlands, end of 1952). (These are both pamphlets printed in the Netherlands.)

109 P. 44 above.

110 For a study of the development of separate Chinese churches, see the theological dissertation by Pouw Boen-Giok, *De Kerkrechtelijke Positie van een ethnisch bepaalde kerk in een ander ethnisch bepaald milieu* (Utrecht, 1952).

111 102 297 Chinese citizens left Indonesia in 1960—H. Feith, 'Indonesia', in G. McT. Kahin (ed.), *Governments and Politics of Southeast Asia* (Ithaca, 1964, 2nd ed.), p. 253; of these some 96 000 arrived in China within the same year—Skinner, 'The Chinese Minority', p. 115.

112 Estimates of numbers of Chinese Muslims are widely divergent—a report in *Harian Indonesia*, 3 April 1967, cited a leader of the Perkumpulan Islam Tionghoa Indonesia (PITI) as saying that there were 100 000 Chinese Muslims in Indonesia by 1966; on the other hand, another PITI leader two years later only claimed 10 000—*Pos Indonesia*, 30 October 1969.

113 *Assimilasi dalam Rangka Pembinaan Kesatuan Bangsa* (Deppen, Penerbitan Chusus 259, Djakarta, 1963). Somers's monograph, p. 38. Sukarno's speech to the opening of the Baperki congress in March 1963 was published as *Baperki supaja mendjadi sumbangan besar terhadap revolusi Indonesia* (Deppen, Penerbitan Chusus 255), pp. 15–16.

114 Hildred Geertz, 'Indonesian Cultures and Communities', in McVey, *Indonesia*, pp. 35–41. Most writing on assimilation presupposes a 'master

cultural mould', or a 'core society and culture' to which minorities might assimilate—see, e.g. Milton M. Gordon, *op. cit.*, p. 72. The problem of applying these concepts to a 'new nation' with frail national integration, like Indonesia, has not been faced squarely by the assimilationists. Baperki members, however, have given more thought to this type of problem; see *Simposion Baperki tentang Sumbangsih apakah jang dapat diberikan oleh Warganegara2 keturunan Asing kepada pembinaan dan perkembangan kebudajaan nasional Indonesia* (Djakarta, 1957). *Star Weekly*, 26 March 1960.

115 Yap Thiam Hien's views appeared in a series of three articles under the title 'Dua Therapy'—*Star Weekly*, 16 and 30 April and 21 May 1960. Siauw's reply appeared in *Star Weekly*, 22 April 1960.

116 This was the Urusan Pembinaan Kesatuan Bangsa (UPKB), set up under the army front organisation Badan Pembina Potensi Karya (body to develop the potential of the functional groups)—see *Inti Masalah 'Minorita'*, pp. 4–5. On the early history of the assimilationist movement, see *Lahirnja Konsepsi Assimilasi* (Djakarta, 1962) and *Inti Masalah 'Minorita'* (Djakarta, 1962?).

117 H. Feith, 'Indonesia's Political Symbols and their Wielders', *World Politics*, October 1963, p. 88n.

118 It had been decided in December 1962 that, following the successful prosecution of the campaign over West Irian, the 'state of emergency' would be terminated by 1 May 1963 at the latest—Muhono, *Ketetapan MPRS dan Peraturan Negara Jang Penting Bagi Anggauta Angkatan Bersendjata* (1966), p. 577. On 13 February 1963 President Sukarno gave his backing to the 'Panca-Program' (Five Programmes) of the National Front. *Ibid.*, pp. 789 ff. One of the targets of the National Front was the elimination of the army's rival front organisation (the BPPK—see note 116) and its incorporation within the National Front itself. *Ibid.*, p. 804. The approach by the assimilationists to the President took place on 22 February 1963— see *Assimilasi dalam rangka pembinaan kesatuan bangsa, op. cit.*

119 Somers's monograph, pp. 42–4. On the formation of LPKB, see *Assimilasi dalam rangka pembinaan kesatuan bangsa, op. cit.*

120 In 1968 the Indonesian Department of Home Affairs kindly allowed me to have access to the LPKB files. Some of the material which follows is based upon data from the files, and some too from interviews conducted during my periods of field research in Indonesia.

121 For the President's speech to Baperki congress, see *Baperki supaja mendjadi ..., op. cit.*

122 Partindo was a small party which had been formed in 1958 as a breakaway from the PNI. It was leftist and claimed a special relationship with President Sukarno. On PPKK, see *Madju Terus Pantang Mundur* (Djakarta, 1964), pp. 63–5.

123 See *Assimilasi dalam rangka pembinaan kesatuan bangsa* (Deppen, Penerbitan Chusus 326, 2nd revised ed., 1964), pp. 12 and 125–7. Also interviews, Jakarta, December 1968.

124 Siauw Giok Tjhan, *Gotong Rojong Nasakom Untuk Melaksanakan Ampera*, pp. 107, 108–9, citing *Bintang Timur*, 23 July 1963.

125   Muhono, *op. cit.*, pp. 539–68; the reference to Nasakom-phobia and LPKB are at pp. 559–60.

126   For text, Muhono, *op. cit.*, pp. 1141–76; the references to LPKB are at pp. 1167–8. For an example of the bowdlerised version published by LPKB see *Pembinaan Kesatuan Bangsa dalam rangka Nation-building dan Character-building* (Djakarta, 1964), p. 16.

127   Not so Baperki; an estimate by the Baperki central leadership on 9 August 1965 put the total membership of Baperki at 284 799, in 409 branches, excluding those at provincial level. (Cf. the 1955 figures given on p. 46 above.) The membership was heavily concentrated in Java (75.9 per cent) and Sumatra (18.6 per cent). The 1965 figures do not give the proportion of members who are of Chinese origin.

128   The abortive coup of 1 October 1965; for a collection of documents, see *Indonesia*, 1 (April 1966), pp. 131–204.

129   For text of this statement see *LPKB Ganjang Gestapu* (Djakarta, 1966?), p. 5.

130   *Fakta2 Persoalan Sekitar 'Gerakan 30 September'* (Puspenad, Penerbitan Chusus, Nos 1, 2 and 3, Djakarta, 1966), pp. 40–1.

131   Baperki statement of 4 October: mimeo copy in my possession—numbered K/K 1847/1965.

132   *Fakta2* ..., *op. cit.*, p. 75.

133   Copy in my possession, numbered K/1881/1965.

134   LPKB's second press release: *LPKB Ganjang Gestapu, op. cit.*, pp. 6–7. Cf. Berita Yudha editorial of 5 October: *Fakta2* ..., pp. 79–81.

135   *LPKB Ganjang Gestapu*, pp. 8–11.

136   *Indonesia*, I (April 1966), p. 154.

137   Text of KOTI radiogram in *LPKB Ganjang Gestapu*, pp. 36–7.

138   An abbreviated form of the letter appears in *LPKB Ganjang Gestapu*, p. 12.

139   *Ibid.*, pp. 15–17.

140   Part of the campaign was the distribution of the booklet *Baperki Membahajakan WNI 'Keturunan Tiong Hoa'* (Baperki endangers Indonesian citizens of 'Chinese origin') (Djakarta, 1965).

141   Western observers have put the numbers of those killed in the post-coup massacres at between 200 000 and 500 000 people. (Nicholas Turner, *Guardian*, 7 April 1966; special correspondent of London *Times*, 13 April 1966; C. L. Sulzberger, *New York Times*, 13 April 1966; Robert S. Elegant, *Los Angeles Times*, 22 April 1966; and Stanley Karnow, *Washington Post*, 4 and 5 May 1966.) It is commonly believed outside Indonesia that the Chinese were particularly badly hit—in an extreme example, the Australian edition of *Life* of 22 July 1968 says that 'hundreds of thousands of Chinese' were massacred. I have found no-one in Indonesia who subscribes to this view, even among Chinese who are far from reluctant to complain about persecution. On anti-Chinese violence, see ch. 3.

142   KOTI (Supreme Operations Command) was a top-level military organisation installed on 19 July 1963 with very wide terms of reference. Its section V (GV) covered 'political, economic and social' fields. Muhono, *op. cit.*, pp. 805–6.

143   See the third anniversary publication *Buku Peringatan Dies Natalis III Universitas Trisakti (29 Nopember 1965–29 Nopember 1968)* (Djakarta 1968). Selection of students at the university 'is based upon academic considerations by means of entrance examinations and upon political considerations in order to maintain the continued existence of Trisakti University and to create a harmonious atmosphere in the promotion of national unity' (*ibid.*, p. 47). Alien students are only to be admitted with the approval of the Government, and even this is limited to inter-governmental cultural agreements, scholarships and student exchanges (*ibid.*, p. 76). This effectively excludes alien Chinese residents in Indonesia.

144   Coppel, 'Indonesia: Freezing Relations with China', *Australia's Neighbours*, 4th series, no. 54–55, March/April 1968.

145   This situation was brought about by a MPRS decision in July 1966, which limited the number of press publications in foreign languages which (like Chinese) did not use Latin script, to one only, and that one to be published by the government: see *Ketetapan2 MPRS Hasil2 Sidang Umum ke-IV Tahun 1966* (Djakarta, 1966), p. 138. In practice, there have been two such publications, both government-controlled, issued under the same name, *Harian Indonesia*; the fiction is maintained that these are two editions of the same newspaper, one the North Sumatra edition, and the other the Jakarta edition, but in fact their management is quite separate. The North Sumatran edition was subsequently closed.

146   At the time of their closure, official statistics showed that there were 667 such schools, attended by 276 382 students, of whom 272 782 were Chinese citizens. (Source: Bureau of Foreign Education, Department of Education and Culture, 11 April 1966.)

147   See Mely G. Tan and Leo Suryadinata, 'The "Special Project National Schools" in Djakarta', paper delivered at the 28th Congress of Orientalists, Canberra, January 1971.

148   The total numbers of Chinese who left Indonesia during the upheaval which followed the attempted coup are unknown. Although they may be quite substantial, it seems clear that the figure must be appreciably less than the mass exodus of 1960.

149   One Jakarta newspaper which has had the temerity to publish some details of cukong arrangements and even to suggest that the cukongs have a share in determining Indonesian government policy is the daily *Nusantara*—e.g. the issue for 1 February 1971.

150   This section is based upon interviews in Jakarta in December 1968, April 1969 and November 1970.

151   In fact, even among the Taiwan-oriented group, those chosen as members of the BKUT do not seem to have been particularly prominent.

152   See my 'The National Status of the Chinese in Indonesia', *Papers on Far Eastern History*, no. 1 (March 1970), esp. pp. 126–35.

153   The Psychology Faculty of Padjadjaran University, Bandung, made a survey of this phenomenon within a month after the event—see *Laporan Projek Penelitian Tentang Perkembangan Proses Asimilasi Sesudah Peristiwa Gestapu/P.K.I. Di Kotamadya/Kabupaten Sukabumi* (n.d.). The research was

funded by the central **LPKB** and **KOGAM-GV**, and the research team
headed by Drs J. Wullur (Oei Tjin San), who, in addition to being on the
staff of the Psychology Faculty, was a leading figure in LPKB and its West
Java branch.

154   Keputusan no. 127/U/Kep/12/1966. 232882 WNI Chinese: *Kompas*, 28
August 1969.

155   Instruksi no. 31/U/In/12/1966.

156   *Ketetapan2 MPRS* ..., pp. 141–4.

157   *Ibid.*, pp. 31–5. Roger Paget, 'The Military in Indonesian Politics: The
Burden of Power', *Pacific Affairs*, Fall and Winter 1967–68, p. 307.

158   OPSUS is an abbreviation for Operasi Chusus (Special Operations), an
intelligence organisation headed by the President's personal assistant,
Major Gen. Ali Murtopo. One of his right-hand men is a young Chinese
Catholic called Liem Bian Kie. OPSUS is widely credited with successfully
manipulating elections and appointments within several political parties
and other organisations. These moves have given support to the widespread belief that OPSUS is highly antagonistic to militant Islam. Liem
Bian Kie's brother, Lim Bian Koen, is assistant to Major Gen. Sudjono
Humardhani, another close associate of the President. These generals (and
the President) are all believed to have close ties with Chinese businessmen
(or cukongs).

159   Rosihan Anwar in *Harian KAMI*, 13 October 1969; reproduced with a
reply by Arief Budiman in *Komunikasi*, 25 October 1969.

160   Lea Williams, *The Future of the Overseas Chinese in Southeast Asia* (New York,
1966), p. 105. My criticism of it first appeared in *Australian Outlook*
(August 1969), pp. 194–6. For his definition of 'political assimilation', see
p. 74n.

161   *Ibid.*, p. 86.

162   *Ibid.*, p. 114.

163   *Ibid.*, p. 114.

164   Above, p. 71.

165   See note 3, above.

166   Michael Leigh, 'Party formation in Sarawak', *Indonesia*, 9 (April 1970),
pp. 189–224.

167   Some Chinese influences from outside Indonesia have grown in recent
times, however; in the form of books, periodicals and films from Taiwan,
Hong Kong and Singapore.

168   The discussion in this paragraph owes much to a discussion with Leo
Suryadinata in Melbourne in the latter part of 1969, but responsibility for
any deficiencies in the extended presentation given here is entirely mine.

3   ANTI-CHINESE OUTBREAKS IN INDONESIA 1959–68

1   No satisfactory account of the role and predicament of the Overseas
Chinese in Indonesia during the Revolution has yet appeared. Some of
them sided with the Republic, others openly supported the Dutch: most
seem to have tried to avoid taking sides while waiting to see who would
win, for which they were accused of opportunism by Indonesian nationalists. The main highlights of the period are sketched in Victor Purcell,

The Chinese in Southeast Asia (London, 2nd ed., 1965), ch. 49: a more balanced and deeply researched account is given by Mary Somers Heidhues in her Peranakan Chinese Politics in Indonesia (Ph.D. dissertation, Cornell University, 1965), pp. 110–28.

2   Ruth McVey, 'Indonesian Communism and China', in Tang Tsou (ed.), *China's Policies in Asia and America's Alternatives* (Chicago, 1968), vol. II, p. 359.

3   Herbert Feith, 'The Political Dynamics of Guided Democracy', in Ruth McVey (ed.), *Indonesia* (New Haven, 1963), p. 349. The left-right dichotomy was not quite as tidy as this: some members of the so-called 'national-communist' or 'Trotskyist' Murba Party sometimes revealed strongly anti-Chinese inclinations, although its founder, Tan Malakka, was notable for his cordiality towards Chinese.

4   W. F. Wertheim, *East-West Parallels* (The Hague, 1964), p. 76.

5   *Ibid.*, p. 79.

6   The Siauw Giap, 'Group Conflict in a Plural Society', *Revue du Sudest Asiatique*, vol. 2, 1966, p. 19.

7   The contrast between Buddhist Thailand and Muslim Indonesia in this respect was well stated by G. W. Skinner in 'Change and Persistence in Chinese Culture Overseas; a Comparison of Thailand and Java', *Journal of the South Seas Society*, vol. XVI, 1960.

8   While the *prima facie* evidence seems to support the view that anti-Chinese feeling is less intense among the non-*santri* Javanese than among the more 'fanatical' Muslims such as the Acehnese, Madurese, Bugis-Makassarese, etc., Indonesian Chinese often say they find it easier to establish cordial business and social relations with the latter than with the reserved and culturally self-assured *priyayi* Javanese, who make a great virtue of not displaying their feelings, even when they may be harbouring deep resentments and hostility. One can easily imagine the complexity of the psychological mechanisms operating in a matter such as this.

9   This was the assessment of G. W. Skinner shortly afterwards; see his 'The Chinese Minority', p. 115. The inference that the Chinese had few friends at court after 1959 turned out to be too pessimistic, however, for President Sukarno and the PKI proved able to curb any overt manifestation of anti-Chinese sentiments until 1965.

10   *Surat Keputusan Menteri Perdagangan* no. 2933/M. 14 May 1959. Some notion of the scope of the ban may be obtained from the fact that there were 209 *kabupaten* in 1960, with an average size of about 800 000 in Java, but less than 300 000 in the outer islands.

11   The term 'national businessmen' was a euphemism in common use between 1956 and 1960 to refer to the group of indigenous (asli) businessmen only. The 'Assaat movement' and its policies are sketched briefly by Ralph Anspach in Golay (ed.), *Underdevelopment and Economic Nationalism in Southeast Asia* (Ithaca, 1969), pp. 186–7.

12   Regulations obliging all alien-owned or partly alien-owned businesses to register with the Department of Trade had been passed in 1958. For details of this and other measures against the Chinese in 1957–8, see Skinner, *op. cit.*, p. 114: also Anspach, *op. cit.*, pp. 111–203.

13 See *Harian Rakjat*, 5 September 1959, for a favourable comment on Sukarno's Manipol reference to 'progressive foreign capital'.

14 For an excellent account of this relationship, see Feith, *op. cit.*, pp. 336–42. A more detailed narrative of the events of mid-1959 is given by Daniel S. Lev, *The Transition to Guided Democracy: Indonesian Politics, 1957–1959* (Cornell, 1966), ch. 6.

15 David Mozingo puts great stress on the residence bans as 'the real irritant' to the Chinese and 'the main issue in dispute between the Peking and Jakarta governments': see his Ph.D. dissertation, Chinese Policy in Indonesia, 1949–1967 (University of California, Los Angeles, 1971), ch. 6.

16 According to figures made available by Mr K. D. Thomas, the amount of working capital needed if indigenous businesses (co-operatives or capitalists) were to take over the function of the Chinese traders was estimated at Rp. 27 billion (approx. $200 million at the prevailing black market value of the Rupiah).

17 *Nusantara*, 6 October 1959.

18 See above, pp. 9–11.

19 Mozingo, *Sino-Indonesian Relations* ..., pp. 22–5. See also his dissertation, ch. 6.

20 According to a report by Dennis Bloodworth in the *Observer* (London) on 6 November 'the Chinese treated Dr Subandrio like a delinquent brought before an outraged magistrate. Chou En-lai spoke to him so insultingly that Dr Subandrio had to stop the discussion, remind the Chinese premier that he was the representative of a friendly power, and threaten to leave if he continued in that tone'. Subandrio officially denied the truth of the report, but I have been told that unofficially he admitted that it was substantially correct.

21 The full text of the Joint Statement was published in *Harian Rakjat*, 13 October. (It was surprisingly hard to find copies of it in other Indonesian newspapers. In fact, press reports of the entire episode were extremely sketchy and an account based solely on what was printed at the time would be quite misleading; both *Harian Rakjat* and several right-wing papers were banned temporarily in October–November and the other papers were obviously afraid of taking risks of saying the wrong thing.)

22 *Duta Masjarakat*, 14 October; *Suluh Indonesia*, 13 October; *Pedoman*, 13 October. Subandrio said in Hong Kong that agreement had been reached on fundamental issues, but that practical difficulties remained to be settled; some papers took this to mean that he had made concessions to the Chinese. He made a firmer statement on his return to Jakarta on 22 October, which removed the earlier doubts, but by this time the press was thoroughly roused on the issue.

23 *Harian Rakjat*, 2 November; *Duta Masjarakat*, 3 November.

24 For the text of PP 10, see *Business News*, 23 November; for the little-known supplementary regulation of 12 November, see *Suara Rakjat* (Surabaya), 21 November.

25 Mozingo, Ph.D. dissertation, ch. 6. For the full text of the West Java Military Commander's regulation of 12 November, see *Harian Rakjat*, 21 November.

26 Press reports of the Cibadak incident were scanty in the extreme; *Harian Rakjat*, 17 November, carried, without comment, an official account by the information officer of the West Java military command, Major Nawawi Alif, who claimed that the movement of 81 aliens from Cibadak on 3 November was carried out smoothly, except for one incident in which a Chinese assumed an 'attitude of opposition to the instructions and warnings given to him' and an officer became angry and hit him; his wounds were described as not serious, but the officer concerned was allegedly subjected to disciplinary action. No other such incidents were reported.

27 See *Pedoman*, 31 November, and *Suluh Indonesia*, 16 November, on the Hong Kong reports; *Nusantara*, 14 November, for the Bloodworth story; *Abadi*, 16 November, for a 'shocked' reaction to the latter. For Subandrio's pleas to play down the tension and prevent exaggerations by both sides, see *Pedoman*, 17 November.

28 Huang Chen's repudiation of Subandrio's press statement was apparently directed against the implication that he supported the implementation of the residence ban; see *Harian Rakjat*, 18, 19 November, *Kedaulatan Rakjat*, 20, 21 November. He met Prime Minister Djuanda and President Sukarno during the next three days and seems to have soothed their feelings on the issue somewhat; shortly before this incident he had travelled to Cirebon in the Presidential party for a ceremony there. It may be misleading to put too much stress on the tensions aroused by this issue at the time, for other controversial questions were attracting just as much attention in the Jakarta press.

29 The PKI Politbureau's official statement on the issue was published in *Harian Rakjat* on 23 November 1959: the PNI newspaper, *Suluh Indonesia*, came out openly in favour of the ban on 16 November, after having avoided taking sides clearly on the issue previously; it had made a non-committal comment on 11 October and in mid-November the PNI published a speech made in June 1957 by Subagio Reksodipuro in parliament as material for the 'guidance' of PNI members on the Overseas Chinese question: see *Kedaulatan Rakjat*, 21 November.

30 Mozingo, Ph.D. dissertation, ch. 6.

31 For stories of Chinese consular intervention and transgression of the ban on their movements in West Java, see *Kedaulatan Rakjat*, 21 November, *Abadi*, 10 and 14 December, and *Pos Indonesia*, 1 December.

32 Mozingo, Ph.D. dissertation, ch. 6; however, Stephen Fitzgerald attributes the Chinese response to Indonesia's measures to quite different motives, principally to 'the magnitude and the nature of the discrimination (which) made it almost impossible for the Chinese to ignore'. *China and the Overseas Chinese* (Cambridge, 1972), pp. 152–4. Repatriation was not a new policy directed against Indonesia, but one which Peking had announced several years previously.

33 For example, the Masyumi newspaper, *Abadi*, 14, 15, 16 December, alleged that China's behaviour was evidence of her expansionist tendencies and claimed that the PKI was linked with Peking's attacks on Indonesia's good name in the world.

34 The several Notes exchanged between Chen Yi and Subandrio between December and March are published in G. V. Ambedkar and V. D. Divekar, *Documents on China's Relations with South and Southeast Asia, 1949–1962* (Bombay, 1964), pp. 240–61. Chen Yi's three proposals of 9 December were: (i) immediate ratification and implementation of the Dual Nationality Agreement; (ii) protection by Indonesia of the rights and interests of Chinese nationals, whom China would encourage to respect the laws of Indonesia; (iii) repatriation of those Chinese who did not wish to remain in Indonesia.

35 The black market rate of the Rupiah had been Rp. 94 to the $US at the end of September 1959: it then climbed to Rp. 250 by the end of December and Rp. 310 in March, but fell back to about Rp. 200 later in 1960. Presumably the sudden outflow of 'hot money' after PP 10 was largely responsible for the jump.

36 An account of the rise and fall of the Democratic League is given in Feith, 'Dynamics of Guided Democracy', *op. cit.*, pp. 343–4.

37 Mozingo, Ph.D. dissertation, ch. 6.

38 *Ibid.*, p. 16.

39 In West Java the residence ban on aliens in rural areas had not been put into effect at the end of 1959, its implementation having been postponed till 30 June 1960. According to the Indonesian explanation of the Cimahi incident, the Overseas Chinese in Cimahi had made no efforts to move up till that time and on 1 July their leaders refused to obey a police summons to explain why they had not moved; the police were attacked and withdrew. When they returned on 3 July with military support a struggle broke out in which shots were fired and two women were killed. The *Peking Review* of 12 July alleges that *all* Overseas Chinese in Cimahi were being forcibly evacuated, although this is barely credible, since Cimahi is a fair-sized town with a large Chinese population, almost on the outskirts of Bandung. The Indonesian Foreign Ministry expressed its regret over the incident in a Note to the Chinese government, but stated that there was 'incitement from outside' (a Chinese Embassy official was in near-by Bandung at the time): see *Pedoman* 5, 7 July 1950: *Suluh Indonesia*, 28 July; cf. *Peking Review*, 12 July 1960.

40 Mary Somers Heidhues, *Peranakan Chinese Politics in Indonesia*, pp. 208–9. See also her *Chinese Minorities in Southeast Asia* (Longmans, 1974), ch. 7.

41 Mary Somers Heidhues, *Peranakan Chinese Politics*, pp. 210–11.

42 *Ibid.*, pp. 203–14.

43 *Ibid.*, pp. 16–18 and 203–40; cf. also Giok-lan Tan, *The Chinese of Suka-bumi: a Study in Social and Cultural Accommodation* (Cornell Modern Indonesia Project, Monograph Series, 1963), ch. 1.

44 Selo Soemardjan, cs, *Gerakan 10 Mei 1963 di Sukabumi* (The 10 May 1963 Movement in Sukabumi) (P.T. Eresco, Bandung, n.d.). This is the printed version of the report published by a group of social scientists from the National Economic and Social Research Institute (LEKNAS—hereafter referred to as the Leknas Report) on the background to the Sukabumi riots. It was originally circulated in mimeographed form under the title *Laporan Umum, Pilot Survey 'Pusaka Djiwa' tentang faktor-faktor mengandung*

potensi gerakan kerukunan di kota Sukabumi. While the report suffers from some shortcomings which are due in part to the political constraints applying in the late Guided Democracy period, it was in several respects a daringly independent piece of research into an unusually sensitive subject. A brief summary of its findings is given in The Siauw Giap, 'Group Conflict in a Plural Society', *loc. cit.*

45 Leknas Report, pp. 203–4. Outbreaks occurred at Sindanglaut, Kuningan, Palimanan, Blambangan, Jatiwangi, Jambang and Plered between 29 March and 1 April; at Tegal, Pagongan, Slawi, and Bandung between 5 and 10 May; and at Solo, Bogor, Cipanjung, Tasikmalaya, Garut, Singaparna, Surabaya, Malang, Medan, Cianjur, Cibadak and Sukabumi between 11 and 20 May.

46 Mozingo, *Sino-Indonesian Relations: an Overview*, p. 60 ff.

47 The jaundiced attitude towards Indonesia of several key Congressmen and Senators in Washington was making it extremely doubtful that the State Department could get a substantial foreign aid appropriation for Indonesia accepted in the face of Sukarno's bellicosity towards Malaysia. The complex interplay of external and internal politics in Indonesian-US relations in early 1963 is spelled out fully in Frederick Bunnell, The Kennedy Initiatives in Indonesia 1962–1963 (Ph.D. thesis, Cornell University, 1969), ch. 3–4.

48 On the Baperki-LPKB rivalry, see above, p. 53 ff, and Mary F. Somers, *Peranakan Chinese Politics in Indonesia*, ch. 3.

49 This estimate of the duration of the Cirebon rioting has been queried by one Indonesian informant who blamed the security authorities for negligence in not taking firm action more promptly. For a fuller account, cf. Leknas Report, p. 203–4, and The, *op. cit.*, p. 5.

50 According to the *Age* (Melbourne), 15 May 1963, 177 vehicles and 28 buildings, including government buildings, were damaged. This and the following paragraph are based on material derived from the Leknas Report and personal communications from Professor Herbert Feith, to whom I am also indebted for much other information in the following pages.

51 Personal communications from Mr Stuart Graham and Dr Ulf Sundhaussen.

52 *Age* (Melbourne), 15 May 1963.

53 The question of whether responsibility rested with the civil or military authorities to take action against the rioters does not seem to have been a significant factor behind the failure to take more prompt or vigorous action on 10 May. Troops were called in toward the end of the day. The Siliwangi Division commander, Major General Adjie (a man who got on well with the Chinese), happened to be out of Bandung at the time: his Chief of Staff, Col. Ishak Djuarsa, was said to be strongly anti-Chinese, but what role he played in the tortuous politics of the affair is not known to me.

54 According to one report, Governor Mashudi spoke in too placatory a vein to deter the rioters ('I understand your sentiments, but . . .') although he went on to threaten that arrests would be made if the rioting did not stop. Some arrests were made; according to the *Age*, 15 May 1963, 350 people were held for interrogation. Several were later brought to trial, but rather

half-heartedly, owing to the complex political overtones of the whole affair.

55   For the main official statements, see below, pp. 107–8.

56   In this account of the rioting in Sukabumi, I have drawn heavily on a study by Jean Taylor, Inter-communal Antagonisms in Indonesia: a Study of the 1963 Riots (BA Hons thesis, University of Melbourne, 1966), which is also based primarily on the Leknas Report, supplemented by newspaper accounts.

57   The, *op. cit.*, p. 11.

58   These allegations may well have had some basis of truth, for it would have been reasonable for the Chinese to look for help in those quarters. But in the atmosphere of tension and xenophobia then prevailing, the most sinister interpretations could easily be attached to quite innocent actions and anti-Sukarno groups would have been eager to find opportunities for generating suspicion of collusion between the Chinese and government officials to whom they were opposed.

59   The total damage was officially estimated at Rp. 2.5 billion (approx. $US 7–8 million at the overvalued official rate of the Rupiah at that time, but less than $2 million at the black market rate), but this figure was a gross underestimate.

60   *Harian Rakjat*, 20 May.

61   *Suluh Indonesia*, 13 May.

62   *Harian Rakjat*, 13 May; *Duta Masjarakat*, 13 May.

63   *Harian Rakjat*, 13 May.

64   *Harian Rakjat*, 14 May.

65   *Harian Rakjat*, 17 May; *Duta Masjarakat*, 17 May.

66   *Duta Masjarakat*, 29 May.

67   Leknas Report, p. 28.

68   Leknas Report, p. 46: The Siauw Giap is sceptical of this conclusion, which runs counter to his own interpretation in terms of economic competition as the decisive factor, but he provides no specific evidence to the contrary.

69   I am indebted to Herbert Feith for this point and to Ulf Sundhaussen and Stuart Graham for data on which other parts of this paragraph are based.

70   For much of the information contained in the following section I am indebted to Herbert Feith and Charles Coppel, although they bear no responsibility for the interpretation given here. Numerous accounts of the coup and the events which led to the gradual transfer of power from President Sukarno to Lt General Suharto have appeared: one of the most readable and less highly partisan versions which may be recommended to the reader who is unfamiliar with the general political background of this period is John Hughes, *Indonesian Upheaval* (New York, 1967). The main events of 1966–68 are well summarised by Herbert Feith, 'Suharto's Search for a Political Format', *Indonesia*, no. 6, October 1968.

71   A series of inflammatory articles in the daily newspaper *Api Pantjasila* in October 1965 were an outstanding instance of this kind of mischief-making.

72   Some of these are quoted in Rafe de Crespigny, 'Chinese Newspaper

Reports of the Changes in Indonesia, September to December 1965', *Australian Outlook*, vol. 20, no. 2, August 1966.

73 It was reported that the army leaders had refused to allow Dr Subandrio, who was still the Foreign Minister, to leave Indonesia to attend the Standing Committee meeting. Indonesia was represented by a junior official and played a very subdued part at the meeting.

74 Charles A. Coppel, 'Indonesia: Freezing Relations with China', *Australia's Neighbours*, 4th series, nos 54–55, March–April 1968, p. 5.

75 The Chinese government also seems to have hoped the axis could be maintained until about that time; on 20 November, it announced that Chinese technicians working in Jakarta on the Conefo building were to be withdrawn, but this may have been done to avoid undesirable incidents as much as to signal Peking's displeasure.

76 de Crespigny, *op. cit.*, p. 198.

77 See above, p. 64.

78 There were some puzzling aspects to the long and unedifying wrangle that dragged on over the question of repatriation of Chinese nationals throughout the following months. China only made available one ship, the *Kuang Hua*, which took only four shiploads, approximately 4 250 persons, during the 15-month period from September 1966 to the end of 1967. The various pinpricking delays and protests (on both sides) during that period may have been a sign that neither government was really keen to encourage large-scale emigration of Chinese nationals from Indonesia, but could not afford to say this openly. Alternatively, they may have simply meant that neither government was willing to make any concessions to the other on a matter in which national pride and 'face' were so heavily involved.

79 Although the number of alien Chinese in Aceh dropped sharply in 1966 (from more than 21 000 in 1965 to a mere handful of aliens and around 4 000 'stateless' in 1966), there were still almost 6 000 alien and 'stateless' Chinese there in 1967, mostly the former, according to official statistics made available to me by Charles Coppel. An account of refugee camps in North Sumatra and Aceh is given in a report by Ian Brodie in the London *Daily Express*, 21 September 1966.

80 Accounts of the appalling conditions in the Medan refugee camps may be found in the *New York Times*, 23 October 1966 (according to which 6 000 Chinese were expelled from Aceh to Medan) and in reports by Philip Koch of the ABC in November 1966.

81 For the Chinese version of these incidents, which occurred at a time when the Cultural Revolution was at its height, see *Hsinhua*, 18 September, 2 October and 25 November 1967.

82 For a good survey of the Suharto government's economic rehabilitation programme of October 1966 and its apprehensions about the disruptive effect of anti-Chinese actions, see the 'Survey of Recent Developments' in *Bulletin of Indonesian Economic Studies*, no. 6, February 1967, pp. 2–15, and no. 7, June 1967, pp. 9–10.

83 Suharto promised that the government 'would continue to oppose racialism and will take firm measures against any individual or group which

directly or indirectly inflames or carries out racialist actions which are not in accordance with the spirit of Pantja Sila'. He did not refer to China or the Chinese by name, but merely alluded to 'the problem of citizens of a country that has a hostile attitude to Indonesia'.

84   Coppel and Suryadinata, 'The Use of the Terms "Tjina" and "Tionghoa" in Indonesia; An historical survey', *Papers on Far Eastern History*, no. 2, September 1970.

85   The number of Chinese who actually left Indonesia in those years is almost impossible to estimate with any precision. The official figures for alien and 'stateless' Chinese show a perceptible decline between 1967 and 1969 (from 1 115 781 to 994 754), the fall occurring mostly in Sumatra, as one would expect; but it is not clear how much of this decline was due to emigration or how much to conversion to Indonesian citizenship or to mere failure to register. The judgement of Charles Coppel, who has supplied me with these figures, is that the number of emigrants was probably a good deal less than the 100 000 or so who left in 1959–60, but one cannot say much more than that.

86   According to some reports, attempts were made to have the ban applied to Chinese-owned businesses of all kinds outside the city of Surabaya as well; the regulations required that Chinese businesses were to be sold by 15 February and the proceeds deposited in blocked accounts in the banks so as to prevent an outflow of capital.

87   *Bulletin of Indonesian Economic Studies*, June 1967, no. 7, pp. 9–10.

88   On 8 February Acting-President Suharto announced that 'No action should be taken against foreigners which will disrupt economic activity'; cf. also a statement in the same vein by the Minister of Trade at a Governors' Conference on 13 March.

89   See *ibid.* for a press report in May that there had been inadequate follow-up on the East Java regulations and that the economic activities of the Chinese were continuing as usual.

90   Brig. General Rijacudu announced in November 1966 that PP 10—and a residence ban—would be applied against Chinese nationals in West Kalimantan, where many of the Chinese who had been living there for several generations had not taken the necessary steps to opt for Indonesian nationality under the Dual Nationality Treaty in 1960–62 and were therefore subject to these bans. Attempts to apply the ban failed, however, and the Chinese returned to their villages in the first half of 1967, until the Dayak attacks of October–November, described below.

91   Herbert Feith, who was in Jakarta at the time and has supplied background information on these events, speculated that some Chinese Embassy personnel may have played a part in this display of strength.

92   In Peking, an anti-Indonesian rally was held on 27 April at which Suharto's effigy was burnt, and several demonstrations against the Indonesian Embassy occurred. Two Indonesian diplomats who were ordered to leave China after being declared *persona non grata* were pushed around and spat upon by Red Guards at Canton, actions which inevitably inflamed the passions of KAPPI militants in Indonesia even further. Indonesia retaliat-

ed by declaring the Chinese Chargé d'Affaires and Consul General *persona non grata* likewise.

93 The State Committee was set up to investigate all aspects of the Chinese problem, with Brig. Gen. Sunarso as Chairman and Lt Col. Drs W. D. Sukisman (a sinologist) as Secretary. Its importance is not attributable to any radically new policy recommendations except the establishment of SCUT and BKUT (see above, pp. 66–7), but rather to the fact that it asserted the need to reach an integral settlement of the problem and to avoid unco-ordinated and ad hoc measures against the Chinese, such as various regional commanders and New Order activists had attempted. It was apparently on the basis of the Committee's review of the citizenship legislation and the Dual Nationality Treaty that the government later revoked the Treaty (in April 1969), depriving certain nationals of the right to opt for Indonesian citizenship on attaining their majority; thus naturalisation was henceforth the only means open to non-citizen Chinese to become citizens. While this seems to have been a restrictive and retrograde measure, the Committee made recommendations for a 'domestic foreign capital' law (i.e. capital held in Indonesia by Chinese nationals) which opened the way to a satisfactory settlement of their economic position. We can date the subsidence of agitation against the Chinese on these issues from about the time of the Committee's report to the Presidium in June 1967.

94 Even this resolution was a watered-down version of a more uncompromising one; it was criticised by Muslim groups as 'too defensive'.

95 Although each government felt obliged to take diplomatic action of some kind in retaliation against the 'insults' of the other, their gestures were frequently kept to a minimum; for instance, when the Indonesian government decided to withdraw its diplomats from Peking to Hong Kong in June 1967 on grounds of inadequate protection, it avoided publicising its action for several weeks.

96 Coppel, 'Indonesia: Freezing Relations with China', *loc. cit.*

97 The fact that the Jakarta military commander found it necessary to issue a strong denunciation of extortionate practices in February 1968 is an indication that they were still widespread.

98 The 'Glodok incident' of 25 January 1968 was an ugly episode which flared up several days after an RPKAD paratrooper was beaten up by five Chinese who accused him of extortion; two truckloads of paratroopers retaliated by ransacking shops and beating up Chinese in the area concerned. Scores of students began smashing Chinese motor cycles and other property, but were curbed by troops firing shots in the air. Fortunately the incident did not spread beyond that. The Surabaya episode was a response to the Singapore government's gratuitously provocative action in hanging four Indonesian marines who had been sentenced to death for acts they had committed during Confrontation, more than three years earlier. Here too the outbreak was confined to one city.

99 For the background of the Chinese in the Sarawak-West Kalimantan region in the 1960s, see J. M. van der Kroef, 'The Sarawak-Indonesian

Border Insurgency', *Modern Asian Studies*, vol. II, no. 3, July 1968, pp. 245–65.

100 *Hsinhua*, 30 August. An Indonesian account of the military background to these events was given in a series of articles in *Pelopor Baru*, 22 November to 11 December.

101 *Herald* (Melbourne), 18 November 1967; *Kami*, 14 November 1967.

102 *Kami*, 15 April 1968. For accounts of conditions in the camps, see the *Herald* (Melbourne), 18, 21 and 22 November.

103 *Far Eastern Economic Review*, 25 January 1968. Feith suggested that the Dayak attacks on the Chinese may have been instigated or controlled by a leading Dayak political leader prominent in the Sukarno era but later displaced, J. C. Oevang Oeray, in a bid to regain a position of influence.

104 *Pelopor Baru*, 23 November 1967.

105 *Sinar Harapan*, 11 and 20 March 1971.

106 A somewhat similar approach to this may be found in Selosoemardjan's introductory chapter of the Leknas Report, pp. 45–6, where he identifies five 'potential factors' contributing to aggressive actions in the Sukabumi situation of 1963. Mary Somers Heidhues has compiled a valuable generalised survey of theories of anti-Sinicism throughout Southeast Asia as a whole in a study which has appeared since this chapter was written, *The Chinese Minorities in Southeast Asia* (Longmans, 1974), in which she examines explanations in terms of economic exploitation, economic competition, religious and cultural differences, nationalism and political manipulation ('deflection') and 'vacuum of power' as the 'spark in the tinder-box'.

107 See pp. 5, 9–10 above.

108 The emergence in the early twentieth century of what we commonly call Indonesian nationalism or Chinese nationalism among the Overseas Chinese (which were initially marked by attempts to unify diverse groups fragmented by other primordial attachments through appeals of a nationalist character) tended to elevate the racial factor as a key element in the new nationalism and to reinforce the sense of ethnic differences between Indonesians and Chinese. Indonesian nationalists were given pause to wonder just what the basis of the 'Indonesian nation' (*bangsa Indonesia*) was to be: see above pp. 35–8 and Leo Suryadinata, *op. cit.*, p. 80 ff.

109 On China's policies towards the Overseas Chinese and the 'fifth column' argument, see Stephen Fitzgerald, *op. cit.*

110 The *Benteng* system was the most blatant set of measures involving preference for ethnic Indonesians and it was modified in 1954 to avoid discriminating against WNI Chinese; see above pp. 13–14.

111 Before one draws too many optimistic conclusions from this proposition, however, it is necessary to keep in mind the fact that Chinese businessmen are still subject to a good deal of 'squeeze' in periods of relative prosperity precisely because they are thought to be making huge profits. Conversely, as soon as any contraction of business activity or of credit availability occurs, Indonesian businessmen are bound to be the most severely hurt and are likely to revive their demands for discriminatory policies reminiscent of Assaatism.

112 For fuller details see Harold Crouch, 'The "15 January" Affair in Indonesia', *Dyason House Papers*, vol. 1, no. 1, Aug. 1974; also *Far Eastern Economic Review*, 25 Feb. 1974, pp. 12–14, and 15 July 1974, pp. 31–4.

4 THE CHINESE IN THE SOUTH SUMATRAN RUBBER INDUSTRY: A CASE STUDY IN ECONOMIC NATIONALISM

1 In Indonesia, the distinction between estate and smallholder rubber depends on the type of land lease (unlike Malaysia where the distinction is one of size). For a short note on types of leases see K. D. Thomas, *Smallholders Rubber in Indonesia* (Jakarta, Institute for Economic and Social Research, University of Indonesia, 1957), p. 5.

2 South Sumatra was divided into three residencies in the colonial period (Palembang, Lampung and Bengkulu). After independence these were termed *keresidenan* until the 1960s, when they were raised to provincial status (*Daerah Swatantra I*), the residency of Palembang becoming the province of South Sumatra.

3 V. Purcell, *The Chinese in Southeast Asia* (London, Oxford University Press, 2nd ed., 1965), p. 16.

4 The statistics for 1912 and 1915 are taken from G. F. de Bruyn Kops, *Overzicht van Zuid-Sumatra* (Amsterdam, J. H. De Bussy, 1919), pp. 162–3.

5 Data from the 1930 census are taken from J. W. J. Wellen, *Zuid-Sumatra, Economisch Overzicht* (Holland, H. Veenman and Zonen, 1932), pp. 152–5. The percentage increase in the Chinese population of South Sumatra greatly exceeded the growth rate of population as a whole (253 per cent compared with 64 per cent). Migration must have been a crucial factor in both cases, but especially for the Chinese.

6 Petroleum is not included in this list, which is confined to agricultural products. By 1928 the value of petroleum products exported from Palembang exceeded the combined value of coffee, rubber and pepper by some 12 million guilders (petroleum exports were fl. 39.5 million).

7 J. H. Boeke, *Economics and Economic Policy of Dual Societies, as exemplified by Indonesia* (Haarlem, H. D. Tjeenk Willink & Zoon N.V., 1953), p. 124. Presumably, Boeke was referring to the study of Palembang in the seven volume report on the smallholder rubber industry in Indonesia compiled in the mid1920s, *De Bevolkings-rubbercultuur in Nederlandsch-Indie* (Weltevreden, Departement Van Landbouw, Nijverheid en Handel, 1927). The report on Palembang in Volume IV was written by C. N. Warren, and was based on field work carried out in April and May 1925.

8 I.e. those Chinese resident in Indonesia who did not become Indonesian citizens.

9 In the remilling process the slabs were put through a series of power-driven machines, each unit consisting of two rollers to tear them apart while water was sprayed on them so that as much dirt as possible was washed out. Several slabs were put through the machine at once and as they were ripped apart the rubber was bound together into long thin strips. Slabs, about 80 cm long, 40 cm wide and of varying thickness, were transformed by the milling machines into a blanket of about 4 to 5 metres in length and

5 mm thick. The blankets were hung in a drying room for 15–20 days, depending on the drying system. The process is still the same today. About 40 per cent of the latex from the tree is water, so the process of turning a slab into a blanket involves getting rid of any impurities in the slab and then reducing the water content. The blanket is then ready for the world market. There are several grades of blanket, the quality depending largely on the quality of the slab. The problems of assessing the quality of slab rubber are discussed on pages 156–9.

10 To make sheets, latex is sieved to get rid of dirt, then poured into a pan to coagulate. Once coagulated, the rubber is tipped onto a bench and kneaded to make it thin enough to put through hand mangles. These mangles, similar to those used in household laundries, squeeze out as much water as possible. Two steel rollers are used, one smooth and the other grooved. When the rubber passes through the grooved mangle, the rubber sheet has a pattern on it from which it takes its name *ribbed* sheet—the pattern exposes more of the surface than if the sheet were plain, thus assisting in the drying process. The sheets are hung in a *smokehouse* where they are completely dried by smoke channelled into the house via pipes. Some smokehouses are large structures with several compartments but, large or small, the principle is the same. Smoking takes 4 to 5 days, or 30 per cent of the drying time for blankets, mainly because sheets are smaller than blankets (1.40 metres by 40 to 50 cm).

11 In the Banjarmasin area, smallholders often made their own smokehouses, primitive structures with *atap* roofs. The resulting smoked sheet was of very low quality and often had to be re-processed in the port.

12 Whether the interest rates on such loans was exorbitant is a matter for considerable debate and is central to the attack on the role of the Chinese.

13 In the mountainous areas of Palembang residency and more particularly in the Lampung residency the shifting cultivator planted coffee instead of rubber.

14 The (ethnic) Chinese dominated this level at least until 1959. Changes have occurred since then and are discussed below.

15 Pribumi traders did operate at these levels, but only in small numbers. Even before the war, however, the Dutch shipping company (KPM) extended credit to indigenous traders in rubber.

16 Kops's description of a *toko* is a useful one, namely 'a Chinese toko is more than a bazaar, a department store in the small, in which a most heterogeneous assortment of goods are sold such as drapery, various products made of iron and copper, glassware and china, leather goods, foodstuffs, drinks, kerosene. This is in contrast to the establishments of the Arabs in the Indies which specialise in the sale of drapery only'; *ibid.*, p. 158.

17 Not until the remilling factories were set up in the Lampung (especially around Panjang) did the railways come to play an important part in the trading network.

18 It is worth noting that although remilling exports reached 46 000 tonnes in 1941 there were still only five remilling factories in Palembang.

19 Exports increased sharply to 85 000 tonnes in the following year. The potential production (assuming satisfactory prices) of smallholders cannot

be estimated with any degree of accuracy, owing to lack of reliable data on the area of mature rubber. Throughout the 1930s more and more trees planted in the previous decade became tappable, but the Restriction Scheme, commenced in 1934, kept them out of production.

20   Before the war Kian Gwan had a registered capacity of 12 000 tonnes, and Hok Tong of 9 000 tonnes. Total capacity was listed at 37 000 tonnes. See K. T. Kiet, 'Rubberbedrijven in Zuid Sumatra', *Gema* (the Magazine of the *Oei Tiong Ham* Concern Club in Indonesia), no. 16, March 1956, p. 6.

21   For a study on Kian Gwan see J. Panglaykim and I. Palmer, *Entrepreneurship and Commercial Risks: the Case of a Schumpeterian Business in Indonesia*, Occasional Papers 2, Institute of Business Studies, Nanyang University (Singapore, 1970).

22   For lower quality blankets and sheets, Singapore buyers sometimes re-sorted the shipment, often re-processing the rubber before exporting it. As can be seen in Table 1, the volume of slabs in Palembang's exports declined in the transition to blanket and sheet export.

23   Some pribumi no doubt owned their own mangles and smokehouses, buying rubber from their neighbours as well as processing rubber from their own gardens, but this group was small in number.

24   The reasons for this failure will be considered later; see pp. 159 ff. One remiller told us that he had tried to produce sheets after the war but could not compete with the demand for slabs. The implication is that slab buyers paid more for rubber than those who purchased sheets. How they could do this when sheets brought a higher price on the world market requires a consideration of the wide variety of ways of falsifying export documents.

25   N.V. is the Dutch abbreviation for *Naamloze Vennootschap*, equivalent to a Limited Liability Company.

26   In private interview, January 1956.

27   Its actual capital was well below even this small amount.

28   For a discussion of the nature of this rift, see pp. 168 ff.

29   This comment should be qualified as far as the role of the extension service is concerned. Information was provided to the smallholder on methods. Even so, such information would have accomplished little without the complementary roles of those who purchased the mangles to make the sheets, usually owners of warong, and the traders who marketed the finished products. No extension service can function in a market economy without the assistance of others, a point to which we return later.

30   Profitability appears to be the operative word here, but profitability in the Indonesian context is an elusive concept. From our discussions with remillers and businessmen connected with the rubber industry, we have been forced to the conclusion that any attempt to calculate profitability solely by reference to world market price is a somewhat futile exercise. For example, one Singapore merchant told us that there have been times when the price of flat bark, the lowest quality of remilled rubber, has been higher than that of Blanket C. No businessman could be expected to reveal the many trade secrets involved in getting round such discrepancies and it would be presumptuous for an outsider to attempt to estimate the degree of profitability. For this reason, we have not tried to analyse the fluctuating

price differentials between the various qualities of rubber, particularly RSS III and Blanket C. (To complicate matters still further, we were also told by the same informant that the prices quoted in the *Rubber Statistical Bulletin* were not necessarily the prices at which the rubber changed hands.) A similar problem arises in attempting an analysis of prices on the basis of data collected by the Department of Trade in Palembang. The department records the price at which transactions between the motor boat trader and the remiller or buyer in the towns take place. An informant advised us that this price is recorded for taxation purposes and bears little relationship to the actual price at which rubber is traded. Sophisticated techniques to analyse such price data would hardly be warranted in such circumstances. The period between 1950 and 1965 was not generally conducive to the conduct of business along 'normal' lines in Indonesia, especially after 1960. There was a de facto devaluation almost every year between 1955 and 1965, inflation was ever-present and became especially severe after 1961. The transport system was allowed to deteriorate, and in South Sumatra both rail, river and road transportation suffered from neglect and became increasingly costly. Hidden taxes became more and more prevalent under the '*tahu-sama-tahu*' system: see M. A. Jaspan, 'Tolerance and Rejection of Cultural Impediments to Economic Growth', *Bulletin of Indonesian Economic Studies*, no. 7, June 1967, pp. 38–59. During research in a South Sumatran village in 1963, one of us was told that the official cost of renting a government-owned railway truck for transporting rubber from Prabumulih to Panjang was Rp. 1000. By the time the rubber reached its destination Rp. 9000 had been added to transport costs.

31   For more details on the price disparity phenomenon see K.D. Thomas, 'Price Disparity in Export Trade', *BIES*, no. 4, June 1966, pp. 101–2.

32   Mansjurdin Nurdin argues in favour of the 'single buyer' hypothesis in his Master's thesis (unpublished) on Masalah Sheet versus Non-Sheet di Sumatra Selatan (Agricultural Institute, Bogor, 1965). No evidence is presented in support of this claim.

33   In this paper we concentrate only on rubber marketing and processing. It is worth noting that the numerous attempts to establish a planting programme for rubber similar to that in Malaysia were doomed to fail for the same reasons that attempts to upgrade qualities were. The collection of a cess on rubber to finance a planting programme was unrealistic when inflation was running above 100 per cent per annum!

34   In the post-war period almost all the requirements for production of high quality blankets and sheets have generally been neglected by the South Sumatran farmer. It is essential that the rubber tapper should use only clean equipment to collect the latex. The spout along which the latex flows from the tree into the cup must be kept clean, as well as the cup and the collecting bucket. Care must be taken not to allow leaves, twigs or any foreign matter to become mixed with the latex. But the equipment used is often rudimentary and not kept clean. Instead of metal spouts leaves are often used, the cups are often half a coconut shell and are not rinsed out. Scraps of rubber which coagulate in the cup are often ripped out and

dropped into the bucket with the latex. So too is the coagulated rubber which drips down and collects at the foot of the tree, even though it may have dirt in it and leaves and twigs sticking to it. (The scraps of rubber from the cup and along the tapping cut should be collected and kept separate from the latex, along with the earth rubber at the foot of the tree. Where sheets are made, these other rubbers are sold in separate lots, but there is no market for such scraps in the slab areas.) As the tapper goes from tree to tree he makes little attempt to prevent leaves and twigs dropping into his bucket.

35 Stories of farmers putting iron bars in the slabs are common, and the remilling factories often have a heavy-duty mangle through which the slab is put just in case such items are in the slab.

36 Mellor argues that 'the profits of the traders ... [are] related largely to their skill in trading; there is little monopoly profit', J. W. Mellor and others, *Developing Rural India* (Ithaca, NY, Cornell University Press, 1968), p. 67. The example of Lele's study of agricultural marketing in Sholpur is cited along with the work done by Cummings in north India, Dewey in Java, and Bauer in Africa. On the other hand, Mellor does point out that exploitation of the economically weak by the trading class is most likely to occur where the farmer has small quantities to market.

37 Mellor (*idem*) points out that exploitation of the economically weak by the traders is most likely where the farmer has small quantities to market. Such a situation may apply to rubber trading in South Sumatra. But a whole range of factors tends to weaken the bargaining power of the farmer, including a very poor transportation network which tends to discourage market entry in such services as credit, provision of a wide range of essential goods as well as the purchase of the tani's rubber. The trader's role is multi-faceted and any attempt to replace him should take this into account. Overall development of the area may serve the farmers' interests in the long run better than attempts to tackle the issue of 'exploitation' head-on.

38 The Chinese rubber traders have often been criticised for keeping the farmers' incomes low, but it is difficult to assess the validity of these charges for lack of adequate data; see, for example, some calculations of the distribution of incomes between various sectors of the smallholders' rubber industry included in a report forming part of the *Agro-Economic Survey of Indonesia* conducted by the Bogor Agriculture Faculty in 1966–67 by R. S. Sinaga and Kasryno, *Pengusaha dan Tataniaga Karet Rakjat di Sumatera Selatan dan Kalimantan Selatan* (Smallholder Rubber Traders and Trading in South Sumatra and South Kalimantan), 1, Jakarta, 1969. We have omitted the information contained in their report for a variety of reasons which go beyond the scope of this essay. Suffice it to note that their survey of the Palembang area was carried out in a rather short period at a time of both political and economic instability, neither of which are given prominence in the report; nor is any mention made of the tensions between the various groups in the rubber industry. In particular, no mention was made of the conflict between the remillers and the Rubber Co-operative

Associations (GAKKA) over the *wajib giling* issue. (Under the wajib giling regulations, remillers were obliged to remill the slabs of other parties on a contract basis. See pp. 181 ff. for a more detailed discussion of this matter.) It is not clear what sources of information were used for the tables showing the relative share of incomes derived from rubber and the various marketing charges for the crucial months December 1966 and August 1967. In view of the uncertainties and price rises of that period, it would be risky to generalise on the basis of those months and it could be argued that the government was simply in no position at that stage to formulate a well-conceived policy on rubber. The team was in Palembang at a time when the ex-Malaysia remilling factories, *Hok Tong* and *Sumatra Rubber*, were under government control, when a study of the marketing operations of those firms could have thrown considerable light on the extent to which the remillers and traders exploited the peasants; but unfortunately this opportunity was missed.

39   Myrdal, G., *Asian Drama, An Inquiry into the Poverty of Nations* (NY, Pantheon, 1968), ch. 20.

40   Whether there really was a decline in quality, or merely a statistical illusion due to under-invoicing, must remain an open question.

41   For a detailed discussion of this conflict and the relevant literature see B. Glassburner, 'Economic Policy-Making in Indonesia, 1950–1957', *Economic Development and Cultural Change*, vol. 10, no. 2, January 1962, pp. 113–33.

42   The confusion surrounding the government nationalisation of the Dutch companies is discussed in K. D. Thomas and B. Glassburner, 'Abrogation, Take-Over and Nationalisation: the Elimination of Dutch Economic Dominance from the Republic of Indonesia', *Australian Outlook*, vol. 19, no. 2, August 1965, pp. 158–79.

43   A good summary of the main points of the Declaration can be found in L. Castles, 'Socialism and Private Business: The Latest Phase', *Bulletin of Indonesian Economic Studies*, no. 1, 1965, pp. 33–4. For the May Regulations see also K. D. Thomas, 'Recent Developments in Indonesia', *Australia's Neighbours*, 4th series, no. 11–12, January–February 1964.

44   *Penelitian Untuk Menindjau Kemungkinan Menaikkan Produksi Karet Rakjat Dalam Kwantitas Dan Mutu Di Sumatra Selatan* (An Investigation into the Possibility of Raising Production of Smallholder Rubber in Quantity and Quality in South Sumatra), Team Fakultas Pertanian, Institut Pertanian, Bogor, April 1965, section III (4).

45   At a cabinet meeting on 23 July it was decided that rural co-operatives should replace the alien traders: cf. also the wording of the 16 May Ministerial Decision and PP 10 (see above, pp. 82–97). For a fuller discussion see K. D. Thomas, Indonesia's Approach to Socialism, 1950–1960: An Historical Analysis in Political Economy (MA thesis, University of California, Berkeley, 1962).

46   The reports about large numbers moving out of the rural areas and into the city were of course unquantified, but there was general consensus on the matter.

47 One of those interviewed said that, as conditions improved under the Suharto government during 1968, the WNI Chinese were going back to the warong and were also operating along the rivers once again.

48 We have yet to see evidence that the pribumi trader acts any differently towards the farmer than his Chinese counterpart.

49 To some extent the regional government itself was responsible for some of the shortcomings alleged by the Committee. For example, it held the majority of the shares of the N.V.Karet and had some say in the running of the departments concerned with the rubber industry. There must have been some serious political implications in the Committee's early sections of the report, but only the records of the DPRD-GR debates will reveal this.

50 Quotation of this article tended to gloss over the debates which had resulted from it; as a guide to action it had little meaning in itself, all depended on who interpreted it! For one such discussion see *The Socio-Economic Basis of the Indonesian State*, Cornell Modern Indonesia Project, Translation Series (Ithaca, 1959), which contains a translation of the debate between Mr Wilopo and the then young economist Widjojo Nitisastro.

51 Strictly speaking this system of buying refers to the selling of rice as a cash crop. In effect, the farmer pledges to sell his rice to a certain trader while it is still green (*hijau-ijon*), i.e. still growing. Of course, the farmer then receives a lower price. In the case of rubber, the farmer gets credit from a trader on condition that he later sells his rubber to that trader. The abuses possible in the rice trade are less likely with rubber because it is tapped every day. To suggest that the farmer gets his money quicker by making sheets is to ignore the fact that markets are usually held once a week. Traders' operations were under attack even in those areas where sheet production was prevalent, i.e. almost everywhere except the Riau Island group.

52 This phrase was first used by the President in his Independence Day speech in 1959. At that time the President was concerned to harness the talents of the Chinese who were to be excluded from the rural retail trade if they were aliens in industry. It is probable that Lim saw Sukarmin's proposals not only as an attack on the freedom of operations of the remillers, but also as an attack on their ethnic background.

53 There are two points to note here. The slabs become drier as they get older or if they are piled on top of one another so that some water is squeezed out. Offsetting this improvement is the fact that they become lighter with less water. A price-fixing committee would have to assess both factors in determining price at village level.

54 The exact implications of this term were vague. The first firms 'taken over' by the Indonesian government were those owned by the Dutch in 1957. After much debate, these firms were eventually nationalised. In the early 1960s other foreign firms were 'taken over' but their exact status was not specified. Given the trend of the late Sukarno period it was natural then to assume that such firms would not be returned to their former owners.

55 All shares in *P.T. Peksin* (Indonesian Export Development Company) were held by five state banks but it was legally organised as a private

corporation. See Panglaykim, 'Some Notes on the Administrative Aspects of Indonesian State Trading Corporations', *Maandschrift Economie*, Tilburg, October 1964.

56   This decision is found in Instruction No. 17/Opess/64 dated 19 December 1963 and was presumably issued by the regional government.

57   We could find out very little about this organisation, which had its head office in Jakarta and branch offices in the rubber producing areas. During research into the rubber industry in 1965 we were unable to speak with the directors because the co-operative was in the process of liquidation as a result of alleged involvement of its top personnel in corrupt practices. Members of the group no doubt allied themselves with the Extension Service in Palembang in opposition to the remillers and the N.V.Karet; in particular they would have supported the proposals of Sukarmin in the ad hoc Committee. But its political influence must have been negligible.

58   KOTOE was one of the numerous 'command' organisations set up during Confrontation when para-military organisations seemed to proliferate, bringing civilians and the armed forces together in a wide range of activities.

59   *Penelitian untuk Menindjau Kemungkinan Menaikkan Produksi Karet Rakjat dalam Kwantitas dan Mutu di Sumatra Selatan*, Team Fakultas Pertanian (Institut Pertanian, Bogor, April 1965), p. 154.

60   We should emphasise that little has been written on smallholder rubber during Confrontation. While there are intriguing aspects it is difficult to get concrete data. We are in the process of preparing a paper on the period.

61   According to Drs Alwi of Sriwijaya University factories were often unable to produce to capacity because of shortages of spare parts and raw material required for producing blankets or because the companies had not installed equipment to the amount indicated by their licences. He also attempted to assess the potential output of slabs for the Palembang region and concluded that even had the Palembang factories been equipped to operate at capacity there would have been a shortage of slabs amounting to around 50 000 tonnes. One must make heroic assumptions to attempt a calculation of slab production on the basis of an estimate of the area under rubber. No census on rubber acreage in the region has been taken since 1940 and the fact that the census produced a figure almost double the area which had been assessed in the 1936 census should indicate the enormous difficulties in arriving at a reliable figure for potential slab production! (Continuous planting in the shifting cultivation cycle would ensure an increasing proportion of young rubber trees with higher yields even where plant material was taken from old strains, see K. D. Thomas, 'Shifting Cultivation and the Production of Rubber in a South Sumatran Village', *Malayan Economic Review*, vol. X, no. 1, April 1965, p. 107.) In any case, attempts to relate remilling capacity to potential slab production tends to imply that licences were in fact issued on the basis of such calculations. We believe that this is far from the truth and that the motives behind the extension of remilling capacity were a mixture of personal and party or group gain.

62   As the production of the 'ex-Malaysia' factories declined, the clients of

those remillers might have transferred their allegiance to the newcomers, the only change being between the old-established *pedagang motor* and the new remiller. But there are many possibilities at the lower levels in the trading channels.

63 *Straits Times*, 10 December 1968.

64 *Agro-Economic Survey* (1968), p. xxvi.

65 Foreign investors would, moreover, be at a disadvantage, compared to the local Chinese with their years of experience in handling a product which must be collected from many growers scattered over a wide area and for which a sound knowledge of local conditions is necessary. The failure of the Dutch remilling company in the 1930s provides a salutary lesson in this case.

66 *Ibid.*, p. xxv-xxvi.

67 The minimum outlay for a crumb rubber plant built by Guthrie and Co., with a capacity of 100 tonnes of rubber a month, is $6000, see *Straits Times*, 10 December 1968.

68 Both Shell and Stanvac had similar enclaves in Palembang itself complete with shops, churches, club house with swimming pool and electric generators. The state-owned fertiliser plant, Pusri, emulated these examples.

69 The authors of the survey were less dogmatic on the question of location. They recommended *research* into the *possibility* of establishing crumb rubber factories in the interior, see the *Agro-Economic Survey* (1968), p. 73.

70 No 'aliens with domestic capital' (i.e. alien Chinese businessmen, in effect) were involved in remilling in Palembang by the late 1960s, nor were any of them among the applicants for crumb rubber licences, though that opportunity was open to them.

71 In 1961 the output of both was slightly in excess of 2 million tonnes. In 1970 the output of NR was 2.9 million tonnes compared to an SR output of 4.5 million tonnes.

72 For a dissenting view on the price 'trend' see P. W. Allen, 'Analysing Price Patterns', *Rubber Developments*, vol. 22, no. 4, 1969, pp. 122–5. In spite of our attitude on price trends we share Dr Bateman's view that 'history and present perception tell that natural rubber will (with all round modernisation) continue to pay off well in good times and pay its way in bad', 'Natural Rubber can meet the Synthetics Challenge', *Rubber Developments*, vol. 22, no. 4, 1969, p. 121.

73 Although Palembang was also the centre for the operations of the Shell and Stanvac petroleum companies, they were the concern of the politicians in Jakarta rather than of the regional politicians, except in September 1963 when the local trade unions and some politicians were involved in the short-lived takeover of Shell installations.

74 See K. D. Thomas, *Smallholders Rubber in Indonesia*, especially the section on the Smallholder Rubber Foundation, p. 35 ff.

75 One aspect of the future of natural rubber and its possible effect on the position of the Chinese is ominous, however. Present trends in rubber technology are labour saving. The crumb rubber process requires only about 30 per cent of the labour force of a remilling factory. In the short run, where Palembang has an employment problem, expansion of both

industry and agriculture will be required initially to absorb the labour made redundant by the developments in the rubber industry itself. Only after the potential backwash effects of trends in the rubber industry have been taken care of will economic expansion in other fields absorb *new* job seekers. Dismissal of labour from work in rubber processing could be a source of friction which might be used against the ethnic Chinese business community even though such dismissals may be essential for the strength of the industry as it competes with synthetics. Policies for the region should be designed to take this possibility into account; otherwise the tensions of the recent past may well be repeated.

76 Soedjatmoko, 'Foreign Private Investment in a Developing Nation', *Quadrant*, vol. xiii: 5, September–October 1969, pp. 106–7.

77 The success of the Suharto government in controlling inflation may already have improved the real income of the farmer as the rice-rubber terms of trade turn in favour of the rubber tappers.

78 In this essay we have focused our attention on the role of the Chinese in the rubber industry in one region, concentrating on the ways in which the Chinese accommodated themselves to the changing political power structure in Jakarta and in the region as they went about their business of trading and processing rubber. It should now be clear that even in Palembang the Chinese do not represent a homogeneous group and that competition among them cuts across the lines of the division between citizen and alien. We have concluded our discussion on an optimistic note on the assumption that President Suharto's concern for economic development will encompass the development of the South Sumatran region. Much will depend on the opportunities available. Palembang has considerable potential for industrial development and if the region does develop, the economic reasons for the pressure on the Chinese ethnic minority should be reduced. On the other hand, in considering the potential for regional development we must also assess the prospects for natural rubber. This issue extends beyond the scope of this present essay in which we have been attempting to strike a balance between the role of the Chinese in the rubber industry and a study of the rubber industry itself. Men engaged in the industry, both in Indonesia and Malaysia, are confident that with the new crumb rubber process natural rubber can maintain its position in competition with synthetics. The outcome of this competition will be a further chapter in the history of the Chinese in the smallholders' rubber industry. And if smallholders' rubber is to have any chance of survival in Indonesia, much will depend on the co-operation of all those in the industry, including a well-trained and well-paid extension service, especially with regard to a new and replanting programme for the smallholders that takes their interests into account. The Chinese have a future in the industry as traders and processors only if there is a steady flow of rubber from the villages.

79 It should be emphasised that what matters for the easing of ethnic tensions is the development of the regions where the Chinese are resident. If Indonesia develops but South Sumatra stagnates, for example, the regional legislature and the pribumi community of that province will continue to regard the economic position of the WNI Chinese with concern.

5 'ARE INDONESIAN CHINESE UNIQUE?': SOME OBSERVATIONS

1 Outside Southeast Asia, only Mauritius has a distinctive Chinese community which forms about 3 per cent of the total population. I recently visited sections of that community and still keep in touch with some of its members, but the community is a rather exceptional case and does not, I feel, help the comparisons made here. When the Chinese elsewhere are well under 1 per cent of the total population, there is no serious 'Chinese problem'.

2 'Chinese Politics in Malaya', *The China Quarterly*, no. 43, July–Sept. 1970, pp. 1–30; and 'Political Chinese: an aspect of their contribution to modern Southeast Asian history', in Bernard Grossmann (ed.), *Southeast Asia in the Modern World* (Hamburg, 1973), pp. 115–28.

3 The 'nationalist' pattern described actions based on identification with China while the three 'integration-assimilation' patterns concerned the politics of the Netherlands East Indies or of Indonesia. The officer system, however, operated well when the community was locally domiciled but politically either non-committal or not yet acceptable to the Dutch, the Japanese or the Indonesian.

4 The main variants in the traditional officer system are outlined in Victor Purcell, *The Chinese in Southeast Asia* (London, 2nd ed., 1965), chs on Thailand, Indochina states, Malaya and Singapore, Indonesia and the Philippines. Among many fuller studies, one may mention treatments by G. William Skinner, *Chinese Society in Thailand: an Analytical History* (Ithaca, NY, 1957), ch. 1, and *Leadership and Power in the Chinese Community of Thailand* (Ithaca, NY, 1958), ch. 1; W. E. Willmott, *The Political Structure of the Chinese Community in Cambodia* (London, 1970), chs 1–5, and the comparisons in ch. 12; Tsai Mawkuey, *Les Chinois au Sud-Vietnam* (Paris, 1968), ch. 1; C. S. Wong, *A Gallery of Chinese Kapitans* (Singapore, 1963), parts I and II; Song Ong Siang, *One Hundred Years' History of the Chinese in Singapore* (Singapore, reprint, 1967); Donald E. Willmott, *The National Status of the Chinese in Indonesia, 1900–1958* (Ithaca, NY, rev. ed. 1961); G. William Skinner, 'Java's Chinese Minority: Continuity and Change', *Journal of Asian Studies*, vol. 20, no. 3, May 1961, pp. 353–62; Leo Suryadinata, *The Pre-World War II Peranakan Chinese Press of Java: A Preliminary Survey* (Athens, Ohio, 1971); and E. Wickberg, *The Chinese in Philippine Life, 1850–1898* (New Haven, 1965), chs 5–7.

5 V. Purcell, *The Chinese in Southeast Asia*, provides a sober account of these interventions throughout the region. Two notable studies are Lea E. Williams, *Overseas Chinese Nationalism* (Glencoe, Ill., 1960), and Antonio S. Tan, *The Chinese in the Philippines, 1898–1935: A Study of their National Awakening* (Quezon City, 1972). There is a considerable literature in Western languages emphasising the alarming activities of the Chinese; see bibliography in Purcell. There is an equally large body of writings in Chinese reporting the discriminatory practices of colonial and national governments; some are listed in N. Uchida, *The Overseas Chinese: A Bibliographical Essay* (Stanford, 1959); but fuller lists are found in Hsu Yun-ts'iao, 'Nan-yang wen-hsien hsü-lu ch'ang-pien', *Nanyang Yen-chiu*, vol. I, 1959, pp. 1–170, and Nanyang University Southeast Asia Institute,

Index to Chinese Periodical Literature on Southeast Asia, 1905–1966 (Singapore, 1968). I have discussed aspects of this 'nationalist' pattern in a recent paper, 'The Limits of Nanyang Nationalism, 1912–1937' (to be published in a forthcoming *Festschrift* to D. G. E. Hall).

6   G. William Skinner on Thailand and E. Wickberg on the Philippines (see note 4 above) describe varieties of 'assimilation' but do not draw attention to the stages which Coppel outlines, the earlier stages of which are described in greater detail in Leo Suryadinata, *Peranakan Chinese Press* and can be discerned in his invaluable reference work, *Prominent Indonesian Chinese in the Twentieth Century: A Preliminary Survey* (Athens, Ohio, 1972).

7   The resistance to assimilation and re-sinicisation has yet to be independently studied. Four works of special interest are Kwee Tek Hoay, *The Origins of the Modern Chinese Movement in Indonesia* (first published in 1936–39), trans. by Lea E. Williams (Ithaca, NY, 1969); Li Ch'uan-shou, 'Yin-tu-ni-hsi-ya hua-ch'iao chiao-yü shih', *Nan-yang Hsueh-pao* (Singapore), vol. 15, part 1, July 1959, pp. 1–14; The Siauw Giap, 'Group Conflict in a Plural Society', part II, *Revue de Sudest Asiatique* (Brussels, vol. 2, 1966), pp. 185–218; and the recent article by Leo Suryadinata, 'Indonesian Chinese Education: past and present', *Indonesia*, no. 14, October, 1972, pp. 49–71. The literature on the peranakan is growing. Among the peranakan themselves, the following should be mentioned: Liem Thian Joe, *Riwajat Semarang, 1416–1931* (Semarang, 1933); Kwee Hing Tjiat, *Doea Kepala Batoe* (Berlin, 1921); Kwee Kek Beng, *Doea Poeloe Lima Tahon sebagi Wartawan* (Batavia, 1948); Nio Joe Lan, *Riwajat 40 Taon dari Tiong Hoa Hwe Koan-Batavia 1900–1939* (Batavia, 1940); and more recently, Tan Giok-lan, *The Chinese of Sukabumi* (Ithaca, NY, 1963); The Siauw Giap, 'Religion and Overseas Chinese Assimilation in Southeast Asian countries', *Revue de Sudest Asiatique* (Brussels), vol. 2, 1965, pp. 67–83; and the yet unpublished MA thesis by Leo Suryadinata, The Three Major Streams in Peranakan Chinese Politics in Java, 1917–1942 (Monash University, 1969). In addition, there are studies by G. William Skinner (note 4 above), Donald E. Willmott's *The Chinese in Semarang* (Ithaca, NY, 1960) and Mary F. Somers's *Peranakan Chinese Politics in Indonesia* (Ithaca, NY, 1964).

8   These two are the most obvious and the most commented upon; e.g. G. William Skinner, 'Change and Persistence in Chinese Culture Overseas: A Comparison of Thailand and Java', *Nan-yang Hsueh-pao*, Singapore, vol. 16, 1960, pp. 86–100.

9   This subject first engaged Western scholars and journalists and then those indigenous to Southeast Asia. Fear of Overseas Chinese subversion probably reached its peak about the time Robert S. Elegant published his *The Dragon's Seed: Peking and the Overseas Chinese* in 1959, and had a different emphasis during the Cultural Revolution in China and the long years of the Vietnam War. A major study of the problem as seen from the China end is that recently published by Stephen Fitzgerald, *China and the Overseas Chinese: A Study of Peking's Changing Policy, 1949–1970* (Cambridge, 1972).

10 I discuss this more fully in my paper, 'The Peranakan Phenomenon in Southeast Asia' (presented at the 29th International Congress of Orientalists, Paris, 16–22 July 1973).

11 This is not peculiar to the peranakan in Indonesia. It is largely a product of those colonial policies which distinguish between 'Foreign Orientals', Chinese Mestizo, Anglo-Chinese groups and the native peoples, and the resultant Westernised Chinese often arouse the ire of indigenous nationalists.

12 The papers by Coppel and Mackie are the most recent writings touching on the Baperki and the politics of the 1950s and 1960s. For earlier studies, see Mary F. Somers, *Peranakan Chinese Politics*; G. William Skinner, 'The Chinese Minority', in Ruth T. McVey (ed.), *Indonesia* (New Haven, 1963), pp. 97–117; Go Gien Tjwan, 'The Assimilation Problem of the Chinese in Indonesia', *Culture et developpement* (Louvain), vol. 1, no. 1, 1968, pp. 41–59.

13 Traditionally, the language group one belonged to was crucial to the kinds of business one could profitably enter. Innumerable writers have commented on this during the nineteenth century and the first half of the twentieth century. This factor is still relevant everywhere, but in the large cosmopolitan trading centres like Hong Kong, Singapore, Jakarta and cities linked to them and in large-scale industries involving international contacts, especially the newer multi-national organisations, such traditional ties and obligations have been found to be too restrictive. It is still too early to say if new generations of Chinese businessmen will eschew language group operations altogether in favour of modern economic organisations.

14 'Ali-Baba' businesses are supposed to have appeared in the 1950s first in Indonesia and then in Malaysia. Through usage, they imply businesses where the 'Baba' (Chinese) runs the show while 'Ali' (Indonesian pribumi or Malay) provides contacts with the indigenous elites and shares the profits, but is often a sleeping partner in practice, lending protection and respectability to Chinese businessmen. In fact, there is no reason why such organisations should not develop into viable instruments in both assimilating the Chinese and involving the pribumi in capitalist enterprises.

15 In my 'Political Chinese' article in Grossmann, *op. cit.*, I argue that the Chinese have contributed to the political history of Southeast Asia, but the process has been mainly indirect if not involuntary. Few Chinese have had political ambitions outside Singapore and Malaysia and when they did, as in Thailand and the Philippines, it was when they were thoroughly assimilated and were no longer seen as Chinese. What is more interesting is that the Chinese have had little chance to gain social respectability without wealth, whether among the Chinese themselves or among the indigenous peoples, and wealth produced a dubious if not precarious kind of respectability. Modern efforts to gain respectability through the professions have been unsuccessful except in the medical profession.

16 'The devil of *suku*-ism' has been attacked from several angles, by pribumi and Chinese alike, from Sukarno and Professor Prijono to Onghokham

to Siauw Giok Tjhan; see H. Feith and L. Castles (eds), *Indonesian Political Thinking, 1945–1965* (Ithaca, NY, 1970), pp. 316–54. But the fact that many suku exist, are locally important and form the original amalgam that is Indonesia has always highlighted the scattering of 'foreign orientals' like the Chinese who have no suku-region to call their own. Concerning 'Tjina' or 'Tionghoa', see Charles A. Coppel and Leo Suryadinata, 'The Use of the Terms "Tjina" and "Tionghoa" in Indonesia: An Historical Survey', *Papers on Far Eastern History*, no. 2, Sept. 1970, pp. 97–118.

6

SELECT BIBLIOGRAPHY ON
THE INDONESIAN CHINESE

Charles A. Coppel

It would be an enormous undertaking to compile a comprehensive bibliography of the Chinese in Indonesia. Not only is the material relating to them written in a number of European and Asian languages, but much useful information is to be found in publications concerned more generally either with the Overseas Chinese or with Indonesia. Furthermore, much valuable material exists but is to be found in relatively inaccessible places. For example, the newspapers and periodicals published by the Indonesian Chinese often contained invaluable data about their group, particularly in the special numbers customarily published at the beginning of the Chinese New Year. Similarly, Chinese associations of many kinds often published newsletters and periodicals as well as commemorative publications celebrating an anniversary of their association. Moreover, there must be still a considerable volume of material which is unavailable outside Indonesia, and even within the country much that can only be found in private collections. There is no doubt that a great deal was destroyed because of fear on the part of the owners during the Japanese occupation and during more recent political disturbances, and of course much too has deteriorated over time because of lack of proper care. But much material must still be in existence.

The listing which follows is more limited in its scope. Because of the linguistic deficiencies of the bibliographer, works published in Chinese or Japanese, for example, are not included. What is included are works written either in Indonesian or in western European languages (usually English or Dutch). The reader will find some guidance for works in other languages in the first section of the bibliography, which lists some valuable bibliographies on the Overseas Chinese. These bibliographies will also lead him to most publications dealing generally with the Overseas Chinese, rather than specifically with the Chinese in Indonesia, and consequently, with the exception of some which are too recent to have been listed there, these have been excluded also from the present bibliography. Similarly, publications dealing generally with Indonesia, rather than specifically with the Indonesian Chinese, have not been included, but the reader is warned that a general history like J. S. Furnivall's *Netherlands India: a Study of Plural Economy* (Cambridge University Press, Cambridge, 1939) or a study of a particular industry, such as Lance Castles's study of the *kretek* cigarette industry of Kudus, contain much valuable material about them [*Religion, Politics and Economic Behaviour in Java: The Kudus Cigarette Industry* (Southeast Asian Studies Cultural Report No. 15, Yale University, New Haven, 1967)].

So as to reduce the bulk of what follows to a manageable size, certain categories of material have been excluded. First, material of a purely journalistic or ephemeral character has been jettisoned. Secondly, most of the output of Chinese associations, schools and the like has been omitted. Thirdly, the considerable volume of translations into Indonesian of works in Chinese, more often than not by Indonesian Chinese translators, has been excluded. These exclusions, with some reluctance, were made to conserve space. There must, however, be much in Chinese (especially peranakan Chinese) newspapers and periodicals published in Indonesia which has not found a place in what follows, simply because of the ignorance of the bibliographer. One valuable guide to this storehouse is the study by Leo Suryadinata of the pre-Second World War peranakan Chinese press of Java (listed in section XV below) which includes as an appendix a list of the holdings of the Museum library in Jakarta. In addition, some post-war publications of the same kind should be mentioned here, such as *Star Weekly*, *Pantjawarna*, and *Sin Tjun*. A substantial proportion of the latter publications has become available recently on microfiche, thanks to the reproduction by IDC of Cornell University library holdings. Monash University library has also recently acquired sets of the pre-war weeklies of *Sin Po* and *Star Magazine* as well as a large proportion of the numbers lacking in the Cornell holdings of *Star Weekly*.

Finally, a word about the ordering of the bibliography. It appears in sections according to subject matter. Within each section the items are listed in order of known (or estimated) date of publication. At the end of all but two sections there is a brief annotation relating to that section, but individual works are not annotated separately. Although some entries are duplicated under more than one heading, the reader is warned that many others contain much that is useful in fields other than those under which they are classified. The bibliography concludes with an alphabetical index of author's names so that those seeking a work by a particular author may locate it quickly.

I BIBLIOGRAPHIES ON OVERSEAS CHINESE

1   Oey Giok Po. *Survey of Chinese language materials on Southeast Asia in the Hoover Institute and Library.* (Cornell University Southeast Asia Program. Data Paper No. 8, Ithaca, 1953.)

2   Uchida, Naosaku. *The Overseas Chinese: a bibliographical essay with supplementary bibliography by Eugene Wu and Hsüeh Chün-tu.* (Stanford University 1959. Hoover Institute bibliographical series 7.)

3   Williams, Lea E. *Overseas Chinese Nationalism: The Genesis of the Pan-Chinese Movement in Indonesia 1900–1916.* (Free Press, Glencoe, 1960.) Bibliography, pp. 211-29.

4   Freedman, Maurice, and Willmott, William E. 'Recent research on racial relations: Southeast Asia with special reference to the Chinese', *International Social Science Journal*, 23/2 (1961), pp. 245-70.

5   Purcell, Victor. *The Chinese in Southeast Asia.* (Oxford University Press, London, 1965. 2nd edition.) Bibliographies compiled by the author and Hugh D. R. Baker, pp. 574-610.

6   Shu, A. C. W., and Wan, W. W. L. *Twentieth Century Chinese Works on Southeast Asia: A bibliography.* (Annotated bibliography series No. 3, East-West Center, Honolulu, 1968.)

7   Nevadomsky, J. J., and Li, A. *The Chinese in Southeast Asia: a selected and annotated bibliography of publications in Western languages 1960–1970.* (Occasional paper No. 6, Center for South and South East Asia Studies, University of California, Berkeley, 1970.)

II INDONESIAN CHINESE—GENERAL

1   Borel, Henri. *De Chineezen in Nederlandsch-Indie.* (L. J. Veen, Amsterdam, 1900.)

2   de Veer, W. *Chineezen onder Hollandsche Vlag.* (Scheltema en Holkema, Amsterdam, 1908.)

3   van Sandick, L. H. W. *Chineezen Buiten China: hunne beteknis voor de ontwikkeling van Zuid-Oost Azie, speciaal van Nederlandsch Indie.* (M. van der Beek, The Hague, 1909.)

4   Sim Ki Ay. *De Chineesche Nederzetting in Nederlandsch-Indië.* (Clausen, Amsterdam, 1918?)

5   Moll, J. Th. *De Chineezen in Nederlandsch-Indie.* (J. van Druten, Utrecht, 1928.)

6   Moerman, J. *De Chineezen in Nederlandsch Oost-Indie.* (P. Noordhoff, Groningen-Batavia. 1933-34.)

7   Jansen, Gerard. *Vreemde Oosterlingen.* (W. van Hoeve, Deventer, 1935?)

8   Ong Eng Die. *Chineezen in Nederlandsch-Indie: Sociografie van een Indonesische bevolkingsgroep.* (van Gorcum, Assen, 1943.)

9   Liem Khiam Soen. *Kedoedoekan Bangsa Tionghoa di Indonesia.* (*De positie der Chineezen in Indonesie.*) (Sawahan Chung Hua Hui, Soerabaia, 1946.)

10 Veldhuysen, F. *Hoa-Kiao, Chineezen in Indonesie.* (Keizerskroon, Amsterdam, 1948.)

11 Toer, Pramudya Ananta. *Hoa Kiau di Indonesia.* (Bintang Press, Djakarta, 1960.)

12   Indonesia. *Angkatan Darat. Staf Umum.* '*Masalah Tionghoa' di Indonesia.* (Djakarta, 1961.)

13   Skinner, G. William. 'The Chinese Minority', in Ruth T. McVey (ed.), *Indonesia.* (HRAF, New Haven, 1963.)

14   Mabbett, Hugh, and Ping-Ching. 'The Chinese community in Indonesia', in *The Chinese in Indonesia, The Philippines and Malaysia* (Report No. 10, Minority Rights Group, London, 1972).

NOTE: The best short survey of the Indonesian Chinese is undoubtedly Skinner (II/13) which also contains a valuable but very brief annotated bibliography. Of the pre-independence studies, the most useful are van Sandick (II/3) and Ong Eng Die (II/8). Pramudya Ananta Toer's work (II/11), which was banned in Indonesia soon after publication, is remarkably sympathetic to the Chinese. The Mabbetts' piece (II/14) is a brief but very readable account of the position in the early 1970s.

III   HISTORY OF INDONESIAN CHINESE BEFORE THE TWENTIETH CENTURY

1   Ong Tae Hae. *The Chinaman abroad; or, A desultory account of the Malayan Archipelago, particularly of Java* (trans. W. H. Medhurst, Shanghai, 1849). [Also available in Dutch under the title, *Chineesche aanteekeningen omtrent Nederlandsch Indie* (The Hague, 1858).]

2   Millies, H. C. *De Chinezen in Nederlandsch Oost-Indie en het Christendom. Eene schets.* (Amsterdam, 1850?)

3   Groeneveldt, W. P. 'Notes on the Malay archipelago and Malacca', in *Verhandelingen van het Bataviaasch Genootschap van Kunsten en Wetenschappen,* 39 (1880). Reprinted for *JRASSB,* London, 1888 and as *Historical Notes on Indonesia and Malaya, compiled from Chinese sources.* (Bhratara, Djakarta, 1960.)

4   Liem Thian Joe. *Riwajat Semarang 1416–1931.* (Ho Kim Yoe, Semarang, 1931.)

5   Verboeket, K. 'Geschiedenis van der Chineezen in Nederlandsch Indie', *Koloniale Studien,* 20/5 and 6 (1936).

6   Vermeulen, J. T. *De Chineezen te Batavia en de troebelen vàn 1740* (Leiden, 1938). English translation in *Journal of the South Seas Society* 9/1 (June 1953).

7   Vermeulen, J. T. 'Remarks about the Dutch East India Company's Administration of Justice for the Chinese community in the Seventeenth and Eighteenth Centuries', *Jade,* 12/2 (1948).

8   Liem Thian Joe. 'Pengaroeh Tionghoa di Java', *Jade* 12/2 (1948).

9   Bastin, J. 'The Chinese estates in East Java during the British Administration', *Indonesie,* 7 (July 1954).

10   Williams, Lea E. 'Indonesia's Chinese educate Raffles', *Indonesie,* (October 1956).

11   Williams, Lea E. 'The Chinese in Indonesia and Singapore under Raffles', *Far Eastern Economic Review,* 33 (July 1957).

12   Williams, Lea E. 'The ethical program and the Chinese of Indonesia', *Journal of Southeast Asian History,* 2/2 (1961).

13   Heidhues, Mary F. Somers. 'Dutch Colonial and Indonesian Nationalist

Policies toward the Chinese Minority in Indonesia', *Verfassung und Recht in Übersee*, 3/3 (1972).

NOTE: The most substantial of these studies are the Vermeulen dissertation (III/6), Liem's history of Semarang based on local Chinese sources (III/4) and Groeneveldt's pioneering collection of extracts from Chinese sources. Ong Tae Hae's travel notes throw valuable light on the Chinese in eighteenth century Java (III/1).

IV TWENTIETH CENTURY POLITICAL DEVELOPMENTS AMONG INDONESIAN CHINESE

1 Fromberg, P. H. *Verspreide geschriften* (Leidsche Uitgeversmaatschappij, Leiden, 1926), especially *De Chineesche Beweging op Java* (1911) pp. 405-47.

2 Tjoe Bou San. *Pergerakan Tionghoa di Hindia Olanda dan Mr. P. H. Fromberg.* (*Sin Po*, Batavia, 1921.)

3 M. H. *De Chineesche Kwestie*. (Papyrus, Batavia, 1913.)

4 Douwes Dekker, E. F. E. *Het Chineezen vraagstuk onder Nationaal Indische belichting*. (Schiedam, 1914.)

5 Kwee Hing Tjiat. *Doea Kapala Batoe*. (Berlin, 1921.)

6 Kwee Tek Hoay. 'Atsal Moelahnja Timboel Pergerakan Tionghoa jang Modern di Indonesia', *Moestika Romans* (1936–1939). (More readily available in English translation and edited by Lea E. Williams under the title *The Origins of the Modern Chinese Movement in Indonesia* (Cornell Modern Indonesia Project Translation Series, Ithaca, 1969).)

7 Nio Joe Lan. *Riwajat 40 Taon dari Tiong Hoa Hwe Koan-Batavia (1900–1939)*. (THHK, Batavia, 1940.)

8 Kahin, G. McT. The Political Position of the Chinese in Indonesia. (Unpublished MA thesis, Political Science, Stanford University, 1946.)

9 Kahin, G. McT. 'The Chinese in Indonesia', *Far Eastern Survey*, 15 (1946) pp. 326-9.

10 Glover, Clive. Reactions of the Indonesian Chinese to Two Years of Dutch-Indonesian Conflict. (Research paper for Prof. Kahin's seminar, John Hopkins University, 1950.)

11 Tan Eng-kie. 'The question of minorities', in *Perspective of Indonesia* (*Atlantic Monthly* Supplement, 1956?).

12 Hanssens, V. 'The Campaign against Nationalist Chinese in Indonesia', in B. H. M. Vlekke (ed.), *Indonesia's Struggle 1957–1958* (The Hague, 1959).

13 Mackie, J. A. C. 'The Chinese in Indonesia', *Australia's Neighbours*, 102 (December, 1959).

14 Williams, Lea E. *Overseas Chinese Nationalism: The Genesis of the Pan-Chinese Movement in Indonesia* 1900–1916. (Free Press, Glencoe, 1960.)

15 Willmott, Donald E. *The National Status of the Chinese in Indonesia 1900–1958.* (Cornell Modern Indonesia Project Monograph Series, Ithaca, 1961, revised edition.)

16 Somers, Mary F. *Peranakan Chinese Politics in Indonesia*. (Cornell Modern Indonesian Project Interim Reports Series, Ithaca, 1964.)

17 Somers, Mary F: Peranakan Chinese Politics in Indonesia. (Unpublished Ph.D. thesis, Cornell, 1965.)

18 Somers, Mary F. 'Die Chinesische Minderheit Im Politischen Leben Indonesiens', *Zeitschrift für Politik*, 15/3 (September 1968).

19 Suryadinata, Leo. The Three Major Streams in Peranakan Chinese Politics in Java. 1917–1942. (Unpublished MA thesis, Monash University, 1969.)

20 Lie Tek Tjeng. *Masalah WNI dan Masalah Huakiau di Indonesia.* (Lembaga Research Kebudajaan Nasional, LIPI, Djakarta, 1969.)

21 Lie Tek Tjeng. 'The Chinese problem in Indonesia following the September 30 movement: A personal view', *Internationale Spectator*, 24/12 (1970).

22 Coppel, Charles, and Suryadinata, Leo. 'The Use of the Terms "Tjina" and "Tionghoa" in Indonesia: An historical survey', *Papers on Far Eastern History*, 2 (September, 1970).

23 Go Gien Tjwan. 'The role of the Overseas Chinese in the Southeast Asian revolutions and their adjustment to new states', in Leifer, M. (ed.), *Nationalism, Revolution and Evolution in Southeast Asia.* (Centre for Southeast Asian Studies, Hull, 1970.)

24 Feith, H., and Castles, L. (eds). *Indonesian Political Thinking 1945–1965.* (Cornell University Press, Ithaca, 1970), ch. 11.

25 Suryadinata, Leo. 'Pre-war Indonesian Nationalism and the Peranakan Chinese', *Indonesia*, 11 (April 1971).

26 Go Gien Tjwan. 'De historische wortels van de Baperki-beweging', in *Buiten de Grenzen: sociologische opstellen aangeboden aan Prof. Dr. W. F. Wertheim.* (Boom, Meppel, 1971.)

27 Heidhues, Mary F. Somers. 'Dutch colonial and Indonesian nationalist policies toward the Chinese minority in Indonesia', *Verfassung und Recht in Übersee*, 3/3 (1972).

NOTE: The Fromberg volume (IV/1) is the collected works of a Dutch lawyer and great friend of the Chinese. Tjoe Bou San (IV/2) and Kwee Hing Tjiat (IV/5) are examples of writings by leaders of the Chinese nationalist movement when it was at its peak, showing that their demands went well beyond what Fromberg thought them to be. Kwee Tek Hoay (IV/6) and Nio Joe Lan (IV/7) look back at the origins of the nationalist movement more reflectively. Lea Williams (IV/14), Mary Somers Heidhues (IV/17), and Leo Suryadinata (IV/19) are three pioneering theses on the politics of the Indonesian Chinese. Go Gien Tjwan and Lie Tek Tjeng are two contemporary scholars who were actual participants in the political struggles of their time.

V CHINESE AND THE LAW: NATIONAL STATUS

1 Groot, J. J. M. de. *Eenige aantekeningen omtrent Chineesche gerechtelijke eeden in de Nederlandsche koloniën. Een poging tot oplossen van de vraag, welke eed aldaar den Chineezen voor de rechtbanken behoort te worden afgenomen.* (Batavia, 1883.)

2 Cordes, J. W. C. *De Privaatrechterlijke Toestand der Vreemde Oosterlingen op Java en Madoera.* (Doctoral dissertation, Leiden, 1887.)

3   Albrecht, J. E. *Soerat Ketrangan dari pada hal kaadaan bangsa Tjina di negri Hindia Olanda.* (Batavia, 1890.)

4   Faber, G. von. *Het familie- en erfrecht der Chineezen in Nederlandsch-Indie.* (Utrecht doctoral dissertation, Leiden, 1895.)

5   (Paets tot Gansoijen, A.) *Eenige opmerkingen over het ontwerp eener nieuwe regeling van den privaatrechtlijken toestand der Chineezen in Nederlandsch-Indie.* (Soerabaia, 1897.)

6   Heeckeren, C. W. van. *Beschouwingen over het voor Chineezen op Java geldende recht.* (Semarang-Soerabaia, 1901.)

7   Wiggers, F. *Hak Poesaka boeat Orang-orang Bangsa Tiong Hoa.* (Taman Sari, Batavia, 1907.)

8   Cordes, J. W. C. *Ontwerp eener regeling van den privaatrechtlijken toestand der Chineezen in Nederlandsch-Indie.* (Weltevreden, 1914.)

9   (Heyman, B.) *Ontwerp van een reglement op het houden der registers van den burgerlijken stand voor de Chineezen in Nederlandsch-Indie.* (Kolff, Batavia, 1914.)

10 Brokx, Wouter. *Het recht tot wonen en reizen in Nederlandsch-Indie.* (Doctoral dissertation, Leiden University, publ. 's-Hertogenbosch, 1925.)

11 Fromberg, P. H. *Verspreide Geschriften.* (Leidsche Uitgeversmaatschappij, Leiden, 1926.) Various essays.

12 Bertling, C. T. 'Gelijkstelling van Chineezen met Europeanen', *Koloniale Studien*, 11/4 (1927).

13 van der Valk, M. H. 'De rechtspositie der Chineezen in Nederlandsch-Indie', *Koloniale Studien*, 20/5 and 6 (1936).

14 Han Swie Tian. *Bijdrage tot de kennis van het familie- en erfrecht der Chineezen in Nederlandsch-Indie.* (Amsterdam, 1936.)

15 Ko Swan Sik. *De Meervoudige Nationaliteit.* (Leiden, 1957.)

16 Sasmojo. *Menjelesaikan Masalah Dwikewarganegaraan RI-RRT.* (Djambatan, Djakarta, 1959.)

17 Baperki. *Segala Sesuatu tentang Kewarganegaraan RI.* (Baperki, Djakarta, 1960?)

18 Gouw Giok Siong. *Warga Negara dan Orang Asing.* (Keng Po, Djakarta, 1960—second edition.)

19 Liem Tjing Hien-Kho. *Perdjandjian Dwi-kewarganegaraan RI-RRT dan Pelaksanaannja.* (Keng Po, Djakarta, 1961.)

20 Mozingo, David. 'The Sino-Indonesian Dual Nationality Treaty', *Asian Survey*, 1/10 (1961).

21 Willmott, Donald E. *The National Status of the Chinese in Indonesia 1900–1958.* (Cornell Modern Indonesia Project Monograph Series, Ithaca, 1961—revised edition.)

22 Susanto Tirtoprodjo. *Hasil Kerdja Panitya Bersama.* (Djambatan, Djakarta, 1961.)

23 Somers, Mary F. *Peranakan Chinese Politics in Indonesia.* (Cornell Modern Indonesia Project Interim Reports Series, Ithaca, 1964.)

24 Somers, Mary F. Peranakan Chinese Politics in Indonesia. (Unpublished Ph.D. thesis, Cornell, 1965.)

25 Coppel, Charles A. 'The National Status of the Chinese in Indonesia', *Papers on Far Eastern History*, 1 (March 1970).

26 Coppel, Charles A. 'The position of the Chinese in the Philippines, Malaysia and Indonesia', in *The Chinese in Indonesia, The Philippines and Malaysia.* (Report No. 10, Minority Rights Group, London, 1972.)

NOTE: Willmott (V/21) gives the most convenient extended discussion of the complex issues associated with the dual nationality problem; Coppel (V/25) outlines the more recent developments. Ko Swan Sik (V/15) and Gouw Giok Siong (V/18) are substantial works by Indonesian Chinese jurists. Of the earlier works, Brokx (V/10) and Fromberg (V/11) are particularly valuable.

VI SINO-INDONESIAN RELATIONS

1 T. Sung Fartsan. 'A brief historical sketch of the Chinese Consulate-General at Batavia, Java'. (*Sin Po Jubileum Nummer 1910-1935*).

2 Mozingo, David. 'New developments in China's relations with Indonesia', *Current Scene*, 1 (1962).

3 Williams, Lea E. 'Sino-Indonesian Diplomacy: A study of revolutionary international politics', *China Quarterly*, 11 (July/September 1962).

4 van der Kroef, J. M. 'The Sino-Indonesian Partnership', *Orbis*, (Summer, 1964).

5 Mozingo, David. *Sino-Indonesian Relations : An Overview 1955-1965.* (RAND, Santa Monica, 1965.)

6 Heidhues, Mary F. Somers. 'Peking and the Overseas Chinese: The Malaysian Dispute', *Asian Survey*, 6/5 (May 1966).

7 van der Kroef, J. M. 'The Sino-Indonesian Rupture', *China Quarterly*, 33 (January/March 1968).

8 Coppel, Charles A. 'Indonesia: Freezing Relations with China', *Australia's Neighbours* (March/April 1968).

9 Mozingo, David. 'China's Policy towards Indonesia'—and McVey, Ruth T. 'Indonesian Communism and China' in Tang Tsou (ed.), *China in Crisis*: vol. 2: *China's Policies in Asia and America's Alternatives.* (University of Chicago, Chicago, 1968.)

10 Simon, S. W. *The Broken Triangle: Peking, Djakarta and the PKI.* (Johns Hopkins, Baltimore, 1969.)

11 Mozingo, David. Chinese Policy in Indonesia, 1949–1967. (Ph.D. dissertation, University of California, Los Angeles, 1971: publication forthcoming by Cornell University Press.)

NOTE: The various works of David Mozingo and Ruth T. McVey are by far the most valuable in this section. Parts of Stephen Fitzgerald's *China and the Overseas Chinese* (Cambridge University Press, Cambridge, 1972) are of direct relevance to this subject, although not primarily concerned with it.

VII RACE RELATIONS IN INDONESIA AND THE CHINESE

1 Tan Hong Boen. *Peroesoehan di Koedoes.* (Batavia, 1920.)

2 Wertheim, W. F. *Het rassenprobleem : De ondergang van een mythe* (Albani, The Hague, 1949), especially ch. 5.

3 van der Kroef, J. M. 'Social conflict and minority aspirations in Indonesia', *American Journal of Sociology*, 55 (1949–50).
4 Tabrani, M. *Soal Minoriteit Dalam Indonesia Merdeka*. (Djokjakarta, 1950.)
5 van der Kroef, J. M. 'Minority problems in Indonesia', *Far Eastern Survey*, 24 (1955).
6 Assaat. *Perlindungan Chusus bagi Usaha Nasional*. (Djakarta, 1956.)
7 Badan Pekerdja KENSI Pusat, *KENSI Berdjuang*. (Djambatan, Djakarta, 1956.)
8 Muaja, A. J. *The Chinese Problem in Indonesia*. (New Nusantara, Djakarta, 1958.)
9 Wertheim, W. F. 'The Trading Minorities in Southeast Asia', in his *East-West Parallels: Sociological Approaches*. (The Hague, 1964.)
10 Selo Soemardjan cs. *Gerakan 10 Mei 1963 di Sukabumi*. (Eresco, Bandung, 1964?). [Also as Selo Soemardjan, *Pilot Projek Survey 'Pusaka Djiwa' tentang Faktor2 jang mengandung Gerakan Kerukunan dalam Masjarakat di Kota Sukabumi*. (Departemen Urusan Research Nasional, Madjelis Ilmu Pengetahuan Indonesia, Lembaga Ekonomi dan Kemasjarakatan Nasional, Djakarta, 1965.)]
11 *Peristiwa '10 Mei' Dalam Penelitian*. (LPKB survey, KOTI, Djakarta, 1965.)
12 The Siauw Giap. 'Group Conflict in a Plural Society', *Revue du Sudest Asiatique* (1966) pp. 1-31, 185-217.
13 Taylor, Jean. Inter-Communal Antagonisms in Indonesia: a Study of the 1963 Riots. (BA Hons. thesis, University of Melbourne, 1966.)

NOTE: The writings of W. F. Wertheim on this subject (VII/2 & 9) have been very influential; The Siauw Giap's article is a fuller development of his approach (VII/12). The two works listed as VII/10 & 11 are both officially-sponsored surveys, of which the former is by far the more valuable. The growth of anti-Chinese sentiment in the late 1950s is well reflected in VII/6, 7 & 8; Pramudya Ananta Toer's book (II/11) should be seen as a reply to them.

VIII CHINESE AND THE INDONESIAN ECONOMY

1 (E.) *Twee brieven over de Chineezen en hun landbezit op Java*. (Tiel, 1861.)
2 *Reglement voor de aanwerving van arbeiders in China, om onder contract voor een bepaalden tyd, veld- of fabriekarbeid to verrigten, in Nederlandsche kolonien*. (Peking, 1873.)
3 (Meeter, P.) *Advies van een deskundige in zake boekhouding en faillissementen van Chineezen*. (Soerabaia, 1881.)
4 Thomas, Theodoor. *Eenige opmerkingen naar aanleiding van het pachtstelsel op Java*.
5 Gutem, V. B. van. 'Tjina Mindering', *Koloniale Studien*, 3/1 (1919).
6 Vleming, J. L. Jr. *Het Chineesche Zakenleven in Nederlandsch Indie*. (Landsdrukkerij, Weltevreden, 1926.)
7 Djie Ting Liat. *De economische positie der Chineezen op Java*. (Chung Hwa Hui, Semarang, 1933.)

8   Phoa Liong Gie. 'De economische positie der Chineezen in Nederlandsch-Indie', *Koloniale Studien*, 20/5 and 6 (1936).

9   Cator, W. J. *The Economic Position of the Chinese in the Netherlands Indies.* (University of Chicago, Chicago, 1936.)

10 (Liem Thian Joe.) *Boekoe Peringetan 1907–1937, Tiong Hwa Siang Hwee, Semarang.* (Semarang, 1937.)

11 Nederlandsch Indie. Dienst der Belastingen. *De boekhouding van Chineezen, Japanners, Britsch-Indiers en Arabieren.* (Landsdrukkerij?, Batavia, 1937.)

12 Liem Twan Djie. *De distribueerende tusschenhandel der Chineezen op Java.* (Nijhoff, The Hague, 1947.) English abridged trans. by E. P. Wittermans, under the title *The distributive intermediate trade of the Chinese of Java.* (Institute of Advanced Projects, East-West Center, Honolulu, 1964.)

13 Williams, Lea E. 'Chinese entrepreneurs in Indonesia', *Explorations in Entrepreneurial History* (1st series), 5/1 (October 1952).

14 Palmier, L. H. 'Batik manufacture in a Chinese community in Java', in Higgins, B. H. et al., *Entrepreneurship and labor skills in Indonesian economic development.* (Yale University Southeast Asia Studies Monograph Series no. 1, New Haven, 1961.)

15 Tjoa Soe Tjong. 'OTHC—100 jaar. Een stukje economische geschiedenis van Indonesia', *Economische-Statistische Berichten* (June/July 1963).

16 Liem Thian Joe. Riwajat Kian Gwan. (Unpublished MS, held by Monash University Library.)

17 Panglaykim, J. and Palmer, Ingrid. 'Study of entrepreneurialship in developing countries: the development of one Chinese concern in Indonesia', *Journal of Southeast Asian Studies*, 1/1 (March 1970). An expanded version of this appears under the title *Entrepreneurship and Commercial Risks: The Case of a Schumpeterian Business in Indonesia.* (Occasional Paper No. 2, Institute of Business Studies, Nanyang University 1970.)

18 Go Gien Tjwan. 'The changing trade position of the Chinese in Southeast Asia', *International Social Science Journal*, 23/4 (1971).

NOTE: Considering their dominant position in the Indonesian economy, remarkably little has been written about the Chinese economic role since 1945; for hard research, as distinct from broad assertion, it is necessary to turn to articles on particular industries or aspects of economic life in Indonesia. Cator (VIII/9) and Ong Eng Die (II/8) are among the few (but now dated) attempts to provide a comprehensive survey. Liem Twan Djie (VIII/12), Djie Ting Liat (VIII/7) and Vleming (VIII/6) all contain much useful information. The story of the giant Oei Tiong Ham Concern (Kian Gwan) is told in VIII/15 to 17; Liem Thian Joe (VIII/16) was commissioned by the firm to write its history in anticipation of its centenary, but it was not published because the firm was nationalised.

IX   STATISTICAL AND DEMOGRAPHIC MATERIAL ABOUT INDONESIAN CHINESE

1   *Uitkomsten der in de maand November 1920 gehouden Volkstelling.* (Ruygrok, Batavia, 1922.) Inter alia, this 1920 Census provides useful information on language use.

2 Nederlandsch Indie, Department van economische zaken. *Volkstelling 1930, Deel VII, Chineezen en andere Vreemde Oosterlingen in Nederlandsch-Indie.* (Landsdrukkerij, Batavia, 1935.) By far the most detailed source of statistical and demographic material on the Indonesian Chinese.

3 *Penduduk Indonesia* (Biro Pusat Statistik, Seksi Demografi) is the title of the serial published by the Central Bureau of Statistics in the late 1950s, which tabulates the registered population giving figures for the Chinese. The years for which this publication appeared were 1956, 1957 and 1958; it reappeared in 1971 giving the 1968 figures, but, unlike the earlier publications, no breakdown for the Chinese is given in the figures for 'WNI of foreign descent' and 'WNA'. In all years, data for Chinese outside Java are very skimpy.

4 Baks, C. 'Chinese communities in Eastern Java: A few remarks', *Asian Studies*, 8/2 (August 1970).

X CHINESE CULTURE AND SOCIETY IN INDONESIA

1 Doren, J. B. J. van. *Bijdragen tot de kennis der zeden, gewoonten en geaardheid der Chineezen in het algemeen, doch van die op Java en onderhoorigheden in het bijzonder.* (Utrecht, 1853.)

2 Schlegel, G. *Chineesche Begrafenis- en Huwelijksonderneming (gevestigd te Soerabaya).* (Leiden, 1855, 2nd edition.)

3 Young, J. W. *Uit de Indo-Chineesche Samenleving.* (Honig, Utrecht, 1895.)

4 Moerman, J. *In en om de Chineesche Kamp.* (G. Kolff and Co., Batavia, 1929.)

5 Kwee Kek Beng, 'Het culturele leven der Chineezen in Nederlandsch Indie', *Koloniale Studien*, 20/5 and 6 (1936).

6 Tjan Tjoe Som, 'De culturele positie der Chinezen in Nederlandsch Indie', *Indonesie* (July 1947).

7 van der Kroef, J. M. 'Chinese Assimilation in Indonesia', *Social Research*, 20 (1953); the same piece appears in his *Indonesia in the Modern World* (Bandung, 1954), vol. 1, with footnotes, under the title 'Problems of Chinese Assimilation'.

8 *Simposion Baperki tentang: sumbangsih apakah jang dapat diberikan oleh warganegara2 Indonesia keturunan asing kepada pembinaan dan perkembangan kebudajaan nasional Indonesia.* (Baperki, Djakarta, 1957.)

9 Skinner, G. William. 'The Chinese of Java', in Morton H. Fried (ed.) *Colloquium on Overseas Chinese.* (Institute of Pacific Relations, New York, 1958.)

10 Skinner, G. William. 'Change and Persistence in Chinese Culture Overseas: A comparison of Thailand and Java', *Journal of the South Seas Society*, 16 (1960).

11 Skinner, G. William. 'Java's Chinese Minority: Continuity and Change', *Journal of Asian Studies*, 20/3 (May 1961).

12 Ryan, Edward J. The value system of a Chinese community in Java. (Unpublished Ph.D. thesis, Harvard, 1961.)

13 Nio Joe Lan. *Peradaban Tionghoa selajang pandang.* (Keng Po, Djakarta, 1961.)

14 The Siauw Giap. 'Religion and Overseas Chinese Assimilation in Southeast Asian countries', *Revue du Sudest Asiatique* (1965).

15 Go Gien Tjwan, 'The Assimilation Problem of the Chinese in Indonesia', *Cultures et developpement*, 1/1 (1968).

16 Weldon, Peter. *Indonesian and Chinese Status Differences in Urban Java*. (University of Singapore, Department of Sociology, Working Paper No. 7, Singapore, 1973.)

17 Coppel, Charles A. 'Mapping the Peranakan Chinese in Indonesia', *Papers on Far Eastern History*, 8 (September 1973).

NOTE: Skinner's works (X/9 to 11) are the most influential in this field; The Siauw Giap (X/14) provides an interesting qualification of his ideas. The Ryan thesis is another impressive study of Chinese culture in Java (X/12) as also are several of the studies of the Chinese in Java listed in section XI below. Reflections by peranakan Chinese intellectuals on their cultural situation may be found in X/5, 6, 8 and 13. A fascinating outsider's picture is given by Moerman (X/4).

XI CHINESE IN PARTICULAR AREAS OF INDONESIA

1 Java
(a) *Semarang*
   1 Liem Thian Joe, *Riwajat Semarang 1416-1931*. (Ho Kim Yoe, Semarang, 1933.)
   2 Willmott, Donald E. *The Chinese of Semarang: A Changing Minority Community in Indonesia*. (Cornell University Press, Ithaca, 1960.)
(b) *Sukabumi*
   1 Tan Giok-lan. *The Chinese of Sukabumi: a study in social and cultural accommodation*. (Cornell Modern Indonesia Project Monograph Series, Ithaca, 1963.)
(c) *Tanggerang*
   1 Go Gien Tjwan. *Eenheid in verscheidenheid in een Indonesisch dorp*. (Amsterdam University, Sociologisch-Historisch Seminarium voor Zuidoost Azië, Publication No. 10, Amsterdam, 1966.)
(d) *'Modjokuto'*
   1 Ryan, Edward J. The value system of a Chinese community in Java. (Unpublished Ph.D. thesis, Harvard, 1961.)
(e) *East Java*
   1 Baks, C. 'Chinese communities in Eastern Java: A few remarks', *Asian Studies*, 8/2 (August 1970).

2 Sumatra
(a) *East coast*
   1 Bool, H. J. *De Chineesche immigratie naar Deli*. (Landsdrukkerij, Batavia, 1903?)
   2 de Bruin, A. G. *Der Chineezen ter Oostkust van Sumatra*. (Brill, Leiden, 1918.)
   3 Reid, Anthony. 'Early Chinese migration into North Sumatra', in J. Ch'en

and N. Tarling (ed.), *Studies in the Social History of China and Southeast Asia* (Cambridge University Press, Cambridge 1970).

(b)   *Palembang*

1   Hoeven, Jac. M. van der. *De Chinezen van de stad Palembang. Een marginale situatie. Bevindingen van een onderzoek gedurende 8 maanden in de Zuid Sumatraanse stad Palembang, November 1969–Juni 1970.* (N.pl.c. 1970.)

3   Kalimantan (Borneo)

(a)   *East Kalimantan*

1   Bertling, C. T. 'De Chineezen op de Oostkust van Borneo', *Koloniale Studien*, 9/1 (1925).

(b)   *West Kalimantan*

1   Veth, P. J. *Borneo's Wester-afdeeling.* (Zaltbommel, 1854–6.)

2   van Rees, W. A. *Montrado: Geschied- en krijgskundige bijdragen betreffende de onderwerping der Chineezen op Borneo.* (Rotterdam, 1860.)

3   de Groot, J. J. M. *Het kongsiwezen van Borneo, eene verhandeling over den grondslag en den aard der Chineesche politiek vereeningen in der kolonien.* (Nijhoff, The Hague, 1885.)

4   Schlegel, G. 'L'organization des kongsis à Borneo', *Revue Coloniale Internationale* (Amsterdam), 1 (1885).

5   Kielstra, E. B. *Bijdragen tot de geschiedenis van Borneo's Westerafdeeling.* (Leiden 1889, 1890, 1893—reprinted from *De Indische Gids*.)

6   Schaank, S. H. 'De kongsis van Montrado', *Tijdschrift voor Indische Taal-Land- en Volkenkunde* (1893).

7   Adriani, P. *Herinneringen uit en aan de Chineesche Districten der Wester-Afdeeling van Borneo, 1879–1882.* (Campagne, Amsterdam, 1900.)

8   Brouwer, P. M. van Meeteren. 'De geschiedenis der Chineesche districten der Westerafdeeling van Borneo van 1740–1926', *De Indische Gids*, 2 (1927).

9   Jackson, J. C. *Chinese in the West Borneo goldfields: a study in cultural geography.* (Occasional paper in geography No. 15, University of Hull, 1970.)

4   Sulawesi (Celebes)

(a)   *Makassar*

1   Lombard-Salmon, C. 'La communauté chinoise de Makasar, Dieux et sociétés', *T'oung Pao*, 15 (1969).

2   Lombard-Salmon, C. 'La communauté chinoise de Makasar, Vie collective et organisations', 23/2, *France-Asie* (1969).

NOTE: It is most striking that social scientists studying particular Indonesian Chinese communities have concentrated their energies heavily on Java. The works listed here have enriched our understanding enormously, but it should not be thought that the Chinese in Java are at all representative of Chinese elsewhere in Indonesia. Hearteningly, some recent shorter studies have now appeared based on research among the Chinese of Palembang and Makassar. On the other hand, the works listed for the East Coast of Sumatra and West Kalimantan all relate to the earlier periods of Chinese settlement in those regions. Of these, de Groot (XI, West Kalimantan/3) deserves special mention.

XII   BIOGRAPHY OF INDONESIAN CHINESE

1   Hoetink, B. 'So Bing Kong, het eerste hoofd der Chineezen te Batavia (1619–1636)', *Bijdragen tot de Taal- Land- en Volkenkunde*, 73 (1917).

2   Hoetink, B. 'Ni Hoe Kong, Kapitein der Chineezen te Batavia in 1740', *Bijdragen* etc., 74 (1918). Translated into Indonesian by Liem Koen Hian under the title *Ni Hoe Kong—Kapitein Tiong Hoa di Batavia dalam tahon 1740* (Batavia, 1923).

3   Hoetink, B. 'Chineesche Officieren te Batavia Onder de Compagnie', *Bijdragen* etc., 78 (1922).

4   Tan Hong Boen. *Orang-orang Tionghoa Jang Terkemuka di Java.* (Biographical Publishing Centre, Solo, 1935.)

5   *Pedoman Kampanje Perdjoangan Badan Permusjawaratan Kewarganegaraan Indonesia (Baperki) Dalam Pemilihan Umum.* (Pengurus Harian Baperki Pusat, Djakarta, 1955?)

6   Tio Ie Soei. *Lie Kim Hok (1852–1912).* (L.D. 'Good Luck', Bandung, 1959.)

7   Suryadinata, Leo. *Prominent Indonesian Chinese in the Twentieth Century: a preliminary survey.* (Athens, Ohio, 1972.)

NOTE: Tan Hong Boen (XII/4) and Leo Suryadinata (XII/7), although both heavily Java-centric, together provide something like a twentieth century *Who's Who Among the Indonesian Chinese*? Biographical data for Baperki's candidates in the 1955 Indonesian elections may be found in XII/5. Tio Ie Soei's biography of Lie Kim Hok, an important journalist and writer of the late nineteenth and early twentieth centuries, throws much light on the language, literature and press of the peranakan Chinese in that period (XII/6). Hoetink's writings all focus on the 'officers' appointed by the Dutch East India Company from among the Batavia Chinese in the seventeenth and eighteenth centuries (XII/1 to 3).

XIII   MEMOIRS BY INDONESIAN CHINESE

1   Kwee Hing Tjiat, *Doea Kapala Batoe.* (Berlin, 1921.)

2   See, C.S. *Hoe Een Chinees de Wereld Beziet.* (Kedirische Sullper, Kediri, 1938.)

3   Koo, Hui lan (Oei). *An autobiography, as told to Mary van Reusselaer Thayer* (Dial Press, New York, 1943.)

4   Nio Joe Lan. *Dalem Tawanan Djepang.* (Lotus, Djakarta, 1946.)

5   'Tjamboek Berduri'. *Indonesia dalem Api dan Bara.* (Malang, 1947.)

6   Kwee Kek Beng. *Doea Poeloe Lima Tahon sebagi Wartawan.* (Kuo, Batavia, 1948.)

7   Kwee Kek Beng. *Ke Tiongkok Baru.* (Kuo, Djakarta, 1952.)

8   Saw, G.C. *Around Three Continents.* (New China Times, Medan 1955— revised edition.)

9   Kwee Kek Beng. *50,000 Kilometer Dalam 100 Hari.* (Lauw Putra, Palembang, 1965.)

10 Thung Liang Lee. *The Fundamental Problem of the Indonesian Chinese.* Series of 37 articles in *Djakarta Times* (17 April–5 June, 1972).

NOTE: Four of those listed here are really descriptions by Indonesian Chinese of their overseas travels (XIII/2, 7, 8 & 9). Kwee Hing Tjiat XIII/1) is particularly valuable for his first-hand account of the important 1917 Semarang conference of Chinese leaders from all over Java and his pungent comments on some of them. Nio Joe Lan (XIII/4), 'Tjamboek Berduri' (XIII/5) and Kwee Kek Beng (XIII/6) tell of their different experiences during the Japanese occupation and, in the case of 'Tjamboek Berduri', the Indonesian revolution. The Kwee Kek Beng is in fact an extended memoir by a man who was for a long time editor-in-chief of the Indonesian language edition of *Sin Po*. Thung Liang Lee (XIII/10) tells the story of an Indonesian Chinese who was born in Indonesia, had a Dutch secondary education there, then graduated at the University of London's school of economics, and went on to China to become a close associate of Wang Ch'ing Wei and a junior cabinet minister in the Chinese government. After the Second World War, he returned to Indonesia and, recanting his former espousal of Chinese nationalism, identified himself with Indonesia. Koo Hui-lan (XIII/3) was a daughter of the Semarang tycoon Oei Tiong Ham who married Wellington Koo, Chinese envoy to the 1919 Versailles peace conference.

XIV CHINESE EDUCATION IN INDONESIA

1 Kwee Tek Hoay. 'Onderwijs Hoakiauw di Indonesia', *Panorama*, (7 August–24 September 1931).

2 (?), 'Onderwijs Tionghoa di Indonesia', *Sin Po Jubileum-Nummer 1910–1935*, (Batavia, 1935).

3 van Diffelin, R. 'Het onderwijs voor Chineezen', *Koloniale Studien*, 20/5 and 6 (1936).

4 Nio Joe Lan. 'De eigen onderwijsvoorziening der Chineezen', *Koloniale Studien*, 23/1 (1939).

5 Nio Joe Lan. *Riwajat 40 Taon dari Tiong Hoa Hwe Koan-Batavia 1900–1939*. (THHK Batavia, 1940.)

6 Soeto Tjan. 'Rentjana Pengoebahan Peladjaran di Sekolah Tionghoa Masa Ini', *Jade*, 12/1 (July 1948).

7 Tan Njoek Fa. 'De onderwijsvoorziening Aan de Chinese Groep', *Jade*, 12/1 (July 1948).

8 Sie Boen Lian. 'Tjita-tjita Pengadjaran Tionghoa di Indonesia', *Sinar* (Nomor Kongres 1950).

9 *Hari Ulang Ke-50 Tiong Hoa Hwee Koan Djakarta (3 Juni 1900–3 Juni 1950)*. (Djakarta, 1950.)

10 Lie Tjwan Sioe. 'Perguruan Tionghoa di Indonesia', *Pantjawarna*, 5/60–6/64 (September 1953–January 1954).

11 Indonesia. Departemen Pendidikan, Pengadjaran dan Kebudajaan—bersama Staf Penguasa Perang Pusat, *Pengawasan pengadjaran asing*. (Djakarta, 1959?)

12 Somers, Mary F. Peranakan Chinese Politics in Indonesia. (Unpublished Ph.D. thesis, Cornell, 1965), ch. 2.

13 Clark, Marilyn Alice (Williams). *Overseas Chinese education in Indonesia;*

minority group schooling in an Asian context. (US Government Printing Office, 1965.)

14 Tan, Mely G. L., and Suryadinata, Leo. 'The special project national schools in Indonesia.' (Paper delivered to 28th Congress of Orientalists, Canberra, January 1971.)

15 Suryadinata, Leo. 'Indonesian Chinese Education: Past and Present', *Indonesia,* 14 (October 1972).

NOTE: The most valuable English-language treatments of the subject are those of Mary Somers Heidhues (XIV/12) and Leo Suryadinata (XIV/15); mention should also be made of an important article by Murray, Douglas B. 'Chinese Education in Southeast Asia', *China Quarterly* (October–December 1964). The Indonesian government produced a White Paper on Chinese education in 1959 (XIV/11) and this too is an invaluable source for its period. For the earlier period, reference should be made to the series of articles by Kwee Tek Hoay (XIV/1) and the thesis by Lie Tjwan Sioe (XIV/10); the latter was also published in Chinese translation in the Singapore *Journal of the South Seas Society* in 1959. Much important information can also be found in two histories of the Djakarta Tiong Hoa Hwee Koan (XIV/5 & 9).

XV CHINESE PRESS IN INDONESIA

1 Kwee Kek Beng. 'De Chineesche Pers in Nederlandsch-Indie', *Koloniale Studien,* 19/1 (1935).

2 Liem Thian Joe. 'Journalistiek Tionghoa-Melajoe', *Sin Po Wekelijksche Editie,* Nos. 840–845 (May/June 1939).

3 Kwee Kek Beng. *Doea Poeloe Lima Tahon sebagi Wartawan.* (Kuo, Batavia, 1948.)

4 Tio Ie Soei. 'Pers, Melaju Betawi dan Wartawan', *Istimewa,* (monthly, Surabaja, 1 August 1951).

5 Soedarjo Tjokrosisworo (S.Tj.S.). 'Pers Tionghoa ditengah Revolusi', *Sunday Courier* (16 August 1953).

6 Nio Joe Lan. 'Dari harian Tionghoa-Melaju mendjadi harian Indonesia Nasional', in Sudarjo Tjokrosisworo (ed.), *Kenangan Sekilas Perdjuangan Suratkabar* (Djakarta, 1958).

7 S.Tj.S. 'Hapusnja Pers Tionghoa Melaju', *Pos Indonesia* (18 August 1959).

8 Suryadinata, Leo. *The Pre-World War II Peranakan Chinese Press of Java: a preliminary survey.* (Athens, Ohio, 1971.)

NOTE: Leo Suryadinata's survey of the pre-war peranakan Chinese press deserves special mention (XV/8); he also provides a useful listing of the holdings of peranakan Chinese newspapers in the Museum library in Jakarta.

XVI PERANAKAN CHINESE LITERATURE IN INDONESIA

1 Tio Ie Soei. *Lie Kim Hok (1852–1912).* (L.D. 'Good Luck', Bandung, 1959.)

2 Nio Joe Lan. *Sastera Indonesia-Tionghoa.* (Gunung Agung, Djakarta, 1962.)

NOTE: Both books deal extensively with the literature written and enjoyed by the peranakan Chinese of Java in the late nineteenth and early twentieth centuries.

XVII   CHINESE RELIGION

1   Tjoa Tjoe Koan. *Hari Raja Orang Tjina.* (Albrecht, Batavia, 1887.)
2   Ezerman, J. L. J. F. *Beschrijving van den Koan Iem tempel 'Tiao Kak Sie' te Cheribon.* (Weltevreden, 1920.) Indonesian trans. by S. M. Latif under title *Peri hal kelenting Koan Iem 'Tiao Kak Sie' di Tjeribon.* (Weltevreden, 1922.)
3   Jansen, Gerard. *De Andere Helft.* (Kohler, Medan, 1934.)
4   Pouw Boen-giok. *De kerkrechtelijke Positie van een ethnisch Bepaalde kerk in een Ander Ethnisch Bepaald Milieu.* (Smits, Utrecht, 1952.)
5   Tju Kie Hak Siep. *Riwajat Sam Poo Tay Djien.* (Semarang, 1954?)
6   Kam Seng Kioe. *Sam Po.* (Liong, Semarang, 1955?)
7   Willmott, Donald E. *The Chinese of Semarang: A changing minority community in Indonesia.* (Cornell University Press, Ithaca, 1960), ch. 9.
8   Nio Joe Lan. *Peradaban Tionghoa selajang pandang.* (Keng Po, Djakarta, 1961.)   .
9   Lombard-Salmon, Cl. 'A propos de quelques cultes Chinois particuliers à Java', *Arts Asiatiques,* 26 (1973).
NOTE: The chapter of Willmott's book on the Chinese of Semarang which deals with Chinese religion and magic (XVII/7) is the best treatment in English so far. Pouw Boen-giok's thesis (XVII/4) traces the history of the Chinese Protestant churches in Java. Nio Joe Lan (XVII/8) is a wide-ranging discussion of Chinese religion and culture by a prominent peranakan intellectual.

AUTHOR INDEX TO BIBLIOGRAPHY

Clark, Marilyn Alice (Williams). XIV/13
Coppel, Charles. IV/22, V/25 and 26, VI/8, X/17
Cordes, J. W. C. V/2 and 8
Diffelin, R. van. XIV/3
Djie Ting Liat. VIII/7
Doren, J. B. J. van. X/1
Douwes Dekker, E. F. E. IV/4
Ezerman, J. L. J. F. XVII/2
Faber, G. von. V/4
Feith, H. IV/24
Freedman, Maurice. I/4
Fromberg, P. H. IV/1, V/11
(Gansoijen, A. Paets tot.) V/5
Glover, Clive. IV/10
Go Gien Tjwan. IV/23 and 26, VIII/18, X/15, XI (Tanggerang) /1
Gouw Giok Siong. V/18
Groeneveldt, W. P. III/3
Groot, J. J. M. de. V/1, XI (West Kalimantan) /3
Gutem, V. B. van. VIII/5
Han Swie Tian. V/14
Hanssens, V. IV/12
Heeckeren, C. W. van. V/6
Heidhues, Mary F. Somers. (see Somers, Mary F.)
Heyman, B. V/9
Hoetink, B. XII/1, 2 and 3
Hoeven, Jac. M. van der. XI (Palembang) /1
Indonesia. Angkatan Darat. Staf Umum. II/12
—— Biro Pusat Statistik. IX/3
—— Departemen P, P and K bersama Staf Penguasa Perang Pusat XIV/11
Jackson, J. C. XI (West Kalimantan) /9
Jansen, Gerard. II/7, XVII/3
Kahin, G. McT. IV/8 and 9
Kam Seng Kioe. XVII/6
KENSI (Kongres Ekonomi Nasional Seluruh Indonesia). VII/7
Kielstra, E. B. XI (West Kalimantan) /5
Ko Swan Sik. V/15
Koo Hui-lan (Oei) XIII/3
Kroef, J. M. van der. VI/4 and 7, VII/3 and 5, X/7
Kwee Hing Tjiat. IV/5, XIII/1
Kwee Kek Beng. X/5, XIII/6, 7 and 9, XV/1 and 3
Kwee Tek Hoay. IV/6, XIV/1
'Leknas Report'. VII/10
Li, A. I/7
Liauw Kian Djoe (see Suryadinata, Leo)
Lie Tek Tjeng. IV/20 and 21
Lie Tjwan Sioe. XIV/10
Liem Khiam Soen II/9
Liem Thian Joe. III/4, VIII/10 and 16, XI (Semarang) /1, XV/2

Liem Tjing Hien-Kho. V/19
Liem Twan Djie. VIII /12
Lombard-Salmon, Cl. XI (Makassar) /1 and 2, XVII/9
L.P.K.B. (Lembaga Pembinaan Kesatuan Bangsa). VII/11
Mabbett, Hugh and Ping-ching II/14
Mackie, J. A. C. IV/13
McVey, Ruth. VI/9
Meeter, P. VIII/3
Millies, H. C. III/2
Moerman, J. II/6, X/4
Moll, J. Th. II/5
Mozingo, David. V/20, VI/2, 5, 9 and 11
Muaja, A. J. VII/8
Nederlandsch Indie. Departement van economische zaken. IX/2
—— Dienst der Belastingen. VIII/11
Nevadomsky, J. J. I/7
Nio Joe Lan. IV/7, X/13, XIII/4, XIV/4 and 5, XV/6, XVI/2, XVII/8
Oey Giok Po. I/1
Ong Eng Die. II/8
Ong Tae Hae. III/1
Palmer, Ingrid. VIII/17
Palmier, L. H. VIII/14
Panglaykim, J. VIII/17
Phoa Liong Gie. VIII/8
Pouw Boen-giok. XVII/4
Purcell, Victor. I/5
Rees, W. A. van. XI (West Kalimantan) /2
Reid, Anthony, XI (Sumatra East Coast) /3
Ryan, Edward J. X/12, XI ('Modjokuto') /1
Sandick, L. H. W. van. II/3
Sasmojo. V/16
Saw, G. C. XIII/8
Schaank, S. H. XI (West Kalimantan) /6
Schlegel, G. X/2, XI (West Kalimantan) /4
See, C.S. XIII/2
Selo Soemardjan. VII/10
Shu, A. C. W. I/6
Sie Boen Lian. XIV/8
Sim Ki Ay. II/4
Simon, S. W. VI/10
Skinner, G. William. II/13, X/9, 10 and 11
Soedarjo Tjokrosisworo (S.Tj.S.). XV/5 and 7
Soeto Tjan. XIV/6
Somers, Mary F. III/13, IV/16, 17, 18 and 27, V/23 and 24, VI/6, XIV/12
Sung, T. Fartsan. VI/1
Suryadinata, Leo (Liauw Kian Djoe). IV/19, 22 and 25, XII/7, XIV/14 and
    15, XV/8
Susanto Tirtoprodjo. V/22

GLOSSARY

abangan
: Javanese who are merely nominal Muslims adhering to syncretist practices and beliefs of pre-Islamic (i.e. animist, Hindu or Buddhist) origin

Ali-Baba firms
: firms in which an Indonesian (Ali) obtains the licences, while a Chinese (Baba) provides the capital and trading connections

asing
: foreign, alien

asli
: indigenous; cf. *pribumi*—both being terms used to distinguish ethnic Indonesians from WNI Chinese (q.v.)

atap
: roof of palm leaves

Baperki (Badan Permusjawaratan Kewarganegaraan Indonesia)
: Consultative Body for Indonesian Citizenship, a Chinese political organisation formed in March 1954

becak
: pedicab

BKUT (Badan Kontak Urusan Tjina)
: Contact Body for Chinese Affairs; formed mid-1967

bulanan
: monthly

bupati
: head of the administrative division, *kabupaten*

cap go mei
: Chinese New Year festival

CHH (Chung Hwa Hui)
: Chinese Association; the first integrationist party, formed in 1928

CHTH (Chung Hua Tsung Hui)
: Federation of Chinese Organisations, replacing the HCTH in 1945

cukong
: originally a Chinese word, now commonly used in Indonesian, from the words for 'boss' and

	'grandfather', formerly used to refer to a backer or patron-adviser of a business associate, connoting something like the Mafia 'godfather' relationship, although without such sinister overtones; in the contemporary Indonesian context, however, the Chinese cukong who provides the capital or business contacts often stands on a footing of less than equality with the Indonesian who provides the essential political influence or protection
Dekon (Deklarasi Ekonomi)	Economic Declaration
Dinas Karet	Smallholder Rubber Office, the extension service for small rubber producers
DKR (Djawatan Karet Rekjab)	Smallholder Rubber Office (see Dinas Karet)
DPRD-GR (Dewan Perwakilan Rakyat Daerah-Gotong Royong)	Regional Representative Council
Dwikora (Dwikomando Rakyat)	People's Twofold Command; Sukarno's speech of 3 May 1963 proclaiming Indonesia's objectives in the 'confrontation' of Malaysia
dusun	village
GAKKA (Gabungan Koperasi Karet)	Rubber Cooperative Association
Gestapu (Gerakan September Tiga Puluh)	the movement responsible for the abortive coup attempt of 1 October 1965
Harian Rakjat	People's Daily; PKI daily newspaper
HCS (Hollands Chineesche Scholen)	Dutch language primary school, established in 1908 exclusively for Chinese children
HCTH (Hua Ch'iao Tsung Hui)	Federation of Chinese Associations, established after July 1942
IEV (Indo-Europeesch Verbond)	Indo-European Union
ijon	the practice of selling crop in the field before the harvest (lit. 'green')
jus sanguinis	the principle by which nationality is determined by descent, not birthplace
jus soli	the principle by which nationality is determined by one's place of birth
kabupaten	district—administrative subdivision of a residency
KAMI (Kesatuan Aksi Mahasiswa Indonesia)	Indonesian Students Action Front; a federation of anti-Communist university students organisations formed in 1966
KAPPI (Kesatuan Aksi Pemuda dan Peladjar Indonesia)	Indonesian Youth and Students Action Front; similar to KAMI but at secondary school level
karet	rubber

kecamatan	subdistrict—territorial division embracing a number of villages
kepercayaan	mutual trust
keresidenan	residency
kiyayi	general term applied to Muslim leaders or scholars
KOGAM (Komando Ganjang Malaysia)	'Crush Malaysia Command'—the name applied to KOTI after February 1966
kongsi	informal business associations
KOTI (Komando Tertinggi)	Supreme Operations Command, established April 1962; (G-V) Gabungan V was the section responsible for social and political affairs
KOTOE (Komando Tertinggi Operasi Ekonomi)	Supreme Economic Operational Command
kuasai	to control, take over
kuo-yu	the Chinese national language (Mandarin)
langganan	customer
LPKB (Lembaga Pembinaan Kesatuan Bangsa)	Institute for Promotion of National Unity, an assimilationist body formed in July 1963
Manipol-Usdek (Manifesto Politik-USDEK)	the Political Manifesto of Sukarno of 17 August 1959 designed to serve as the programme and philosophy of Guided Democracy; USDEK, an acronym referring to its five main features
mingguan	weekly
MPRS (Madjelis Permusjawaratan Rakjat Sementara)	Provisional People's Consultative Assembly
Nan Yang	'the South Seas' (Chinese)
Nasakom	'Nasionalisme - Agama - Komunisme' — an acronym referring to the principle of co-operation between nationalist, religious and Communist streams, advocated by Sukarno as the basis for national unity, especially between 1960–65
Nekolim	an acronym referring to 'neo-colonialism, colonialism and imperialism'
NU (Nahdatul Ulama)	Muslim political party
N.V. Karet	Rubber Corporation, established 1955 in South Sumatra
panglong	timber and fuel business
Partindo (Partai Indonesia)	originally, the successor in 1931–33 to Sukarno's banned PNI; later, a party founded in 1958 as an embodiment of Sukarno's left-wing radical-nationalist but non-Communist ideology
pedagang dusun	rubber trader in the village without a shop

pedagang motor	rubber trader using a motor boat
pedagang pucuk	rubber traders in the *kecamatan* towns, usually owning a shop
pedagang talang	rubber trader around the rice-rubber villages
pedagang warong	rubber buyer in village with a shop
peranakan	term referring to Chinese communities in Indonesia characterised by use of the vernacular language and a distinctive set of cultural traits neither wholly Chinese nor wholly Indonesian
Perseroan Terbatas (PT)	Limited Company
PGRS (Pasukan Geriljawan Rakjat Sarawak)	the rebel force in West Kalimantan, largely made up of Sarawak opponents of Malaysia who took refuge in Indonesia in 1963–65 and fled to the jungle after the 1965 coup
PKI (Partai Komunis Indonesia)	Indonesian Communist Party
PNI (Partai Nasional Indonesia)	Indonesian Nationalist Party
PPMI (Perkumpulan Perhimpunan Mahasiswa Indonesia)	Federation of Indonesian Student Associations
pribumi	indigenous Indonesian (lit. 'son of the soil')
PRIKA (Primer Koperasi Pertanian Rakjat)	Primary Cooperative
priyayi	term for class of government official in Java; lit. the aristocracy, descendants of a prince or regent. In general the upper strata of the non-santri stream in Java
PRRI-Permesta (Pemerintah Revolusioner Republik Indonesia)	the 1957–58 regional dissident movements in Sumatra and Sulawesi
PSI (Partai Sosialis Indonesia)	Indonesian Socialist Party
PSII (Partai Sarikat Islam Indonesia)	Muslim political party
PTI (Partai Tionghoa Indonesia)	Indonesian Chinese Party formed 1932, an integrationist party
rakyat	the (ordinary) people
RPKAD (Resimen Parakomando Angkatan, Darat)	Army Para-commando Regiment
santri	devout Muslim; in general the more self-consciously Muslim stream among the ethnic Javanese
SCUT (Staf Chusus Urusan Tjina)	Special Staff for Chinese Affairs, formed mid-1967

sia hwee (Tionghoa)	unified Chinese community
siang hwee	Chambers of Commerce of the Netherlands Indies
Sin Po	Malay language Chinese-oriented daily, Jakarta
Soe Po Sia	reading clubs established by supporters in Indonesia of Sun Yat Sen and his fellow revolutionaries
suku	Indonesian ethnic group
tahu-sama-tahu	(lit.) 'know-together-know'—implying reciprocal knowledge and mutual exoneration of unlawful or corrupt actions
talang	a temporary settlement
tani	farmer
THHK (Tiong Hoa Hwe Koan)	the earliest pan-Chinese (political) organisation in Batavia, established 1900
toko	city store or shop
tongkang	river barge
totok	(lit. of pure blood) term referring to group of Chinese in Indonesia made up of those who had recently immigrated, who spoke Chinese and were currently oriented towards China
UPBA (Urusan Peranakan dan Bangsa Asing)	Indonesian government's Bureau of Peranakan and Alien Affairs
Volksraad (People's Council)	representative body with limited powers established by the Dutch in 1917
wajib giling	compulsory remilling on a contract basis
warong	small retail store
WNI (Warganegara Indonesia)	term commonly applied to Chinese who are Indonesian citizens

INDEX

Contributors

J. A. C. Mackie worked in the Indonesian State Planning Bureau from 1956 to 1958; was subsequently head of the Department of Indonesian Studies at University of Melbourne; and since 1968 has been Research Director of the Centre of Southeast Asian Studies at Monash University.

Charles A. Coppel, who has just completed at Ph.D. thesis at Monash University on the position of the Indonesian Chinese under the Sukarno and Suharto governments, is Lecturer in the Department of Southeast Asian Studies at Melbourne University.

Dr J. Panglaykim was formerly a Professor in the Economics Faculty at the University of Indonesia; later a member of the Department of Economics at the Australian National University. He is now a staff Member of the Centre for Strategic and International Studies, Jakarta.

K. D. Thomas spent several years at the University of Indonesia during the 1950s carrying out research on the smallholder rubber industry; he is now Senior Lecturer in Economics at La Trobe University.

Professor Wang Gungwu, formerly Professor of History at the University of Malaga, is now Professor of Far Eastern History in the Research School of Pacific Studies, Australian National University.